The A~Z
of the 1960s

The A~Z
of the 1960s

Ann & Ian Morrison

Breedon Books

First published in Great Britain by
The Breedon Books Publishing Company Limited
44 Friar Gate, Derby DE1 1DA
1989

ISBN 0 907969 60 7

Printed by Butler and Tanner Limited, Frome.
Jacket designed by Graham Hales and printed by Arkle Print,
Northampton.

CONTENTS

WE stand here today on the edge of a new frontier. The frontier of the 1960s. A frontier of unknown opportunities and perils. A frontier of unfulfilled hopes and threats.

John F.Kennedy, July 1960.

Acknowledgements

Barrie Weekes of Southport for his invaluable help.
Jane Steer, Production Secretary, BBC Television.
Sue Curtis, the Austin-Rover Group.
J.H.Dalton, Barclaycard.
The Central Statistical Office, London.
Reg Harwood for the loan of his old newspapers.
The staff at Warrington and Manchester reference libraries.
Nicola Rippon at Breedon Books for her additional research.

Photographic research by Neil Simpson
Photographs supplied by Popperfoto

Bibliography

Changing Trends in Fashion (Batsford)
Who's Who in Pop Radio (Four Square Books)
The Miss World Story (Angley Book Co.)
Longmann Dictionary of 20th Century Biography (Longmann)
The International Who's Who (Europa)
Who's Who in Modern History (Weidenfeld & Nicholson)
The International Dictionary of 20th Century Biographies (Sidgwick & Jackson)
The International Dictionary of Films and Film-makers (St James Press)
Who's Who on Television (Michael Joseph)
Hutchinson 20th Century Encyclopedia (Hutchinson)
Daily Mail Yearbooks
British Hit Singles (Guinness Books)
Who's Really Who (Sphere Books)
The Book of Golden Discs (Barrie & Jenkins)
Chambers Biographical Dictionary (Chambers)
Chronicle of the 20th Century (Longmann)
The Oxford Companion to Film (Oxford University Press)
Halliwell's Television Companion (Paladin)
Radio Times
TV Times
Who Did What (Michael Beazley)

Introduction

IT has often been said that, if you remember the 1960s, then you did not *live* them. And there is no doubt that, as you go through the pages of this book, recalling some of the well-known events and people that affected your life during the decade, there will also be names and events that you will have forgotten — because you were *enjoying* the 1960s. We hope that this look back at one of the most momentous decades of the century will remind you that there was life beyond the swinging days of the early 1960s and the flower-power era of the latter years.

Perhaps distance really does lend enchantment, but back in the 1960s it seemed that people had an extra spring in their step. The era seemed to bring out the better side of human nature. Suddenly the world was a great place to live in. It was a playground for enjoyment and the universe seemed to have been specially created for those of us lucky enough to have been around at the time.

Of course that was essentially a young person's view of life, for the 1960s had their fair share of tragedy, disaster and scandal. Indeed, in many ways it was *the* most scandalous of decades — but even that had its entertaining side.

We both started our teenage years in the early 1960s and ended them in the latter half of the decade. It was a period which had a great influence on our lives and some of the more arbitary entries in our book no doubt bear the hallmark of our own reminiscences. Nevertheless we hope that you will enjoy this look at a very special time.

Ann and Ian Morrison
August 1989

Rescue workers pause from their harrowing task at Aberfan.

ABERFAN

ONE of the most tragic disasters to hit Britain devastated a small Welsh mining community near Merthyr Tydfil on 21 October 1966 when the Aberfan village school was buried underneath tons of slurry from a rain-soaked coal tip which slid down upon it.

Entombed were 150 children. Mercifully, some escaped, but many did not. Rescue workers formed human chains as they attempted to bring people out alive, but as the day and night wore on, their task became increasingly grim as they passed dead bodies along the chain. The first death toll was reported at 83 but, inevitably, it rose as rescuers worked well into the night. The final figure was 116 children and 28 adults. Many of the children were buried as they had lived and died, together, in a mass grave.

As it made its rush towards the school, the slide also destroyed a cottage, and six more cottages in the adjacent Moy Street were engulfed in the mass, claiming other lives. An eyewitness, Mr Gwyn Brown, a National Coal Board crane driver, described the incident: "There was a big roar and the tip lifted itself and moved. It was all over in a matter of seconds."

In August 1967, a coroner's verdict of 'accidental death' was recorded after a tribunal inquiry. The memory of that October when a whole generation of children was wiped out has never been erased from the minds of the people of that close-knit community.

The people of Aberfan felt a great anger towards the Coal Board, who were blamed for the disaster. The miners who worked at the Merthyr Vale Colliery were blameless and in 1989, the local people fought to keep open their pit, which had been in the village for nearly 120 years, as its demise became imminent. Coal was the cause of one of the worst tragedies in British history, but the people of Aberfan also recognized that the community was built because of its existence.

ABORTION ACT

THE Medical Termination of Pregnancy Bill, renamed the Abortion Bill, was passed in Parliament on 25 October 1967, thanks to the efforts of Liberal MP David Steel. Legalized abortions came into effect on 27 April 1968.

Abortions can only be carried out by the National Health Service or at a Ministry of Health approved clinic and provided that two doctors agree that the pregnancy would cause injury (physical or mental) to the mother or that there was a risk that the child would be born with serious physical or mental disability. Doctors and other medical staff are not obliged to participate in abortions if they do not wish to, due to religious or other grounds.

The first abortion clinic opened in London in October 1968.

ADDAMS FAMILY

THIS popular black and white TV series was launched in 1964 and was based on the works of cartoonist Charles Addams in the *New Yorker*. The stories centred around the macabre events in the life of a family of ghouls.

The Addams family consisted of the father Gomez, played by John Astin, who kept a pet octopus called Aristotle. Gomez was married to Morticia, played by Carolyn Jones, and there was also Uncle Fester who was played by the child star of the 1920s and '30s, Jackie Coogan. The son Pugsley (Ken Weatherwax) had a favourite toy — an electric chair — and daughter Wednesday (Lisa Goring) had a black widow spider called Homer. The last member of the family was Grandma, played by Blossom Rock. But perhaps the best-known of the cast was the butler, Lurch, played by the seven-foot tall Ted Cassidy, and his catch phrase of 'You Raaaang', when beckoned by the family, became one of the sayings of the day.

> Thing, *a hand which lived in a gold box and was on call as a servant to members of the family, was the hand of Ted Cassidy.*

Morticia and Gomez went to a cave in Death Valley for their honeymoon. Gomez's favourite pastime was blowing up his model train set and when Morticia spoke to him in French he became very passionate.

ADENAUER, Konrad

GERMAN statesman Konrad Adenauer was born in Cologne in

1876 and became Lord Mayor of his home town in 1917. For being a fierce opponent of the Nazi movement, he was imprisoned upon orders from Hitler in 1933. After the war he became head of the Christian Democratic Union and was Chancellor of the Federal Republic (West Germany) from 1946-1963. He was the man who led Germany to prosperity after the hostilities.

A great believer in the unity of European nations, he was an advocate of the Common Market and backed Britain's entry. He also constantly worked for the unification of Germany, despite Soviet criticism.

He retired in 1963 at the age of 87 and was replaced by Ludwig Erhard. Adenauer died at his home near Bonn on 19 April 1967.

ALI, Muhammad

IF you asked anybody at random to name a sports personality of the 1960s, it is a sure bet that the most popular answer would be Muhammad Ali. He was the most exciting boxer of all time and was so outrageously extrovert that he suddenly made people more aware of the sport. Every time Ali was fighting, people sat glued to their television sets, always expecting the unexpected. And they were rarely disappointed.

Born Cassius Marcellus Clay at Louisville, Kentucky, on 17 January 1942, he won the Olympic light-heavyweight title at Rome in 1960. He had his first professional fight in October that year when he beat Tunney Hunsaker on points over six rounds.

He was given his first crack at the World title in February 1964 when he challenged Sonny Liston, who Clay labelled the 'Big Ugly Bear'. That became one of Clay's trademarks, insulting opponents before each contest. Pre-fight predictions were also a common feature of the build-up to his fights.

Clay predicted he would beat Liston, despite being 8-1 against with the bookies. But what an upset it caused when Liston failed to come out for the seventh round. Fifteen months later, after joining the Muslim

faith and changing his name to Muhammad Ali, he retained his title by beating Liston in one round.

Light on his feet, his footwork was exceptional. And that helped his stay at the top of heavyweight boxing until 1967, when the authorities took his title away from him after he was sentenced to a five-year prison term (which he never served) for failing to join the US forces and serve in Vietnam. "No Vietcong ever called me a nigger," he commented at the time.

Ali regained the title in 1974 and then, remarkably, became the first man to regain the title a second time

World heavyweight champion Muhammad Ali towers over the fallen Sonny Liston at Lewiston, Maine, in May 1965. Ali knocked out Liston in one minute of the first round to retain his crown.

when he beat Leon Spinks in 1978. His last contest was in 1981 and today, the ageing Muhammad Ali is showing the signs of nearly 15 years at the top of world heavyweight boxing.

ALLEN, Dave

IRISH-BORN comedian Dave Allen brought a new dimension to comedy in the 1960s. There was no slapstick to his style, nor did he need a straight man. He was a solo artiste and sat casually on his high stool with a cigarette in one hand and a glass of whiskey in the other, rattling off story after story.

Religion and politics received the brunt of his gags and at times his religious jokes got him into trouble, despite his being brought up as a devout Roman Catholic.

Born on 6 July 1930, he was raised in the Dublin area and surprised his family by becoming a junior reporter on a local newspaper rather than join

Muhammad Ali's world title fights in the 1960s:

Date	Opponent	Venue	Result
25 Feb 1964	Sonny Liston	Miami Beach	Won TKO Rd 7
25 May 1965	Sonny Liston	Lewiston, Maine	Won KO Rd 1
22 Nov 1965	Floyd Patterson	Las Vegas	Won TKO Rd 12
29 Mar 1966	George Chuvalo	Toronto	Won PTS 15 Rds
21 May 1966	Henry Cooper	London	Won TKO Rd 6
6 Aug 1966	Brian London	London	Won KO Rd 3
10 Sep 1966	Karl Mildenberger	Frankfurt	Won TKO Rd 12
14 Nov 1966	Cleveland Williams	Houston	Won TKO Rd 3
6 Feb 1967	Ernie Terrell	Houston	Won PTS 15 Rds
22 Mar 1967	Zora Folley	New York	Won KO Rd 7

the priesthood. From there he became a Redcoat at Butlins, Skegness, where he assumed his now famous stage name of Dave Allen. His real name is Tynan O'Mahoney!

One of Allen's famous lines was the one with which he used to close his show: "Goodnight. Good luck. And may your God go with you."

AMERICAN RACE RIOTS

RACIAL unrest was nothing new to the citizens of the United States, but in September 1962 there started a series of riots in Mississippi that were to prove the bloodiest ever seen. Sadly, racial riots were rife in the 1960s.

It all started on 1 February 1960 when four negroes sat down at the counter of Woolworths, South Elm Street, Greensboro, North Carolina. They asked for coffee and were refused. They returned each day, their numbers swelling. It was the first black demonstration of the sixties and the start of a 'whirlwind' that would sweep across America. The negroes had started their freedom campaign.

On 20 September 1962, the Mississippi State Governor defied a court order and refused to allow negro James Meredith to enter the University of Mississippi. Ten days later, when Meredith enrolled, angry whites stormed the campus and, despite the efforts of more than 700 Federal Marshalls, they could not prevent a riot which resulted in three deaths and many more injuries.

On the instructions of President Kennedy, Meredith had a personal escort to his enrolment. When Meredith attended his first class the following day there were more than 200 arrests.

As the unrest continued, Martin Luther King Junior became a prominent Civil Rights leader and led many marches. When he headed a march in Alabama in 1963 it was intended to be peaceful but, following his arrest, fighting broke out between police and 2,000 black protestors, resulting in many injuries. Another march on Alabama ten days later resulted in 1,000 arrests.

President Kennedy sent Federal troops into the area to help stop the riots and Robert Kennedy was given the task of working out a peace deal between the black and white leaders. Matters were not eased when Alabama Governor, George Wallace,

defied a court order which allowed negroes to enter Alabama University and when two enrolled in June 1963, President Kennedy ordered the National Guard to protect them.

The shooting of Civil Rights leader, Medgar Evans, two days later, sparked off renewed rioting in the South.

On 28 August 1963, more than 200,000 people marched on Washington in the biggest demonstration pressing for civil rights. It was a peaceful demonstration and the one where Martin Luther King made his famous 'I have a dream' speech.

Back in Alabama, Governor Wallace ordered State troopers to seal off the Tuskegee High School to prevent integration of students, but President Kennedy took control of the Alabama National Guard whose task it was to make sure integration was carried out. While all this was taking place, James Meredith received his diploma at Mississippi University.

The greatest act of provocation against the blacks came on a Sunday morning in September 1963, when a bomb exploded during a church service in Birmingham, Alabama. Four negro girls were killed and 23 people injured. Despite the appalling atrocity, Martin Luther King appealed to the blacks to remain non-violent.

Mounted policemen charge into a band of negroes in the Bedford-Stuyvesant area of Brooklyn on the night of 22 July 1964.

1966 and 4,000 National Guards were called in to try to prevent a sniper campaign against the local police. In the final shoot-out, two blacks were killed and six police injured. In Cleveland, the death of a young black mother by police gunfire sparked off rioting which resulted in two more deaths.

In November 1966, Edward Brooke became the first black senator since direct senatorial election was introduced 55 years earlier. Thurgood Marshall was appointed the first black member of the US Supreme Court in June 1967 and Carl Stokes was appointed the Mayor of Cleveland, also in 1967. He was the first negro to become mayor of a major American city. At last, there seemed to be signs that integration was working after all. But the following month Detroit was to see some of the worst riots since the latest period of unrest between blacks and whites. It resulted in 42 people being killed and $50 million-worth of damage to property. What was the cause of this latest riot? Police were called to a noisy party being thrown to celebrate the return of a black soldier from Vietnam. Between 1964-67 rioting in 58 cities had resulted in 147 deaths and 4,500 serious injuries.

> The phrase 'Black Power' was first coined by Stokely Carmichael.

Hopes of bringing an end to the rioting received a serious set-back on 4 April 1968, when Martin Luther King Junior was gunned down by an assassin at Memphis (See 'Assassinations'). Within hours of his death riots broke out in dozens of towns and cities throughout the United States.

Happily, the rioting quelled towards the end of the decade as more American states moved towards integration of blacks and whites. There is still unrest between the two factions, but nothing like that which constantly made the headlines in the 1960s.

Nearly 200 negroes were arrested in a protest at Alabama as the unrest spread. King was arrested again after he tried to force the integration in a Florida restaurant.

In July 1964, the new President, Lyndon B. Johnson, signed the Civil Rights Act which prohibited discrimination in employment, accommodation and other areas. It was the most sweeping Civil Rights Bill in US history. But it did not stop the rioting.

Thousands rioted in Harlem two weeks after the signing of the Act and Governor Rockefeller was forced to send in the National Guard to Rochester, New York, where law and order had completely broken down. There were more than 500 arrests and a curfew was imposed.

For his part in attempting to bring peace to the rioting, Martin Luther King Junior was awarded the Nobel Peace Prize in October 1964. But, despite his efforts, the riots continued.

Twenty-five thousand marchers, led by King, petitioned the grievances of blacks to Governor Wallace and the marchers had the protection of nearly 3,000 troops, ordered in by President Johnson. Trouble spread to the west and troops were called in after three days of fighting in Los Angeles. On 15 August 1965, the worst racial riots in recent history broke out at Watts, Los Angeles.

It happened after a negro was arrested for drunken driving. Snipers fired at police, thousands of fires were started and the net result was 28 deaths and nearly 700 injured.

Twenty thousand National Guardsmen were called into the area and over 2,000 looters were arrested. The cost of the damage was estimated at $175 million.

Chicago had its share of rioting in

Washington DC, April 1968. A National Guardsman patrols a ruined street after a day of arson, looting and violence in the wake of Dr Martin Luther King Jnr's assassination.

ANDREWS, Eamonn

EAMONN Andrews was synonymous with *What's My Line* and *This Is Your Life* in the 1960s. But his broadcasting background extended beyond those two successful programmes.

Born on 19 December 1922, he was educated by the Christian Brothers in Dublin. His first love was boxing and he was a national junior middleweight champion. He spent ten years as a commentator with Radio Eireann before getting his break to cover a boxing match for the BBC in 1951. From there his sporting knowledge took him to BBC Radio's *Sports Report* where he was the front man, before he became the first presenter of ITV's *World Of Sport*. He was also one of the presenters on BBC's *Crackerjack*.

But it was as the host of *This Is Your Life* that he is best remembered. The show was launched in the autumn of 1955 and ran until Michael Aspell took over in 1987. Eamonn opened the famous red book on hundreds of unsuspecting personalities from all walks of life and was, himself, once the subject when David Nixon took charge of the famous book.

As the chairman of *What's My Line* he kept such notable personalities as Lady Isobel Barnet, Barbara Kelly and Gilbert Harding in check each week as they sought to outwit the challenger by guessing his or her occupation. Eamonn was also a competent chat show host and writer. He died on 5 November 1987 after a short illness.

ANDREWS, Julie

BRITISH-BORN Julie Andrews starred in two of the biggest box office successes of the 1960s, *Mary Poppins* and *The Sound Of Music*.

Born Julia Wells at Walton-on-Thames on 1 October 1935, she starred in the Broadway production of *The Boy Friend* in 1954 and portrayed Eliza Doolittle in the stage version of *My Fair Lady* before venturing into her first film part as the magical nanny in *Mary Poppins* in 1964. She won an Oscar that year as best actress. The following year she missed out on a second Oscar, but *The Sound Of Music*, which featured her as Maria the nun, who later became governess of Colonel Von Trapp's seven children, before

becoming Mrs Von Trapp, was the Best Film of the Year. Both films gave Julie the chance to display her singing talents.

Other films, like *The Americanization Of Emily* (1964) and *Thoroughly Modern Millie* (1967), saw her playing comedy roles, to which she adapted well. But her portrayal of Gertrude Lawrence in *Star* (1967) was not as successful.

ANIMALS, The

A MALE vocalist and instrumental group originally called the Alan Price Combo, all the members hailed from the Newcastle-upon-Tyne area and were one of the many groups that had Mickey Most as their recording manager. Their only number-one hit, and first million seller, was *House Of The Rising Sun* in 1964. Arranged by Alan Price, it was an adaptation of a negro folk song. It was twice subsequently reissued and reached number 25 in the charts in 1972 and ten years later got to number 11.

The members of the Animals were: Alan Price, Chas Chandler, Hilton Valentine, Eric Burdon (the lead singer) and John Steel. As a solo artiste, Eric Burdon had several records, the best of which was *San Franciscan Nights* which reached number seven in 1967. Alan Price left the group in 1965 and was replaced by Dave Rowberry. As a solo artiste, Price had top ten hits with *I Put A Spell*

On You, Simon Smith And His Amazing Dancing Bear, The House That Jack Built and *The Jarrow Song*, all between 1966 and 1968. Georgie Fame and Alan Price together took *Rosetta* to number 11 in 1971.

Top Ten hits of the Animals in the 1960s:

Year	Record	Pos
1964	House Of The Rising Sun	1
1964	I'm Crying	8
1965	Don't Let Me Be Misunderstood	3
1965	Bring It On Home To Me	7
1965	We've Gotta Get Out Of This Place	2
1965	It's My Life	7
1966	Don't Bring Me Down	6

APOLLO MISSIONS

THE FIRST Apollo mission was a scheduled manned spaceflight but on 27 January 1967 it ended in tragedy when its three astronauts, Virgil Grissom, Ed White and Roger

The manned Apollo missions of the 1960s were:

Apollo 7	11-22 Oct 1968	Wally Schirra, Donn Eisele, Walt Cunningham
Apollo 8	21-27 Dec 1968	Frank Borman, James Lovell, William Anders
Apollo 9	3-13 Mar 1969	James McDivitt, David Scott, Russell Schweickart
Apollo 10	18-26 May 1969	Thomas Stafford, Eugene Cernan, John Young
Apollo 11	16-24 July 1969	Neil Armstrong†, Buzz Aldrin†, Michael Collins
Apollo 12	14-24 Nov 1969	Charles Conrad†, Alan Bean†, Richard Gordon

† Indicates: Walked on the moon.

Chaffee, lost their lives in a fire aboard the craft during a practice countdown. The next five Apollo missions were cancelled and it was not until 1968 that another manned flight was undertaken.

The Apollo flights were to play a significant role towards man's first step on the moon. *Apollo 8* was the first craft to take men into lunar orbit and sent lunar pictures back to earth; *Lunar 9* was the first manned flight of the lunar module; and *Apollo 10* was the first lunar module orbit of the moon. But the important mission was *Apollo 11*.

Apollo 11 blasted off from Cape Kennedy on 16 July 1969 and on 20 July, *'Eagle'*, the lunar module, landed on the moon's surface. (See *Armstrong, Neil*, for further details of the first moon walk.)

Apollo 12 was the last mission in the 1960s, and was also a moon landing. There were five other Apollo flights, the last being *Apollo 18* in 1975 when American and Russian astronauts met in space.

All Apollo flights were powered by the Saturn rocket.

ARCHIES, The

AMERICAN group who had a number-one hit with their only hit single in Britain, *Sugar Sugar* in 1969. It spent 26 weeks in the charts and sold over three million copies in the United States.

The Archies were, in fact, cartoon characters: Archie Andrews, Mr Weatherbee, Betty Copper, Veronica Lodge, Reggie Mantle and Jughead Jones, who appeared on a Saturday morning CBS show. The record was made by studio singers and topped the British charts for eight weeks, selling a million copies. Worldwide sales reached almost six million, making it the top single of 1969.

Their follow-up record *Jingle Jangle* was a million-seller in the United States but did not reach the charts in Britain. All the session singers remained anonymous with the exception of Ron Dante, who was later revealed as the lead singer of the Archies, and Barry Manilow who appeared on *Sugar Sugar*.

ARKLE

THE greatest steeplechaser of all time, Arkle was foaled in April 1957 at Ballymacoll Stud, County Meath, by Archive out of Bright Cherry.

Anne, Duchess of Westminster, bought him in 1960 for 1,150 guineas and Tom Dreaper was his trainer. He ran three flat races, six over hurdles and 26 steeplechases. Of the latter he won 22. His clashes with Mill House were truly great sporting moments of the 1960s. Despite winning the

Arkle's major triumphs:	
Cheltenham Gold Cup	1964, 1965, 1966.
Irish Grand National	1964.
Hennessey Gold Cup	1964, 1965.
Whitbread Gold Cup	1965.
George VI Chase	1965.
Leapordstown Handicap Chase	1964, 1965, 1966.

Cheltenham Gold Cup three years in succession he never entered the Grand National. In every race over fences he was ridden by Pat Taaffe and had his last race on Boxing Day 1966, in the King George VI Chase at Kempton Park. A leg injury forced his retirement. Arkle was put down on 31 May 1970.

ARMSTRONG, Neil

NEIL Armstrong is immortalized in world history as the first man to walk on the moon when, in July 1969, he took that 'one small step for man but one giant leap for mankind'.

Born at Wapokoneta, Ohio, in 1930, he obtained a pilot's licence at the age of 16 and served in Korea from 1949 to 1952. He joined NASA as a test pilot and became an astronaut in 1962. His first space flight was in *Gemini 8* (with David Scott) on 16 March 1966 and lasted slightly less than 11 hours. His next flight, however, was the historic one that took him on to the moon's surface.

On 16 July 1969, *Apollo 11* left Cape Kennedy. Four days later, *Eagle* touched down on the moon's surface, and at 3.56am BST, on 21 July, Armstrong took that first step on to the moon.

Armstrong's first words after the lunar module, *Eagle*, touched on the moon's surface, were: "Houston. Tranquility Base. The Eagle has landed."

Armstrong never made another space flight, but continued working on the US space programme at NASA.

ASSASSINATIONS

THE 1960s will be remembered for three major assassinations:

PRESIDENT KENNEDY

They say everybody remembers exactly where they were at the moment they heard the news of President Kennedy's assassination. There can be few other world events, if any, about which that can be said. This highlights the magnitude of the disaster that fateful day at Dallas in 1963.

Dallas is famous for its oil, the Ewings and the Dallas Cowboys. But on 22 November 1963 it received worldwide notoriety as the place where John Fitzgerald Kennedy, 35th President of the United States, lost his life.

Whilst on his way to make a speech at a political festival, the car carrying the President, his wife Jackie and Texas Governor John Connally, was hit by a hail of bullets.

The President slumped into the arms of his wife after being hit twice in the head. He was rushed to Parkland Hospital where he received a blood transfusion and the last rites. But 25 minutes after being hit, he was pronounced dead.

Later that day, 24-year-old former marine Lee Harvey Oswald was

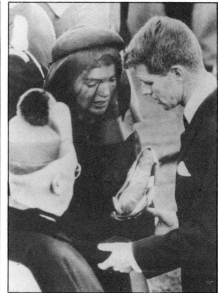

Jacqueline Kennedy clutches the flag that draped her husband's coffin. Bobby Kennedy, the murdered President's brother, offers comfort.

arrested in a local cinema following the shooting of a policeman nearby. He denied all knowledge of the crime and of the killing of the President, but was charged with the murder of the policeman. He was later charged with the assassination of the President.

Two days after Oswald was charged, and as he was being transferred from Dallas police headquarters to the county gaol, Dallas strip club owner 52-year-old Jack Rubenstein (known as Jack Ruby) leapt from a crowd waiting in the underground car-park at the police station and shot Oswald at point-blank range with a single shot into his ribs. Millions saw the incident live on television.

The funeral of President Kennedy took place on 25 November 1963. His body was carried on a gun carriage led by six grey horses. Behind the procession a single soldier led a

Nightclub owner Jack Ruby fires his revolver into Lee Harvey Oswald, the alleged assassin of President Kennedy.

riderless horse, with boots reversed in the stirrups — a sign of a fallen warrior. Ninety-three nations were represented at the funeral as the President was laid to rest at the Arlington National Cemetery.

Oswald never admitted to the killing of the President and in the quarter of a century since the assassination, there still remains speculation as to the identity of President Kennedy's murderer. Oswald was a former chairman of the pro-Castro 'Fair Play for Cuba' committee and in 1959 defected to the Soviet Union before returning in 1962 with his Russian-born wife. He had appropriate credentials, but those were not proof that he was the murderer. As for Jack Ruby, he was sentenced to death in March 1964, but died of a blood clot in the lung on 3 January 1967 while awaiting a retrial.

MARTIN LUTHER KING JUNIOR

Dr Martin Luther King Junior was gunned down while he stood on his Memphis hotel balcony in 1968 on yet another Civil Rights mission.

On 4 April 1968, King returned to Memphis seven days after leading a march on behalf of the city's 3,000 dustmen who were on strike. That march ended violently and saw a 16-year-old negro girl killed, 62 injured and 200 arrests.

When he returned a week later, Dr King arrived at the Lorraine Motel on Mulberry Street in the morning and stayed in his first-floor room, number 306, all day. At about 6.00pm he came to his balcony to talk to fellow Civil Rights workers on adjacent balconies; among them was Jesse Jackson, the man who ran for President in 1988.

As King was talking, a shot rang out from the other side of the street and hit him in the face. The 39-year-old

was rushed to the St Joseph's Hospital where he was pronounced dead. King's wife, Coretta, and two of his children were in Alabama at the time and they immediately rushed to Memphis, but it was too late.

The assassination brought about renewed violence on the streets, both in Memphis and across the United States. Four thousand National Guardsmen were called to Memphis as a curfew was imposed on the city where 40% of the 550,000 population were negroes.

King's assassin, James Earl Ray (alias Eric Galt), was captured in London and in March 1969 was sentenced to 99 years imprisonment.

ROBERT KENNEDY

Having defeated Senator Eugene McCarthy in the Californian Presidential Primary on 5 June 1968, Senator Robert Kennedy addressed a crowd of 2,000 cheering and enthusiastic supporters and helpers in the Embassy ballroom of the Ambassador Hotel, Los Angeles.

He left the ballroom via the kitchen at the back of the stage just after midnight. He was accompanied by a party of about eight people, including his wife Ethel. Kennedy stopped to shake hands with a waiter who offered

his congratulations, and then continued on his way towards a lift. A man who was leaning over a long table suddenly leapt on to the table brandishing a .22 calibre pistol. He jumped down and fired three shots into the Senator from point-blank range. As Kennedy slumped against a freezer, the gunman rained five more shots into the crowd.

Two members of the Senator's party, ex-American footballer Roosevelt Grier (6ft 4in and 22st) and former Olympic decathlete Rafer Johnson managed to apprehend the gunman and bring him to the ground.

The Senator was taken to the Good Samaritan Hospital where surgeons fought for 25 hours to save his life, but at 1.44am on 6 June, Robert Kennedy died. The bullet which killed him entered his brain through the right mastoid.

The assassin, Sirhan Sirhan, was initially charged with the attempted murder of Kennedy. This charge was later changed to murder. At the time of the shooting he said: "I did it for my country." Kennedy's assassination coincided with the anniversary of the Six Days' War and during his campaign he had expressed his support for Israel and for the

Other notable assassinations of the 1960s include:

17 Jan 1961 — Patrice Lumumba, ex-premier of the Congo
30 May 1961 — Rafael Trujillo Molina, Dominican dictator
2 Nov 1963 — Ngo Dinh Diem, President of the Republic of Vietnam, killed in a coup. His brother Ngo Dinh Nhu was also killed.
21 Jan 1965 — Hassan Ali Mansour, Iranian Premier
21 Feb 1965 — Malcolm X, Black Nationalist
6 Sep 1966 — Hendrik Verwoerd, South African Prime Minister

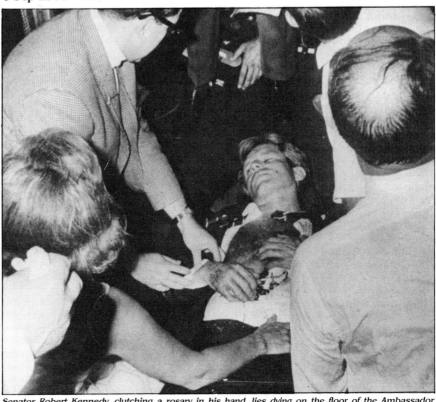

Senator Robert Kennedy, clutching a rosary in his hand, lies dying on the floor of the Ambassador Hotel, Los Angeles, moments after being shot by Sirhan Sirhan.

15

continued supply of arms to the country.

Kennedy was buried alongside his brother at Arlington National Cemetery on 8 June 1968. Sirhan was found guilty of the killing and on 23 April 1969 was sentenced to death in the gas chamber. The sentence was later commuted and in 1989 Sirhan was considered for parole.

ATTENBOROUGH, Sir Richard

SIR Richard Attenborough, or just plain Dickie to his friends, has been a stalwart of the British film industry for nearly 50 years.

Born on 29 August 1923, Attenborough starred in his first film *In Which We Serve* in 1942. He soon established himself as a promising British actor and, in 1952, played the part of the detective in the first stage performance of the long-running *Mousetrap*.

He later turned his attention to producing, after the formation of his own production companies, Beaver Films and Allied Film Makers. *The Angry Silence* and *Seance On A Wet Afternoon* were two of his films of the 1960s. He also produced and starred in *10 Rillington Place,* the story about the Christie murders.

Attenborough also turned his hand to directing and the first film under his direction was *Oh What A Lovely War* in 1969.

Despite his long career in the theatre and film business, it was not until 1982 that his talents received their just rewards when his film *Gandhi* won eight Oscars, including a personal one for Sir Richard as best director. It is the most Oscars ever won by a British film and it ended a 20-year dream he had of making the film.

His younger brother, David, was a familiar face on television in the 1960s, hosting wildlife programmes.

AVENGERS, The

The Avengers made its debut in 1961 and was born out of a former series called *Police Surgeon* which starred Patrick MacNee and Ian Hendry, making its debut a year earlier.

The new series was popular

Honor Blackman and Patrick McNee, alias Kathy Gale and John Steed.

because of the absurdity of some of the plots. Nevertheless, most of the stories were clever, well written and well acted and this kept the large number of viewers happy.

The Avengers team was led by John Steed (played by Patrick MacNee) and over the years he was assisted by a variety of attractive and willing helpers whose tasks were to solve bizarre crimes and plots against the Government.

Steed's first assistant was Honor Blackman, who played Kathy Gale and was popular for her leather outfits and judo skills. He was next aided by Diana Rigg in the guise of Emma Peel. The humour between Steed and Peel, together with Steed's steel-rimmed bowler, were hallmarks of the success at that time.

Linda Thorson, as Tara King, replaced Diana Rigg and she was Steed's last partner until the series re-emerged in 1976 as *The New Avengers* when John Steed was joined by Gambit (Gareth Hunt) and Purdy (Joanna Lumley).

AVERAGE WAGE

THE average weekly wage throughout the sixties, based on the earnings of manual workers over the age of 21, was as follows:

1960	£14 10s 8d
1961	£15 6s 10d
1962	£15 17s 3d
1963	£16 14s 11d
1964	£18 2s 2d
1965	£19 11s 9d
1966	£20 6s 1d
1967	£21 7s 6d
1968	£22 19s 11d
1969	£24 16s 5d

All figures were calculated as at October each year. Unlike today the principal Government figures did not include service industries.

BACHELORS, The

AMIDST the hysteria of the Beatles, Rolling Stones and Gerry and the Pacemakers, there emerged an Irish trio of lads whose style was so different to many of the groups of the 1960s, but was just as popular. Those three lads were The Bachelors.

They first hit the charts with *Charmaine* and, after two other hits, climbed to number one with their only million-seller, *Diane*. It spent 19 weeks in the charts and topped the hit parade for one week on 20 February 1964.

That hit was followed up by other well-known songs like *I Believe, Ramona* and *I Wouldn't Trade You For The World*. They remained popular throughout the 1960s and had no fewer than 17 chart hits. Their last chart entry was *Marta* in 1967; it reached number 20.

The group consisted of brothers Con and Dec Clusky, and John Stokes. They all came from Dublin and formed in 1953 when they called themselves the Harmonicordes and in the late 1950s appeared in America's popular chat programme the *Ed Sullivan Show*.

Still around in the 1980s, the personnel has changed slightly and the temples have got a bit greyer, but the distinctive sound of The Bachelors remains.

Top Ten hits for the Bachelors in the 1960s:

Year	Record	Pos
1963	Charmaine	6
1964	Diane	1
1964	I Believe	2
1964	Ramona	4
1964	I Wouldn't Trade You For The World	4
1964	No Arms Can Ever Hold You	7
1965	Marie	9
1966	The Sound Of Silence	3

BAD WEATHER 1962-63

THE BAD weather in the winter of 1962 was the worst since 1947. It started at the beginning of December with dense fog in London, the worst for ten years, with visibility virtually down to nil in places. Gale-force winds of 100mph in mid-December then caused widespread damage. And on 23 December the snow and ice followed.

By the end of December, all English counties were affected by snow and on 30 December the worst blizzard for 15 years swept across the south and west of England, causing road and rail chaos, not to mention the problems livestock faced. Farmers were forced to throw away thousands of gallons of milk as churns could not be delivered. And many industries allied to agriculture were forced to close.

Stories of people being stranded were commonplace and major roads were cut off. Virtually all roads connecting England and Scotland were impassable.

There was a slight thaw in mid-January, but then the snow and ice returned with a vengeance and by 17 January, 49 counties in England and Wales were affected once more. In London, the temperature had not risen above 3°C since 23 December. There were the inevitable power cuts and stories of railway engines freezing up while moving!

On 8 February it was reported that 108 main roads were still blocked as the RAF continued to help out with the delivery of food supplies in isolated areas. And at the Fylingdales early-warning station, they helped with the airlift of nearly 300 men who had been stranded for three days.

Sport was seriously affected, particularly horse racing and soccer. The FA Cup tie between Lincoln City and Coventry City was postponed 15 times and on 9 February 1963, a total of 57 first-class games in England and Scotland were called off. Between 12 January and 2 February 1963, only four Football League games were played. By early February the total of race meetings cancelled surpassed the 1946-7 record total of 69. More than 100 meetings were lost and racing did not return to England until 8 March, when Josh Gifford rode Hamanet to victory in the Burford Novices Steeplechase at Newbury. It was the first English meeting since 22 December, although one day's racing had been possible at Ayr on 5 January.

Once the thaw set in, it brought the inevitable burst pipes and flooding. The cost of the bad weather was then counted and estimated in millions of pounds. The cost of damage to roads alone was put at £20 million. Unemployment reached new peaks in January 1963, as many firms had been forced to close during some of the worst weather conditions on record.

BAILEY, David

AS THE fashion boom took off in the 1960s, so did the need for the professional photographer. Good quality photographs were the way of projecting the models of the day to the teenage girl via the glossy (and some not-so-glossy) magazines.

The top models of the 1960s were Jean Shrimpton and Twiggy, and the man who photographed these girls countless times was David Bailey.

Born the son of an East Ham tailor in 1938, his first photographic job was as the assistant to the *Daily Express* fashion photographer in 1959. He later set up on his own and secured a contract with *Vogue* where his pictures of 'The Shrimp' (Jean Shrimpton) turned her into one of the leading models of the decade.

Bailey gained a reputation for working with models who portrayed strong sexual feeling and gave the provocative look.

When David married his second wife, French actress Catherine Deneuve, in August 1965, the best man was Mick Jagger and, as you would expect, the dress was casual — jeans and round-necked sweaters.

Bailey was the inspiration behind Antonioni's 1967 cult film *Blow Up*, starring Vanessa Redgrave, David Hemmings, Sarah Miles and Peter Bowles.

BAN THE BOMB

THE CAMPAIGN for Nuclear Disarmament was formed in 1958 and at Easter that year 6,000 anti-H-Bomb marchers walked the 50 miles from London to Aldermaston where the Atomic Weapons Research Establishment was situated. Along the way they were joined by other walkers and a total of 12,000 demonstrators joined the protest at Aldermaston.

Six thousand people set off from Aldermaston on a ban-the-bomb march at Easter 1961.

That was the start of a series of CND marches and protests that were commonplace in the 1960s under the cry of 'Ban the Bomb' and to the movement's theme tune 'We Shall Not Be Moved'.

The biggest Ban the Bomb protest ever seen in London was in September 1961 when more than 15,000 demonstrators crammed into Trafalgar Square. Three thousand police clashed with demonstrators as they tried to move protestors who engaged in a sit-in. There were 850 arrests, including such personalities as playwright John Osborne, actress Vanessa Redgrave and musician George Melly. A week earlier, Earl Russell had been jailed following a similar demonstration, also in London.

By 1963, the annual Aldermaston march had swelled its numbers to 70,000, a fair indication as to the growing numbers in favour of nuclear disarmament as the Ban the Bomb campaign reached its peak.

The campaign is still going on today, but there is nothing like the intensity of those Aldermaston marches of the early 1960s.

BANK RATE

THE FIRST post-war change in the Bank Rate was on 7 November 1951 when it went up from 2 to 2½%. This is how it changed in the 1960s:

1 Jan 1960	4%	23 Nov 1964	7%
21 Jan 1960	5%	3 Jun 1965	6%
23 Jun 1960	6%	14 Jul 1966	7%
27 Oct 1960	5½%	26 Jan 1967	6½%
8 Dec 1960	5%	16 Mar 1967	6%
25 Jul 1961	7%	4 May 1967	5½%
5 Oct 1961	6½%	19 Oct 1967	6%
2 Nov 1961	6%	9 Nov 1967	6½%
8 Mar 1962	5½%	18 Nov 1967	8%
22 Mar 1962	5%	21 Mar 1968	7½%
26 Apr 1962	4½%	19 Sep 1968	7%
3 Mar 1963	4%	27 Feb 1969	8%
27 Feb 1964	5%		

The Bank Base Rate (as it is now called) stood at 14% on 23 August 1989.

BARCLAYCARD

The 1980s certainly became the 'age of the credit card'. But how different it was in the 1960s when Barclays Bank launched their Barclaycard, the first British institution to launch a credit card.

After the first half of 1966 had been spent recruiting retail outlets, the Barclaycard was officially launched on 29 June 1966 when cards were sent out to one million customers.

Thirty thousand retailers initially joined the scheme and by the end of 1966 that figure had increased to 35,000. In the words of a Barclays executive, the new form of credit was 'met with a tidal wave of indifference'.

There was not a computer large enough to handle the volume of vouchers that flooded into the Barclaycard offices and they had to be flown to West Germany to be processed! Hardly surprising that the operation ran at a loss to begin with.

There is much talk of credit cards being an expensive way of borrowing money. Today's rate is 2% per month, compared to a Bank Base Rate of 14%. When it was first launched in 1966, the Barclaycard rate was 1½% per month compared to a Bank Rate of 7%. It makes the present-day credit card look cheap.

Barclays were certainly the market leaders in the 1960s. Almost 12 months to the day after the launch of the Barclaycard, they became the first bank to provide a cash dispensing machine when the first one opened at their Enfield branch on 27 June 1967.

Barclaycard information:

Number of Cardholders:	31 Dec 1966, 1,000,000
	31 Dec 1988, 9,010,000

Turnover:	
1967	1988
£10,000,000	£8,341,000,000

Average per Cardholder:	1967:	£ 10.00
	1988:	£925.75
UK Retail outlets:	31 Dec 1966,	35,000
	31 Dec 1988,	306,000

BARDOT, Brigitte

BRIGITTE Bardot was the 'sex kitten' of the silver screen in the 1950s and '60s. Born in Paris in 1934, she was the daughter of a wealthy industrialist.

Having appeared in some minor films in the mid-1950s, she shot to international fame in 1956 with the film *Et Dieu Créa La Femme (And God Created Woman)*. It was directed by

Roger Vadim, the man she had married in 1952.

That film projected Bardot as a sex symbol, a tag she has lived with ever since. She became a blonde, and despite making many more films, none of which can be described as 'blockbusters', she remained popular and appeared in plenty of glossy magazines. Her best film of the 1960s was *Viva Maria!* in 1965.

Two films have been made about her: *I Paparazzi* in 1963, and *Dear Brigitte* (1965) in which she played herself.

A tempestuous private life resulted in a suicide attempt in October 1960.

Her last film was in 1973, which was for her former husband, Vadim, whom she divorced in 1957. Since then she has devoted a large part of her life to animal protection and set up the Bardot Animal Foundation. In 1989, however, she announced plans to come out of her 15-year retirement to make a series of films for television to raise money for the Foundation.

The films of Brigitte Bardot in the 1960s:

Please Not Now	(1961)
La Vérit (The Truth)	(1961)
Le Repos Du Guerrier	(1962)
Love On A Pillow	(1962)
La Vie Privée	
(A Very Private Affair)	(1962)
Le Mépris	(1963)
Contempt	(1964)
Viva Maria!	(1965)
Dear Brigitte	(1965)
Two Weeks In September	(1967)
Shalako	(1968)

BARNARD, Dr Christiaan

SOUTH African Christiaan Barnard and his team of 30 doctors and nurses made history on 3 December 1967 when he successfully transplanted the heart of donor, 25-year-old Denise Ann Darvall, into Louis Washkansky at the Groot Schuur Hospital, Cape Town.

Christiaan Neethling Barnard was born at Beaufort West in 1922 and after graduating from the Cape Town Medical School, spent some time in the United States, where he carried out heart research. When he returned to South Africa he was involved in open-heart surgery and transplant research until fulfilling those years on that historic day in December 1967.

Washkansky, a 53-year-old grocer, died 18 days after his operation as a result of contracting pneumonia. The actual transplant was a success but tissue rejection was a major problem. Barnard's second patient, Philip Blaiberg, was operated on in

January 1968 and survived for nearly 20 months.

Heart and other organ transplants are now commonplace, and the rate of survival is high. Many people owe their lives to the innovative skills of Christiaan Barnard.

BART, Lionel

LIONEL Bart started his musical career writing music and lyrics for *Fings Ain't Wot They Used To Be* which made its debut at the Theatre Royal, Stratford, in 1959. But the following year he wrote the music and lyrics for *Oliver!* the musical based on the Charles Dickens novel *Oliver Twist*, and the one Bart is best remembered for.

The show opened at London's New Theatre on 30 June 1960 and became one of the most acclaimed musicals in London stage history. It ran for 2,618 performances.

It opened at the Curran Theatre, San Francisco, on 26 September 1962 before moving to Broadway's Imperial Theatre on 6 January 1963 where it ran for 774 performances. A film version of *Oliver!* was released in 1968 with Mark Lester playing the lead role.

Bart, born in London in 1930, enjoyed other successes. *Lock Up Your Daughters* and *Blitz*, which like *Oliver!*, won him the Ivor Novello Award, but there were other well-known scores like *Maggie May*, *The Tommy Steele Story* and *Tommy The Toreador*. The musical *Lionel*, which opened in 1977, was based on Bart's career and works.

Bart also penned the title song for the James Bond movie *From Russia With Love*, and also one of Cliff Richard's early hits, *Living Doll*.

BASS, Alfie

ALFIE Bass rose to fame as one of the stars of *The Army Game* which first appeared on British television screens in 1957 and ran until 1962.

Born within London's Jewish community, and of Russian descent, Bass played the part of Private Bisley, better known as 'Excused Boots' or plain 'Bootsie', for more than 150 episodes. Because of his oddly-shaped feet, he could not wear regulation army boots and therefore wore plimsoles — hence his nickname.

Another star of the series was Bill Fraser, who played the part of Sergeant Major Snudge. Bass and Fraser teamed up in a spin-off series called *Bootsie And Snudge* created by Barry Took and Marty Feldman. Set after their demobilization from the army, the two men played similar roles, with Bass as the doorman/odd-job man at a posh London club and Fraser as his superior yet again.

In 1968, Bass played the role of Tevye in *Fiddler On The Roof*. He also appeared in well-known films like *Alfie*, *Up The Junction* and *The Lavendar Hill Mob*. He returned to television in the 1980s in later episodes of *Till Death Us Do Part*.

Alfie Bass died on 15 July 1987. Bill Fraser died seven weeks later.

BASSEY, Shirley

DURING the 1960s, Shirley Bassey became not only one of the top recording artistes of the decade, but also one of Britain's greatest international singing stars.

Brought up in the Tiger Bay area of Cardiff, she appeared at the leading

venues in Las Vegas, New York, Sydney and Monte Carlo, to name just a few. As a recording artiste, she spent a then record 313 weeks in the British singles charts between 1957 and 1973, which included 12 Top Ten entries and two number ones: *As I Love You* in 1959 and the double-sided *Reach For The Stars/Climb Ev'ry Mountain* two years later.

Perhaps surprisingly, the two songs for which she is best known, *Big Spender* and the theme to the James Bond film *Goldfinger*, failed to find a place in the Top Twenty, although worldwide, *Goldfinger* became a million-seller in only five months.

As well as enjoying success with singles, Shirley Bassey has recorded some memorable albums which have helped make her one of the great British female singers of all time.

The private life of Shirley Bassey has not been as happy. She has endured two broken marriages followed by, in 1985, the tragic death of her daughter, Samantha, who fell from the Clifton Suspension Bridge in Bristol.

Top Ten hits of Shirley Bassey in the 1960s:

Year	Record	Pos
1960	As Long As He Needs Me	2
1961	You'll Never Know	6
1961	Reach For The Stars/ Climb Ev'ry Mountain	1
1961	I'll Get By	10
1962	What Now My Love	5
1963	I (Who Have Nothing)	6

BATCHELOR, Horace

THE sounds of the sixties which bellowed out of the 'tranny', courtesy of *Radio Luxembourg* were occasionally broken by advertisements. One of the most famous adverts of the day was that by Horace Batchelor, the man with a system for winning the football pools, who invited you to write to him at PO Box number six, Keynsham, that's K-E-Y-N-S-H-A-M, Keynsham, Bristol.

Not only did Horace help people to win the pools but he certainly put Keynsham on the map.

Born in Bristol, he called his system 'In for a Draw' and he based his operation from a house on Bath Road which he named 'In For A Lodge'. Coincidentally, it was number 321 Bath Road, which was the then points value for draws, aways and homes on the pools.

Batchelor won over one thousand first dividends for himself and many more for his clients, including two first dividend prizes approaching six-figure sums.

After Horace's death in 1981, while in his seventies, his son John carried

on the business but discontinued it a couple of years later and thus brought about the end of Horace Batchelor's famous pools-winning system which had been going for more than 25 years.

BATMAN

THE BATMAN character was created by Bob Kane and made his American television debut in 1965, thanks to ABC TV.

The series came to Britain in the late-1960s and was popular with adults and children alike. The unbelievable stories, which contained villains with such wonderful names as The Penguin, The Riddler, Catwoman, The Bookworm and the Joker, made it good, light-hearted viewing. The dialogue was written by somebody who obviously swallowed the 'Book of Clichés' before each programme, and

Bronco star Ty Hardin was the first choice to play Batman but was not available.

fight scenes would have visual sound effects like 'Zap' and 'Splat' appear on the screen. The first episode was entitled 'Hi Diddle Riddle'.

Only their butler, Alfred, knew the identity of Batman and his sidekick Robin, but the people of Gotham City, police chief O'Hara and Commissioner Gordon didn't care as long as the Caped Crusaders and their Batmobile were on hand to protect the city.

The two central characters of Bruce

The only person to die in a Batman series was Jill St John who played the Riddler's moll. She sneaked into the Bat Cave, slipped and fell into the Bat Generator.

Wayne and Dick Grayson were played by Adam West (Batman) and Burt Ward (Robin). A full-length feature film was made in 1966 — but it wasn't all that successful.

However, the 1989 film starring Michael Keaton in the lead role and Jack Nicholson as *The Joker* was a different story and grossed $40.4 million in its first three months in the United States . . .and that without Robin!

Some of the well-known personalities who appeared in Batman included:-
Talulah Bankhead *The Black Widow*
Roddy McDowall . . .*The Bookworm*
Eartha Kitt . . . .*Catwoman*
Lee Meriweather *also Catwoman*
Liberace . . . .*Chandell*
Vincent Price . . . .*Egg Head*
Otto Preminger . . . .*Mr Freeze*
Eli Wallach . . . .*also Mr Freeze*
Cesar Romero . . . .*The Joker*
Shelley Winters . . . .*Ma Parker*
Zsa Zsa Gabor . . . .*Minerva*
Van Johnson . . . .*The Minstrel*
Burgess Meredith . . . .*Penguin*
Frank Gorshin . . . .*The Riddler*
Michael Rennie . . . .*Sandman*
Cliff Robertson . . . .*Shame*
Joan Collins . . . .*The Siren*

BBC SPORTS PERSONALITY OF THE YEAR

THE VIEWERS' poll to find the most outstanding sports personality of the year was first launched in 1954 and won by athlete Christopher Chataway. During the 1960s the 1st, 2nd and 3rd at each presentation were:

Year	1st	2nd	3rd
1960	David Broome	Don Thompson	Anita Lonsborough
1961	Stirling Moss	Billy Walker	Angela Mortimer
1962	Anita Lonsborough	Dorothy Hyman	Linda Ludgrove
1963	Dorothy Hyman	Bobby McGregor	Jim Clark
1964	Mary Rand	Barry Briggs	Ann Packer
1965	Tommy Simpson	Jim Clark	Marion Coakes
1966	Bobby Moore	Barry Briggs	Geoff Hurst
1967	Henry Cooper	Beryl Burton	Harvey Smith
1968	David Hemery	Graham Hill	Marion Coakes
1969	Ann Jones	Tony Jacklin	George Best

Henry Cooper won the title again in 1970 and is the only dual winner. Bobby Moore is the only footballer to win the title.

BEACH BOYS

AMERICAN vocal and instrumental group, they started life as Carl and the Passions before a brief spell under the name of the Pendletones. They became the Beach Boys in 1961 after the release of their first record, *Surfin!*

The original line-up consisted of three brothers, Brian, Dennis and Carl Wilson. A cousin of theirs, Mike Love, and High School buddy Al Jardine, completed the line-up. When Brian left the group in 1965 after a nervous breakdown, he was replaced by Glen Campbell who stayed for six months before being replaced by Brian Johnston. Even after Brian Wilson's return, Johnston remained and was a vital member of the group.

During the mid-1960s it was British groups who dominated the pop scene, but the Beach Boys were one of the few American groups to break the monopoly and had ten British Top Ten hits. In addition, they had 13 hit albums and their record *I Get Around* was a monster hit in the States. It went to number one on the Billboard charts, as did *Help Me Rhonda* and *Good Vibrations.*

> *Although they earned California a lot of publicity for sun, sand and surfing only Dennis Wilson of the Beach Boys could actually surf.*

The group continued to have success long after the 1960s had gone. In 1976 their album *20 Golden Greats* reached number one in Britain as did the album *The Very Best Of The Beach Boys* seven years later. The group who gave us the West Coast sound of America in the 1960s have certainly stood the test of time.

Top Ten hits of the Beach Boys in the 1960s:

Year	Record	Pos
1964	I Get Around	7
1966	Barbara Ann	3
1966	Sloop John B	2
1966	God Only Knows	2
1966	Good Vibrations	1
1967	Then I Kissed Her	4
1967	Heroes And Villains	8
1968	Do It Again	1
1969	I Can Hear Music	10
1969	Break Away	6

BEATLEMANIA

THE BEATLES attracted an army of fans never before seen in the music world. Everywhere they went there were thousands of fans waiting to get a glimpse of their idols. This new hysteria became known as 'Beatlemania'.

Screaming fans caused traffic jams in Central London when the group were due to top the bill at the Palladium for the 1963 Royal Variety Performance. But when they went to the United States the following year, Beatlemania scaled new heights.

Disc jockeys had been broadcasting updates on the progress of Pan Am Flight 101 that was bringing the Beatles to the States. Thousands of screaming fans greeted them at New York's Kennedy Airport and many of them broke a police cordon and

Beatlemania outside Buckingham Palace. Fans await the Fab Four, who were inside receiving the insignia of their MBEs from the Queen in October 1965.

followed the group to the Plaza Hotel.

Upon their return from the States, the greeting from the British fans at London was equally ecstatic. After only four months back home on English soil, the group was off again, this time to Australia, and again the welcome was staggering as Beatlemania spread to all corners of the globe. They were greeted by 300,000 fans in Adelaide. The following month 10,000 fans turned up to see John, Paul, George and Ringo arrive for the

An American policeman tries to deaden the screams of Beatles fans in Atlantic City.

More than 100,000 Beatles fans welcomed their heroes back to Liverpool for the premier of the film A Hard Day's Night *in October 1964.*

premiere of their film, *A Hard Day's Night,* in the West End.

The Beatles returned to their home town, Liverpool, in July 1964 and 150,000 crammed into the spectator's gallery at Liverpool's Speke Airport. Inevitably, such a large crowd in such a small area brought its problems and 300 fans were treated for injuries. Some were crushed, some fainted with the excitement, and some broken-hearted because they couldn't see the Fab Four.

When the Beatles returned to the United States in 1965 there was little indication that the hysteria had died down and proof that the Beatles were still popular across the Atlantic lies in the fact that 55,000 fans turned out for the concert at New York City's Shea Stadium.

Even Buckingham Palace was not free from Beatlemania. When the group went to collect their MBEs in 1965, hundreds of fans shouted, screamed and waved banners outside the gates of the Royal residence.

Nowhere was free from Beatlemania. Wherever the Beatles went, it went too. The Beatles formally dissolved in 1970 and so brought to an end a great era in music history. It also brought to an end the hysteria that had never been seen before. Nor has it been seen since. Beatlemania was something quite unique.

BEATLES, The

WHAT more can one say about the Beatles that hasn't already been said? They were unquestionably the biggest single happening of the sixties and played such an important role in the music boom of the decade which was to change our lives so much. The Beatles were the forerunners of the so-called 'Mersey Sound' which saw many more top groups emerge from the great city as Liverpool became the music centre of the world.

Bred on the rock and roll music of the fifties, the Beatles used that music as a basis for creating their own unique sounds and covered the whole spectrum of popular music of the day ranging from rock 'n' roll to rhythm and blues, to gentle ballads.

John Lennon was born on 9 October 1940 and formed his first group, the Quarrymen (named after his school, Quarry Bank High School), when he was 15. The other members of the original group were Eric Griffiths, Pete Shotton and Colin Hanson. John was introduced to Paul McCartney (born 18 June 1942) at a church fête in 1956, and the left-handed guitarist joined the group. In 1958 George Harrison (born 25 February 1943), who had previously played with the Les Stewart Quartet and had his own group, the Rebels, also became a Quarryman.

By the end of the fifties the Quarrymen were a trio and entered a talent contest as Johnny and the Moondogs and used other names like the Rainbows and the Silver Beatles. Stu Sutcliffe joined the other three

members in 1960 and they had, by then, settled on the name the Silver Beatles and went on a Scottish tour as the backing group for Johnny Gentle. Later that year they went to Hamburg for the first time and by then had Pete Best on drums.

Playing at the Top Ten Club, they met up with, and backed, singer Tony Sheridan and in 1961 cut their first disc as the backing group to Sheridan. It was a minor hit and was entitled *My Bonnie* and was backed with *When The Saints Go Marching In*. The group were listed as the Beatles on the record label (Polydor).

It was this record that was responsible for the Beatles' career really taking off.

Somebody went into the Liverpool store NEMS and asked for the record. The record department manager, Brian Epstein, had not heard of the record but was interested when he learned the group hailed from Liverpool. He set about tracking them down and watched them play. He was impressed and subsequently became their manager.

He changed their image and smartened up their appearance, but at the same time made sure they retained their individuality. Long hair was still acceptable, but in a tidier form.

Epstein secured a record contract with EMI (on the Parlophone label) as he proved to be the man the Beatles needed to expose their extraordinary talents to the British public. But without the skills of John and Paul as singers and songwriters, Epstein would never have had a marketable product in the first place.

When Epstein took the Beatles under his wing, the group consisted of John, Paul, George and Pete Best. Stu Sutcliffe quit the group in Hamburg and subsequently died of a brain tumour. But shortly after Epstein's arrival, drummer Best was replaced by Richard Starkey on 16 August 1962. Better known as Ringo Starr (born 7 July 1940), he had been the drummer with Rory Storm and the Hurricanes, another of Liverpool's top groups of the day. His arrival was not popular with the Beatles' fans at first but they soon accepted him. Best, on the other hand, joined another Liverpool group, Lee Curtis and the All Stars, before eventually quitting the pop scene in 1968 and earning a living as a baker and then an employment counsellor in Liverpool.

The 'new' Beatles' first record was *Love Me Do;* their first television appearance on 17 October 1962 helped record sales and by December it was in the charts. Within 12 months the Beatles had made the biggest impact on the British charts since the early days of Elvis Presley. By the end of 1963 they had enjoyed three number-one hits: *From Me To You, She Loves You* and *I Want To Hold Your Hand.* They had accounted for record sales of seven million. The Beatles' revolution was on its way.

Wherever they went they were followed by mass hysteria, known as *Beatlemania.* But it was not just the kids that enjoyed the Beatles and their music; their parents enjoyed the new vibrant sound which they brought into our lives.

The Beatles did more than give us wonderful music. They gave us their Beatle haircuts, the Beatle jacket with the rounded neckline and no collar, and the Cuban-heeled Beatle boots.

The Beatles' success was the spur other Liverpool groups needed and

The Beatles in the psychedelic days of the 1960s.

by 1964 the Mersey Beat had taken a hold all over Britain, across Europe, and in the United States where the American pop fans, previously brought up on a staple diet of Elvis Presley and Buddy Holly, immediately fell in love with the new sounds of the Fab Four.

An appearance on the *Ed Sullivan Show* in 1964 helped increase the group's popularity in the States, and sell-out concerts proved that Beatlemania existed on both sides of the Atlantic. Beatles' records dominated both the singles and album charts in the States at the time. They returned to America in 1965 and played in front of 55,000 at New York City's Shea Stadium.

The Beatles were one of Britain's biggest 'exports' and in 1965 were honoured with the MBE, despite the protests of some MPs who thought the award was degraded by honouring members of the pop music world.

Inevitably there was the diversification into the world of films and *A Hard Day's Night,* while not making them Oscar-winning candidates, did show that the Beatles were adaptable and could make the transition from the tiny stage of the Cavern to the silver screen. But it was still their music which people wanted to hear and Lennon and McCartney continued writing hit after hit as they became acknowledged as one of the finest songwriting teams of all time, and that includes the likes of Rodgers and Hammerstein.

Their own publishing company, Northern Songs, was formed but, by 1965, the catchy and simple songs were starting to drift away and were being replaced by more deep and complex lyrics which their albums *Rubber Soul* and *Revolver* highlighted. The introduction of a wide variety of additional musical instruments, like the sitar and string quartet, made the Beatles music so different from the 'Yeah yeah yeah' sounds of the early days. And when they released *Sergeant Pepper's Lonely Hearts Club Band* album in June 1967 they brought together in musical form all the popular ideals of the day which the youth could identify themselves with. And there was more than a hidden reference to one of the big issues of the day, drugs. The album was innovative and probably the most popular of all their albums before or since and considered by many to be an anthem to the whole sixties experience.

The Beatles had by now become hippies and gone into the world of meditation. Their hair was longer and the smart appearance of the Beatle jackets was long gone. By 1967 there were signs that it was gradually coming to an end.

Brian Epstein died in 1967 and the group started to drift away from each other. They were still around, but more as individuals rather than the great group they were five years earlier. They opened their own *Apple* record company in August 1968 and came together to record the *White Album* which, after the electronic wizardry of *Sergeant Pepper,* was a return to the more relaxed Beatles sounds. It was to be one of their biggest-selling LPs. There was another LP in 1969 when they recorded *Abbey Road,* named after their London studios. It was a monster hit and was again reflective of some of the early Beatles material.

But the following year it all came to an end. Their *Let It Be* album was the last they made together.

The four members of the Beatles went their own way and had hit records. John Lennon had his first solo hit in 1969 when *Give Peace A Chance* reached number two in the charts. He also gave us number-one hits with *Imagine, (Just Like) Starting Over* and *Woman* amongst other Top Ten hits. Sadly, the world of pop music was devastated on 9 December 1980 when John Lennon was murdered in cold blood outside his New York apartment.

Paul McCartney is still producing hit records whether they be on his own, with his band Wings, with the Frog Chorus, or with other singers like Michael Jackson and Stevie Wonder. His *Mull Of Kintyre/Girls' School* in 1977 was one of the biggest-selling singles in British chart history and was the first to sell two million copies.

Ringo Starr enjoyed minor success as a singer and had Top Ten hits with *It Don't Come Easy, Back Off Boogaloo, Photograph* and *You're Sixteen.* However, he diversified and became the voice behind the televised children's favourite, *Thomas The Tank Engine.*

And finally, George Harrison. He spent his early post-Beatles days in the world of meditation, but was the first member of the group to have a solo number-one hit when *My Sweet*

In June 1966, the Beatles appeared live on TV for the first time. They took part in the BBCs Top Of The Pops

Lord topped the charts in 1971. It was his only number one and his other big hits were *Bangla Desh, Give Me Love (Give Me Peace On Earth)* and *All Those Years Ago* in 1981. George also had a hit in 1987 with *Got My Mind Set On You*, which went to number two, and followed that with a successful solo album called *Cloud Nine*. He is also a member of the Travelling Wilburys the all-star super-group which included Bob Dylan, Tom Petty, Jeff Lynn and formerly Roy Orbison.

Decca had the chance to have the Beatles under contract but turned them down in January 1962. Their executives felt they were not good enough to make it as chart artistes!

The Beatles were inspirational, not only to other groups but also to the millions of pop music fans of the sixties. They brought a new dimension to the world of music. They brought a new dimension to our lives. Thank you.

Top Ten hit singles of the Beatles in the 1960s:

Year	Record	Pos
1963	Please Please Me	2
1963	From Me To You	1
1963	She Loves You	1
1963	I Want To Hold Your Hand	1
1964	Can't Buy Me Love	1
1964	A Hard Day's Night	1
1964	I Feel Fine	1
1965	Ticket To Ride	1
1965	Help!	1
1965	Day Tripper/We Can Work It Out	1
1966	Paperback Writer	1
1966	Yellow Submarine/ Eleanor Rigby	1
1967	Penny Lane/Strawberry Fields Forever	2
1967	All You Need Is Love	1
1967	Hello Goodbye	1
1967	Magical Mystery Tour (double EP)	2
1968	Lady Madonna	1
1968	Hey Jude	1
1969	Get Back	1
1969	Ballad Of John And Yoko	1
1969	Something/Come Together	4

On 4 April 1964 the US pop charts looked like this:

1.	Can't Buy Me Love	The Beatles
2.	Twist And Shout	The Beatles
3.	She Loves You	The Beatles
4.	I Want To Hold Your Hand	The Beatles
5.	Please Please Me	The Beatles

The album chart looked like this:

1.	Meet The Beatles	The Beatles
2.	Introducing The Beatles	The Beatles

Number-one hits of the four members since leaving the Beatles:

John Lennon
1980 (Just Like) Starting Over
1980 Imagine (re-release)
1981 Woman

Lennon also had three chart-topping albums:-
Imagine (1971), Double Fantasy (1980) and The John Lennon Collection (1982).

Paul McCartney
1977 Mull Of Kintyre/Girls' School
1982 Ebony And Ivory (with Stevie Wonder)
1983 Pipes Of Peace

In addition McCartney has had seven number-one LPs:-
Ram (1971), Band On The Run (1973), Venus And Mars (1975), McCartney (1980), Tug Of War (1982), Give My Regards To Broad Street (1984) and All The Best (1987).

George Harrison
1971 My Sweet Lord

Beatles' marriages of the 1960s:-
Aug 1962 John Lennon to Cynthia Powell
Feb 1965 Ringo Starr to Maureen Cox
Jan 1966 George Harrison to Patti Boyd
Mar 1969 Paul McCartney to Linda Eastman (after years of speculation that his bride would be Jane Asher)
Mar 1969 John Lennon to Yoko Ono (for their honeymoon they spent a week in bed, 'making love, not war' at the Amsterdam Hilton).

BEECHING, Dr Richard

DR BEECHING was chairman of the British Railways Board for four years between 1961 and 1965, but what an impact he made during his short term of office.

Born in 1913, Baron Richard Beeching was a scientist and had two spells as a director of ICI, both before and after his time at British Railways.

But it was as chairman of the Railways Board that he will best be remembered, and notably for his famous Beeching Report of 1963, which suggested a concentration of rail services on Inter-City passenger and freight rail services. At the same time it outlined wholesale cuts in many rural services.

Having been chosen to head a team to look into the British Rail network in 1960, his controversial report was published in March 1963.

The report was headed 'The

Reshaping of British Railways'. It announced plans to close more than 2,000 stations, scrap more than 8,000 coaches and cut 67,700 jobs. The network was reduced by 5,000 miles and passenger services north of Inverness disappeared, as did most branch lines in north and central Wales and the West Country.

Having studied his report, the Government announced 12 months later that it would make wholesale closures as outlined by Beeching. In December 1964, Dr Beeching was sacked as British Railways boss and the following year he returned to ICI. The cuts were still carried out.

BEE GEES

ALTHOUGH they have spent most of their lives living and working in either Australia or the United States, all members of the Bee Gees were brought up in the Manchester area as youngsters. The family emigrated to Australia in 1958 and within three years Barry Gibb and his younger twin brothers, Maurice (who later married Lulu) and Robin, were starring in their own television series. This led to them becoming one of Australia's top groups and they recorded their first song, *Coal Man*.

To further their career they returned to England in 1967 and became contracted to manager Robert Stigwood. Their first British release came out that year and *New York Mining Disaster 1941* reached number 12 in the charts.

But real success came when their own composition, *Massachusetts* reached number one. It heralded the arrival of the Bee Gees as singers and songwriters. They had one more number one before the 1960s were out, but they became truly inter-national stars in the 1970s with many US chart-topping singles. Their writing skills enabled younger brother Andy to have his first three singles all go to the top of the charts in America — a unique feat.

They also became well-known for their compositions for the hit movies *Saturday Night Fever* and *Grease,* and leading solo artistes like Frankie Valli, Barbra Streisand, Kenny Rogers, Dionne Warwick and many more have benefited from Bee Gees material.

Robin left the group following an argument in 1969 and followed a solo career. But less than a year later he returned. In 1987 they topped the British charts again 20 years after their first success when *You Win Again* went to number one.

Top Ten hits of the Bee Gees in the 1960s:

Year	Record	Pos
1967	Massachusetts	1
1967	World	9
1968	Words	8
1968	I've Gotta Get A Message To You	1
1969	First Of May	6
1969	Don't Forget To Remember	2

BEEHIVE HAIRSTYLE

A POPULAR woman's hairstyle in the early half of the 1960s, it was so called because of its beehive shape.

The hair was back-combed (teased) towards its roots and this helped to create the required height. It was then smoothed over and vast quantities of hair lacquer applied to hold it in place. Special back-combing combs were available and these incorporated little nodules on the teeth. Because of the beehive, and also the wearing of stiletto-heeled shoes, girls in the 1960s were anything up to a foot taller than their normal height!

Typical Press sensationalism of the day reported various insects, and even mice, living in some beehive hairstyles!

BERLIN WALL

ON 30 August 1960, the East Germans closed their border with West Berlin. This led to the construction of the Berlin Wall a year later.

On the morning of 13 August 1961, East German soldiers divided the east and west sectors with rolls of barbed wire. Some 50,000 East Germans who worked in West Berlin were not allowed to pass. Work then started immediately on the building of the 28¼ mile (45km) long wall which now divides the city in two, West and East Berlin. The latter is the Communist sector.

Concrete barriers placed in the American sector to prevent Allied vehicles patrolling this section of the Berlin Wall.

The wall was made with prefabricated concrete blocks and every possible loophole was blocked by the East Germans. However, many have tried to find a route to freedom in West Berlin. Some have succeeded, but many have failed and been shot on sight as they tried to make their way through, under or over the wall.

> *Extract from J.F.Kennedy's 'Berlin Wall' speech on 26 June 1963:-*
> *"All free men, wherever they may live, are citizens of Berlin. And therefore as a free man I take pride in the words: 'Ich bin ein Berliner' "*

BEST, George

ARGUMENTS have raged for many years as to who was the best British footballer. Those arguments will never end but when you look at the wealth of talent around in the sixties, there were plenty of candidates, and there was none stronger than Ulsterman George Best.

Born in Belfast in 1946, he joined Manchester United as a 15-year-old and made his debut in 1963. During the next ten years, many of them tempestuous, Best played more than 450 games in the famous red shirt of United and scored nearly 200 goals. One of the most important was two minutes into extra-time of the 1968 European Cup Final at Wembley when he side-stepped the Benfica defence to put United 2-1 ahead and set up their eventual 4-1 victory, making them the first English winners of the trophy.

Best helped United to win two League Championships, in 1965 and 1967, but, following a series of disagreements with the new management teams at Old Trafford, he moved

on to pastures new in 1975 when he joined nearby Stockport County. Since then he has tried to resurrect his career at Fulham, Bournemouth, Hibernian and across the Atlantic in the North American Soccer League.

Sadly he slumped to an all-time low in the 1980s when he had to endure a spell in prison which was a tragedy for the man who had everything required of the 'complete' footballer. He had control, speed, craft and above all, that insatiable appetite for

scoring goals. Those who saw George Best play will not entertain any other candidate for the 'Best Ever British Footballer' title.

BETTING SHOPS

THE MODERN-DAY betting shop consists of several television screens displaying latest odds and broadcasting races via a wide range of satellites and cable television links. But 30 years ago there was no such thing as a betting shop. The only legal betting on race horses was on-track betting. That is not to say off-course betting didn't take place — but it shouldn't have! One London bookmaker welcomed the legalizing of betting shops because he had been paying fines of £400 per year for running his business — mind you, his 2,000 bets a day comfortably paid the fine.

Off-course betting was legalized on 1 May 1961 when the Betting and Gaming Act came into force and this made betting shops legal. The first shops opened in London but they were not easy to find at first because the laws forbade them to display spectacular advertising.

Since then, however, the betting shop has become a more comfortable place to visit, even if the end product is still the same as it was in 1961!

Bookmakers in a mock funeral procession to 'bury' the proposed betting tax.

IT IS amazing how many shows of the 1960s are enjoying a second life in the 1980s. *The Beverly Hillbillies* is enjoying as much success the second time around as it did the first.

The series is based on the story of the Clampetts, a four-strong family of hillbillies from Bugtussle in the Ozarks, who find oil on their land. With their new-found wealth they set out for Bel-Air and Beverly Hills.

The weekly stories revolved around their adjusting (or not, as the case was) to life amongst the rich in Beverly Hills, whilst still maintaining their rural image. There was the other aspect to the stories; how did the local people adjust to them? The local banker's wife, Margaret Drysdale, wanted them out of town, while husband Milburn wanted them to stay — he held their account.

The cast comprised: Jed Clampett (played by Buddy Ebsen), Granny Moses (Irene Ryan), Jethro Bodine (Max Baer Jnr), Elly May Clampett (Donna Douglas), Milburn Drysdale (Raymond Bailey) and Margaret Drysdale (Harriet MacGibbon). Max Baer Junior is the son of former world boxing champion, Max Baer.

There was also Cousin Pearl who was played by Bea Benaderet, who also appeared in *Petticoat Junction*. Ebsen, a well-known dancer who appeared with Shirley Temple in *Good Ship Lollipop*, went on to play *Barnaby Jones*. Irene Ryan died in 1973.

BEWITCHED

THIS popular series ran from 1964 to 1972. It was the story of Darrin and Samantha Stephens. Darrin was an advertising executive with 'McCann & Tate' while Samantha was a witch. But it was only on their wedding night that she broke the news to her husband.

They lived at 1164 Morning Glory Circle, and despite pleas from her husband, Samantha could not resist the temptation to keep up her practice which, by the twitching of her nose, could cause all sorts of mysterious happenings. When baby Tabitha came along, it did not help matters, and there was further unrest for Darrin when Samantha's mother, Endora (Agnes Moorhead), and scheming cousin, Serena, made regular visits to the household.

Elizabeth Montgomery played the role of Samantha and also that of cousin Serena. Darrin was played by Dick York from 1964 to 1969, and then by Dick Sargent.

In the 1980s *Bewitched* has enjoyed a rebirth of popularity with the British TV fans.

BIAFRA

FAMINE has been a fact of life for as long as anyone can remember. In the 1980s we have had the much-publicized Ethiopian famine, and in the 1960s there was the equally well-publicized starvation of thousands of Biafrans. The differences between the two were, firstly, there was no Bob Geldof at the time of the Biafran famine, and secondly, the Biafran problem was totally man-made.

The troubles started in 1966, six years after Nigeria became an independent republic. In that year an army coup led to much bloodshed and the Ibo race, who lived in the eastern region, felt threatened. In May 1967, Colonel Ojukwu announced independence for the eastern region which would become known as the Republic of Biafra.

The region contained rich oil reserves and the Nigerian Government sent in troops to invade the new republic. Nearly 3,000 British and American residents fled as the fighting continued.

During the bloodshed, Colonel Ojukwu asked British oil companies drilling in the area to pay all royalties directly to him. They agreed. But then the Federal authorities imposed a blockade on all oil exports.

Nigerian troops pictured as they take Enugu airport in the Biafran capital.

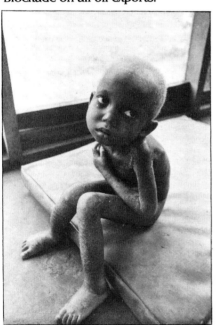

Above and opposite: Innocent victims of the Nigerian civil war.

As the war reached the middle of 1969, and with more than 2,000 men, women and children massacred, there developed another problem — starvation amongst the survivors.

The Nigerian Government banned night flights of Red Cross supplies because they maintained the Biafrans were using this as a cover to fly in arms. In turn, the Biafrans refused to allow daytime flights on to their airstrip. Consequently, there was mass starvation. The Red Cross were ordered out of Nigeria for flying relief missions to refugees. The Biafrans were literally being starved out and on 12 January 1970, Ojukwu surrendered. The British Government immediately announced £5-million worth of aid to the starving as 300,000 Biafrans left the refugee camps and

made their way back to their homes. They were the lucky ones. In the days leading up to the surrender, there were mass killings, raping and looting.

Ojukwu was granted asylum on the Ivory Coast.

BIBA

AS BOUTIQUES became the mode of the 1960s, there was, firstly, Mary Quant's *Bazaar* and then came *Biba*.

Biba was the idea of Barbara Hulanicki, the daughter of a Polish diplomat. Born in 1938, she moved to England at the outbreak of the war and as a teenager studied at the Brighton School of Art. Her first job was as a fashion artist.

With the fashion boom taking off, she started designing clothes that would appeal to the new teenager, but more importantly, would be inexpensive. She set up a mail-order operation and it was so successful that she opened her *Biba* boutique in Abingdon Road, London, in 1963. Her ultra-modern clothes made her a cult figure in the fashion business.

After several moves she opened her famous department store in Kensington High Street, in 1969. It became affectionately known as the 'Dolly Birds' Department Store'. The store had an all-black decor and was designed in the 1930s style. The

success was instant, and it became a big tourist attraction.

Like Mary Quant she diversified into cosmetics and when the store eventually closed in 1975, she sold the cosmetics empire to Dorothy Perkins. The following year Barbara Hulanicki moved to Brazil in the hope of starting the fashion revolution all over again.

BIGGS, Ronnie

RONNIE Biggs is the most celebrated of the Great Train Robbers and, apart from a spell of a little over 12 months in prison, has had his freedom ever since that day in August 1963 when he and other members of the daring gang got away with £2.6 million.

Ronald Arthur Biggs, the then 34-year-old joiner from Redhill, was sentenced to 30 years imprisonment in April 1964. But on 8 July 1965 he was 'sprung' from Wandsworth Prison, when he and three others escaped up a rope ladder thrown over a 20ft wall while they were having their afternoon exercise at 3.05pm. From there they dropped into the open top of a removal van parked on the other side of the wall, and escaped.

The others who escaped with Biggs were Robert Anderson, serving 12 years for conspiracy to rob; Eric Flower, also 12 years for armed robbery and conspiracy to rob; and

Anthony Jenkins, serving four years for conspiracy to rob.

Biggs has since enjoyed his freedom but has spent a large part of his share of the robbery spoils on arranging false passports etc.

> Biggs was the second Great Train Robber to escape from prison. The first was Charles Wilson who escaped from Winson Green Prison, Birmingham, almost a year to the day after the robbery, on 12 August 1964. He was recaptured at Rigaud, Quebec, Canada, on 25 January 1968.

Ronnie Biggs on his way to court.

At first he fled to Australia where he met up with his wife, Charmaine, but when the police were hot on his trail he skipped the country and ended up in Brazil. He was forced to leave his wife and has since set up home in his new country without her.

He was about to be deported on a technicality in 1974 but it was discovered that his girlfriend, Raimonda, was pregnant and, consequently, Biggs was allowed to stay in the country as the father of a Brazilian child.

Since then his son Michael has become one of Brazil's top pop singers and Biggs has never re-married.

BIKILA, Abebe

IN 1960 Abebe Bikila made history by becoming the first Ethiopian to win an Olympic gold medal when he pounded his way through the streets of Rome to win the marathon, one of the most prestigious of all Olympic events. Furthermore he covered the 26 miles 385 yards barefoot. Four years later in Tokyo he became the first man to win the Olympic marathon title twice.

Before he won the 1960 title, Bikila was an unknown, and had only raced in two previous marathons; both only a couple of weeks before the Games! He was an Imperial Bodyguard to Emperor Haile Selassie and when he returned home he was proclaimed a national hero. The Emperor duly

promoted him from private to sergeant.

When he retained his title four years later, he did so with the biggest winning margin for 40 years, and set a new Olympic record. This time he wore shoes, but six weeks before the race he had his appendix removed! When he returned to his homeland he was promoted once more, this time to lieutenant.

A leg injury shortly before the 1968 Olympics forced him to pull out of the race after ten miles and thus thwarted what could have been one of the greatest Olympic hat-tricks of all time . . .and possible further promotion!

His running career came to an end in 1969 when he was involved in a car crash in Addis Ababa. He was confined to a wheelchair and convalesced at Stoke Mandeville Hospital, where he competed in the paraplegic Olympics. He died of a brain haemorrhage on 25 October 1973.

BILK, Acker

THINK of a bowler hat, a multi-coloured waistcoat and a clarinet and who immediately springs to mind? Acker Bilk, the man who found everlasting fame with the Top Ten hit *Stranger On The Shore*.

Born in Somerset in 1929, his real name is Bernard Stanley Bilk, but he took the name Acker which is Somerset slang for 'mate'. He learned to play the clarinet while serving a three-month prison sentence in an army jail in 1947. He received the sentence for falling asleep while on guard!

His monster hit was released in 1961 and spent a staggering 55 consecutive weeks in the British charts, yet, remarkably, never reached number one. It also spent 21 weeks in the US charts and sold more than four million copies in five years.

The song was written by Bilk and originally called Jenny after one of his daughters. It was renamed after it was used as the theme tune for a BBC TV children's series entitled *Stranger*

On The Shore. The record credits Mr Acker Bilk with the Leon Young String Chorale.

Acker and his band, the Paramount Jazz Band, became a big attraction in the 1960s either at live concerts, or on radio and television.

He returned to the charts in 1976 with *Aria.*

Top Ten hits of Acker Bilk in the 1960s:

Year	Record	Pos
1960	Summer Set	5
1960	Buona Sera	7
1961	That's My Home	7
1961	Stranger On The Shore	2

BLACK, Cilla

BORN Priscilla Maria Veronica White in Liverpool on 27 May 1943, she changed her name to Cilla Black on the advice of her manager Brian Epstein, who signed her in 1963. On leaving school Cilla was a typist and secretary, but spent whatever time she could at the famous Cavern were she was a coat check-out girl before being given the chance to grace the stage which housed many of the great Liverpool groups of the era who later became top stars.

Red-headed Cilla's first record was a Lennon/McCartney composition called *Love Of The Loved* and was released in 1963. She sang it on her television debut on *Ready Steady Go.* It was only a minor hit but her next two records *Anyone Who Had A Heart* and *You're My World* both reached number one for the girl dubbed 'The female Beatle'. Both records sold over a million copies worldwide and *Anyone Who Had A Heart* was the biggest selling single for a female singer in the 1960s.

She had countless more Top Twenty hits but towards the end of the decade started to diversify and the BBC eventually gave Cilla her own show. It was a huge success and she has continually appeared on the television screens in a wide range of variety programmes such as *Blind Date* and *Surprise, Surprise* which have brought a 'lorra, lorra' pleasure to millions.

Cilla married her agent-manager Bobby Willis in 1970. They have three sons and live in a mansion in Buckinghamshire — a far cry from Cilla's 'Scottie Road' roots, but roots she has never forgotten.

Top Ten hits of Cilla Black in the 1960s:

Year	Record	Pos
1964	Anyone Who Had A Heart	1
1964	You're My World	1
1964	It's For You	7
1965	You've Lost That Lovin' Feelin'	2
1966	Love's Just A Broken Heart	5
1966	Alfie	9
1966	Don't Answer Me	6
1968	Step Inside Love	8
1969	Surround Yourself With Sorrow	3
1969	Conversations	7

BLACKBURN, Tony

TONY Blackburn, the man with the ultra-white teeth, started his disc-jockeying career on the 'pirate' radios before having the honour of playing the first record on Radio One in 1967 when he spun *Flowers In The Rain* by The Move.

The son of a doctor, Blackburn was born at Guildford in 1943 and was educated at Millfield School where classmates included the top sports personalities Mary Rand and Mike Sangster. Despite his education, Blackburn's first job was as a guitarist and singer with the Ian Ralfini Orchestra in Bournemouth, which became his new home town.

He joined Radio Caroline in 1964 after they placed an advert in one of the music papers of the day. From there he moved to another 'pirate' station, Radio London (no relation to the present-day BBC Radio London where he continues his radio career).

Appearances on Radio Luxembourg and the old Light Programme enhanced his career before he got the

Breakfast Show slot on the new Radio One in 1967.

He later moved to the mid-morning and afternoon shows before joining Radio Two. He has appeared on a wide range of television programmes as a guest.

In addition to playing records, Blackburn has cut a few discs in his time and enjoyed minor success in the late sixties with *So Much In Love,* which reached number 31 in 1968, and *It's Only Love,* number 42 in 1969.

The ever-smiling Blackburn was once married to actress Tessa Wyatt, who later set up home with her *Robin's Nest* co-star, Richard O'Sullivan.

BLAKE, George

GEORGE Blake was charged with offences under the Official Secrets Act on 18 April 1961 but details of the actual charges were withheld.

A month later he was sentenced to a record 42 years imprisonment and the actions of the self-confessed spy were described as one of 'treachery' by Lord Chief Justice Parker.

Blake was 38 at the time and had been passing information to the Soviets for nine years. He was captured by them during the Korean War while serving as the British Vice Consul in Seoul. During his three years in captivity he was believed to have been 'brainwashed'.

On 22 October 1966 Blake escaped from Wormwood Scrubs with, it is said, with Soviet aid. He was never recaptured. Blake died in the Soviet Union in 1989.

BLUE STREAK

ON 13 April 1960 the British Government announced that it was scrapping the £65 million Blue Streak project, a decision which brought uproar in the House of Commons.

The development of the ballistic missile, the major weapon in Britain's planned independent nuclear strike force, was first announced in the 1950s and as recently as February 1959 the annual White Paper on defence said: 'The Government have recently reviewed the British ballistic rocket programme and have concluded that, on present knowledge, *Blue Streak* is of the type of missile best suited to British needs. The development of this weapon is therefore continuing.'

When issued the following February, the next White Paper said: 'The development of the British missile *Blue Streak* is continuing'. But two months later the embarrassing job of pronouncing it obsolete fell to Harold Watkinson, the Conservative Minister of Defence.

Blue Streak's problem was that it could only be launched from a static site, which was being developed at Woomera in Australia. However, as Mr. Watkinson said in his speech: "The vulnerability of missiles launched from static sites, and the practicability of launching missiles of considerable range from mobile platforms, has now been established."

At the time of the announcement, the project had cost the nation £65 million but, as Mr Watkinson said: "The cost of completing it would be between £500-600 million. In other words, the project has been stopped when something like only one-sixth of the expense has been incurred." This comment from the Minister brought hoots of laughter from Labour members.

Blue Streak was, however, used as the first stage of a satellite launcher by the European Launcher Development Organization (ELDO) and the 92-ton rocket was launched for the first time from Woomera in 1964.

BOARD, Lillian, MBE

THE death of Lillian Board from cancer at the age of 22 in 1970 shocked the whole nation. She had become popular, not only with fellow athletes, and track and field fans, but also with the average man in the street. Her rise to the top of British athletics was a quick one.

Born in Durban, South Africa, in 1948 and one of twin sisters, she was a talented sprinter and long-jumper at school. Her first coach was her father and in 1966, after the family moved to England, she was picked to make her international debut in the USA versus British Commonwealth match in Los Angeles. She was the only British winner.

Lillian Board, pictured at Heathrow Airport in October 1968, wearing her Olympic silver medal. Also in the picture is Britain's gold-medallist, David Hemery.

The following year Lillian won the 400 metres in the European Cup, but at the Mexico Olympics in 1968 she was deprived of a gold medal in the last couple of strides by French girl Collette Besson. However, she won gold in the 800 metres at the European Championships a year later.

When she came third in the WAAA's 800 metres in June 1970, the first signs of her illness were showing. She experienced great pain, particularly in her back, and Crohn's Disease was diagnosed. The illness caused her to withdraw from the Commonwealth Games. By October her parents, relatives and friends all knew the seriousness of her illness. When Lillian found out she announced that she was 'going to fight and beat the disease'. But, despite a visit to Dr Isschel's Bavarian clinic, Lillian Board died on 26 December 1970.

In her four brief years at the top of British athletics she had captured the hearts of the British people with her bubbly nature. She had also been awarded the MBE. Cruelly, her chances of more track honours were taken away from her.

BOGARDE, Dirk

IT IS hardly surprising film star Dirk Bogarde changed his name; he was born as Derek Julius Gaspard Ulric Niven van den Bogaerde at Hampstead, London, on 29 March 1921. With a mouthful like that, by the time his name had been added to the film credits there wouldn't be much room for any other stars. So, plain Dirk Bogarde he became.

The son of a *Times* editor, he started acting in 1939 but then spent five years in military service, mostly in the Far East. Upon his discharge he appeared in small productions. After a West End appearance in 1947 he was given a contract with the Rank Organization. His first film was *Dancing With Crime* in 1947.

In the 1950s he starred in such films as *The Blue Lamp* and portrayed the likeable Dr Simon Sparrow in the *Doctor* films. Sparrow was just one of the roles he played in the 1960s as *We Joined The Navy* and *Doctor In Distress* featured Bogarde's character.

The portrayal of a suspected homosexual in the 1961 film *Victim* received acclaim and in 1963, Bogarde won the Best British Actor award from the British Academy for his part as Melville Farr in *The Servant*. He received the same award two years later for his role as Robert Gold in the John Schlessinger film *Darling* opposite Julie Christie.

The films of Dirk Bogarde in the 1960s:

The Wind Cannot Read	(1960)
The Angel Wore Red	(1960)
Song Without End	(1960)
The Singer Not The Song	(1961)
Victim	(1961)
HMS Defiant (Damn The Defiant!)	(1962)
The Password Is Courage	(1962)
We Joined The Navy	(1962)
The Mind Benders	(1962)
I Could Go On Singing	(1962)
Doctor In Distress	(1963)
The Servant	(1963)
Hot Enough For June	(1963)
King And Country	(1964)
The High Bright Sun	(1964)
Darling	(1965)
Modesty Blaise	(1966)
Accident	(1966)
Our Mother's House	(1967)
Sebastian	(1968)
The Fixer	(1968)
Oh! What A Lovely War	(1969)
Justine	(1969)
The Damned	(1969)

BONANZA

ONE of the most popular westerns to hit the British television screens was *Bonanza*. It was first seen this side of the Atlantic in 1960, a year after American viewers were first treated to it.

It told stories of the life of the Cartwright family on their Ponderosa ranch near Virginia City, Nevada, during the Civil War.

The family consisted of thrice married widower Ben Cartwright (Lorne Green). Each of his wives bore him a son: Adam (Pernell Roberts), Eric, nicknamed 'Hoss' (Dan Blocker) and the youngest, Little Joe, played by Michael Landon who later starred in the 'weepie' western *The Little House On The Prairie* and also *Highway To Heaven*. Pernell Roberts pursued a stage career after leaving the programme before turning up as *Trapper John MD* in the series of the same name.

> *Unlike the Southfork ranch in Dallas, The Ponderosa never existed. It was a stage set at the Paramount studios.*

Even after Roberts left the cast of *Bonanza* in 1965 the show retained its popularity and was the first western to be shown in colour. Filming eventually ended in 1972 after Dan Blocker tragically died and Lorne Greene suffered a mild heart attack. Canadian-born Greene eventually died in 1987 at the age of 72.

Bonanza became the trendsetter for other such popular family western series as *The Big Valley* and *The High Chaparral*. Furthermore many people in Britain and the United States renamed their houses *Ponderosa*.

BOSTON STRANGLER, The

BETWEEN June 1962 and December 1964 a total of 13 women are believed to have died at the hands of the Boston Strangler. All but two bore the Strangler's trademark — a single stocking tied tightly around their necks. His victims were killed in their own homes; most had been sexually abused and their bodies were left in obscene poses. However, some police officers were not of the opinion that one man killed all 13. The Strangler was never caught or positively identified.

In January 1967, Albert DeSalvo, a former United States Army middle-weight boxing champion, was sentenced to life imprisonment for a series of burglaries, assaults and sex attacks against four women unrelated to the 13 murders 'accredited' to the Boston Strangler. At first he was ruled mentally unstable to stand trial, but he was eventually brought to justice. However, a month after starting his sentence, he, along with three other inmates of the Bridgewater State Hospital, escaped but were recaptured shortly afterwards.

Upon his recapture, DeSalvo was sent to the Walpole State Prison and it was while there that he confessed to a psychiatrist that he was in fact the Strangler. The details he gave of the crimes led police to believe his statements to be true. However, he later retracted his 'confession'.

DeSalvo was never brought to trial for the 13 killings, because, on 26 November 1973, the 40-year-old was stabbed to death by another inmate following a row over drugs.

Tony Curtis played the part of DeSalvo in the 1968 film The Boston Strangler.

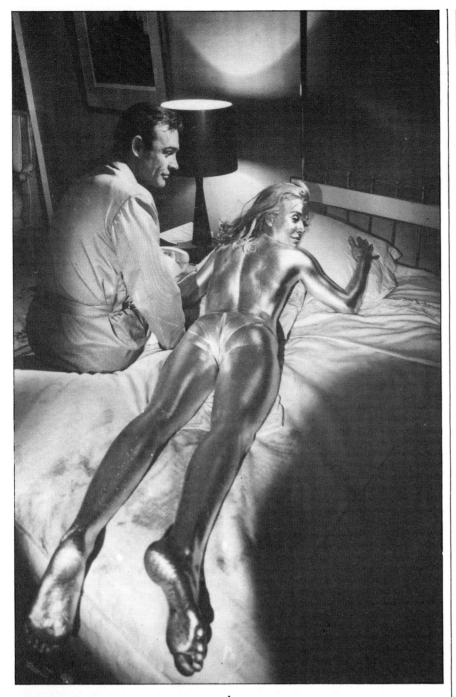

James Bond, played by Sean Connery, pictured in the film Goldfinger *with actress Shirley Eaton.*

BOND FILMS

THE James Bond films brought to the silver screen the character invented by Ian Fleming in the early 1950s. Tongue-in-cheek thrillers, they were lavish productions which captured the public's imagination and are still as popular in the 1980s.

The first sixties Bond film was *Dr No* in 1962 and the main character was played by Sean Connery, who fitted ideally into the Bond person-ality. He portrayed Agent number 007 in the next four films; *From Russia With Love* (1963), *Goldfinger* (1964), *Thunderball* (1965) and *You Only Live Twice* (1967). But he opted out of the next one, *On Her Majesty's Secret Service* (1969) which featured George Lazenby in the part of Bond.

The success of the films not only stemmed from the cool character as portrayed by Connery, but also from the array of leading ladies who appeared alongside him. There was Ursula Andress in *Dr No*, Honor Blackman in *Goldfinger* and George Lazenby had Diana Rigg as his leading lady in his only portrayal of Bond.

Connery returned to play the lead in *Diamonds Are Forever* in 1971 but then handed the role of Bond to Roger Moore who, like Connery, slotted into the role ideally. Connery returned in 1983 to play Bond once more in *Never Say Never Again*.

There was a spoof version of *Casino Royale* in 1967 with a variety of leading actors, including Peter Sellers, taking turns to play the part of Bond.

BREATHALYSER

ON 29 January 1966, Parliament passed the new Road Safety Act that, 18 months later, saw the introduction of the breathalyser which had been invented in the United States and used in other countries.

It set a limit of 80 milligrammes of alcohol in 100cc of blood and it became an offence to drive, or even attempt to drive, with a higher level of alcohol content.

Understandably, the motor asso-ciations objected to the Bill on the grounds it was an infringement of personal liberty. The Pedestrians' Association, meanwhile, welcomed the new law.

Anybody found guilty would be fined up to £100 or imprisoned and received an automatic one-year ban from driving. Second and subsequent offences carried even more severe penalties.

Then Minister of Transport, Barbara Castle, said it was: "the start of a social revolution" and believed it would bring a change in social habits. She was right.

The first statutory breath test was carried out just after midnight on 8 October 1967, when an unnamed youth, who had been involved in an accident at Redhill, near Bristol, was tested. He was later taken to Flax Bourton police station about 12 miles away where a second test was carried out and a blood sample taken. Elsewhere around the country, it was not until around 3.00am that further tests were carried out.

The Hatfield Hotel in Lowestoft was quick to provide their customers a way of beating the breathalyser. They laid on a free bus service.

BURTON, Richard

RICHARD Burton, the 12th of 13 children, was born as Richard Jenkins in the Welsh mining community of Pontrhydfen in 1925. After his mother's death he lived with his sister and was befriended by his English schoolteacher Phillip Burton, who was Richard's inspiration. It was after his teacher that Burton took his stage name.

He won a scholarship to Oxford at the age of 18 and made his first stage appearance in *Druid's Rest* at Liverpool's Royal Court Theatre. Burton served in the RAF but returned to the stage in 1948. The following year he was hailed as a great actor both in the West End and on Broadway. He also captivated audiences at Stratford-upon-Avon.

Burton made his Hollywood debut in *My Cousin Rachel* in 1952 but he enjoyed alternating his film roles with Old Vic productions. He became established as one of the great modern-day Shakespearian actors.

In the 1960s, Burton hit the headlines because of his much-publicized romance, and subsequent marriage in 1964 to Elizabeth Taylor after they had met on the set of *Cleopatra* the year before. The romance cost Burton a 'few bob'

because he bought Liz the 33-carat Krupp diamond. However, he got the money back because *Cleopatra* was the film that launched him into the top bracket of the film industry when he was reported to be earning £1 million per appearance.

Other notable Burton films of the sixties included the much-acclaimed *Becket, The Spy Who Came In From The Cold* and *Who's Afraid Of Virginia Woolf?* which also starred Elizabeth Taylor. But sadly, his critics were quick to point out that he was not intent on stretching his ability to its fullest and undertook roles which were not suitable to his great talent.

Burton received six Oscar nominations without ever winning one of the coveted awards.

Sadly, over-indulgence, particularly of drink, was to see his talent wasted and shortly after making his 50th film he died of a cerebral haemorrhage at his Swiss home on 5 August 1984.

The films of Richard Burton in the 1960s:

The Longest Day	(1962)
Cleopatra	(1962)
The VIPs	(1963)
Becket	(1964)
The Night Of The Iguana	(1964)
The Sandpiper	(1964)
The Spy Who Came In From The Cold	(1965)
Who's Afraid Of Virginia Woolf?	(1966)
The Taming Of The Shrew	(1967)
Dr Faustus	(1967)
The Comedians	(1967)
Boom	(1968)
Where Eagles Dare	(1968)
Candy	(1968)
Staircase	(1969)
Anne Of The Thousand Days	(1969)

Richard Burton and Elizabeth Taylor arriving at London's Adelphi Theatre in January 1965. They were going to see Rachel Roberts playing the title role in Maggie May.

BYRDS, The

FORMED in Los Angeles in 1964, they are often referred to as the band who originated 'folk rock music'.

The original line-up consisted of the former cowboy and founder of the Flying Burrito Brothers, Chris Hillman, ex-New Christy Minstrel Gene Clark, drummer Mike Clarke, David Crosby, who later found fame with Crosby, Stills, Nash and Young, and the founder Jim McGuinn. By 1969, McGuinn was the only surviving member of the original Byrds.

The group will best be remembered for their interpretation of the Bob Dylan song *Mr Tambourine Man* which topped the charts both sides of the Atlantic, and was one of the classics of the 1960s.

It was their only number one in

Britain, but in the States they had another chart-topper with *Turn, Turn, Turn.* It was written by Pete Seeger, who adapted the words from the Book of the Ecclesiastes from the Bible, which makes the lyrics the oldest ever to top the charts!

Top Ten hits of The Byrds in the 1960s:

Year	Record	Pos
1965	Mr Tambourine Man	1
1965	All I Really Want To Do	4

CAINE, Michael

MICHAEL Caine was born as Maurice Micklewhite on 14 March 1933. He is the son of a Billingsgate porter and a charlady and hailed from the East End of London — roots of which he is very proud.

After spending ten years in repertory he changed his name after watching the film *The Cain Mutiny.* He made his film debut in *A Hill In Korea* in 1956. He had only a bit part (not a lot of people know that), but it was an appropriate debut because Michael had served with the Royal Fusiliers during the Korean War in the 1950s.

Caine had other minor film and television roles, but his career took off in 1963 when he was given the part of one of the officers in the acclaimed *Zulu.* Since then Michael Caine has been one of the biggest box office names.

He followed *Zulu* by playing the part of spy Harry Palmer for the first time in *The Ipcress File* and he then played the part of the cheeky Alfie in the film of the same name. For that role he received the first of his three Oscar nominations. In those three films alone he had shown his true versatility, allied with a great sense of humour.

Harry Palmer was to appear in two more 1960s films and in 1969 Caine played the part of Charlie Croker in *The Italian Job.*

Michael Caine has remained one of Britain's top actors in the quarter of a century since *Zulu* and his portrayal of Milo Tindle opposite Laurence Olivier in *Sleuth* won Caine a second Oscar nomination in 1972. A third nomination followed after his brilliant performance as the alcoholic lecturer opposite Julie Walters in the 1984 film *Educating Rita.*

Michael Caine once attempted to get out of the crippling taxation system in England by taking his family to California. But his love of the English countryside saw him return. Furthermore, he was missing the roast beef and Yorkshire pud.

The films of Michael Caine in the 1960s:

Foxhole In Cairo	(1960)
The Bulldog Breed	(1960)
The Day The Earth Caught Fire	(1961)
Solo For Sparrow	(1962)
The Wrong Arm Of The Law	(1962)
Zulu	(1963)
The Ipcress File	(1965)
Alfie	(1966)
The Wrong Box	(1966)
Gambit	(1966)
Funeral In Berlin	(1966)
Hurry Sundown	(1966)
Billion Dollar Brain	(1967)
Woman Times Seven	(1967)
Deadfall	(1968)
Play Dirty	(1968)
The Magus	(1968)
The Italian Job	(1969)
Battle Of Britain	(1969)
Too Late The Hero	(1969)

CAMPBELL, Donald

SINCE Donald Campbell's tragic death in 1967, attempts on the world water speed record hold little interest for the British people. But in the 1960s attempts by Campbell in his famous *Bluebird* attracted a great deal of public interest.

Donald's love of speed came from his father, Sir Malcolm Campbell, who, like his son, held world records on both land and water. But it was on water that Donald Campbell was invincible during the 1960s.

Born in 1921, he was a qualified engineer and nine months after his father's death in 1949, Donald made his first attempt on the world water speed record. That, like the next two, was unsuccessful. It was not until after the launch of *Bluebird III*, a hydroplane made entirely of metal and powered by a turbo-jet engine, that he eventually wrested the world record from Stanley Sayers in 1955. After that Campbell kept increasing

Above: Bluebird III pictured at Goodwood, Sussex, in July 1962. Opposite: Donald Campbell.

the world record and in November 1958 became the first man to exceed 400kph. On 17 July 1964, at Lake Eyre (salt) in Australia, he captured the world land speed record, after several unsuccessful attempts. He returned to the water and uniquely broke both world records in the same year, 1964.

In 1967, Campbell wanted to take the water speed record through the 300mph barrier and late in 1966 he set up a base at Coniston Water in the Lake District. And on 4 January 1967 came the last fateful run of Donald Campbell. As he pushed the craft to the limit it suddenly left the water and somersaulted. Campbell's body was never recovered.

Donald Campbell had a great love of life. He was a showman but at the same time did not take uncalculated risks. His daughter Gina has followed family tradition and made attempts on the world water speed record.

The world records of Donald Campbell:
Water

Year	mph	Location
1955	202,32	Ullswater
1955	216,25	Lake Mead, Nevada
1956	225,63	Coniston Water

THE Labour Member of Parliament for Blackburn, she was born as Barbara Betts in 1911. She married journalist Edward Castle in 1944. During the 1960s she held three Cabinet posts, as Minister of Overseas Development, Transport and Employment.

The woman who ousted Manny Shinwell from Labour's National Executive Committee in 1951, she was best remembered as the Minister of Transport in Harold Wilson's Cabinet (even though she did not have a driving licence), a post she held controversially from 1965 to 1968.

In 1967 she announced that the 70mph speed limit imposed on motorways would stay. It is still in force today. The same year she also announced the introduction of the breathalyser.

In April 1968 she was appointed head of the new Department of Employment and Productivity, which incorporated the old Labour Ministry. Her White Paper *In Place of Strife*, which proposed a ballot of union members before a strike, was abandoned because it was felt to be too controversial. It caused a rift in the Labour Party which resulted in Wilson removing James Callaghan from the 'inner' Cabinet.

In Callaghan's Cabinet, Barbara Castle was the Minister of Health and Social Security until being dropped. In 1979 she turned her attention to Europe and became vice-chairman of the Socialist Group in the European Parliament.

1957	239,07	Coniston Water
1958	248,62	Coniston Water
1959	260,35	Coniston Water
1964	276,33	Lake Dumbleyung, Western Australia

Land
| Year | mph | Location |
| 1964 | 403,10 | Lake Eyre, South Australia |

CARNABY STREET

A BACK STREET behind London's famous Regent Street, and not far from Oxford Circus, Carnaby Street became the fashion centre for the Mods of the sixties as shop after shop turned into a boutique.

The leading stockist and seller of Mod gear was John Stephen, a grocer's son from Glasgow. He owned ten shops on Carnaby Street and did more than anyone to promote the area. He owned a further 14 shops, known as John Stephen Boutiques, in the London area.

Carnaby Street became one of the great fashion centres of the world in the mid-sixties, particularly amongst the young, and Stephen wanted it to be a fashion centre for men as well as women. He succeeded in that aim and ever since, the male has been as fashion-conscious as his female partner.

Miniskirts were, of course, to be seen everywhere. So too was the kaftan coat, which was very much part of the hippie outfit. And there were the hipsters, Cuban-heeled boots and brightly printed round-collared shirts.

Carnaby Street became such a tourist attraction that the shops geared themselves accordingly and started selling plastic London buses, Tower of London ashtrays and dolls dressed up as Yeomen. It is still very much like that today, but it remains a tourist attraction as visitors to the Capital can say they have been to Carnaby Street, one of the world's best-known thoroughfares in the 1960s.

CASTRO, Fidel

AFTER two unsuccessful coups (in 1953 and 1956) against the Cuban dictatorship of Batista, Fidel Castro eventually mustered an army of 5,000 which successfully overthrew Batista in 1959, when Castro was installed as Prime Minister. His brother Raul, who was with him during his previous

Fidel Castro, surrounded by heavily-armed 'barbudos' — 'the bearded ones' — enters Havana.

unsuccessful coups, was made Minister of the Armed Forces.

Castro nationalized all private businesses and then upset the United States by nationalizing all US-owned properties in Cuba in retaliation for the financial restraints put on Cuba by the US.

Cuba, and Castro, attracted a great deal of worldwide attention in 1962 when the Cuban crisis came to a head and nuclear war was very much a possibility. Cuba was used as a Russian missile base which, in view of its close proximity to the United States, was a potential recipe for disaster.

Castro has seen some troubled times since then but remains in power and is a popular leader with the Cuban people.

CATHY COME HOME

CATHY Come Home was first shown on BBC television on 16 November 1966. It went out at 9.05pm and the 65-minute play told the story of a happy-go-lucky Cathy (played by Carol White) and her husband Reg (Ray Brooks), who found both money and housing in short supply. Written by author Jeremy Sandford, the story set out to shock. Sandford succeeded as the deeply moving story saw Cathy's plight go from bad to worse as she was forced from slum to slum. It culminated in her two children being taken away from her.

Sandford clearly got the message across and the programme aroused such public interest and comment that it led to the formation of *Shelter*, the help-the-homeless group.

CAVERN

LIVERPOOL'S Cavern Club was damp, dingy, sweaty and often overcrowded. But who cared? The atmosphere was electric as Merseyside teenagers crammed into the cellar to see the top local bands in the early 1960s. Regularly appearing at the Cavern were groups like The Merseybeats, The Big Three, Undertakers, Fourmost and, of course, The Beatles. The girl who took your coat off you as you went in was none other than Cilla Black.

Daytime and evening sessions at the Cavern, situated at 10 Matthew Street, were a regular haunt particularly with those kids who 'sagged' off school. Alcoholic beverages were not available at the Cavern, only soft drinks. The girls used to dance on the floor in front of the tiny stage, while all the lads used to lean against the pillars deciding who they were going to 'split up'.

The Cavern opened as a jazz club on 16 January 1957 and was in the basement of an old warehouse. The Beatles made their debut on 21 March 1961 and appeared at the famous club nearly 300 times. More often than not they were introduced by the club's resident DJ, Bob Wooler.

For safety reasons the Cavern was forced to close at the end of the Merseybeat era, but reconstruction of the old club was incorporated in the new Cavern Walks project in the 1980s. It will never be possible, however, to recreate those great days down at the Cavern in the early 1960s.

CENTRE POINT

CENTRE Point was the 34-storey, 385ft West End office block built by Harry Hyams in 1964. But it attracted a great deal of attention by the fact that it was largely unoccupied throughout the 1960s at a time when there was an outcry about the plight of the homeless in the Capital.

Built by Hyams' Oldham Estates, and situated near Tottenham Court Road, it was not until 1979, by which time the Co-operative Insurance Company had a controlling interest, that the premises became occupied when the Confederation of British Industries (CBI) took a lease and based their headquarters there. Shortly before the CBI took occu-

pation it had been used as an overnight shelter for homeless young people.

The fact that such a building should stay empty for so long was one of the great scandals of the sixties — and the seventies.

CHARLES, Ray

WHILE Ray Charles has been acknowledged as one of the finest singers for more than 30 years, his days as a chart-topping recording artist disappeared in the early 1960s when the groups took over. But he will be remembered for his classic *I Can't Stop Loving You* which topped the hit parade in 1962.

A pianist, saxophonist, clarinetist and organist, Ray Charles was also a singer of rhythm and blues, soul, jazz, pop, and country and western, something rare for a coloured singer. Remarkably, Charles' success has been achieved despite the handicap of blindness.

Born at Albany, Georgia, on 23 September 1932, he went blind at the age of six, was orphaned at 15 and was penniless at 18. By the time he was 26 he was a singing sensation. In terms of British chart success one might review Ray Charles as a failure. But on the contrary, he was the inspiration to many singers and groups of the 1960s. In the United States, as well as being inspirational, he also had eight golden discs including *I Can't Stop Loving You, Georgia On My Mind* and *Hit The Road Jack*.

With his group the Raelets he became one of the most sought after cabaret artistes in the 1960s. More than 25 years later he is still demanding that same attention.

Top Ten hits of Ray Charles in the 1960s:

Year	Record	Pos
1961	Hit The Road Jack	6
1962	I Can't Stop Loving You	1
1962	You Don't Know Me	9
1963	Take These Chains From My Heart	5

CHARLTON, Bobby, OBE

BOBBY Charlton was the ultimate professional footballer and one who graced soccer pitches the world over for nearly 20 years. For those who watched football in the sixties they were fortunate enough to see one of the game's gentlemen and prolific goalscorers in his prime.

Born in Ashington, County Durham, he was the younger brother of fellow-professional Jack, who spent all his playing career at Leeds United. Bobby, however, was one of the 'Busby Babes' at Manchester United and, after surviving the horrific Munich air disaster in 1958, was a vital member of the playing staff around whom the rebuilding programme took place.

Charlton helped United to win the FA Cup in 1963 and the League Championship in 1965 and 1967. In between he was a member of the England team which beat West Germany to lift the World Cup at Wembley in 1966. Charlton's great goals in the semi-final against Portugal were two to savour.

Matt Busby, and Manchester United, had been chasing a European dream for more than ten years and at Wembley on a May night in 1968 it all came good for the club and skipper Charlton as they beat Benfica 4-1 after extra-time. Charlton scored one of his two goals with a rare header.

The Footballer of the Year and European Player of the Year in 1966, Bobby was also honoured with the OBE in 1969 for his services to football. He played his last game for United in April 1973 and became manager of Preston North End where he could not match his playing skills. Now a director at Old Trafford, he is still a very popular figure. His tally of 49 goals for England remains an all-time record.

Charlton's daughter, Suzanne, is an ITV weather forecaster.

CHECKER, Chubby

FORMER chicken-plucker Chubby Checker was responsible for introducing the biggest dance craze of the 1960s, the Twist.

His first record *The Twist* was released in 1960 and topped the American charts. Two years later it became the first record ever to enter the US charts twice. The song was written and first recorded by Hank Ballard and the Midnighters in 1958.

So that American teenagers would know how to do the dance the record company issued detailed instructions with each copy of the record!

The craze took off in Britain when the follow-up record *Let's Twist Again* was released in 1961 and went to number two in the charts. In total it spent 34 weeks in the British charts in the sixties and another ten weeks in the seventies. It was Checker's only Top Ten hit in Britain in the 1960s. However, in 1975 both records were re-released as a double-sided disc and reached number five. A remix of *The Twist* by the Fat Boys and featuring Chubby Checker reached number one in Britain in 1988.

Checker, who was born as Ernest Evans in Philadelphia in 1941, derived his name after somebody said he looked like a 'mini-Fats Domino'. He married former Miss World, Catherina Lodders of Holland, in 1962.

Now, nearly 30 years after the birth of the Twist, it is still popular at parties and dances amongst all age groups and for many years people will carry on doing the Twist, just as they did last summer, and the summer before, and the summer before . . .

CHERRY B INCIDENT

ON Monday, 17 June 1963, HRH Prince Charles went to the cinema with four other boys from Gordonstoun School. They were accompanied by a detective. Before setting off the pupils went for a meal at the Crown Hotel, Stornaway, and Prince Charles ordered a 2s 6d, Cherry B from the hotel bar. The Prince was only 14 at the time and news of the 'scandal' leaked out. Initially it was denied by Buckingham Palace but, two days later, they admitted that Charles had bought the drink and they expressed regret that the initial report had been denied.

The next problem lay with Mr F.R.G.Chew, headmaster of Gordonstoun: Drinking by pupils was outlawed, but what action would he take against the Royal Prince? After all, it was Mr Chew who said when Prince Charles first went to the school that he would be treated like any other pupil. Diplomatically Mr Chew announced that whatever disciplinary action had been issued against the Prince was a private affair and would not be disclosed in public. With that the incident was closed.

CHICHESTER, Sir Francis

LONG before his yachting exploits of the 1960s Francis Chichester had the spirit of adventure in him, and his yachting feats were the culmination of many years of adventures.

Born in 1901, he left Britain when he was 18 and headed for New Zealand where he acquired a love of flying. He returned to England in 1929 for a short, but intensive, flying course before setting off for Sydney, Australia, in his own plane, *Gipsy Moth*. Chichester eventually arrived in Oz, and became only the second man to make the trip single-handed.

That was the start of many record-breaking attempts, including one on the round-the-world record. But it sadly ended in Japan when his plane caught some telephone cables and crashed into a harbour.

He eventually returned to England and acquired a boat which he renamed *Gipsy Moth II*. He took part in the 1957 Admiral's Cup races, but a few months later it was discovered he had lung cancer. However, he refused surgery and with determination, and the help of his second wife Sheila, he miraculously overcame the illness.

Chichester won the first single-handed transatlantic yacht race in *Gipsy Moth III* in 1960. In 1966 he embarked on his greatest adventure when he set sail in *Gipsy Moth IV* for a single-handed round-the-world trip. Despite serious bad weather, he completed the first half of the journey on 12 December 1966 when he covered the 13,000 miles from Plymouth to Sydney in 107 days. Despite calls to abandon the return journey because of the treacherous conditions, he kept going and at 8.56pm on 28 May 1967 he completed the second half of his 28,500-mile voyage in 119 days, when he arrived back at Plymouth.

Her Majesty the Queen bestowed a Knighthood on Chichester on the lawns of the Royal Naval College in Greenwich with the same sword used to knight Sir Francis Drake.

His last race was in June 1972 when he was forced to pull out through a combination of bad weather and ill health. Two months later the 70-year-old adventurer died.

Sir Francis Chichester aboard Gipsy Moth III.

CHRISTIE, Julie

JULIE Christie first attracted attention in the 1963 film *Billy Liar*, but it was after her portrayal of a fashion model in the 1965 film *Darling* that she received worldwide attention.

Julie was an actress who fitted in with the theme of the 1960s and consequently, was not as big a success in such films as *Doctor Zhivago*. However, she received rave reviews once more for her part in the 1971 film *The Go-Between*.

The daughter of a tea planter, she was born in India in 1941. Julie studied art in France before finishing her education at the Central Music and Drama School in London. She started acting in 1957 and appeared on television in the early '60s. Her film debut was in *Crooks Anonymous* before she was given her first lead in *Billy Liar*.

But it was for her part in Schlessinger's *Darling* that she gained most acclaim, not to mention an Oscar and Best British Actress award from the British Academy. Astonishingly, she was reputed to have been paid a mere £7,500 for her role in the film.

Her last major success of the sixties was *Petulia* in 1968. And while continuing her acting career in the 1980s she also involved herself with anti-nuclear groups.

The Films of Julie Christie in the 1960s:

Crooks Anonymous	(1962)
The Fast Lady	(1963)
Billy Liar	(1963)
Young Cassidy	(1964)
Darling	(1965)
Doctor Zhivago	(1965)

Julie Christie and Tom Courtney in the film Billy Liar.

Fahreneheit 451	(1966)
Far From The Madding Crowd	(1967)
Tonite Let's All Make Love In London	(1967)
Petulia	(1968)

CHURCHILL, Sir Winston

BY THE time the 1960s came around, Sir Winston Churchill was no longer at the fore of British politics, but his position as one of Britain's finest leaders was still in the memory of those people who lived through the war. Teenagers in the 1960s also knew of Churchill's outstanding

achievements. And when his death came in 1965, at the age of 91, the whole nation mourned.

Born at Blenheim Palace, Oxfordshire, on 30 November 1874, he was educated at Harrow and Sandhurst. Churchill entered Parliament in 1900 as Conservative MP for Oldham. He switched his allegiance to the Liberals in 1906, became Home Secretary and held that post at the time of the famous Sidney Street seige in 1911. He later rejoined the Conservatives and became MP for Epping.

During World War Two, Churchill was asked to form a Coalition Government in succession to Neville Chamberlain and did much for the nation during the war years. While at his political peak, he suffered defeat in the 1945 General Election but remained as Leader of the Opposition. He became Prime Minister again in 1951 at the age of 77, before eventually retiring from his leadership in 1955. He remained a backbencher before eventually bowing out of the House of Commons on 27 July 1964.

Away from politics, the cigar-smoking Sir Winston was a keen artist and writer and in 1953 won the Nobel Prize for Literature for his book *Savrola*.

Often described as the 'Greatest Ever Englishman' his contribution to British history is immense and, while he contributed little in the 1960s, he was still regarded in high esteem by those who lived in the era.

Two 'insulting' quotes from Churchill:-

Nancy Astor once said: "Winston, if I were married to you, I'd put poison in your coffee."

Churchill replied: "Nancy, if you were my wife, I'd drink it."

and ...

Bessie Braddock once said: "Winston, you're drunk."

Churchill replied: "Bessie, you're ugly ...but tomorrow I'll be sober."

CIVIL RIGHTS ACT

SEVEN months after the death of John F.Kennedy, President Lyndon Johnson eventually concluded the work of his predecessor when, on 2 July 1964, he signed the Civil Rights Act.

It was the most far-reaching civil rights law in US history. It set out to end racial discrimination and gave more freedom to blacks on voting, in obtaining public accommodation, using public facilities, obtaining public education and receiving Federal aid. It also gave them improved rights in gaining employment and joining unions and other institutions.

On the day that the Bill came into force, negroes tested the new law immediately. Across America there was a general indication that integration between blacks and whites was taking place. Even in such hotbeds of racial discrimination like Albany, Georgia, there were signs that the new Bill was working. In Kansas, a 13-year-old negro attracted a lot of nationwide publicity when he went into the barbers shop of a local hotel for a haircut. He was duly served. The previous day he had been refused.

The American riots did not disappear completely, nor did the Civil Rights marches. But the Act did help to ease the situation.

CLARK, Jim

MOTOR racing has claimed many lives over the years but the death of Jim Clark at Hockenheim on 7 April 1968 was felt by a whole nation, not just those people involved with, or interested in, motor racing.

The genial Scot, born in Fife in 1936, was unquestionably the finest driver of the era, and probably amongst the top five best of all time.

He spent his entire Formula One career driving for the Lotus team led by his good friend and mentor, Colin Chapman. Clark teamed up with

Chapman in 1960 and had his first grand prix success at Spa, Belgium, in 1962. He was runner-up in the world championship to Graham Hill that year, but 12 months later he took the title after winning a record seven championship races.

Third in the 1964 championship, he took his second title the following year when he won six races on his way to a 14-point victory over Hill. He also conquered America in 1965 when he became the first Briton to win the coveted Indianapolis 500 race.

Clark's death came, not in a Formula One grand prix, but in a Formula Two race on a Sunday afternoon around the tree-lined Hockenheim circuit in West Germany. His car inexplicably left the track. It somersaulted, hit a tree and, in the words of an eyewitness, 'broke into a hundred pieces'. Jim Clark, the greatest motor-racing driver of the decade, was dead.

CLARK, Petula

ALTHOUGH her career spans nearly five decades, it was in the 1960s that Petula Clark became a truly international star.

Born as Petula Sally Olwen Clark at West Ewell, Surrey, on 15 November 1932, she was a child star during the war and appeared in over 500 radio programmes for the BBC. She made her film debut in *Medal For The General* and appeared as Jack Warner's daughter in the popular 1950s series *The Huggetts*. She had her own radio series, *Pet's Parlour*, when she was only 20. She recorded her first British record *Put Your Shoes On Lucy* in 1949 and had her first chart entry five years later with *The Little Shoemaker*.

Her first British number one did not come until 1961 when *Sailor* took her

to the top of the charts. That was to herald the start of seven glorious years which saw Petula top the charts once more with *This Is My Song* and have other such big hits as *Romeo* and the Tony Hatch composition *Downtown* which reached number one in the States and made Petula the first British female singer since Vera Lynn in 1952 to achieve such success.

Her last major hit, until a remix of *Downtown* found its way back into the top ten in 1988-89, was the Charlie Chaplin composition *This Is My Song* in 1967.

Petula married Claude Wolff, the French publicity director for Vogue Records, in 1961 and she made her new home across the Channel where the French people took 'Pet' to their hearts as much as the British did.

Top Ten hits of Pet Clark in the 1960s:

Year	Record	Pos
1961	Sailor	1
1961	Romeo	3
1961	My Friend The Sea	7
1964	Downtown	2
1966	My Love	4
1966	I Couldn't Live Without Your Love	6
1967	This Is My Song	1

COCHRAN, Eddie

IF THE truth be known, Eddie Cochran has been a bigger name in the 1980s than he was in the '60s. But had it not been for a fateful car accident in April 1960 there is no question that Cochran would have been one of the biggest names in pop music during the era heralded as the 'decade of pop.'

Born in Oklahoma City on 31 October 1938, he was only 21 when he died. But in his short life he gave rock 'n' roll music such classics as *Summertime Blues, C'mon Everybody* and his only British number one *Three Steps To Heaven*. Collectors of

rock 'n' roll records make sure these three are most cherished items.

During his short career he also found time to make four films; *The Girl Can't Help It, Untamed Youth, Go Johnny Go* and *Bop Girl*. He made numerous television appearances on both sides of the Atlantic and happily there is plenty of footage to relive the memory of one of the great rock 'n' rollers.

Cochran had the pop world at his feet and when he went on stage at the Bristol Hippodrome on 16 April 1960, he wowed the fans as he had done at every venue on his British tour. Sadly, that was to be the last the world saw of Eddie Cochran. The following morning the London-bound car he shared with Gene Vincent and songwriter fiancée Sharon Sheeley, was involved in an accident at Chippenham, Wiltshire, and on a cold, dark morning, 21-year-old Cochran died in hospital without regaining consciousness.

During 1987 *C'mon Everybody* returned to the British charts after featuring in the successful *Levi 501* TV advertisement.

COMMON MARKET

THE Common Market was formed on 25 March 1957, when six nations, Italy, France, West Germany, Belgium, Holland and Luxembourg, signed the Treaty of Rome. The UK was not one of the founder members and there followed years of debate as to whether we should or should not join.

Many thought Britain should have been one of the founder members but she did not formally apply to join until August 1961. However, General De Gaulle then put the brakes on Britain's membership and it was not until 1967 that Britain made another application to join the EEC. Again De Gaulle said 'non'. However, terms for Britain's entry were agreed in 1971 and on 22 January 1972 the Treaty of Brussels was signed by Edward Heath, who ended a ten-year quest to gain membership.

Britain, Ireland and Denmark all became full members of the EEC on 1 January 1973. They should have been joined by Norway but a referendum in that country a few months

Anti-Common Market demonstrators outside Chequers in April 1967. Inside the house, Premier Harold Wilson and his Cabinet were discussing Britain's entry into Europe

earlier voted against membership and consequently they did not join.

Britain had its own referendum in 1975 after the Labour Party returned to power. Despite a big split in the Cabinet, the referendum went ahead and the British people voted with a two-thirds majority to stay in the EEC.

COMPACT

FOLLOWING the success of ITV's *Coronation Street*, the BBC launched its own twice-weekly soap opera *Compact* on 2 January 1962.

The story of life on a woman's magazine, it was written by Peter Ling

Stars of Compact *celebrate the serial's 100th edition in November 1963. From left: Gussie Brown (played by Frances Bennett), Edmund Bruce (Robert Fleming), Ian Harman (Ronald Allen) and Mark Vicars (Gareth Davies).*

and Hazel Adair who later moved to *Crossroads.* Part of the series' success, which *Crossroads* later adopted, was having real-life stars appear in the programme as themselves.

After 373 episodes, *Compact* came to an end on 30 July 1965 and viewers bid farewell to the likes of Gussie Brown, Edmund Bruce, Ian Harman, David Rome, Alison Morley and Alan Drew. But the final words of the series were left to two of its central characters, the bespectacled Camilla (played by Carmen Silvera) and her television husband Ben (Bill Kerr). Appropriately the final episode was entitled *Journey's End.*

CONCORDE

PLANS to build a supersonic airliner were announced by the Government in February 1960. The estimated cost of each craft would be £5-6 million and it was to be a joint venture between Britain and another country, probably France or the United States. Nearly three years later Britain and France signed an agreement to build the plane, to be called Concorde.

The new plane was put on display for the first time in December 1967, when the French prototype 001 was seen at Toulouse, and even as it was being unveiled there was dispute over the spelling of the plane's name...with or without an 'e'.

People were fascinated by the design of the high-speed plane, particularly its swept-back wings and moveable nose. The maiden flight of 001 was not until 2 March 1969 and the following month, on 9 April, pilot Brian Trubshaw took Britain's prototype, 002, into the air for the first time as he took off from Filton, Bristol, on a flight which lasted 21 minutes.

Although the plane was capable of flying faster than sound and consequently crossing the Atlantic in half the normal time, Concorde had one big drawback — its excessive noise. When it landed at Heathrow for the first time in September 1970 there were many complaints. Because of the noise some of the world's leading airports indicated they would not allow Concorde to land and that affected sales of the plane in its early days.

Concorde eventually went into service on 21 January 1976 when planes took off from Paris and London simultaneously. It was 16 years since the Government first announced its plans for a supersonic airliner. The cost in the meantime had been astronomical, but Concorde (with an 'e') has become an accepted means of travelling across the Atlantic, and to other points on the globe, particularly by those business people who need to save time.

Britain's Concorde takes off on its maiden flight in April 1969.

CONNERY, Sean

NO matter what Sean Connery did before, or has done since, he will always be remembered as James Bond, even though other actors have played the part of Ian Fleming's famous spy.

Connery was born as Thomas Connery in Edinburgh on 25 August 1930. He served in the Royal Navy before being discharged with ulcers. That led to a succession of jobs; lifeguard, milkman, coffin-polisher, body-builder and artist's model — amongst others. He then toured in the chorus of *South Pacific* before going into rep. He played his first film character, Spike, in *No Road Back* in 1957 and in 1962 appeared in *The Longest Day*. That same year he was cast as Bond for the first time in *Dr No*.

He continued to play the character throughout the 1960s, but did not restrict his acting to that of Bond. He also appeared in Hitchcock's *Marnie*, as well as *The Hill* and *The Molly McGuires* amongst others.

After handing over the role of Bond to George Lazenby, Connery returned in 1971 to star in *Diamonds Are Forever* and in 1983 he was tempted back out of '007-retirement' to play the character again in *Never Say Never Again* for which he received a reported £3.5 million.

In 1962 Connery married Diane Cilento. The marriage ended in 1973 but they produced Jason Connery who also took up an acting career like his father and played the part of Robin Hood in *Robin Of Sherwood* on television. Connery married the French-Moroccan Micheline Roqueburn in 1975 and spends much of his time living in Marbella where he is as much at home on the golf course as he is on the film-set, equally adept at golf as he was at playing James Bond.

The films of Sean Connery in the 1960s:

The Frightened City	(1961)
On The Fiddle	(1961)
The Longest Day	(1962)
Dr No	(1962)
From Russia With Love	(1963)
Woman Of Straw	(1964)
Marnie	(1964)
Goldfinger	(1964)
The Hill	(1965)
Thunderball	(1965)
A Fine Madness	(1966)
You Only Live Twice	(1967)
Shalako	(1968)
The Molly McGuires	(1969)
La Tenda Rossa (The Red Tent)	(1969)

COOPER, Henry, OBE

FRANK Bruno has played a big role in putting British heavyweight boxing back on the map in recent years, and has won a lot of fans and friends for his achievements. Despite Frank's efforts, the most popular British heavyweight has always been 'Our 'Enery', Henry Cooper.

Born in 1934, he was brought up in Bellingham and won the ABA light-heavyweight title in 1952. After coming out of the army in 1954 he teamed up with Jim Wicks and turned professional. Wicks, affectionately known as 'The Bishop', remained Henry's manager throughout his career.

Famous for his left hook, known as 'Enery's Hammer', Cooper won his first title in 1959 when he beat Brian London on points to win the British and Empire heavyweight crowns. The European title followed in 1964, when London was again on the receiving end. Henry then set his sights on the world title.

He had fought the future world champion Cassius Clay, at Wembley in 1963. The extrovert Clay came to London announcing that Cooper was: "A bum. A cripple. And I'll take him in five." Well, he did win in five rounds, but not until he overcame one of the biggest scares of his career when Henry floored him at the end of the fourth.

While the shaken Clay was sitting in his corner, his glove was 'mysteriously' torn. This gave the American breathing space and he came out fresh for the next round when he duly stopped Henry.

When the two men eventually met for the world title at Highbury Stadium in 1966, Clay (by now known as Muhammad Ali) had far more respect for his opponent, but bad cuts forced the fight to be stopped in the sixth round and so ended Henry's quest to become the world champion.

Nevertheless, he was gracious in defeat and went on to win three Lonsdale Belts outright; the only person in boxing history to perform this feat.

Henry retired in 1971 after losing controversially to Joe Bugner. But Henry is still around and is as popular as ever, whether it be for his boxing involvement, charity work, or enjoying himself on the golf course, the new sporting love of his life.

Henry Cooper puts Cassius Clay on the canvas at Wembley in June 1963.

COOPER, Tommy

A FORMER Horse Guardsman, the giant Tommy Cooper became one of the best loved comedians in the 1960s, although he had set out to become a serious magician. A member of the Magic Circle, he realized in his early days of variety theatre that he could get laughs from messing up his tricks and so he played on that idea and became a superstar in his field.

Despite his 'failure' to successfully perform his tricks, Cooper was a proficient magician and occasionally he got it all 'wrong' and did a trick properly!

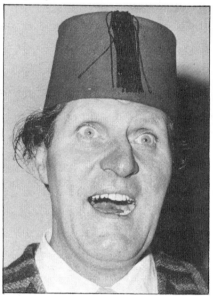

Famous for his red fez and catchphrase 'Just Like That', his appearance on a stage was enough to arouse laughter from his audience. His facial expressions alone were enough to create mirth.

Born in Caerphilly in 1922, Cooper was brought up in Exeter. He was given his first television series, *Life with Tommy* on ITV in 1957 and appeared in many of his own and others' variety shows in the 1960s.

Tommy Cooper was still popular at the time of his sudden death at the age of 62 in 1984. He collapsed on stage during a live television programme from Her Majesty's Theatre. The audience thought it was part of his act. Sadly, they were wrong and Cooper died shortly afterwards. He ended his life just as he would have wished — entertaining his fans.

CORONATION STREET

CORONATION Street was to originally have been called *Florizel Street*. But it was after Agnes, a Granada TV tealady, said the name sounded more like a disinfectant, that the producers changed its name to that of the most famous name in British soap opera history.

This is how the *TV Times* reported the first episode of Coronation Street:

7.0. CORONATION STREET

Every front door hides a story. In this new twice-weekly serial there are seven front doors and more than 20 interesting people. Come down Coronation Street on Wednesdays and Fridays and join the neighbours.

Written by Tony Warren
Designed by Denis Parkin
Directed by Derek Bennett
Producer Stuart Latham
Granada TV Network Production.

And this is how they reported the second episode the following Wednesday, 14 December 1960.

7.0. CORONATION STREET

Cast includes:

Florrie Lindley	Betty Alberg
Elsie Tanner	Patricia Phoenix
Annie Walker	Doris Speed
Christine Hardman	Christine Hargreaves
Harry Hewitt	Ivan Beavis
Jack Walker	Arthur Leslie
Frank Barlow	Frank Pemberton
Kenneth Barlow	William Roache
David Barlow	Alan Rothwell
Linda Cheveski	Ann Cunningham
Ena Sharples	Violet Carson
Esther Hayes	Daphne Oxenford
Minnie Caldwell	Margot Bryant
Ida Barlow	Noel Dyson

Written by Tony Warren
Designed by Denis Parkin
Directed by Derek Bennett
Producer Stuart Latham
Continuing the everyday adventures of the people who live in Coronation Street.
Granada TV Network Production.

Set in the back streets of Salford in the imaginary district of Wetherfield, the first programme went out on Friday, 9 December 1960. It was a twice-weekly serial to begin with, on Wednesdays and Fridays. It was not until 3 May the following year that it was fully networked.

The opening scene saw Florrie Lindley standing outside the corner shop which she had just bought from Elsie Lappin. And it was Lindley, played by Betty Alberg (later Harry Cross's wife in *Brookside*), who had the honour of speaking the first words.

Since then Coronation Street has been shown more than two and a half thousand times and has constantly topped the viewers' ratings as people like Elsie Tanner, Ken Barlow, Ena Sharples, Albert Tatlock, Annie and Jack Walker and Hilda and Stan Ogden have become household names. The wedding of Elsie to Steve

Ena Sharples (played by Violet Carson) (right) and Minnie Caldwell (Margot Bryant) enjoying a drink in the snug of the Rover's Return.

Tanner in 1967 attracted a viewing audience of 20 million.

The world's longest-running twice-weekly soap opera, it now appears on Mondays and Wednesdays with an omnibus edition on Sundays, which was launched in 1989.

mind, the vestries were built by German students and apprentices. The modern interior is noted for John Hutton's glass screen, engraved with the figures of saints and angels. There is also a stained-glass baptistery window designed by John Piper and one of the most striking features of the Cathedral is John Sutherland's tapestry *Christ in His Majesty*. The entrance to the Cathedral has a magnificent Epstein sculpture depicting St Michael treading the Devil underfoot.

Coventry Cathedral, the old and new spires, pictured in May 1962.

In 1965, a residential youth centre, called John F.Kennedy House, was opened by Herr Willy Brandt, thus confirming the Cathedral's reconciliation theme.

CRAZY WORLD OF ARTHUR BROWN

IN comparison to Arthur Brown, many of today's punk rockers are well dressed and sophisticated. In the 1960s he used to wear multi-coloured robes, streaks of make-up down his face, and more often than not, set his hair alight. Arthur and his band were one of the more 'noticeable' groups of the late-60s and his performances were, to say the least, electrifying!

Born in the Yorkshire seaside resort of Whitby in June 1944, he studied law at London University, philosophy at Reading University and had a succession of jobs including teaching, digging holes in roads and washing dishes. Arthur Brown's world was certainly a 'crazy' one even before he entered pop music. His father has a claim to fame; he is purported to be the inventor of the automatic toothbrush.

As a recording artist the Crazy World of Arthur Brown goes down as a 'one-hit wonder'. But that one hit, *Fire,* reached number one in Britain in 1968, and across the Atlantic went as high as number two. It was a million-seller. His only journey into the LP charts was the following year with *The Crazy World Of Arthur Brown;* it reached number two. One of the group members was Carl Palmer, later of Emerson, Lake and Palmer.

COVENTRY CATHEDRAL

THE City of Coventry came in for some heavy German bombing in 1940 and on the nights of 14 and 15 November, the City's 14th-century Cathedral was destroyed.

A competition for the design of a new Cathedral began in 1951 and was won by Basil Spence. His design was to incorporate the remains of the old building. Work started in 1954 and was completed eight years later at a cost of £1.35 million. It was one of the largest and most original in design of all churches built after the war. The new Cathedral was consecrated on 25 May 1962.

The theme of the new Cathedral was reconciliation and, with this in

CREAM

IN terms of chart success, Cream were one of the least successful groups of the sixties, having only three Top Twenty hits, but in terms of music they were the first of the 'Supergroups'.

Founded in 1966, they were the brainchild of music agent Robert Stigwood and he brought together three of the best talents on the British rock scene.

Eric Clapton, previously of the Yardbirds, and one of the country's leading guitarists, was joined by Jack Bruce, formerly of Manfred Mann and the Alexis Korner Blues Band. And finally there was Ginger Baker, who had been the drummer with the grossly underrated Graham Bond Organization, a band that had a tremendous following but enjoyed very little chart success.

Sadly, Cream were together for only two years. But in that short spell they established themselves as one of the top live bands in the country and their music is still much listened to by rock connoisseurs. Wherever they performed, their concerts were a sell-out.

Their best-selling single was *I Feel Free,* which reached number 11 in 1966. But their LP successes were a totally different story. All six of their albums reached the Top Ten and their final album *Farewell* reached number one in 1969. It was a compilation of all their songs played during their various farewell concerts in 1968.

Eric Clapton went on to form the group Blind Faith with Ginger Baker, Stevie Winwood and Rich Grech in 1969 and they had a number-one album. Jack Bruce also had a top-selling solo album that same year. Eric Clapton remains one of the most recognizable, and probably best, rock musicians of our time.

CREDIT CARDS

OPEN your wallet in the early 1960s and what did it contain? A couple of ten-bob notes, the odd pound note and, if you were very, very rich, a fiver. What does the wallet of today look like? Plastic cards . . . and more plastic cards. The 1980s is certainly the age of the credit card. But it was a different story in the 1960s.

The first credit card in Britain was launched by American Express on 10 September 1963, five years after its launch in the United States. But to get hold of one of these new cards, which allowed you to buy goods and services on credit, you needed to earn £2,000 per annum — quite a sum in 1963.

Surprisingly, American Express beat Diners Club to be the first British credit card, Diners were the first to launch a card in America.

The first British institution to issue a credit card was Barclays Bank, who launched their Barclaycard in June 1966. Access did not follow until the 1970s.
(see also BARCLAYCARD)

CROSSROADS

THE Crossroads Motel opened its doors to television viewers on 2 November 1964 when Jill Richardson (played by Jane Rossington) spoke the first words when she said "Crossroads Motel, can I help you?" Jill, later Jill Chance, was, coincidentally, the only surviving member of the first cast when the series folded in 1988.

The original series was written by Peter Ling and Hazel Adair, who had previously written the popular soap opera *Compact.*

Crossroads stars Anthony Morton and Sue Nicholls, who now stars as Audrey Roberts in Coronation Street.

Despite its launch in 1964, it was not until 1972 that *Crossroads* was seen on network ITV when the nation had the chance to see such characters as the wheelchaired Sandy Richardson (Roger Tonge), Amy Turtle (Ann George) and of course the motel owner Meg Richardson. There were other such notable characters as Benny, Carlos and David Hunter — amongst dozens of others over the years.

Meg Richardson was played by Noele Gordon, who portrayed the character more than 3,500 times, but she was written out in 1981 when the motel went up in flames. It was not known for a while whether Meg had been killed in the fire, but she was then seen setting sail on the *QEII* for a new life in Australia. Noele Gordon has since died.

Part of the success of the series was that real-life personalities occasionally 'stayed' at the motel where they played themselves. However, the

Crossroads was set in the fictional Midlands village of King's Oak. The original working title of the series was Midland Road.

Noele Gordon.

programme lost a lot of its appeal after Meg's departure and the doors to television's most famous motel were eventually closed for the last time on 4 April 1988.

Coincidentally, Jane Rossington spoke the last words which were: "How about Crossroads?" when she was discussing the possible name for her new hotel venture. The word 'Crossroads' was therefore the first and last word ever spoken during the series' 23½-year life.

CUBAN MISSILE CRISIS

REVOLUTIONARY Fidel Castro had a rough ride before eventually overthrowing President Batista in 1959. After he announced sweeping changes to education, agriculture and industry, the United States and Cuba fell out and in January 1961 the US broke off diplomatic relations with the island. Rebel forces, inspired and organized by America, then invaded Cuba but Castro and his men successfully shook off the invasion at the Bay of Pigs. The invasion sparked off a row between Kennedy and Khrushchev.

Thereafter, Castro depended on Communist assistance, largely from the Russians, and that did nothing to help the friction between the United States and Soviet Union.

The Cuban Missile Crisis occupied a large portion of the news in 1962 and was the nearest we came to World War Three, a war which would inevitably have been fought with nuclear weapons.

In return for Soviet help, Castro announced on 24 September 1962 that he had granted permission for the building of a £4.2 million port on the island as a base for the Russian fishing fleet. But the Americans rightly suspected it was to be a nuclear base. In view of the proximity to the United States, President Kennedy had to take action. He was given permission by Congress to call up 150,000 reservists if necessary. Khrushchev, on the other hand, was quick to point out that if the Americans invaded Cuba it would lead to a nuclear war. Kennedy was in a delicate position.

On 23 October, the United States announced a blockade on Cuba after they had received firm evidence of the Russians establishing nuclear missile sites on the island. Ships of any nationality were turned away from Cuba if they carried arms. The Soviet leader, Nikita Khrushchev, accused the Americans of dictating to Cuba what weapons she should have in defence of herself.

U Thant, Secretary-General of the United Nations, appealed to the Americans to end the blockade and to the Russians to end the shipment of arms. A week of talks between the two super powers then took place as the world awaited the outcome with baited breath.

On 28 October, Khrushchev agreed to dismantle all missiles and return them to the Soviet Union, an operation which was done under UN supervision. In return Kennedy promised not to invade Cuba and lifted the blockade. Morally it was a victory for the US President.

The whole world, which had teetered on the brink of the ultimate horror, breathed a sigh of relief.

CZECH INVASION

IN January 1968 Alexander Dubček became the first Slav leader of the Czechoslovak Communist Party. A reformer, his attitudes were liberal and one that was not viewed too well by the Soviets, particularly after Dubček had ousted the pro-Russian Antonin Novotny from the leadership.

One of Dubček's first acts was to relax Press censorship as a wave of liberalism swept through the country. The Soviets were alarmed at such rapid developments and they sent tanks across Poland and East Germany to the Czech borders. Dubček had assured the Russians that Czechoslovakia would remain an ally of theirs . . .but they were not very confident of such an assurance.

Despite talks between Soviet Premier Kosygin, Leonid Brezhnev, Dubček and other Warsaw Pact countries, Dubček was not going to retract his new democratic policies which the Czech people supported.

The Russians felt the need to protect themselves from a Western threat and on 21 August 1968 the

tanks moved forward from their 'waiting' positions and crossed the border. The next day they rolled through the streets of Prague.

Demonstrations were plentiful and acts of aggression were seen as the Czech people made their feelings very clear. Soviet troops were attacked with any form of ammunition the people could muster and Prague became a battlefield. Hundreds were injured and there were many fatalities. Jan Palach became a national hero in January 1969 when he set fire to himself in Wenceslas Square, Prague, in protest at the Russian invasion. He was immortalized when Czech people tore down the name of Red Army Square and replaced it with that of Jan Palach Square.

Tass reported to the Russian people that: 'the Czechs are showing gratitude for the timely arrival of Soviet troops' . . .their reporter must have been at a different match!

The tanks paraded the streets of Prague for nearly a month as the country 'returned' to solidarity with Moscow, with Vasiliy Kuznetsov installed as their spokesman.

The protests against the Soviet presence continued and, a year after the first invasion, tanks returned to Prague to curb further demonstrations. In May 1970 the Czechs signed a 20-year friendship treaty with the Soviet Union.

DAILY HERALD

THE *Daily Herald* was born in 1919 and died in 1964. The paper had long been known as the good old-fashioned voice of the trade union movement. After 44 years, the last edition hit the news-stands on Monday, 14 September. Priced at 3d, at the time of its demise, the paper's last front page told the story of an American US Army private who helped an East German to escape to the West over the Berlin Wall. It also revealed that Ringo Starr was going to have his tonsils out!

The *Herald's* circulation at the time of its death was down to 1.3 million. Its successor, *The Sun*, which was Britain's first new national daily since the *Herald*, sold 3.5 million on its first day of publication.

DAVE CLARK FIVE

THE arrival of the Beatles and other Liverpool groups in the early 1960s brought a response from London, which produced the 'Tottenham Sound' via the Dave Clark Five.

The group was formed in 1958 when ex-stuntman Dave Clark got together a group to raise finances to send his local rugby team on a tour of Holland. They were so successful that, by 1961, they had made their first record, an instrumental entitled *Chaquita*. They enjoyed their first chart success in 1963 when *Glad All Over* went to number one.

The group's personnel during their glory days consisted of Rick Huxley, Mike Smith, Lenny Davidson, Dennis Payton and leader and drummer Dave Clark.

In 1964 they followed the Beatles' lead and toured the United States. Their popularity was such that they had 16 Top Thirty hits in the States compared to 14 in Britain. The Dave Clark Five went into the movies in

1965 when they appeared in and wrote the soundtrack for *Catch Us If You Can*.

The group disbanded in 1970 but Dave Clark carried on working in the music industry and in 1986 produced and co-wrote most of the lyrics for the show *Time*, which contained such stars as Laurence Olivier, Cliff Richard and David Cassidy.

Top Ten hits of the Dave Clark Five in the 1960s:

Year	Record	Pos
1963	Glad All Over	1
1964	Bits And Pieces	2
1964	Can't You See That She's Mine	10
1965	Catch Us If You Can	5
1967	Everybody Knows	2
1968	Red Balloon	7
1969	Good Old Rock 'N Roll	7

DAVE DEE, DOZY, BEAKY, MICK AND TICH

IF NOTHING else, Dave Dee, Dozy, Beaky, Mick and Tich had one of the longest names of the many pop groups that appeared in the 1960s. Their name was derived from the nicknames of each member of the band. Dave Harman was Dave Dee, Trevor Davies was Dozy, John Dymond was Beaky, Michael Wilson was Mick and Tich was Ian Amey.

The group hailed from Wiltshire and had enormous hits, not only in Britain but also on the Continent and their smash hit *Bend It* reached number one in the West German charts and sold a million copies in Europe alone.

In Britain they had eight Top Ten hits between March 1966 and July 1968. Their only number one was the powerful *Legend Of Xanadu*. Since the end of the 1960s little has been heard of the group, although Dave Dee is still closely involved with the music business.

Top Ten hits of Dave Dee, Dozy, Beaky, Mick & Tich in the 1960s:

Year	Record	Pos
1966	Hold Tight	4
1966	Hideaway	10
1966	Bend It	2
1966	Save Me	4
1967	Okay!	4
1967	Zabadak!	3
1968	Legend Of Xanadu	1
1968	Last Night In Soho	8

DAY, Doris

ALTHOUGH she was a big hit in the 1950s, Doris Day was still a great box office draw in the 1960s with such films as *Lover Come Back* and *That Touch Of Mink*.

Born as Doris Kappelhoff, in Cincinnati in 1924, she was a singer touring with different dance bands in the 1940s before appearing as a replacement in her first film, *Romance On The High Seas* in 1949. She was an instant success, and her combination of good singing voice, acting ability and fresh approach led to her appearing in the hugely successful musicals *Calamity Jane* and *The Pyjama Game*.

She also displayed her ability to make people laugh and became a noted comedienne for her parts in *The Thrill Of It All* and *Send Me No Flowers*, both 1960s hits.

Doris' third husband, Marty Melcher, died in 1968 and it was revealed at the time that he was in financial difficulties. This led to Doris having a nervous breakdown but she bounced back and the Doris Day Show on American television was a big success in the 1970s.

On the music front she had two British number ones in the 1950s with *Secret Love* and *Whatever Will Be Will Be*. She had a Top Ten hit in 1964 with *Move Over Darling*. More recently she was seen on British TV screens advertising margarine.

The Films of Doris Day in the 1960s:

Please Don't Eat The Daisies	(1960)
Midnight Lace	(1960)
Lover Come Back	(1961)
That Touch Of Mink	(1962)
Jumbo	(1962)
The Thrill Of It All	(1963)
Move Over Darling	(1963)
Send Me No Flowers	(1964)
Do Not Disturb	(1965)
The Glass Bottom Boat	(1966)
Caprice	(1967)
The Ballad Of Josie	(1968)
Where Were You When The Lights Went Out?	(1968)
With Six You Get Egg Roll	(1968)

DE GAULLE, Charles

BORN at Lille on 22 November 1890, Charles André Joseph Marie De Gaulle became the first President of the Fifth Republic of France after a successful military career which saw him serve in World War One.

During the last war, when France fell in 1940, De Gaulle fled to England. He returned to Paris in 1944 as head of a liberation force and became leader of the provisional government. He resigned in 1946 and was in the background of French politics until recalled in 1958 and installed as president in December that year.

He granted independence to all of France's African colonies in 1959-60.

General De Gaulle, President of France, arrives in London in April 1960.

During the 1960s he is best remembered for his handling of the Algerian troubles and for his continued refusal to allow Britain into the Common Market. The students' revolution in 1968 posed particular problems for De Gaulle. Popular support for the students resulted in a series of strikes and at one time ten million workers were reported to have withdrawn their labour. But his position as leader was confirmed after an overwhelming victory in the general election shortly afterwards.

However, De Gaulle was forced to resign as President in 1969, after his proposals for senate and regional reforms were defeated. The following year Charles De Gaulle died on 9 November, two weeks short of his 80th birthday.

DEATH PENALTY

AT THE end of the 18th century, more than 200 crimes carried the death penalty in England and Wales. Execution was by hanging and until 1868 was in a public place. From 1838 the death penalty was virtually for murders only and in 1908 it was abolished for children under 16. The minimum age was raised to 18 in 1933.

The Commons were in favour of abolishing hanging as long ago as 1938 and the campaign which eventually led to its abolition in 1965 started in 1948 through a private members bill from MP Sidney

Silverman. The House of Lords, however, defeated the bill but, after years of campaigning, the bill was eventually passed by both the Commons and the Lords.

The bill was put to the House of Lords in July 1965 and they surprisingly passed it. On 8 November 1965 the Murder Bill (Abolition of the Death Penalty) became law. Ironically, the death penalty was abolished barely two weeks after Ian Brady and Myra Hindley were charged with the Moors murders.

While hanging still exists for such crimes as treason, various motions have been put to the House of Commons to get hanging brought back, but on each occasion it has been rejected.

The last persons to be executed in Britain were Peter Anthony Allen (21) and John Robson Walby (24), alias Gwynne Owen Evans, both from Preston. They had both been convicted of the murder of John Alan West at his Cumberland home on 7 April and their executions were carried out simultaneously on 13 August 1964. Allen's was at Walton Prison, Liverpool, while Walby's was at Strangeways in Manchester.

The last woman to be sent to the gallows was Ruth Ellis on 13 July 1955 when she was executed at Holloway Prison after being found guilty of the murder of her lover David Blakely.

DECIMALIZATION

ALTHOUGH Decimalization Day was not until 15 February 1971, the work towards it started in the 1960s and it was during the decade that the first decimal coins were introduced.

Chancellor of the Exchequer, James Callaghan, first made the announcement of the impending decimalization of the British monetary system on 1 March 1966. And on 23 April 1968 the first new coins were seen when the 5p and 10p pieces were launched. They were replacements for the one and two shilling pieces. The size was the same, but the design was different.

The old halfpenny disappeared in August 1969 and a couple of months later the first totally different coin was minted when the seven-sided 50p piece came into circulation on 14 October. It was to be the eventual replacement for the good old ten-bob note.

DEE, Simon

IN the late 1960s Simon Dee was one of the biggest names on television, but dramatically, he fell out of favour and disappeared from the screens as quickly as he came.

Born as Nicholas Henty Dodd at Ottawa, Canada, in 1935, he was sent to Shrewsbury College for his education at the age of 13. An excellent swimmer, he was in contention for selection for the 1952 Olympic team.

He did National Service in the RAF and appeared on the British Forces Network, but struggled to find work when he came out of the RAF and worked as a photographer, vacuum cleaner salesman, actor, model etc etc. However, he got into disc-jockeying via Radio Luxembourg and the 'pirate' *Radio Caroline* before getting a job with the BBC in 1965 which led him to landing a top job as the host of *Dee Time*, a peak viewing-time Saturday night show that started and ended with Dee leaping into his 'E'-Type Jaguar.

The show originally came from Manchester but eventually moved to London and ran from 4 April 1967 to 20 December 1969.

Dee hosted the 1967 Miss World contest and appeared in the films *Doctor In Trouble* and *The Italian Job*. But since the dramatic ending of his series the world of Simon Dee has fallen apart and in 1981 he reached an all-time low when arrested outside Buckingham Palace trying to deliver a letter to Her Majesty The Queen.

Since then, however, Simon Dee has made a mini-revival and has enjoyed a brief flirtation once more with the world of radio and television.

DEVALUATION OF THE POUND

ON 9 November 1967 the bank rate was increased to 6½%. Less than a week later the October trade figures were released and showed a deficit of £107 million. This resulted in the Chancellor of the Exchequer, James Callaghan, announcing on 18 November that the pound would be devalued by 14.3% and the bank rate increased further to a then staggering 8%.

These measures were introduced in an effort to improve Britain's economic position. Other controls, like stricter hire-purchase restrictions, a reduction in defence spending, abolition of the export rebate and the withdrawal of the Selective Employment Tax (SET) from

non-development areas, were also announced.

New foreign loans and credits were also arranged and although this went against the Government's policy, the measures were necessary.

In a television broadcast Premier Harold Wilson said: "It does not mean, of course, that the pound here in Britain in your pocket or purse or in your bank has been devalued."

The result of the devaluation saw the exchange rate with the dollar drop dramatically from $2.80 to $2.40. The day after the announcement, Spain, Denmark, Ireland and Israel all devalued in line with Britain. But the United States and Common Market countries did not.

All banks and the Stock Exchange were forced to close for a day on 20 November and nine days later, Callaghan resigned after three years as Chancellor and was appointed Home Secretary. Roy Jenkins made the move in the other direction.

DEVLIN, Bernadette

IN 1969, 21-year-old Bernadette Devlin became the youngest Member of Parliament since William Pitt nearly 200 years earlier.

Born at Dungannon into a poor Catholic family in 1948, she won a scholarship to Queen's University, Belfast, where she read psychology. She also joined the People's Democracy, a student protest group.

Standing a little over 5ft tall, Devlin entered Parliament and in her maiden speech fiercely attacked British policies in Northern Ireland. Outspoken and surrounded by controversy, she was arrested for leading rioters in the Bogside battle and subsequently received a nine-month prison sentence while still an MP.

She married teacher Mike McAliskey in 1973 and did not stand at the 1974 General Election. After a few years away from the limelight she returned in the early 1980s when she was seen at demonstrations in support of the IRA hunger strikers. In 1981, Devlin and her husband were both shot while getting their children ready for school. Undeterred by the experience, she continued to campaign for the hunger strikers in the H-block at the Maze Prison.

DIMBLEBY, Richard, CBE, OBE

RICHARD Dimbleby was the 'voice of the BBC' in the 1950s and 1960s. When there was an important State occasion, his voice echoed the tone of the occasion, whether it be joyous or sombre.

Born on 25 May 1913, his first job was with the family newspaper firm of Dimbleby & Sons in Richmond, Surrey. He then worked on the *Southern Daily Echo* in Southampton and the *Advertisers' Weekly* in London, where he was the news editor at 21.

He got his first job with the BBC in 1936 as an 'observer' in the newly-formed news department. He covered such events as the Spanish Civil War, Royal tours and State visits.

During the war Dimbleby spent three years reporting in the Middle East. Afterwards he continued his radio broadcasting with such programmes as *Down Your Way* and *Off The Record*. He moved to television in the early '50s and in 1953 hosted *Panorama*. His first major outside broadcast for the BBC was the Coronation in 1953.

In the 1960s, Richard Dimbleby became one of the leading political interviewers and commentators and his coverage of Princess Margaret's wedding in 1960 and the funerals of President Kennedy in 1963, and Winston Churchill in 1965 highlighted his professionalism. He was awarded both the OBE and CBE, as well as receiving countless radio and television awards.

Dimbleby died from cancer on 22 December 1965. The Dimbleby name is maintained as sons, David and Jonathan, have followed him into broadcasting and have obviously learned a great deal from their illustrious father.

DISNEY, Walt

NO MATTER what decade is written about since the 1920s, the name of Walt Disney is bound to appear. He was unquestionably the finest animator in the history of the movies and gave us such wonderful characters as Mickey Mouse and Donald Duck.

Born in Chicago in 1901, Walter Disney learnt his animation skills from a member of staff at the *Chicago Herald* and in 1923 he took his new found skills to Hollywood. His first character, Oswald the Rabbit, was invented in 1927, but Walt was unhappy with him and so he developed a new character, a small mouse who he named Mortimer. His name was soon changed to Mickey and he was given a girlfriend, Minnie.

Mickey Mouse met with little success originally but when he was transferred to sound cartoons and made the star of *Steamboat Willy* in 1928 the new character became an idol.

Columbia Pictures contracted

Disney to produce a cartoon series called *Silly Symphonies*, which many regard as his finest work. He experimented with colour techniques and soon became the market leader in all forms of cartoons. Gradually he introduced new characters; Goofy, Horace Horsecollar, Pluto and then Donald Duck. He produced the first ever full-length cartoon, *Snow White And The Seven Dwarfs*, in 1937. It was a huge success. Since then Disney films, whether they be cartoon, or in other forms, have proved to be hugely popular with both adults and children, and will continue to entertain for many more years to come.

In 1955 he opened the famous Disneyland at Anaheim, California. In 1982 Disneyworld opened in Orlando and the EPCOT Center followed on the same site. There is a Disney Magic Kingdom in Tokyo, and in 1992 the Euro Disneyland is scheduled to open just outside Paris.

Disney died on 15 December 1966 at the age of 65, but he has left a legacy that will last for many years. Donald Duck and Mickey Mouse will never die.

In the 1960s, Disney made the comedy *The Absent Minded Professor*, starring Fred MacMurray, the box-office smash *Mary Poppins* and the innovative *Jungle Book* which was released the year after Disney's death.

Disney has won more Oscars than any other person. His first was in 1932. He went on to win 26 regular Oscars and six special awards.

DODD, Ken

LIVERPOOL-BORN comedian Ken Dodd added a unique brand of humour to the sixties, the likes of which had not been seen before or since.

Born in 1932, he tried his hand at singing, dancing and ventriloquism as a youngster before becoming a full-time professional comedian in 1954. His trademarks were his teeth, which were insured for £100,000 in the 1960s, and his stand-up hairstyle, which gave a clown-like impression, and that was another of Dodd's ambitions as a youngster, to be a clown.

A brilliant stand-up comedian, he could get laughs without venturing into the area of 'blue' jokes. He was often accompanied on stage by Dickie Mint and the other 'Diddy Men', kings of the Knotty Ash jam butty mines.

Dodd gave us some wonderful catchphrases like "Where's Me Shirt" and "Have you ever been tickled missus" as he waved his familiar tickling stick to the audience.

In addition to his great sense of

Ken Dodd in 1963, making a safety film about using zebra crossings.

laughter and fun, Dodd has a good voice and one of the best selling records of the sixties was *Tears* which spent five weeks at number one in 1965. *Love Is Like A Violin*, *The River (Le Colline Sono In Fioro)* and *Promises* were all Top Ten hits for him during the decade.

The world of Ken Dodd was shattered in 1989 when he appeared in court on tax evasion charges brought against him by the Inland Revenue but, after a lengthy trial, he was found not guilty on all charges.

DOLLAR (US)

IN THE first half of the 1960s a US dollar was always regarded as being worth 7s 3d (36p), and it rarely changed from that figure.

The rate of $2.80 to the £1 remained unaltered until 1966, when it dropped to $2.78. It went up to $2.79 the following year but, following the devaluation of the pound it was down to $2.41 in 1968. At the end of the decade it had dropped even further to $2.39.

DONOVAN

DONOVAN was born with the full name of Donovan Phillip Leitch at Maryhill, near Glasgow, in February 1946. In the 1960s he became simply known as Donovan and was hailed as the 'British Bob Dylan'.

The Leitch family moved to England when Donovan was ten, and after leaving school he became a busker and travelled Britain and the Continent, guitar in hand, seeking to make enough money to survive.

When he was 18 he returned to live in London and met Peter Eden, who became his first manager. Eden arranged for him to appear on *Ready Steady Go* and such was the impact of Donovan that Pye records immediately offered him a contract. In 1965 *Catch The Wind* became the first of his hits.

The following year, his biggest selling record *Sunshine Superman*, reached number two in Britain. More significantly it went to number one in America where he had previously been viewed only as a Bob Dylan imitator.

occasional comedy songs like *Paddy McGinty's Goat* and *Rafferty's Motor Car*.

Val has since enjoyed continued success both on television and in the recording studios. He had eight Top Twenty hit records, the last being *Morning* in 1971.

Top Ten hits of Val Doonican in the 1960s:

Year	Record	Pos
1964	Walk Tall	3
1965	The Special Years	7
1966	Elusive Butterfly	5
1966	What Would I Be	2
1967	If The Whole World Stopped Loving	3

DOUBLE YOUR MONEY

ONE OF the first of the popular television quiz programmes, *Double*

Donovan appeared on the Beatles record *Yellow Submarine* and Paul McCartney reciprocated by doing the whispering of 'Mellow Yellow' on Donovan's hit of the same name.

Donovan's last hit was in 1969 when he combined with the Jeff Beck Group to make *Goo Goo Barabajagal (Love Is Hot)* which reached number 12 in the charts.

Since the '60s Donovan has led a sheltered life, occasionally coming out of 'hibernation' to record albums and to compose movie soundtracks including *Brother Sun, Sister Moon*.

Top Ten hits of Donovan in the 1960s:

Year	Record	Pos
1965	Catch The Wind	4
1965	Colours	4
1966	Sunshine Superman	2
1967	Mellow Yellow	8
1967	There Is A Mountain	8
1968	Jennifer Juniper	5
1968	Hurdy Gurdy Man	4

DOONICAN, Val

VAL Doonican was an 'overnight sensation' who had been around the show business world for 20 years.

Born in Waterford, Ireland, in 1929, he had his first professional engagement as a 17-year-old and in 1951 appeared on Irish Radio. But the big break came in 1964 when he was given his own rocking chair by the BBC and asked to host the *Val Doonican Show*.

His clean-cut image made him an instant success, not to mention his ability to sing ballads and the

Your Money, was launched in 1955 and lasted nearly 20 years with Hughie Green as the regular questionmaster.

Contestants were asked a series of questions on a subject of their choice and the prize money doubled up each time a question was answered correctly, starting at £1 and going up to £32. The £1 question was always so daft that everybody got it right. Green assisted with the answers up to £8, but after that the contestant was on his or her own.

A certain amount of audience participation was involved when the decision to go or not was reached with cries of 'double it' or 'take the money'

would come from the auditorium.

There was a chance to go for a £1,000 jackpot. After winning the £32 prize, a contestant would be asked a test question. If it was correct he or she would go into the famous box where they would sit, wearing headphones, and would be asked tougher questions, firstly for £64, then £125, £250, £500 and finally £1,000. They could either 'stick' after winning any prize or could carry on to the jackpot. However, if they carried on and got the next set of questions wrong they blew it all, except their initial £32.

This treasure trail part of the programme was carried over from week to week when contestants would announce to an eagerly waiting audience if they were going to take the money or carry on. If somebody was already on the treasure trail then other £32 winners were not eligible to have a go for that part of the programme.

> *Once, while taking part in a celebrity programme, footballer Bobby Charlton refused to go into the sound-proof box because of claustrophobia brought on after the Munich air disaster. He reached the jackpot and is the only contestant to do so outside the box.*

Green's assistant was the elfin-like cockney girl Monica Rose who first appeared as a contestant and captured the hearts of the audience. She was invited back to help Green with the introducing of the contestants.

Hughie Green with two Double Your Money hostesses, leaving for Moscow in May 1966, to do the show in Russia. The girl on the right is Monica Rose, the contestant who went on to become a star of the show.

DOUGLAS-HOME, Sir Alec

SIR Alec Douglas-Home was the surprise choice as leader of the Conservatives after the resignation of Harold Macmillan in 1963. Born in London, but heir to the Scottish Earldom of Home, he became the MP for South Lanark in 1931 but spent six years out of Parliament between 1945 and 1950.

He entered, and became leader of, the House of Lords but he renounced his peerage in order to take the Conservative Party leadership. At the time of taking control of the party he was not a member of either House. He gained his seat in the Commons by winning the Kinross by-election shortly after taking office.

Defeat by Harold Wilson in the 1964 General Election resulted in Douglas-Home being replaced as party leader

by Ted Heath the following year. He remained an MP and served as Foreign Secretary in Heath's Government between 1970 and 1974.

In 1974 he became a life peer and returned to the House of Lords. As Lord Dunglass, he played first-class cricket for Middlesex.

DR KILDARE

AN AMERICAN hospital series centred around the Blair General Hospital. Exactly 200 episodes were made for television between 1961 and 1966 and were based on the stories by Max Brand. The first Dr Kildare was seen on the silver screen in 1937 when the title role was played by Lew Ayres.

Richard Chamberlain in a singing role.

The television series saw a new young actor play the part of James Kildare. His name was Richard Chamberlain and he became one of

Two records of the Dr Kildare theme reached the British charts in 1962. The instrumental version by the Johnny Spence Orchestra reached number 15, while the re-titled vocal version, Three Stars Will Shine Tonight, sung by Chamberlain, reached number 12.

the heart-throbs of the era; a tag he had to live with again 20 years later — the series is frequently repeated.

The show also starred Raymond Massey as Dr Gillespie, the man who gave guidance and tuition to the keen young doctor. The series had a large following, particularly with young women, and the programme ensured Chamberlain's future as an actor of star quality both in the movies and on television as his part in *The Thorn Birds* testifies.

DUBCEK, Alexander

ALEXANDER Dubček was the Czechoslovakian leader at the time of the Russian invasion in 1968.

It was shortly after Dubček's rise to First Secretary in January 1968 that he upset the Russian leadership by announcing sweeping economic and political changes. Freedom of speech, the abolition of censorship and the suspension of former Stalinist party leaders were all steps taken by Dubček.

The Russians were none too pleased, even though Dubček assured the Soviets he would still work within a Communist framework. In August 1968, Soviet troops rolled through the streets of Prague and took occupation of Czechoslovakia.

While some sources felt Dubček should have put up more resistance against the Russians, he was retained as First Secretary until replaced by Husak the following year. Dubček was elected president of the First Assembly but was stripped of Communist party membership in 1970. He later worked in a Government motor pool.

DYLAN, Bob

BOB Dylan was the undisputed 'King of Folk Music' in the 1960s and his compositions have been the inspiration for many singers over the past 20 years.

Born Robert Zimmerman in 1941, he changed his surname to Dylan as a tribute to one of his idols, the Welsh poet Dylan Thomas. He turned poetry into music which captured all aspects of love and war, themes which were rife in the 1960s. *A Hard Rain's Gonna Fall* was based on the Cuban Missile Crisis of 1962 and was later a Top Ten hit for Bryan Ferry. His songs

about war often brought him into conflict with the authorities.

Remarkably, Bob Dylan never had a number one hit in either Britain or America, but his albums were a different story and were phenomenally successful. Between 1964 and 1983 he had 29 different LPs enter the British album charts with no fewer than six hitting the top spot. Of these, *The Freewheelin' Bob Dylan*, *John Wesley Harding* and *Nashville Skyline* are classics.

His writing of such great songs as *Blowin' In The Wind*, *Mr Tambourine Man*, *All I Really Want To Do* and *Mighty Quinn* all produced big hits for other artistes. But Dylan returned to the British singles charts in 1988 after an absence of nearly 20 years as a member of the Travelling Wilburys (an all-star 'Supergroup').

Dylan took his inspiration from the legendary Woody Guthrie who taught him the techniques of folk music. Happily Guthrie's protégé did not disappoint.

Top Ten hits of Bob Dylan in the 1960s:

Year	Record	Pos
1965	Times They Are A-Changin'	9
1965	Subterranean Homesick Blues	9
1965	Like A Rolling Stone	4
1965	Positively Fourth Street	8
1966	Rainy Day Women, Nos. 12 & 35	7
1969	Lay Lady Lay	5

'E'-TYPE JAGUAR

THE 'E'-TYPE Jaguar was the ultra high-performance sports car with the sleek profile that nicely fitted into the 1960s image.

It was seen for the first time at the Geneva Motor Show on 16 March

The new E-Type Jaguar pictured at Oulton Park in April 1961.

1961. This attractive-looking addition to the Jaguar range bore a resemblance to the 'D'-Type of the 1950s and came with the 3.8 litre 'S'-Type engine. It was capable of going from 0-100mph in 16 seconds and developed 265bhp at 5,500rpm.

The 'E'-Type came in two choices; the hard-top coupé version at £2,196 19s 2d or the open-top version at £2,097 15s 10d. They may sound cheap now, but at the time it was only the fortunate few who could afford the car of the decade.

EICHMANN TRIAL

ON 11 April 1961, the most famous trial of a Nazi war criminal got under way in Jerusalem. Sitting in the bullet-proof cage in the courtroom was Adolf Eichmann, who was charged on 15 counts with conspiring to cause the death or persecution of millions of Jews. The 15 charges were as follows: four charges of crimes against the Jewish people, seven crimes against humanity, and one war crime. They all carried the death penalty. There were also three charges of belonging to a hostile organization (Nazi SS, Gestapo and Secret Service) which did not carry a death penalty.

In December 1939 there was a mass deportation of Jews from occupied lands under the direction of Eichmann. When he was captured and brought from Argentina, where he was believed to have been living under an assumed name since the war, Eichmann was described by Israel's Prime Minister, David Ben-Gurion, as 'one of the greatest of the Nazi war criminals'.

The trial lasted four months until its conclusion on 14 August 1961. Thirty-nine witnesses were called against Eichmann and on 15 December he was sentenced to be hanged for the murder of millions of Jews during the Nazi occupation of Europe.

Adolph Eichmann in his bullet-proof 'cage' during his trial.

Despite clemency appeals to the Israel Supreme Court, the execution was carried out at Tel Aviv prison just before midnight on 31 May 1962. Eichmann refused to wear the black hood and in his parting words he sent his regards to Germany, Argentina and Austria — "The countries I shall not forget." He also told witnesses at the execution: "We shall meet again, I have believed in God. I obeyed the laws of war and was loyal to my flag." It was certainly contradictory that he should say he 'believed in God' because, when he was called to give evidence at his trial, he refused to take an oath on the Bible.

EMERGENCY WARD 10

TELEVISION'S first twice-weekly soap opera was the popular Emergency Ward 10, set at Oxbridge Hospital. It was first shown on 19 February 1957 and was broadcast on Tuesday and Friday nights. It enjoyed a run of nearly ten years on ITV.

The series was the idea of Tessa Diamond and its success stemmed around two heart-throbs, Dr Alan Dawson, played by Charles Tingwell, who now crops up in many Australian 'soaps', and nurse (later sister) Carole Young, played by the attractive blonde Jill Browne, who was once married to John Alderton.

Also making up the team were Nurse Roberts, played by Rosemary Miller, Simon Forrester, played by Frederick Bartman, who later appeared in *Take The High Road*, and Dr O'Meara, alias Glyn Owen, who later found fame in *Howard's Way*.

The series ended on 1 October 1966 and was replaced by a one-hour serial entitled *Call Oxbridge 2000*, which retained some of the characters from the original series.

Sonia Fox and Ian Cullen, two of the stars of Emergency Ward 10.

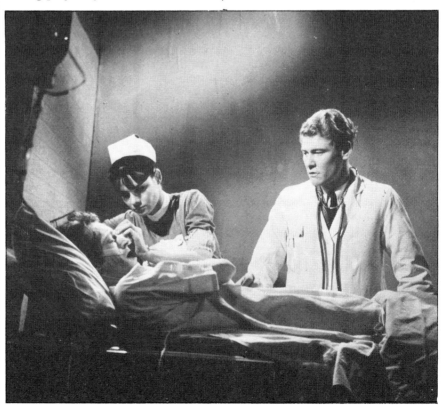

EPSTEIN, Brian

BRIAN Epstein was the man who gave the world The Beatles, Gerry and the Pacemakers, Cilla Black, and many more Liverpool groups and artistes in the 1960s.

Born on 19 September 1934, he entered RADA in 1956 and wanted to pursue a career in the theatre. However, when he returned to Liverpool he took charge of the record department at NEMS, the family's music store. Within two years it had proved so successful that it occupied three floors and employed a staff of 30.

The shop boasted it could obtain a copy of any record and for that reason Brian Epstein's life changed.

On 28 October 1961, he was asked for a copy of *My Bonnie* by Tony Sheridan and the Beatles. Never having heard of the group, nor indeed the record, he discovered that it had been recorded in Germany, but was amazed to learn the group came from Liverpool. They were appearing at the nearby Cavern Club at the time. He went along to see them perform and was impressed. They were just what Epstein needed to restore his involvement with the arts, although it was somewhat different from what he had planned in his RADA days.

Brian Epstein with The Beatles.

Epstein took control of the Beatles and while he did not interfere with their style of music, he got them to change their lifestyle and the way they looked. He took the Beatles music to several top recording companies before being accepted by EMI. The rest is history as 'Eppy' (as the Fab Four called him) helped make the Beatles the biggest ever name in pop music.

On 27 August 1967, Brian Epstein was found dead from a drug overdose at his Belgravia flat. He was only 32 at the time.

EVERLY BROTHERS

DON AND PHIL Everly come from a musical family and, at an early age, used to appear with their parents on a local radio station. At 15, Don even had his own Saturday morning 15-minute slot entitled *The Little Donnie Show*.

Hailing from Kentucky, Don is the eldest of the brothers. He was born

EUROVISION SONG CONTEST

HELD annually since 1956 when Lys Assia of Switzerland won with *Refrains*, the Eurovision Song Contest has survived despite its constant stream of 'knockers'. The most exciting part of the programme is the voting at the end when juries from all over Europe are called upon to give their marks.

There have been few really exciting moments in the event but the voting at the end of the 1969 contest saw four countries challenging for the title going into the last round of votes. And what happened? There was a four-way tie, including our own Lulu with *Boom Bang-a-Bang*. Two years earlier, Sandie Shaw became Britain's first-ever winner of the contest. That honour did not go to Pearl Carr and Teddy Johnson as many people believe.

The winners in the 1960s were:

Year	Song	Singer	Country
1960	Tom Pillibi	Jacqueline Boyer	France
1961	Nous, Les Amoureux	Jean Claude Pascal	Luxembourg
1962	Un Premier Amour	Isabelle Aubret	France
1963	Dansevise	Grethe and Jurgen Ingmann	Denmark
1964	Non Ho L'Eta Per Amarti	Gigliola Cinquetti	Italy
1965	Poupée De Cire, Poupée De Son	France Gall	Luxembourg
1966	Merci Cheri	Udo Jurgens	Austria
1967	Puppet On A String	Sandie Shaw	UK
1968	La La La	Massiel	Spain
1969	Boom Bang-a-Bang	Lulu	UK
	Viva Cantando	Salome	Spain
	Un Jour, Un Enfant	Frida Boccara	France
	De Troubador	Lennie Kuhr	Holland

United Kingdom entrants in the 1960s were:

Year	Song	Singer	Posn in British charts
1960	Looking High High High	Bryan Johnson	20
1961	Are You Sure	The Allisons	2
1962	Ring A Ding Girl	Ronnie Carroll	46
1963	Say Wonderful Things	Ronnie Carroll	6
1964	I Love The Little Things	Matt Monro	-
1965	I Belong	Kathy Kirby	36
1966	A Man Without Love	Kenneth McKellar	30
1967	Puppet On A String	Sandie Shaw	1
1968	Congratulations	Cliff Richard	1
1969	Boom Bang-a-Bang	Lulu	2

Puppet On A String was the first UK entry to subsequently top the British charts.

on 1 February 1937, while Phil was born on 19 January 1939. The two boys were taught the guitar by their father, Ike. They were both left-handed but he made them play right-handed because he was right-handed and could not teach them the other way around!

After the local radio station began to decline, Don and Phil made for Nashville in the hope of selling their music and, thanks to the aid of Chet Atkins, they were given their first recording contract in 1955. They were to take the music world by storm and, with the possible exception of Simon

and Garfunkel, have been the most successful singing duo of all time.

Their first number-one hit in the States was *Wake Up Little Susie* in 1957. By the time the 1960s arrived, Don and Phil had already had four number ones in Britain. In 1960 their own composition *Cathy's Clown* topped the British charts for seven weeks and in the US was number one for five weeks. It was the first disc to simultaneously be number one on both sides of the Atlantic.

By 1966 they found it increasingly difficult to maintain their motivation because of the arrival of so many modern-day groups. While still remaining popular, their relationship became strained and in 1973, while on stage at Beuna Park, California, they split their life-long partnership. The split was to last for ten years. They came to the Royal Albert Hall in 1983 for an emotional reunion concert and earlier that year Phil teamed up with Cliff Richard on the Top Ten hit *She Means Nothing To Me*.

Don and Phil still regularly tour the United States and, happily, Britain. The waistlines are a bit bigger these days and the voices are showing signs of nearly 40 years as singers. But the Everly Brothers are still charismatic.

Top Ten hits of the Everly Brothers in the 1960s:

Year	Record	Pos
1960	Cathy's Clown	1
1960	When Will I Be Loved	4
1960	Lucille/So Sad (To Watch Good Love Go Bad)	4
1961	Walk Right Back	1
1961	Temptation	1
1962	Cryin' In The Rain	6
1965	The Price Of Love	2

FAITH, Adam

ADAM Faith had huge successes in the late 1950s and early 1960s, but he was another of the many top singers to feel the brunt of the pop group invasion. Adam, though, diversified his talents into record production, the theatre, television and even investment management, to maintain his interest in show business.

Born in Acton, West London, in 1940, his real name is Terence Nelhams. He always wanted to be a film editor and worked as a messenger boy for Rank at their Soho offices. However, he was soon influenced by the sounds regularly streaming from the coffee bars in the area and with some workmates formed a group called The Worried Men. In 1959, Adam met musical arranger John Barry and writer Johnny Worth. Between them their talents led to a string of hits. Adam's first record *Runk Bunk Baby* on the Top Rank label didn't exactly go the same way, Mind you . . .what a title!

What Do You Want was his first number one in 1959 and in the early part of the 1960s it seemed that he could not fail to make the Top Ten. Shrewdly managed by Eve Taylor, Adam became one of the biggest-selling solo artistes of the day.

By 1965, despite having a new songwriter, Chris Andrews, and a backing group, The Roulettes, he made the decision to take up acting. He had previously appeared in films, but now wanted to appear on the stage. This ultimately led to his appearance as the likeable rogue in the television series *Budgie*, which first appeared in 1971. Since then he has appeared alongside David Essex in the film *Stardust* and became manager and producer of Leo Sayer. In 1988 he revived *Budgie* in the West End with Anita Dobson, formerly of *EastEnders*, as his co-star, and wrote a weekly financial column in a national newspaper.

Top Ten hits of Adam Faith in the 1960s:

Year	Record	Pos
1960	Poor Me	1
1960	Someone Else's Baby	2
1960	When Johnny Comes Marching Home/Made You	5
1960	How About That	4
1960	Lonely Pup (In A Christmas Shop)	4
1961	This Is It/Who Am I	5
1961	The Time Has Come	4
1962	As You Like It	5
1962	Don't That Beat All	8
1963	The First Time	5

FAME, Georgie

BROUGHT up in the industrial town of Leigh, near Manchester, Georgie Fame was born as Clive Powell on 26 June 1943. After leaving school he worked in a cotton-weaving factory and in his spare time played in a band called The Dominoes.

An accomplished pianist, he was given a job with the Rory Blackwell Band in 1959, after impressing the bandleader during a talent contest at Butlins. This led to his lucky break of meeting impressario Larry Parnes, who advised Powell to change his name to Georgie Fame. Parnes put him into a new group which was later to become the Blue Flames, Georgie's own backing group.

In the early days they acted as a support group to visiting American artistes and were Eddie Cochran's support on his fateful 1960 tour. By 1962, the Blue Flames were resident at London's Flamingo Club and this eventually led to a recording contract. The group recorded 12 discs in the 1960s. Only three of them reached the Top Ten but, remarkably, all three went to number one.

Widely acknowledged as one of Britain's finest rhythm and blues singers, Georgie Fame has continued to find work since those heady days in the 1960s. In 1971 he returned to the charts when he teamed up with Alan Price to record *Rosetta*.

Top Ten hits of Georgie Fame in the 1960s:

Year	Record	Pos
1964	Yeh Yeh	1
1966	Get Away	1
1967	Ballad Of Bonnie & Clyde	1

FARTHING

ONE of the smallest British coins ever minted, the farthing was first seen as a silver coin in the 13th century. It later became a copper coin and in 1860 was struck in bronze. However, the last farthings were minted in 1956 and on 1 January 1961 it ceased to be legal tender.

Its value was ¼d which would today be equivalent to approximately 0.1p. There were 960 farthings in a pound. The reverse of the farthing depicted a wren, not a robin as many people believe.

FASHION

AS history shows, each new decade heralds the start of a new era in fashion. Prior to the 1960s, the greatest new era in fashion-wear was the 'Roaring Twenties'. And now the 'Swinging Sixties' can be compared with that decade. But even the then 'outrageous' styles of the 1920s pale into insignificance in comparison to what the 1960s had to offer.

The 1960s was a period of prosperity and of youth. And it was to the youth that fashion design was aimed. The days when daughters wore similar clothes to their mothers disappeared almost overnight, never to return.

The 'baby-boom' of the immediate post-war years meant there were a lot of teenagers around in the 1960s. These teenagers were prosperous because there was near full-employment. And they sought avenues to spend their cash. Pop music was one outlet of spending, the other was clothes, and in a way that had never been seen before.

It was not just the teenage girl who benefited from the fashion change of the 1960s for the male also became more fashion conscious. However, the biggest fashion trend to hit the decade, or indeed any era, was the showing of the female thigh thanks

to the miniskirt. Previously the female upper leg was a never-to-be-seen domain in public. Now, it was not only the legs and the knee, but also the thigh that was evident wherever you went.

The mini is generally accredited to Mary Quant. It is not known whether she actually designed or made the first one, but there is no doubting her contribution towards popularizing the most adventurous fashion trend ever seen. Mary Quant was an advocate of giving the people what they wanted and at the same time wanted the teenagers to have an identity of their own. She gave them that.

The mini was certainly an eye-catcher and not just with the man in the street. It raised a few eyebrows in Whitehall, particularly amongst the Customs men, who had to have a rethink over the ten-per-cent tax ruling on clothing because of its length. The Customs men got round it by ruling that women's clothing would, in future, be measured on bust size, and not length!

The 'Almost-not-there-look', that's the newest swimsuit from West Coast designer Rudi Gernrich, unveiled in New York in January 1967.

The demand for clothes was greater than ever and this led to Mary Quant's *Bazaar* Boutique, which she opened in the King's Road, Chelsea, in 1955, becoming the centre of London Fashion. Carnaby Street, a run-down back alley off Regent Street, was soon established, largely due to 20-year-old Glaswegian, John Stephen, who acquired his first boutique in 1963. Soon, London was regarded as the fashion centre of the world which both New York and Paris, the two other influential fashion centres, acknowledged.

Boutiques sprang up across the country as the modern teenager became more aware of the changing trends in fashion thanks to the glossy colour magazines that became readily available. And the high street shops acknowledged that fashion was a thing for the masses by stocking the latest designs. The new clothing revolution had well and truly taken a grip.

The new fashions were displayed by models like Jean 'The Shrimp' Shrimpton and Leslie Hornby, better known as Twiggy. These girls became household names and their slim figures, on which hung the modern-day clothes, showed that the bust and waist were things of the past. The 'A' line dresses did nothing to show off the bust and the waist, which just couldn't be seen at all. When wearing trousers the waist was no longer required as the trousers sat on the hips. Consequently they became known as hipsters.

As far as the men were concerned, the mini gave them a chance to see plenty of leg but, as often happens, good news is accompanied by bad. And the bad news in this case was the end of stockings and suspenders although both were making a come-back in the 1980s. In came tights which were an essential accessory with the mini. By the mid-1960s stockings were virtually obsolete. Towards the end of the decade, however, they made a reappearance, but in the self-supporting style. Sorry lads, still no suspenders!

New fabrics helped in the mass production of clothes and the likes of Crimplene, introduced in 1961, was popular in dress and skirt design. But other exciting materials like plastics,

Variations of the 'beehive' hair fashion of the 1960s.

PVC and vinyl were used in clothes manufacture and thus highlighted the space age era that we lived in during the 1960s. In general clothes became much lighter in the decade.

As the mid-1960s approached clothing became more of a unisex nature and at times, particularly from the rear, it was hard to tell which were the boys and which were the girls. T-shirts and hipsters were the vogue with both sexes, and women wore their hair short; in many cases shorter than their male counterparts. Women also wore trouser suits to add to the confusion. The skinny-ribbed jumper was also popular with both sexes and would have either a 'V' or polo neck. Ice blue hipsters and a black polo neck . . .if there was anything guaranteed to pull the girls in the mid-1960s that was the combination!

Italian designer Domenico Albion created this look in 1967. It was made of silver leather strips.

Men's trousers started the decade very tight with 10 or 12-inch bottoms but by the mid-1960s they had become flared. The button-down collared shirts were often patterned and wide 'kipper' ties sometimes matched the pattern of the shirt.

It was still necessary to wear overcoats in times of bad weather. But the thick overcoat disappeared and made way for the shorter car-coat, often made of imitation suede with woollen collar and cuffs. Synthetic leathers were also used and PVC gave the 'wet-look' to raincoats. One thing that was noticeable by its absence in the 1960s was the man's hat. Previous generations had worn hats and caps for whatever occasion. The men of the 1960s wanted to show off their hairstyles, not cover them up.

Pop groups had a big influence on the teenagers of the day and none more than the Beatles. Boys imitated their idols, and the 'Beatle-cut' soon became an established hairstyle. Their collarless Beatle jackets were also imitated. Many groups wore suits

Actress Jane Birken arrived for the premier of the film Slogan *in October 1969 and turned more than a few heads with her see-through dress.*

the decade was no longer a fun-loving era. It was a time for demonstrations, warfare and tragedy. The hippy cult arrived from across the Atlantic and with it came the psychedelic colours of flower power. Flared jeans were popular with both men and women and embroidered Afghan coats and long kaftans arrived. Hairstyles got longer and less clean-cut. The new era heralded a period of extreme casualness.

The miniskirt made the wearing of tights instead of stockings and suspenders an absolute priority for all but the bravest girl.

and the four-button jackets with small, high lapels became popular. But to be trendy you only fastened either the two middle buttons or just the bottom one.

As a complete contrast to the many suit-wearing pop groups, there was (and still is) the Rolling Stones. They, too, had their followers who dressed like their heroes. But in their case it was more of a 'beatnik' look — longer hair, jeans and T-shirts. There were certainly no suits for the Stones fans. Even on his wedding day, Mick Jagger turned up in a sweater and corduroy trousers.

The 1960s was an era of liberation and sensuality and in 1964 the first topless dresses were worn by the more adventurous girls. But it didn't do them much good; indecency charges were inevitably brought against the wearers. However, it led to other adventurous dresses like the bare midriff style and the crocheted see-through dress. Gimmicks like false fingernails were popular in the 1960s, and there was nothing more gimmicky than disposable paper knickers!

Swimwear went through a period of change in the 1960s and the bikini became very popular. And in 1964 Rudi Gernrich designed the topless swimsuit (for girls that is!). Gernrich also designed the 'no-bra' bra and body stocking.

The late 1960s brought about another period of change. By 1968

The first open-air show of 'hippy' fashions in London's Fulham Road in September 1967.

With the advent of psychedelic colours and designs the Beatles opened their Apple boutique in London's West End in 1968. Many of the clothes were designed by Dutch hippie designers, Simon and Marijke. But their prices were too steep for the average man or woman and the boutique became a tourist attraction rather than somewhere the trendy youngsters went to buy their latest wardrobe.

Also in 1968 the miniskirt took on a new look…it became the microskirt which can best be described as a 'big belt'. However, it was to signal the beginning of the end for the mini as the long straight midiskirt covered both thighs and knees yet again, and in 1969 the ankle-length maxiskirt arrived. For those who wanted to carry on wearing the mini there was a compromise; a short skirt worn underneath the long maxicoat which was virtually floor length. It was the longest style of coat seen in Britain since before World War One . . .how fashion changed dramatically in less than ten years.

FELDMAN, Marty

MARTY Feldman, born in Canning Town 1934, died in Mexico City in 1982. That is the sort of inscription the zany Feldman would have wished for on his tombstone.

The man with the 'pop' eyes and a broken nose brought a new kind

Marty Feldman and his wife, Loretta.

of humour to the television screens in the late-1960s and early '70s.

Feldman left school at 15 to become a messenger boy and part-time jazz trumpeter. Over the next two years he had a succession of jobs including assistant to a sideshow act, racetrack tipster and 'book thief'. He entered variety theatre with an act named Morris, Marty and Mitch, joining the BBC as a staff writer in 1957. Feldman's wit led to him writing for *Round The Horne* between 1965-69. He won the Writers' Guild Award in 1967.

He became the chief writer for *The Frost Report* and wrote and appeared in *At Last The 1948 Show* which also starred John Cleese, Tim Brooke-Taylor and Graham Chapman. His own show *Marty* was extremely popular and attracted an average of 15 million viewers. It won a BAFTA Award in 1969.

In the mid-1970s, Feldman left Britain for Hollywood, where he starred in several movies including the role of Eye-gore the hunchback in *Young Frankenstein.*

Feldman died on 21 December 1982 on the day he completed the making of the film *Yellowbeard.* He had a unique sense of fun and made the most of his 'oversized' eyes which were affected by a thyroid problem. Typical of the humour of the man, he was a vegetarian who married a butcher's daughter!

FILMS

WITH the coming of the sixties there came a boom in the British film industry with the so-called 'Kitchen Sink Dramas', as films like *Saturday Night And Sunday Morning, A Taste Of Honey* and *This Sporting Life* dealt with life at 'grass roots' in working class areas. The stars of these films, like the characters they portrayed, often came from similar backgrounds. Albert Finney, Rita Tushingham and Richard Harris were all outstanding examples of such performers.

The early years of the sixties soon gave way to the pop era and with the coming of the Beatles and the like, there was a demand for films with plenty of music and not a lot of story line. But this didn't matter as long as these new found heroes of the silver screen were projected to their masses of fans.

The Beatles, of course, paved the way with *Help* and *A Hard Day's Night*, while Cliff Richard also starred in one of the sixties' 'great' pop movies, *Summer Holiday.*

Following closely on the heels of pop movies were the spy thrillers which became immensely popular in the sixties and of course the market

leader in this respect was Sean Connery, alias James Bond. He made his debut as Bond in *Dr No* in 1962. Michael Caine, as Harry Palmer, and Richard Burton as Lemus in *The Spy Who Came In From The Cold* were two other prominent British actors who tried their hand at spy movies, but not with the same success as Connery and Bond.

Worldwide, the film-makers of the 1960s brought us some classics and blockbusters that will stand the test of time.

In terms of Oscar wins, the Rex Harrison/Audrey Hepburn musical *My Fair Lady* and the brilliant Walt Disney production *Mary Poppins* were the top films of the decade, and Julie Andrews, star of *Mary Poppins,* also figured in the other sixties blockbuster *The Sound Of Music,* the biggest grossing movie of the decade. Rex Harrison followed up his musical success by playing the role of Doctor Dolittle, the former Harley Street doctor who could talk to animals, including the legendary 'Push-me-pull-you', Che Che the chimp, Polynesia the parrot and Sophie the seal. The film was made in the picturesque town of Castle Combe

Peter O'Toole (right) in Lawrence Of Arabia.

Newman/Robert Redford classic Butch Cassidy And The Sundance Kid showed in the latter half of the sixties. But for real cowboy action there was no better film than the 1960 classic, The Magnificent Seven, directed by John Sturges.

The Magnificent Seven were:	
Charles Bronson	Bernardo
Yul Brynner	Chris
Horst Bucholz	Chico
James Coburn	Brit
Brad Dexter	Harry
Steve McQueen	Vin
Robert Vaughn	Lee

Adventure films like The Great Escape and The Guns Of Navarone were big box office successes as was the classic love story Doctor Zhivago, directed by David Lean and starring the good looking Omar Sharif and Julie Christie. From it came one of the sixties most popular tunes, Lara's Theme.

So far we have had the pop movies, the spy thrillers, cowboys, musicals and love stories. But there was still more. There were the epics like Lawrence Of Arabia and Zulu, the film which launched the wonderful career of Michael Caine, the cheerful Cockney who made a name for himself as Alfie, a part he got only after Anthony Newley, James Booth, Terence Stamp and Lawrence Harvey had all turned it down.

And let's not forget the spaghetti westerns, popularized by Clint Eastwood, the man who made his name in the TV series, Rawhide. These new westerns were so called because they were made by the Italian producer Sergio Leone. The first one was Per Un Pugno Di Dollari — better known as A Fistful Of Dollars.

For outstanding individual performances, Paul Schofield gave a terrific performance as Sir Thomas More in A Man For All Seasons and

which became known as Puddleby-on-the-Marsh in the film.

Musicals were popular during the sixties, the non-pop kind, that is. In addition to those already mentioned,

Scene from My Fair Lady with Audrey Hepburn and Rex Harrison.

there was West Side Story and Lionel Bart's Oliver! just to mention two other big box office successes.

The Western type of film was still popular in the sixties as The Alamo, starring John Wayne, showed in the early part of the decade, and the Paul

won an Oscar for his efforts. John Wayne at last got his hands on that elusive Oscar for his performance in *True Grit,* and amongst the women, the only outright dual Oscar winner of the sixties was Elizabeth Taylor for two contrasting roles; firstly as a nymphomaniac in *Butterfield 8* and then as the foul-mouthed Martha in *Who's Afraid Of Virginia Woolf* in what was one of the finest performances of her career. Taylor was, of course, one half of the great real-life love affair of the sixties, with fellow-star Richard Burton.

Sixties films also played a part in inspiring fashion. Berets became popular after Faye Dunaway wore one in *Bonnie And Clyde.* Blonde streaks in brunette hair became all the vogue after Audrey Hepburn set the pace in *Breakfast At Tiffanys* and knee-length vinyl boots became the craze after Jane Fonda appeared in them in *Barbarella.*

Jane Fonda as Barbarella.

> *The 1961 film* The Misfits *was the last completed film for both Clark Gable and Marilyn Monroe.*

Jane Fonda also starred in *They Shoot Horses Don't They?* the first Hollywood film to be shown on Russian television. The Russian censors liked the film because it showed the American depression. What they didn't know, however, was that the main story was about a dance-hall marathon!

A couple of boobs from sixties films: a clip from *The Sound Of Music* shows an orange box marked 'Jaffa Oranges. Produce of Israel'. The film was set in the late 1930s and the State

of Israel was not formed until 1948! The 1968 film *Krakatoa, East Of Java* was hopelessly mis-titled; Krakatoa is WEST of Java.

The sixties was quite a memorable era for movies. We had love and sex, goodies and baddies, comedy and tragedy, and of course we had the musicals, pop or otherwise. It is little wonder the decade is remembered so affectionately.

FLEMING, Ian

ONE of the biggest names in the film world in the 1960s was Sean Connery for his portrayal of James Bond. But, by the time Bond hit the silver screen, the character was ten years old. Devised by author Ian Fleming, Bond first appeared in 1953 when he made his debut in *Casino Royale,* a hardback which sold for 7s 6d (37½p)

Ian Fleming was born in 1908, the son of a banker and later MP. He was educated at Eton, Sandhurst and the Universities of Munich and Geneva. His first job was with Reuters and then in banking and stockbroking. But during World War Two he worked in Naval Intelligence which no doubt inspired many of his spy thrillers.

He got a job as the foreign manager with Kemsley newspapers after the war and his contract allowed him two months off each year, which he would spend at his Jamaican home 'Golden-eye' to write his books.

While his early Bond novels were immensely popular, they were also surrounded with controversy and many felt his descriptive narratives of torture, gambling and promiscuity were outrageous.

He decided to devote himself full-time to his books in 1959, and with the success of the film *Dr No,* there was a new-found interest in his books. In March 1964, Fleming sold 51% of

future royalties (excluding film rights) of all Bond books to the investment company, Booker Bros.

While his Naval intelligence background may have helped in writing the Bond stories, Fleming always maintained his inspiration came from his wife Anne, Viscountess Rothermere. Fleming died at Canterbury on 12 August 1964 at the age of 56, just before the release of the third Bond film, *Goldfinger,* and shortly after the completion of his last novel, *The Man With the Golden Arm.* Altogether he wrote 13 Bond books which sold over 40 million copies.

FOOT AND MOUTH EPIDEMIC

THE world's first recorded outbreak of foot and mouth disease was in France in 1773. Britain first suffered the disease in 1839, when foot and mouth was recorded at Stratford, London. The worst outbreak known in Britain, prior to 1967, was in 1871, when 42,000 farms were hit. But it must be remembered that farms were considerably smaller in those days. However, the 1967 epidemic was far greater in terms of overall loss.

The problem was not restricted to Britain. It became a serious problem worldwide in the early '60s and in 1964 Russia was hit by the disease for the first time. It spread from the Ukrainian borders into neighbouring European countries. By 1965 some 30,000 outbreaks were recorded in 20 European countries. Almost half the cases were in West Germany. By 1966 the disease had spread even further afield and the Type-A virus was seen in south-east Africa for the first time ever.

By 1967 the epidemic was described as reaching epizootic proportions. There had been isolated outbreaks in Britain in Bedfordshire, Devon, Stratford-upon-Avon, Warwickshire, Westmoreland and Northumberland. But on 25 October 1967 a farm at Llanyblodwell, Shropshire, was hit by the disease. Two days later the Ministry of Agriculture said the situation was 'under control'. But on 29 October, it spread to the two adjoining farms. The disease was soon out of control and within weeks it had become the worst outbreak British farmers had ever encountered and the worst epidemic of the 20th century.

By mid-November more than 80,000 animals had been slaughtered in 21 affected counties in England and Wales. Restrictions were placed on the movement of animals, and indeed, the movement of people into affected areas. By the end of November, all of Britain, with the exception of Northern Ireland, was a restricted area. Zoos, like Whipsnade, were forced to close and the outbreak took its toll on the world of sport. The RAC motor rally was cancelled and horse racing ground to a standstill on 28 November. The ban was not lifted until January. The day before racing ended, however, Rondetto beat Stalbridge Colonist to win the Hennessy Gold Cup at Newbury.

The cost to the farmers was astronomical and some suffered the loss of cattle that had been restocked not once, but twice. The Government announced a ban on meat imports from all countries other than those where foot and mouth disease was unknown, or where they had a long history of freedom from it.

The total number of outbreaks by 25 November was reported as 963. Two weeks later that figure was up to 1,730. By the end of the month the number of reported cases was over 2,000.

By March the outbreak seemed to have been curbed and restrictions came to an end. There were still isolated outbreaks but they did not gain a hold. The end officially came on 25 June 1968. There had been a total of 2,364 outbreaks with the loss of 429,632 animals. The cost was put at approximately £150 million.

FORD CORTINA

THE FORD Cortina merits a special place in this book as the car that went on to become a British institution. And like so many 'institutions' it started its life in the sixties.

Ford launched the car, described as having the comfort of a bigger car and economy of the smaller car, in 1962. It was Ford's reply to the success of the Mini and became one of the biggest-selling cars during its 20-year life-span. Indeed, in its early days it was the fastest-selling car ever built in Britain.

Correctly known as the Consul Cortina, it came with an 1198cc engine. The 1500cc engine model and the estate car and de luxe and Super versions followed later. There was also the powerful and popular Lotus Cortina.

Ford Cortina, four-door de luxe.

The Mk.I Cortina sold more than a million models before being

replaced by the redesigned Mk.II in 1966. That lasted until 1970 when the Mk.III made its bow and finally the Mk.IV arrived on the scene in 1976. The Cortina eventually made way for the Sierra and Orion in 1982.

FORDYCE, Keith

LIKE so many stars of radio and television in the sixties, Keith Fordyce started his broadcasting career with the British Forces Network. From there he moved on to *Housewives' Choice* and *Two Way Family Favourites* where he was one of the link-men with the London-based Jean Metcalfe.

Born in Lincoln in 1928, he was the Lincolnshire Junior Tennis champion in 1946. Fordyce obtained an honours degree in law from Cambridge but he sought to make his career in broadcasting and it was as the co-presenter of *Ready Steady Go* with Cathy McGowan that he is best remembered in the 1960s.

Fordyce also hosted the Miss World contest and appeared on the other pop programmes of the decade, *Juke Box Jury* and *Thank Your Lucky Stars*.

FORSYTE SAGA

THE LAST major British drama series to be filmed entirely in black and white, *The Forsyte Saga* was shown in Britain in 1967 and gathered quite a following. It is based on the trilogy of John Galsworthy books and is about the lives of a family of London merchants from 1870 to 1920.

Each programme lasted 50 minutes and made compulsive viewing for 26 weeks. It was also sold

to many overseas countries and *Time* magazine referred to it as being 'The greatest soap opera ever filmed'. Mind you, they hadn't seen *Neighbours* at that time!

The plot centred around the deeds, good or bad, of Soames Forsyte (Eric Porter), his wife Irene (Nyree Dawn Porter) and their daughter Fleur (Susan Hampshire). All the ingredients for a good soap were to be found and an already strong cast was well complemented with other such fine stars as Kenneth More, Fay Compton and Margaret Tyzack. It was hardly surprising that the series won a BAFTA award in 1967.

FORSYTH, Bruce

BORN in Edmonton on 22 February 1928, Bruce Forsyth left school at the age of 14 and entered show business as 'Boy Bruce, the Mighty Atom'. From there he went on to work at the Windmill Theatre between 1945 and 1951, with the exception of two years' RAF service. He then worked on the holiday camp and summer season circuits. It was while compering in Devon during summer of 1958 that he got the call to be compere at the London Palladium in succession to Tommy Trinder, where his all-round skills made him an ideal candidate for the job. That was the launch of his career which has kept him working at the highest level for the last 30 years.

His television career has seen him host such programmes as *The Bruce Forsyth Show, The Generation Game, Play Your Cards Right* and *Bruce's Big Night*. He was responsible for the catch phrases "I'm in Charge" and

From left: Eric Porter, Nyree Dawn Porter and Kenneth More in The Forsyte Saga.

"Nice to see you, to see you, nice" . . .amongst others.

He has been married three times and after having five daughters, three with first wife Penny, and two with his ex-*Generation Game* partner Anthea Redfern, Bruce has, at last, at the age of 60, got a son thanks to his third wife, the former Puerto Rican Miss World, Wilnelia Merced.

Away from the world of entertainment, Bruce's great love is golf, where his handicap is down to single figures.

FOUR FEATHER FALLS

THE first of the popular children's puppet series of the sixties, *Four Feather Falls* ran from 25 February to 17 November 1960.

The stories told of the exploits of Sheriff Tex Tucker who was given four feathers by an Indian chief after Tex saved his son's life. The feathers gave Tex magical powers, provided he wore them in his stetson, including the ability to make his two deputies, his dog Dusty and his horse Rocky, talk. Tex's guns also had magical powers and could swivel on their own — wow!

The talking voice of Tex Tucker was done by Nicholas Parsons while the singing voice belonged to Michael Holliday. Kenneth Connor was the voice behind Dusty and Rocky. Other characters included Pedro, Grandpa Turink, Fernando, Ma Jones and Little Jake.

FOUR SEASONS, The

THE Four Seasons were one of the few American groups to withstand the onslaught of the Beatles and other top British groups in the sixties.

Hailing from New Jersey, they

In 1965 Frankie Valli recorded a falsetto version of Bob Dylan's Don't Think Twice. *He used the pseudonym 'Wonder Who'. It was only a minor hit.*

started life as The Variatones and The Four Lovers before taking their new name from a local bowling alley. The line-up consisted of songwriter Bob Gaudio, who wrote their first hit *Sherry*, Nick Massi, Tommy de Mito and the lead singer with the high-pitched voice, Frankie Valli, whose real name was Frank Castelluccio.

Despite topping the charts in the States with *Sherry, Big Girls Don't Cry, Walk Like A Man* and *Rag Doll,* their first British number one was not until 1976 when *December '63 (Oh What A Night)* went to the top of the charts. It was an amazing comeback for a group that had not charted in Britain since 1967.

At the peak of their career in 1964, Vee Jay Records released an LP entitled *Battle Of The Bands* which was a compilation of Beatles and Four Seasons records.

The Four Seasons provided America with its East Coast sound while the Beach Boys provided the West Coast sound. In 1984 they got together to record a song *East Meets West* which brought together the harmonies of both sounds.

Top Ten hits of the Four Seasons in the 1960s:

Year	Record	Pos
1962	Sherry	8
1964	Rag Doll	2
1965	Let's Hang On	4

FOUR TOPS

LEVI Stubbs, Abdul Fakir, Lawrence Payton and Renaldo Benson must be unique in the annals of popular music history. Some 35 years ago these four Detroit schoolmates formed a group called The Four Aims. Today they are still together, as the Four Tops, and have been one of the leading groups in four decades . . .and soon to be five!

Their first British chart entry was *I Can't Help Myself* which reached Number 23 in 1965. In 1966 they had their first, and only, British number one with the Holland, Dozier, Holland composition *Reach Out I'll Be There*. It also topped the American charts.

One of the backbones of the Motown record label, they left the company in 1973. Record sales dwindled but they remained as popular as ever on the cabaret circuit. They were back in the British charts in 1981 with *When She Was My Girl* and in 1988 and 1989 have re-found chart success with, firstly, a re-release

---

of *Reach Out I'll Be There,* and then *Loco In Acapulco* which reached number three.

Top Ten hits of the Four Tops in the 1960s:

Year	Record	Pos
1966	Reach Out I'll Be There	1
1967	Standing In The Shadows Of Love	6
1967	Bernadette	8
1967	Walk Away Renee	3
1968	If I Were A Carpenter	7

Four Tops singer Levi Stubbs appeared in the 1987 film Little Shop of Horrors *as a man-eating plant!*

FRANKLAND, Rosemarie

ROSEMARIE Frankland was the toast of Britain in 1961 when she became the first United Kingdom winner of the Miss World title.

Eighteen-year-old Rosemarie, from Lancaster, had won the Miss United Kingdom title before taking on, and beating, the world.

She was the youngest winner of the title at the time and was one of the best-looking winners in the sixties. A model, she weighed 8st 12lb, stood 5ft 6in tall and had measurements of 36-22-36.

Rosemarie continued her modelling profession after being crowned Miss World, and also embarked on a brief acting career.

FRASER, Bill

SCOTTISH-born Bill Fraser played the part of the raucous Sergeant-Major Snudge in one of the first great British television comedy series *The Army Game* which ran from 1957 to 1962. His character was a powerful one and lent a great deal to the programme's success.

From there Fraser moved on to the spin-off series with Alfie Bass, also a star of *The Army Game,* and enjoyed a second successful series with *Bootsie And Snudge.*

Born in Perth on 5 June 1908, Fraser loved the theatre and was capable of playing either straight or comedy roles on stage or television. He died on 5 September 1987 at the age of 79 and was working right up to the time of his death, appearing in London's West End. He was still a familiar TV face appearing in *The Secret Diary Of Adrian Mole.*

Ironically, both Bass and Fraser, who shared many great moments together, died within seven weeks of each other.
(See also BASS, Alfie)

FROST, David, OBE

DAVID Frost started his television career as a reporter for *This Week* but gained fame as one of the stars of the great sixties satire show, *That Was The Week That Was.* Since then Frost has become one of the biggest earners on television and has fronted such programmes as *A Degree Of Frost, The Frost Report, Frost Over England, The Frost Programme* and *Frost Over America,* and has shown his versatility as a serious interviewer as well as a satirist.

Born in Kent in 1939, the son of a Methodist minister, he was educated at Cambridge and then spent a year teaching in Northampton. As an 18-year-old he was offered terms as a professional footballer but

decided on a career in the world of entertainment. David Frost became one of the wealthiest men in the television business and was one of the co-founders of London Weekend Television. In recent times he has figured on ITV's breakfast television, where he was their first presenter, and host of the TV-AM Sunday show. He has also fronted the *Guinness Book Of World Records* and *Through The Keyhole* in recent years.

Over the years Frost's name has been associated with some glamorous women and for a while he was married to Lynne Frederick, the former wife of Peter Sellers. But in 1983 he joined the aristocracy when he wed Lady Carina Fitzalan-Howard, daughter of the Duke of Norfolk.

Well known for his catch phrase, "Hello, good evening and welcome," he was awarded the OBE for his services to broadcasting. He is reputed to have made more transatlantic flights on Concorde than any other passenger.

FUGITIVE, The

THE story of David Janssen as Indiana doctor, Dr Kimble was one of the most compelling of the many American television series in the sixties.

Remember the story? Well, this is how it went:

Kimble returns to his home to see a one-armed man running away. When he goes inside he finds his wife Helen has been murdered. Kimble becomes number-one suspect and is eventually charged with her murder and sentenced to death. On his way to the State penetentiary, fate intervenes and the train on which he is travelling is derailed and Kimble escapes.

Our hero is pursued across America, and even into Mexico and Canada, as he seeks to find the only man who can prove his innocence, the one-armed man, alias Fred Johnson, played by Bill Raisch. The man constantly chasing Kimble was police officer Lieutenant Philip Gerard, played superbly by Barry Morse.

> *The narrator on* The Fugitive *was William Conrad, the man who played TV detective* Cannon *in the 1970s.*

After four years (and 120 episodes) on the run, during which time Kimble had been hounded by police, shot, stabbed, beaten up and temporarily blinded, the series ended in August 1967 when, inevitably, Kimble and Johnson came face to face.

Their meeting was at an amusement park and they met each other on top of a water tower. They fought,

and just as Kimble was about to be thrown to his death, a shot rang out and Johnson fell to the ground.

Kimble's saviour was Lieutenant Gerard and Johnson made a dying confession. At last! We all breathed a sigh of relief as Dr Kimble was a free man again.

FURY, Billy

BORN Ronald Wycherley in the Garston district of Liverpool in 1941, but brought up in the tough Dingle area, Billy Fury 'lived for every day' after hearing a doctor tell his mother that her son was unlikely to live beyond 30. As a child he was plagued by ill health and this eventually led to a heart complaint which killed him.

Fury's rock'n'roll career started in the late-1950s and he was one of the first British artistes to break the US domination of the British charts. However, his hair-style, gold lamé suits and gyratory actions had the critics labelling him as the English version of Elvis Presley. Billy would be the first to admit that he styled himself on his idol, Elvis.

With his backing group, The Gamblers, he gained widespread success with songs like *Like I've Never Been Gone* and *Halfway To Paradise* which followed up his first chart success *Maybe Tomorrow* as he moved more towards ballads.

He had limited success across the Atlantic but was a huge success in Britain and was part of the fateful Eddie Cochran tour of 1960. He also appeared in the films *Play It Cool, I've Gotta Horse* and in the David Essex film *That'll Be The Day* in the 1970s. He enjoyed 30 British chart hits but never had a number one. But the hits stopped coming and in 1978 he was declared bankrupt after owing £16,000 in back taxes. He became a lover of country life and lived in rural Wales. Billy Fury died on 28 January 1983. He was 42 and at least enjoyed 12 years more than a doctor had predicted for the young Ronnie Wycherley.

Top Ten hits of Billy Fury in the 1960s:

Year	Record	Pos
1960	Colette	9
1961	Halfway To Paradise	3
1962	Jealousy	2
1961	I'd Never Find Another You	5
1961	Last Night Was Made For Love	4
1962	Once Upon A Dream	7
1963	Like I've Never Been Gone	3
1963	When Will You Say I Love You	3
1963	In Summer	5
1964	It's Only Make Believe	10
1965	In Thoughts Of You	9

GAGARIN, Yuri

THE Russians took a giant leap forward in the space race on 12 April 1961 when 27-year-old Major Yuri Alekseyevich Gagarin created history by becoming the first man in space.

While the superpowers had both mooted a man in space in the early 1960s, it still came as a surprise to the average man in the street who could hardly believe the news as it made the front pages of all the world's newspapers.

Gagarin had been interested in flying as a youngster and qualified as a pilot in 1957. In 1961 he took the trip into space that had only been a vision of such authors as Jules Verne, one of Gagarin's favourite writers.

The famous flight lasted a mere 108 minutes, during which time Gagarin, in his *Vostok 1* capsule, orbited the earth at between 109-187 miles high.

After landing, he walked to a waiting helicopter, obviously none the worse for his experience. In Moscow he was given a hero's welcome and was littered with honours. It was the same story wherever he went. In England he met the Queen and the Prime Minister and when he went to Manchester was made an honorary member of the Foundryworkers Union . . .Gagarin used to be a foundryworker in Lyubertsy.

One of the truly great heroes of the 1960s, he was made welcome in every country he visited. He later became a trainer and advisor to future cosmonauts and, despite his fame and adulation, humbly admitted: "I am still an ordinary mortal and I have not changed in any way."

Ironically Gagarin lost his life in a plane crash on 27 March 1968 at the age of 34. An obsolete MiG-15 jet trainer he was piloting lost height and crashed 40 miles north of Moscow.

He was finally intered in the Kremlin Wall.

Timetable of Gagarin's first space flight:
12 April 1961
0707: *Vostok 1* launched into elipticial orbit from launch pad at Tyuratum space centre in Central Asia.
0722: Reported he was flying over South America and said: "I feel fine."
0815: Over Africa and Asia Minor he reported: "I am withstanding the state of weightlessness well."
0825: Descent starts.
0855: *Vostok 1* landed safely at Smelouka and Gagarin said: "Please report to the party and government, and personally to Mr Khrushchev that the flight was normal. I feel well. I have no injuries or bruises. The completion of the flight opens new perspectives in the conquering of the cosmos."

Gagarin toured Manchester in 1961 in an open-top Rolls-Royce car whose registration number was YG 1. It had been loaned from television and film celebrity Sabrina.

GAITSKELL, Hugh

LEADER of the Labour Party from 1955 until his death, Hugh Gaitskell was at the helm of a troubled and torn party as the 1960s loomed.

Born in 1906, he was educated at Oxford University. He entered Parliament in 1945 as the Member for South Leeds. He took up his first Cabinet post two years later as Minister of Fuel and Power and, in 1950, became Minister of Economic Affairs before becoming Chancellor of the Exchequer in 1951. The Party started to split and Gaitskell's rivalry with Aneurin Bevan was well documented at the time.

Bevan, together with Morrison and Gaitskell, were the three candidates to succeed Clement Attlee as Party leader in 1955 and Gaitskell won, again amidst controversy involving Bevan.

Gaitskell was involved in further disagreements over a change of Party policy and unilateralism, and there was every chance he would lose the election to keep hold of the party leadership in 1960. But he retained his position. He kept the Party together and, as Labour started to gain in popularity, Gaitskell was expected to be the next Prime Minister when the 1964 Election came around. But Hugh Todd Naylor Gaitskell died suddenly after a brief illness on 18 January 1963. A month later Harold Wilson was elected as his successor and it was Wilson who became Britain's next Socialist premier.

GARDINER, Toni

TONI Gardiner was the 20-year-old telephonist from Stratford-upon-Avon who fulfilled the dream of many young girls to be a real-life Princess, in 1961, when she became King Hussein of Jordan's second wife.

King Hussein's first marriage, to Princess Dina Abdel Hamid, lasted

from 1955 to 1957 and she bore him a daughter.

His engagement to Antoinette Avril Gardiner, the daughter of Lieutenant-Colonel Gardiner of the Royal Engineers, was announced on 1 May 1961. Three weeks later, on 25 May, at Hussein's mother's palace, the two were married and Toni Gardiner became Princess Muna al Hussein. Her Majesty the Queen and the Duke of Edinburgh, and President Kennedy sent wedding gifts to the newly married couple.

Princess Muna gave Hussein his son and heir, Abdulla, in 1962, and had a second son, Faisal, the following year. She also had twin daughters, Zein and Aisha, born in 1968.

The couple were divorced on 21 December 1972 and four days later Hussein married 24-year-old Alia Toukan who became Queen Alia.

GERRY and the PACEMAKERS

GERRY Marsden founded the Pacemakers, originally called The Mars Bars, in 1959, together with his brother Freddie and John Chadwick. Along with many other Liverpool groups of the time they accepted an offer to appear at Hamburg's Top Ten Club. Returning to Merseyside, they recruited Les Maguire and, touring many North-West clubs, found themselves regularly sharing the bill with other aspirants such as The Beatles and The Searchers.

In 1962 they signed a contract with Brian Epstein and the following year became the first of the Merseyside groups to have a number-one hit (that honour didn't fall to The Beatles) when the lively *How Do You Do It?* topped the charts.

By the end of the year Gerry and the Pacemakers had become the first act in the history of the British charts to see their first three records all go to number one.

Gerry's most famous song was the Rodgers & Hammerstein production *You'll Never Walk Alone* from the musical *Carousel.* Little did they know

it would become the 'hymn' of Liverpool Football Club. Other clubs have since adopted it.

Gerry re-recorded it to raise money for the Bradford City fire disaster in 1985 when, once again it topped the charts. And in 1989 it was sung at church services and at the FA Cup Final to commemorate the dead from the Hillsborough tragedy. Another Gerry and the Pacemakers hit of the 1960s, *Ferry Across The Mersey*, was re-recorded by Gerry and other Merseyside stars in aid of the Hillsborough Disaster Fund.

Top Ten hits of Gerry and the Pacemakers in the 1960s:

Year	Record	Pos
1963	How Do You Do It?	1
1963	I Like It	1
1963	You'll Never Walk Alone	1
1964	I'm The One	2
1964	Don't Let The Sun Catch You Crying	6
1964	Ferry Across The Mersey	8

GOLDIE THE EAGLE

GOLDIE the eagle enjoyed two spells of freedom from his home at London Zoo in 1965. His first spree lasted ten days and caused a great deal of public interest.

After obtaining his freedom, seven-year-old Goldie, from Finland, set up home in Regent's Park and daily thousands tried to get a glimpse of the new national hero. On one day alone in March 1965, a crowd of 5,000 filled the park and Goldie did not disappoint his admirers. He played to the crowd and flew low over them as he moved from one tree to another as his army of 'fans' followed him.

During his spell of freedom he would occasionally venture away from Regents Park and take a trip to St John's Wood, Little Venice and Marylebone. Despite the numerous offers of food and the appearance of his mate, Goldie was still not recaptured. However, finally succumbing to the temptation of food, he was caught by his keeper, Joe McCorry, on 10 March. McCorry grabbed Goldie by the foot after the eagle had come down to eat some meat put down as bait.

Nine months later Goldie was off again when, on 15 December, he fooled his keeper and flew out of his cage when the door was opened after feeding time. This time his freedom lasted only four days before new keeper Derek Wood retrieved him. Again it was the temptation of food as bait which lured Goldie into his keeper's arms.

Not Goldie, but another golden eagle brought along to try and lure the errant bird down from his perch. The ploy failed.

After the event . . .police guard the train that was robbed.

GREAT TRAIN ROBBERY

AT 3.10am on 8 August 1963, one of the most daring robberies in British history was carried out when the Glasgow to London mail train was held up by a band of masked men.

The robbery had been well planned and the thieves knew that more than £1 million in used bank notes, on their way to London to be destroyed, would be on the train. They must have been surprised to learn that their net haul was £2.6 million.

At least 15 men took part in the raid on the 12-coach train, D326, which had left Glasgow at 6.50pm the previous evening. Driver Jack Mills from Crewe brought the train to a halt as a result of a red light rigged up by the gang at Sears Crossing near Cheddington in Buckinghamshire. The locomotive and the first two carriages were uncoupled and Mills was made to move them 800 yards along the track to Bridego Bridge, 200 yards from the Leighton Buzzard to Tring road. When the four GPO sorters became aware of what was happening they tried to barricade themselves in their carriages, but they could not halt the determined efforts of the gang, who forced their way through a communicating door. One hundred and twenty bags were thrown 15 feet down the embankment and loaded on to a lorry waiting nearby.

Five days after the robbery, while engaging in one of the biggest man hunts ever seen in Britain, police came across Leatherslade Farm which the gang had used as their hideout both before and after the robbery.

The massive police operation paid dividends and on 22 August one of the ring leaders, Charlie Wilson, was charged. The trial of him and other members of the gang began at Buckinghamshire Assizes on 20 January 1964. The trial lasted 51 days and the jury took a record 66 hours to reach their verdicts. Ronald Biggs was one of 12 men found guilty of plotting to steal mailbags containing £2.6 million and on 16 April 1964, a total of 307 years imprisonment was imposed on the members of the gang.

Ronald Christopher 'Buster' Edwards, the Great Train Robber whose exploits inspired a feature film starring Phil Collins.

Wilson and Biggs both escaped from prison. Wilson was recaptured in Canada in 1968 and Biggs fled to Australia and was subsequently forced to leave his wife before finding refuge and immunity in Brazil.

The driver of the train, Jack Mills, was knocked unconscious by a blow to the head during the raid. He died

Charles Wilson escaped from Winson Green prison on 12 August 1964 and Biggs was 'sprung' from Wandsworth the following July. Wilson was recaptured in Quebec, Canada, in January 1968. Biggs is still free and is living in Brazil. Bruce Reynolds, the member of the gang sought by the police for five years, was eventually caught at Torquay on 8 November 1968. Ronald Christopher Edwards, whose story inspired the film Buster, went into hiding in England, France and Mexico, eventually giving himself up in London.

The 12 men who received a total of 307 years imprisonment on 16 April 1964 were:

Term	Name	(age)	Occupation	Address
30	Ronald Arthur Biggs	(34)	Joiner	Redhill, Surrey
30	Douglas Gordon Goody	(34)	Hairdresser	Putney
30	James Hussey	(30)	Painter	East Dulwich
30	Roy John James	(28)	Racing driver/ silversmith	SW London
30	Robert Welch	(34)	Club proprietor	Islington
30	Charles Frederick Wilson	(31)	Bookmaker	Clapham
30	Thomas William Wisbey	(33)	Bookmaker	Camberwell
25	Brian Arthur Field	(29)	Solicitor's Clerk	Whitchurch Hill, Oxon
25	Leonard Dennis Field	(31)	Merchant seaman	Harringay
24	William Boal	(50)	Engineer	Fulham
20	Roger John Cordrey	(42)	Florist	East Molesey, Surrey
3	John Denby Wheater	(41)	Solicitor	Ashtead, Surrey

a few years later and it is believed his death was attributable to the injuries sustained in the robbery.

The exact total of men who carried out the Great Train Robbery was never truly established. But it took military-style precision to plan and carry out. The story of the robbery has since been told numerous times in book form and on film. It was the most daring robbery of its time and it was a stroke of luck for the thieves that the usual high-security carriages were out of service for repair when the 6.50 left Glasgow on the night of 7 August 1963 . . .or maybe the robbers knew that?

GREEN, Hughie

HUGHIE Green was responsible for giving us one of the top television catch phrases of the sixties: "I mean that most sincerely friends", which he used to say regularly when introducing contestants on the talent show *Opportunity Knocks*.

Although born in London in 1920, Green was brought up in Canada and he served with the Canadian RAF during the war. He had a spell in Hollywood as a youngster and appeared in *Lassie* films. He returned to Britain where he became a teenage actor but got his big break as a television host when he became the quizmaster on *Double Your Money*, one of the first TV quiz games in Britain. It was launched in 1955 and ran for almost 20 years with Green as its host.

In 1956 Green became the host of the new talent show *Opportunity Knocks*. It lasted more than 20 years, and thanks to the two popular programmes, he became one of the best known faces on British television.

Since both programmes came off the air in the mid-seventies, little has been seen of Hughie Green on British television.

Hughie Green and Monica Rose took Double Your Money *to Moscow. It was quite a coup for the show to be invited to Russia, for these were pre-Glasnost days in the Soviet Union. In August 1989, four Law Lords ruled that Green did not own the copyright of the idea, opening up the way for television stations to produce that kind of show without paying royalties to him.*

HAILWOOD, Mike

BRITAIN has a fine record for producing top-class motor cyclists and one of the finest was Oxford-born Mike Hailwood.

Known as 'Mike the Bike', he was the best known of all British motor cyclists and in the sixties was invincible as he dominated both the world championship and the Isle of Man TT races.

He won his first grand prix, the Ulster Grand Prix, at the age of 19 and at 20 became the youngest rider of a works team when he joined Honda. The first of his nine world titles was for the Japanese manufacturer in 1961 when he won the 250cc title. Between then and 1967 he won eight more world titles including four 500cc titles for MV.

But it was around the gruelling 37½-mile Isle of Man TT course that Hailwood was in his element. He won the senior, lightweight and ultra-lightweight titles in 1961 and when he won his last TT race in 1979 he had amassed an all-time record 14 wins around the island. His three wins in 1961 and again in 1967 have only been equalled in recent years by Joey Dunlop (1985 and 1988) and Steve Hislop (1989).

Hailwood turned to motor racing in 1967 but was forced to retire after a bad accident at the Nürburgring in 1974. However, in 1978 he was back on a bike and returned to his beloved Isle of Man where he won the Formula One title. A year later he won the prestigious Senior TT.

On 23 March 1981 Hailwood and his daughter were killed when his car was involved in an accident with a lorry near his Birmingham home. They had been to get some fish and chips. How ironic that a great champion should die in such a way after flirting with death for so many years.

HAIR

THE tribal rock musical *Hair* first hit Broadway on 29 April 1968 after a spell playing at Greenwich Village. And on 27 September that year it opened at London's Shaftesbury Theatre. Coincidentally, the previous day saw the abolition of play censorship and on the opening night, 13 members of the cast performed naked for a brief moment during a scene at the close of the first half, when they appeared from under a huge blanket. The full frontal scene didn't last long because the lights were dimmed and the curtain came down almost simultaneously.

The play highlighted the permissiveness of the era and in addition to the nudity there was a barrage of four-letter words, a display of

Paul Nicholas in a rehearsal of Hair.

rebellion against authority and, of course, there was that great hippie belief of the day — make love, not war. Those issues brought a lot of attention to *Hair* but its music was also a major reason for the show's success. Some of the songs became classics in the late-1960s. The title song *Aquarius*, and *Let The Sunshine In* were hits both sides of the Atlantic and the LP of the original Broadway show sold over five million copies. There were other songs appropriate to the theme of the play like *Welcome Carbon Dioxide*.

The book and lyrics of *Hair* were written by two actors, Gerome Ragni and James Rado. They showed their script to leading author Nat Shapiro and he suggested that Galt Mac-Dermot write the music for the play. And so *Hair* was born.

The play was eventually seen in all corners of the globe and in every major city across the United States and Canada.

HANCOCK, Tony

TONY Hancock was a genius whose humour was well ahead of its time. He was individual and despite the attempts of many to copy him, none have been successful. Yet most modern-day comedians will point to Hancock as their inspiration.

Born in Birmingham on 12 May 1924, he got his first taste of show business after his father took a Bournemouth guest house and stars of the 1940s like Elsie and Doris Waters would stay there and take the youngster backstage. He joined the RAF in 1942 and became a member of Ralph Reader's *Gang Show*.

After the war, Hancock got regular work doing pantomimes and summer seasons and in 1948 became the resident comedian at the Windmill Theatre, London. From 1951-53 he appeared in radio's *Educating Archie* and in 1954 got his own radio series *Hancock's Half Hour* when he was joined by Sid James in a series of classic half-hour shows. It was transferred to television in 1956 and out of it came such great scripts as *The Radio Ham* and *The Blood Donor*. The character portrayed by Anthony Aloyisius Hancock was a man who suffered from delusions of grandeur.

Hancock made two films, *The Rebel* and *The Punch And Judy Man*. He returned to television in 1963 and made *Hancock* for ITV but it was not as successful as the BBC series.

In January 1968 he was admitted to a Bournemouth nursing home after an attack of pneumonia. In March that year, Hancock left for Australia to work on a proposed comedy series for Australian TV. Soon afterwards he was taken to a Sydney hospital with a mystery illness. He was released but a month later he was found dead in a Sydney flat. Tony Hancock, the man with the oversized coat and black homburg, had committed suicide.

HANRATTY, James

THE A6 lay-by murder trial, as it became known, was one of the longest and most controversial murder trials in legal history. It still remains controversial and the leading question that was asked at the time was: 'Was petty criminal James Hanratty wrongly executed for the murder of 38-year-old scientific worker Michael Gregsten?'

The murder took place in a lay-by on the A6 at Dead Man's Hill, near Bedford. Gregsten's body was found at 6.45 on the morning of 23 August 1961. His car, a grey Morris Minor, registration number 847 BHN, was found abandoned some 40 miles away at Ilford.

Gregsten, a married man, was in the car with 23-year-old Valerie Storie, who worked with Gregsten at the Road Research Laboratory in Slough. They had set out the night before to plan the route for a car rally.

On the evening of 22 August, Gregsten parked up his Morris Minor in a cornfield at Dorney Reach alongside the Thames between Windsor and Maidenhead. He and Storie were interrupted by a man brandishing a .38 Enfield revolver. He sat in the back of the car and made Gregsten drive aimlessly through the streets of London before reaching the A6 where he told Gregsten to pull in at the lay-by after a 43-mile trip. It was there that he shot Gregsten twice in the head and forced Miss Storie into the back seat where he raped her and shot her. She did not die from her wounds but was confined to life in a wheelchair.

After a murder hunt that lasted seven weeks, James Hanratty was arrested in Blackpool on 9 October. Miss Storie failed to pick him out from an identity parade, but on hearing his voice, immediately recognized him as the murderer. The trial started on 22 January 1962 and Miss Storie came under attack from the defence for failing to identify Hanratty at the ID parade. Hanratty, however, did not do his cause any good by a succession of lies, cockiness and insolence while in the witness box.

The prosecution's case was not, perhaps, watertight, but they did enough to convince the jury and on 4 April 1962 the 25-year-old Hanratty was executed at Bedford prison despite last-minute appeals and Hanratty's constant protests of his innocence.

Peter Alphon.

Peter Louis Alphon

ON the morning of 22 September 1961 Scotland Yard issued a statement that they wished to interview Peter Louis Alphon, alias Frederick Durrant, in connection with the A6 murder. Later that day Alphon walked into Scotland Yard saying he had nothing to hide.

He was subsequently released but two days later was charged with causing grievous bodily harm to a German woman, Mrs Meike Dalal of East Sheen. On 3 October he was discharged and awarded 50gns costs. He subsequently issued a writ against Superintendant Robert Acott of Scotland Yard for alleged defamation and false imprisonment.

Alphon was back in the news in March 1962 when he was remanded at Bow Street Magistrates accused of being drunk and disorderly outside the Regent Palace Hotel. On 3 April he was cleared when the case was dismissed. This was the day before Hanratty was executed.

Four months later, the wife of James Hanratty, Mrs Mary Hanratty, was granted a summons by Bow Street Magistrates against Alphon who was alleged to have assaulted her at Green Park Underground on 23 August.

But Alphon really hit the headlines on 12 May 1967.

A warrant was issued against him for a breach of recognizance made against him in August 1966 to stop pestering Earl Russell of Liverpool with telephone calls. Earl Russell was writing a book about the A6 murder at the time. However, Alphon could not be found to face these charges. But he turned up in France when he gave a press conference at a Paris hotel and admitted to the A6 murder. He said: "I did in fact do the A6 murder. I killed Gregsten and half-killed Miss Storie — it's not my fault, I can't shoot a gun very well. This is my confession. I have never confessed before. There's a time and a place to do it." He said he confessed because he wanted to drag British justice through the mud. A detective-sergeant from Scotland Yard was present at the conference.

Alphon appeared on the London Rediffusion television programme Dateline from a Paris hideaway on 17 May and when asked by interviewer Alan Hart if he had shot Gregsten and fired seven shots at Miss Storie, Alphon said: "That is what I said at the press conference and I am going to stand by it."

On 2 September 1967 Alphon appeared in court on the charge of pestering Earl Russell. But no action was brought about his claim that he committed the A6 murder. At the hearing Chief Inspector Mooney of Scotland Yard said Alphon could not have committed the murder because he knew where he was at the time. This was the first time the police had confirmed an alibi for Alphon. Three months later Alphon joined Earl Russell in calling for a public enquiry into the A6 murder.

HARRIS, Rolf, MBE, OBE

ALTHOUGH his parents were from Cardiff, Rolf Harris was born in Perth, Western Australia, in 1930. At the age of 15 he was the junior backstroke swimming champion of Australia. In 1952 he came to England to study art and it is for his cartoons that he is best known although he has many talents, such as painter, sculptor, composer and singer. It was with such songs as *Tie Me Kangaroo Down Sport* which introduced Harris' famous 'wobble board', and *Sun Arise* that he enjoyed chart success in the sixties. However, his biggest hit was *Two Little Boys* which, coincidentally, was the last number-one hit record of the 1960s. Rolf also brought us the three-legged Jake with the song *Jake The Peg*.

During his spell in Britain in the early fifties, he appeared on television, including *Showcase* with Benny Hill. But he returned to Australia in 1959 where he appeared in, and produced, his own television series. He returned to Britain in July 1962 and the BBC gave him the first show of his own when he hosted *Hey Presto! It's Rolf.* He also narrated Anglia Television's *Survival* series for a while.

Since then, Rolf has made his home in Britain and has appeared on countless adult and children's programmes. He was awarded the MBE in 1968 and nine years later received the OBE. Today he is loved by kids for his cartoon character portrayals on the popular *Disney Time,* amongst other programmes.

HARRISON, Sir Rex

BORN at Huyton, Liverpool, in 1908, Rex Harrison made his theatre debut at Liverpool's Playhouse at the age of 16. By the time he made his film debut, in *The School For Scandal* in 1930, he was rapidly establishing himself as a fine stage actor.

After serving in the RAF during the war, Harrison appeared in well-known films like *Blithe Spirit* and *The Rake's Progress*. But in the 1960s he had phenomenal success.

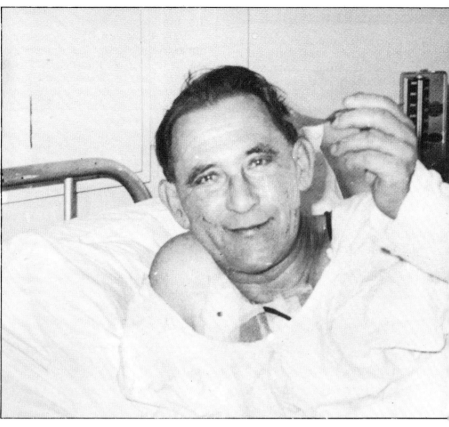

In 1963 he played the part of Julius Caesar in *Cleopatra*. The performance won him an Oscar nomination for best actor. The following year he was chosen to play the part of Professor Higgins in *My Fair Lady*.

Having successfully played the stage role on Broadway in the late 1950s, he was a natural choice for the film and this time his performance yielded that elusive Oscar.

The *Yellow Rolls Royce, The Agony And The Ecstasy* and the part of the man who talked to the animals, Dr Dolittle, in the film of the same name, did nothing but underline Harrison's all-round versatility in the 1960s.

Harrison collected only one Oscar during his illustrious career, but wives were more frequent. He was married to Collette Thomas, Lilli Palmer, Kay Kendall, Rachel Roberts and Elizabeth Harris. He is currently married to Mercia Tinker. He was knighted in June 1989.

His son, Noel, had a smash hit record in 1969 with *Windmills Of Your Mind.*

The films of Rex Harrison in the 1960s:

Midnight Lace	(1960)
The Happy Thieves	(1961)
Cleopatra	(1963)
My Fair Lady	(1964)
The Yellow Rolls Royce	(1964)
The Agony And The Ecstasy	(1965)
Flashes Festivals	(1965)
The Honey Pot	(1966)
Dr Dolittle	(1967)
A Flea In Her Ear	(1968)
Staircase	(1969)

Rex Harrison as Dr Dolittle.

HAWAII FIVE-O

THIS American police series was set in the exotic location of the Hawaiian

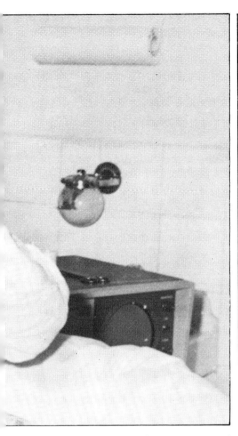

islands. The call sign Five-O stemmed from the fact that Hawaii was the 50th state of America. The programme was first seen in 1968.

It starred Jack Lord as the Honolulu detective Steve McGarrett, and James MacArthur as his sidekick, Danny Williams. McGarrett was rarely out of his blue suit and each series normally ended with him apprehending the 'baddie' and saying to his partner: "Book 'em Danno." McGarrett's arch-rival was master criminal Wo Fat.

The theme music for the series was played by Morton Stevens and is one of the most popular TV themes of all time. It was used in a *Guinness* advert in the 1980s.

Most of the everyday policemen seen in the series were not actors but real-live off-duty Honolulu cops who donated their earnings to the Hawaii Police Department Charity Fund.

HEART TRANSPLANTS

ONE of the most impressive medical breakthroughs of all time took place at the Groot Schuur Hospital, Cape Town, South Africa, on 3 December 1967 when the first human heart transplant operation was successfully completed.

The transplant was carried out by Dr Christiaan Barnard and his 30-strong team. The operation lasted six hours and Barnard successfully transplanted the heart from 25-year-old traffic accident victim Denise Ann Darvall into 53-year-old grocer Louis Washkansky, a diabetic whose fibrotic heart had nearly given up on him.

The donor heart had to be kept in cooled oxygenated blood for more than three hours before its transplant into Washkansky. The donor heart was about half the size of the recipient's and, as Barnard connected up the electrodes to the new heart before getting it to function, he said simply: "It's going to work" . . .and it did. A few days later Washkansky was sitting up in bed, joking with the nurses and eating solid food. Alas, 18 days after the operation the world's first heart transplant patient died after contracting pneumonia.

But Barnard's pioneering opened the door for many similar operations which are commonplace today.

The first British transplant was on 3 May 1968, when surgeon Donald Ross successfully transplanted the heart of 26-year-old donor Patrick Ryan to 45-year-old recipient Frederick West at the National Heart Hospital, Marylebone. Mr West died two weeks later.

May 1968 was quite a month in British transplant history because, in addition to the first heart transplant, there was also the first successful transplant of a liver and lungs, in two separate operations.

On 7 June 1968 Mrs E.Matthews made history in the United States as the first woman to receive a new heart.

By the end of the decade transplant surgery was becoming more common and survival periods were increased. On 17 August 1969, Dr Philip Blaiberg died at the Groot Schuur Hospital 19 months after receiving a new heart. He was the world's longest surviving transplant patient in the sixties.
(See also BARNARD, Dr Christiaan)

HEATH, Ted

THE Ted Heath-Harold Wilson political battles of the 1960s always enlivened the House of Commons.

Ted Heath was born at Broadstairs, Kent, in 1916 and studied at Oxford before entering Parliament in 1950. He was soon heralded as a rising 'star' of the Conservative Party and held a succession of important posts. He was Minister of Labour as the 1960s arrived and then became the chief negotiator for Britain's entry into the Common Market.

In July 1965 he succeeded Sir Alec Douglas-Home as leader of the Tories and in June 1970 became Prime Minister after the Conservative's General Election success.

Ted Heath was 'brought down' by the coalminers in 1973 and the following year the Tories lost two elections. In 1975 Heath suffered the

added embarassment of losing the leadership of the Party to Margaret Thatcher.

A first-class yachtsman, Ted Heath used to sail both competitively and for pleasure in his yacht *Morning Cloud*. He is also an excellent classical pianist and a competent conductor. Heath is still an active Member of Parliament but plays a more passive role these days, occasionally coming out into the open to comment on a crucial issue of the day and is often critical of Premier Margaret Thatcher.

HENDRIX, Jimi

JIMI Hendrix was the man who successfully fused black blues music and white pop music. Nicknamed the 'Psychedelic Superspade' his lyrics were inspired by Bob Dylan and on stage he gave an electric perfor-mance, often playing the guitar with his teeth.

Born in Seattle, Washington, on 27 November 1945 (a date he gave), he was part-negro, part-Cherokee Indian and part-Mexican. As a youngster he appeared in vaudeville and then joined the Isley Brothers backing band. He toured the States with some of the great performers of the era — Sam Cooke, Solomon Burke, Little Richard and Ike and Tina Turner.

Hendrix formed his own band in 1966 and appeared at Greenwich Village. He was spotted at a gig there by Chas Chandler, formerly of the Animals. Chandler became his manager and took him to England and the 'Jimi Hendrix Experience' was formed with 'Mitch' Mitchell and Noel Redding.

Hendrix made full use of amplifi-cation techniques and his frizzy hair

Jimi Hendrix rehearsing for the All-Night Pop Concert at Olympia, London, in December 1967.

style and startling clothes made him quite distinguishable.

When he returned to the United States, Hendrix was banned from touring by the Daughters of the American Revolution, who considered his provocative movements on stage obscene. This only aroused greater interest and a rise in popularity.

He went into partial seclusion in 1969 but returned in 1970 to form a new group, Band of Gypsies. His last appearance was at Ronnie Scott's Club in London. Jimmy Hendrix died from a drug overdose on 18 September 1970. Two months later *Voodoo Chile* became the first number one for Hendrix.

Top Ten hits of Jimi Hendrix in the 1960s:

Year	Record	Pos
1967	Hey Joe	6
1967	Purple Haze	3
1967	The Wind Cries Mary	6
1968	All Along The Watchtower	5

HERMAN'S HERMITS

BEFORE he became one of the pop sensations of the mid-1960s, Peter Noone had enjoyed a successful career on the small screen. As a child star he appeared in *Knight Errant, Saki* and was Len Fairclough's son in *Coronation Street.*

Born in Manchester on 5 November 1947, he got the nickname Herman when he was likened to Sherman, a young colleague of Mr Peabody on the children's television programme *The Bullwinkle Show.*

Herman's pop career started with a Manchester band called The Cyclones. They later became The Heartbeats and it was not until they met Mickie Most that they were persuaded to change their name; and so was born Herman's Hermits. Their first record was the Goffin-King number *I'm Into Something Good* which turned out to be their only British number one.

In America they were a huge success and reached the top of the charts with *Mrs Brown You've Got A Lovely Daughter* (which was not released in Britain) and *I'm Henry The Eighth, I Am* which failed to make the British charts.

The group split up in 1970 but reformed briefly for the reunion tour of 1973. Since then Peter Noone has kept himself busy by song-writing, running a boutique, appearing in Gilbert and Sullivan's *The Pirates Of Penzance* and recording as a solo artiste. But the glory days of the mid-1960s have not returned as far as chart success is concerned.

Top Ten hits of Herman's Hermits in the 1960s:

Year	Record	Pos
1964	I'm Into Something Good	1
1965	Silhouettes	3
1965	Wonderful World	7
1965	A Must To Avoid	6
1966	No Milk Today	7
1967	There's A Kind Of Hush	7
1968	Sunshine Girl	8
1968	Something's Happening	6
1969	My Sentimental Friend	2

HIPPIES

AFTER the Teddy Boys, Beatniks, Mods and Rockers, there then came the Hippies, the breed of youngsters who arrived in the mid-sixties with the motto: 'Make Love Not War'.

The Hippie lifestyle was the ambition of many youngsters. They could wear whatever clothes they wanted, and live in communes, far away from their interfering parents.

Long hair for the men was a 'stipulation' and kaftan coats, beads and flowers in the hair became very much part of the Hippie attire. The hallucinatory drug LSD also became part of the staple diet for many Hippies!

The Hippies would gather at rock concerts when lovemaking, nudity and the smell of cannabis was prevalent. But who cared, everybody was having fun. Occasionally it did get a little bit out of hand.

The Apple Boutique in London's West End became a shrine for Hippies; well at least for those who could afford to buy clothes there. It was run by the Dutch Hippie designers Simon and Marijke.

Some records of the decade were closely associated with the Hippie and Flower Power movement. There was Scott McKenzie's *San Francisco (Be Sure To Wear Flowers In Your Hair)*. There was also the Beatles with their *Sergeant Pepper* album and Procol Harum's *Whiter Shade Of Pale*, both of which seemed to have more than a fleeting reference to pot smoking.

> LSD is short for Lysergic Acid Diethylamide, a drug discovered by a Swiss doctor, Dr Albert Hoffman in the 1930s.

In America, the world of flower power was centred around the Haight-Ashbury district of San Francisco where thousands of Hippies lived from the mid-sixties. But as they grew in media popularity, buses started running a 'Hippie Hop service' to the district on what they advertised as a 'Safari through Psychedelia'. Other big communes were established at Tomkins Square Park in New York's East Village District, and also in Boston and Los Angeles.

HITCHCOCK, Sir Alfred, OBE

ALFRED Hitchcock produced thrillers for more than 40 years and his trade mark was the never-ending trail of twists which left the audience wondering just what was going to happen next.

Two of Hitchcock's best-known films were released in the 1960s. First there was Psycho in which Anthony Perkins portrayed the chilling Norman Bates. It was one of the first films during which cinema owners had, by contract, to refuse admission to the public once the movie had started running.

> The sequel to Psycho, Psycho II *(of course!), also starred Anthony Perkins as Norman Bates. It was made in 1983 and, of course, we have since had* Psycho III. *The first* Psycho *had an orchestral accompaniment composed entirely for stringed instruments, used to achieve a chilling sound designed to frighten the audience . . .*

Hitchcock followed that with *The Birds* in 1963, which portrayed a horrifying attack on humans by flocks of birds. As usual, his techniques were innovative.

But those two were not the extent of the Hitchcock magic. There were dozens more.

Born in Leytonstone, London, on 13 August 1899, his first involvement with films was as a designer of title cards. He directed his first film *The Pleasure Garden*, in 1925 and the following year directed his first thriller, *The Lodger*. It was also the first film in which he made his celebrated 'guest appearances', another Hitchcock trademark.

In 1929, Hitchcock made *Blackmail*, the first British talkie. But in 1938 his skills were required across the Atlantic and he went to Hollywood.

People would flock to the cinema to watch one of his films just because it was a Hitchcock production. Yet, strangely, the man who drew millions through the box office never received an Oscar, although he was awarded the OBE in 1979. Hitchcock died of a heart attack in Los Angeles on 29 April 1980.

The films of Alfred Hitchcock in the 1960s:

Psycho	(1960)
The Birds	(1963)
Marnie	(1964)
Torn Curtain	(1966)
Topaz	(1969)

HOCKNEY, David

BORN in Bradford, West Yorkshire, in 1937, David Hockney became one of Britain's best-known modern-day artists and his work was synonymous with pop art in the 1960s.

A grammar school pupil, Hockney graduated to the Royal College of Art. He was very imaginative and his simplistic style brought a fresh new approach to art, in the same way as Picasso's had done before him. Hockney had his first one-man show in 1963 and the Americans showed great interest in his style. In the mid-1960s he taught in the United States.

He was also sought after as a designer for stage sets at some of the world's great theatres.

Hockney now lives in the United States, although he has a studio in London. His pictures have been seen at all the leading galleries throughout the world and in 1989 a Hockney painting exchanged hands for more than £1 million.

HOLLIES, The

THE HOLLIES were a grossly underrated group in the 1960s. Their record of 15 Top Ten hits during the decade is testament to their talent at a time when there was a lot of competition for places in the charts. Between August 1963 and October 1970 they had 21 consecutive Top Twenty British hit singles.

A Manchester-based group, the original line-up in 1963 consisted of Allan Clarke, Graham Nash, Tony Hicks, Bobby Elliot and Eric Haydock. Bernie Calvert replaced Haydock and in 1969 Nash left to team up with David Crosby (ex-Byrds) and Stephen

Stills (ex-Buffalo Springfield) to form Crosby, Stills and Nash.

Two of the Hollies' best-known numbers were *I'm Alive*, their only number one, and *He Ain't Heavy He's My Brother* which reached number three in 1969. Nineteen years later it became a chart-topper after being featured in the advertisement for Miller Lite beer.

For a quarter of a century the Hollies have been one of the best touring bands in the world of pop music.

Top Ten hits of The Hollies in the 1960s:

Year	Record	Pos
1963	Stay	8
1964	Just One Look	2
1964	Here I Go Again	4
1964	We're Through	7
1965	Yes I Will	9
1965	I'm Alive	1
1966	Look Through Any Window	4
1966	I Can't Let Go	2
1966	Bus Stop	5
1966	Stop Stop Stop	2
1967	On A Carousel	4
1967	Carrie-Anne	3
1968	Jennifer Eccles	7
1969	Sorry Suzanne	3
1969	He Ain't Heavy He's My Brother	3

HOPKIN, Mary

MARY Hopkin was one of the many stars who made their name through the television series *Opportunity Knocks*. Born in Pontadarwe, South Wales, in May 1950, she began singing when she was four and regularly appeared on Welsh television as a youngster, often singing in her native tongue.

After entertaining customers in the working men's and mining clubs around the Rhondda Valley, she got her big break in 1968 when she appeared on the famous television talent show. This led to her being recommended to Paul McCartney by Twiggy. The Beatles new Apple recording label was looking for fresh talent, and Mary became one of the company's first recruits.

Mary Hopkin and Hughie Green.

Her first record for Apple was *Those Were The Days*, which was to become one of the biggest-selling records of the decade, and, ironically, displaced the Beatles' *Hey Jude*, which had been Apple's first chart-topper, from the number-one slot. Mary stayed at the top of the charts for six weeks and a new star was born.

In 1969 her follow-up record *Goodbye* reached number two, as did her Eurovision Song Contest entry *Knock Knock Who's There* in 1970. Since then chart success has eluded Mary Hopkin, although her soft, gentle voice has retained her popularity as a cabaret artiste.

HOVERCRAFT

THE hovercraft (officially called an Air Cushion Vehicle — ACV) was the

The Queen steps aboard for her first trip by Hovercraft. She crossed the Solent from Yarmouth, Isle of Wight, to RAF Thorney Island in July 1965.

brainchild of Suffolk boat-builder Christopher Cockerell. He patented his idea in 1955 after an experiment with an empty food can, a larger Lyons coffee tin, and a vacuum cleaner in which he discovered that the air being passed between the two walls of the tins was being thrust downwards.

His prototype was 30ft long and weighed 3½ tons. It was launched from Cowes, Isle of Wight, in 1959. That same year, his first Hovercraft crossed the Channel. The first regular passenger service was started on 20 July 1962 when the 24-seater British United Airways VA-3 operated on the Dee estuary between Wallasey and Rhyl. The first passengers to cross the Channel did so from Ramsgate to Calais on 6 April 1966, with a regular service starting three weeks later.

The first Channel Hoverferry service was launched on 1 August 1968 when the Mountbatten Class *Princess Margaret* made her maiden crossing. It was capable of carrying 609 passengers or 254 passengers and 30 cars.

Christopher Cockerell was knighted in 1969.

HOWERD, Frankie, OBE

FRANKIE Howerd's trademark is his face. He doesn't have to open his mouth to get laughs — his facial expressions alone do that.

Born in York in 1922, he was brought up in London and made his stage debut at the age of 13. He is best known for his part in the popular television series *Up Pompeii* but his all-round versatility extends to stand-up comedy, television, radio and the movies where he has appeared in such films as *The Ladykillers, Up Pompeii* and a couple of *Carry On* films. He also appeared in *The Great St Trinians Train Robbery*. Most of his film roles have been in risqué films with 'near-the-knuckle' type comedy.

He has appeared in countless Royal Variety Performances and for his services to the industry has been awarded the OBE. He is reported to be the Queen Mother's favourite comedian.

Frankie Howerd belongs to not only the sixties but the fifties, seventies and eighties as well. His comedy can be likened to that of the so-called 'alternative' comedians of today. He is still as good as many of them, and he's been dishing out 'alternative' comedy for more than 50 years.

HUDSON, Rock

ROCK Hudson was one of Hollywood's heart-throbs of the 1950s and '60s. His early movie career saw him playing some dramatic roles but in the 1960s he was better known for his light-hearted romantic/comedy roles and he played opposite Doris Day in *Pillow Talk* (1959), *Lover Come Back* (1961) and *Send Me No Flowers* (1964).

His real name was Roy Scherer and he was born at Winnetka, Illinois, on 17 November 1925. He served in the US Navy before taking up a career in acting. Hudson's film debut was in Raoul Walsh's *Fighter Squadron* in 1949. After playing Bob Merrick in *The Magnificent Obsession* in 1954 he emerged as a major star.

He received one Oscar nomination, in 1956, following his part as Bick Benedict in *Giant*. In the latter part of the '60s he returned to more serious roles in films like *Tobruk* and *Ice Station Zebra*.

In the 1970s Hudson re-found fame in the popular television series *McMillan And Wife* alongside the talented Susan St James. He also appeared in *Dynasty* in the 1980s.

In 1985 it was announced that he had AIDS and his illness attracted a great deal of worldwide attention to the disease. Rock Hudson died on 2 October 1985.

The films of Rock Hudson in the 1960s:

The Last Sunset	(1961)
Come September	(1961)
Lover Come Back	(1961)
The Spiral Road	(1962)
A Gathering Of Eagles	(1963)
Man's Favourite Sport?	(1964)
Send Me No Flowers	(1964)
Strange Bedfellows	(1964)
A Very Special Favor	(1965)
Blindfold	(1966)
Seconds	(1966)
Tobruk	(1966)
Ice Station Zebra	(1968)
Ruba Al Prossimo Two (A Fine Pair)	(1969)
The Undefeated	(1969)

HUMPERDINCK, Engelbert

ENGELBERT Humperdinck followed Tom Jones to the States, and like Jones has wooed the fans at the top US venues. He divides his time between homes in the States and his native Leicester.

'The Hump' started his singing career as Gerry Dorsey. He was born as Arnold George Dorsey in 1936 and was brought up in Leicester, despite being born in Madras, India.

He won a talent contest on the Isle of Man and this resulted in a London agent getting him a recording contract and Dorsey released his first record, *Mister Music Man*, in 1958. But stardom never came and he was living on the breadline and often found it difficult to find the rent for his London flat. However, in 1965 he met up with a former flatmate, Gordon Mills, who had become Tom Jones' manager. Mills took Gerry under his wing and suggested the change of name to Engelbert Humperdinck (borrowed from the turn-of-the-century German composer). That change coincided with his change in fortunes.

He had a couple of hits on the Continent but in January 1967 he recorded *Release Me*. He had a big break when asked to stand in for Dickie Valentine on *Sunday Night At The London Palladium*. He sang *Release Me* and within weeks he had taken the charts by storm. It was one of the best-selling records of the decade and spent six weeks at number one.

His follow-up, *There Goes My Everything* reached number two and then *The Last Waltz* made it to number one. It stayed at the top for five weeks which meant Engelbert was at the top of the charts for 11 of the 52 weeks during 1967, a remarkable achievement for a newcomer to the charts.

By the end of 1967 he had his own television series, *The Engelbert Humperdinck Show*. He had one hit after another before the end of the decade and, like Tom Jones, he amassed an army of female followers. He has not enjoyed a British chart entry since 1973 but that has not detracted from his huge appeal and he remains a popular attraction in America and this side of the Atlantic where he makes all too few appearances these days.

Top Ten hits of Engelbert Humperdinck in the 1960s:

Year	Record	Pos
1967	Release Me	1
1967	There Goes My Everything	2
1967	The Last Waltz	1
1968	Am I That Easy To Forget	3
1968	A Man Without Love	2
1968	Les Bicyclettes De Belsize	5
1969	The Way It Used To Be	3
1969	Winter World Of Love	7

IFIELD, Frank

ASK anybody where Frank Ifield, the man with the yodelling voice, was born and it's a good bet the answer is 'Australia'. In fact Frank was born in Coventry, England, on 30 November 1937 and emigrated to Australia where he developed his singing talent. He was given his own radio and television shows and for several years was one of the country's top entertainers.

To further his career he felt he needed to return to Britain, which he did in 1959. He was given a recording contract with Columbia and this proved to be the springboard for future success. In 1962 and 1963 he was one of the hottest properties around. He had four number-one hits, three of them consecutively, which made him the first English-born singer to achieve this. It took the likes of Elvis and Cliff to displace him.

Since 1964, however, Frank Ifield has enjoyed rare chart success, becoming another victim of the invasion of the '60s groups. He still appears in cabaret.

Top Ten hits of Frank Ifield in the 1960s:

Year	Record	Pos
1962	I Remember You	1
1962	Lovesick Blues	1
1963	Wayward Wind	1
1963	Nobody's Darlin' But Mine	4
1963	Confessin'	1
1964	Don't Blame Me	8

IMMIGRATION BILL

IN THE two years from 1959 to 1961, the number of immigrants into Britain from Commonwealth countries had increased almost five times from 21,000 to 100,000. Consequently, the Government announced measures to control immigration. Part one of the Immigration Bill went through Parliament on 27 February 1962 and at midnight on 30 June it became law.

The new law prevented absolute freedom of immigrants. Although they were entitled entry by right, they had to show they were capable of supporting themselves without a job or, if not, had a voucher showing they either had a job to come to or possessed skills that would be needed in Britain. The prospective immigrant could be refused admission on medical grounds or if he or she had a criminal record.

Many immigrants sought to beat the new legislation by flying in a few days before the act became law. Of the 599 who arrived on the first day of the new law, only 14 were refused entry. An aircraft full of Jamaicans arrived at Belfast just after midnight and although they had arrived without the proper paperwork, they were allowed to stay because their plane was delayed and should have arrived before the midnight deadline.

The new Commonwealth Immigrants Act of 1968 allowed for strict penalties to be imposed on people aiding Commonwealth citizens to enter Britain illegally. The 1971 Immigration Bill was even more restrictive on Commonwealth immigrants and more or less ended the inalienable rights of Commonwealth workers to settle in Britain.

INCOME TAX

THE standard rate of income tax changed only once in the 1960s — 1965-66 when it was increased from 7s 9d in the £ to 8s 3d . . .a standard rate of 41¼%.

INFLATION RATE

THE rate of inflation never once went over 7% during the 1960s and in July 1968 was a mere 0.8%. A far cry from August 1979 when it hit 26.9%. It's highest figure in the sixties was 6.3% in March 1969.

The annual average inflation rate throughout the sixties (from 1963) was as follows:

1963: 2.0%	1965: 4.8%	1968: 4.7%
1964: 3.3%	1966: 3.9%	1969: 5.4%
	1967: 2.5%	

The annual rate of inflation in 1988 was 6.8%.

Scene at Nairobi airport in February 1968 as fleeing Asians arrive at the terminal en route for London in a bid to beat the new Commonwealth Immigrants Act which was about to become law.

INDEPENDENCIES

A 'Wind of Change' certainly blew through Africa in the 1960s as many of the countries became independent. The following is a list of those nations which gained independence during the decade:

1 Jan 1960 Cameroon
27 Apr 1960 Togo
20 Jun 1960 Mali (formerly French Sudan, part of French West Africa)
26 Jun 1960 Madagascar
30 Jun 1960 Zaire (formerly Belgian Congo)
1 Jul 1960 Somalia (formed following merger of the Trust Territory of Somaliland and British Somaliland)
1 Aug 1960 Benin (formerly part of French West Africa it became independent as Dahomey. Changed name to Benin in 1975)
3 Aug 1960 Niger (formerly part of French West Africa)
5 Aug 1960 Upper Volta (formerly part of French West Africa)
7 Aug 1960 Ivory Coast (formerly part of French West Africa)
11 Aug 1960 Chad (formerly province of French Equitorial Africa)
13 Aug 1960 Central African Republic
15 Aug 1960 Congo (formerly part of French Equitorial Africa as Middle Congo)
17 Aug 1960 Gabon (formerly part of French Equitorial Africa)
20 Aug 1960 Senegal (formerly part of French West Africa)
1 Oct 1960 Nigeria
28 Nov 1960 Mauritania (formerly part of French West Africa)
27 Apr 1961 Sierra Leone
9 Dec 1961 Tanganyika (merged with Zanzibar in 1964 to form Tanzania)
1 Jul 1962 Ruanda (formerly part of Ruanda-Urundi)
1 Jul 1962 Burundi (formerly part of Ruanda-Urundi)
3 Jul 1962 Algeria
9 Oct 1962 Uganda
10 Dec 1963 Zanzibar (merged with Tanganyika in 1964 to form Tanzania)
12 Dec 1963 Kenya
6 Jul 1964 Malawi (formerly Nyasaland)
24 Oct 1964 Zambia (formerly Northern Rhodesia)
18 Feb 1965 Gambia
11 Nov 1965 Zimbawe declared UDI (formerly Southern Rhodesia and just Rhodesia from 1964 until adopting the name Zimbabwe in 1979)
6 Sep 1968 Swaziland
30 Sep 1966 Botswana (formerly Bechuanaland)
4 Oct 1966 Lesotho (formerly Basutoland)

INVENTIONS & DISCOVERIES

LIKE all decades, the sixties was a time for advancement, whether it be in medical or scientific fields. Many of the new technological advancements are covered elsewhere in this book, but the following are some of the inventions of the 1960s that had an effect on our lives at the time, or have since become an integral and 'taken for granted' part of modern day life.

Naturally, space exploration took pride of place at the top of the 'Inventions and Discoveries' charts in the 1960s but that topic is covered in detail further on in the book.

Barring the exploits of the Americans and Soviets in space, one of the greatest scientific breakthroughs of the decade was the invention of the laser which is now used to carry out a wide range of functions.

It was invented by Dr Charles Townes of the United States and first demonstrated by Theodore Maiman at Hughes Research, Malibu, California, in July 1960. Laser is short for *light amplification by stimulated emission of radiation*. Without the laser just imagine how dull some of the James Bond movies would have been!

The first year of the decade was quite a good one for inventions; the Hawker P1127 vertical take-off aircraft made its debut. Better known as the 'Jump-jet', it was a British invention and swivelled its engines for either vertical or horizontal flight.

But of all 1960 inventions, the one marketed by the Japanese Stationery Company of Tokyo had the biggest influence on everyday life. They gave the world the *Pentel* fibre-tip pen. Can you imagine life before the fibre-tip pen? Just how did we manage? The Japanese also, via Sony, developed the first all-transistor television set in 1960.

Computerized typesetting was introduced at Imprimerie Nationale, Paris, towards the end of 1960. Today, this method of typesetting is commonplace, not only in the production of books (like the one you are reading) but also in the production of newspapers. This is what they now call 'new technology', but the French were at it nearly 30 years ago. Talking of computers, transistors replaced valves in commercial computers in 1960.

Other inventions of 1960 included the across-the-shoulder car seat belt designed by P.O.Wemen and manufactured by Britax. Satellites started to become commonplace in 1960 and the Americans launched *Tiros I* on 1 April. It was the first meteorological satellite. How many there are currently floating around above us in the 1980s is anybody's guess!

Bank Station in London was chosen as the site for the first passenger conveyor. Known as the 'travelator', it was opened on 27 September 1960.

On the medical front the oral contraceptive made its debut in 1960, as did the measles vaccine, which had been developed by American chemist John F.Enders. The Rubella (German measles) vaccine was developed two years later by another American, Thomas H.Weller.

By comparison to a busy 1960 the rest of the decade was quiet . . .on the invention and discovery front, that is!

The first Post Office pay-on-answer phone boxes were installed in 1961 and that same year the identikit, which is now a vital part of police criminal detection work, was launched. The first suspected criminal to be identified by means of this new invention was Edwin Bush. Another major breakthrough in 1961 was the patenting of the electric toothbrush by the Squibb Company of New York . . .wow!

London Underground had its first electric ticket barrier in 1964 when one was installed at Stamford Brook and three months later the first unmanned tube trains appeared on the Central Line. On water, the first British hydrofoil service was introduced from the Channel Isles to France in April 1964. The aviation industry saw its first airliner make an automatic landing when a BEA de Havilland Trident from Paris landed automatically at Heathrow on 10 June 1965.

One of the major discoveries of the decade was of the gas fields in the North Sea. The first gas was piped ashore by BP at Easington, County Durham, from the West Sole field on 7 March 1967.

After that there was very little to enthuse about except, perhaps, the introduction of supersonic flight firstly via the Russian Tu-144 in 1968 and the Anglo-French Concorde a year later.

JACKLIN'S BRITISH OPEN WIN

IT HAD been 18 years since a Briton had won golf's most cherished trophy, the British Open. But at Royal Lytham on a sunny day in July 1969, Tony Jacklin put that right by beating left-hander Bob Charles, a former champion, by two strokes.

Jacklin was starting to earn a reputation for himself in the golfing world by the time the leading players assembled at Lytham. He had won the Dunlop Masters and achieved success on the US Tour in the Jacksonville Open in 1968. Now he was ready to conquer the world.

Jacklin, 25, played four solid rounds and showed great determination as a pack of great players like Roberto de Vicenzo, Christy O'Connor and Peter Thomson pursued him. Despite such notables breathing down his neck, Jacklin hardly put a foot wrong and showed that he could cope with pressure at the highest level.

In winning the Open, Jacklin did more than become the first British winner since Max Faulkner in 1951. He became the man who put British golf on the map and gave it the standing it has today. Suddenly, thousands went out and tried to emulate his feat and Britain has since produced great players like Nick Faldo, Sandy Lyle and Ian Woosnam. As for Jacklin, he twice went close to winning the Open again and has captained Europe to Ryder Cup success over the Americans.

Tony Jacklin with the Open Golf Championship trophy at Lytham in July 1969.

BRITISH OPEN 1969
280 Tony Jacklin (GB)
     68-70-70-72
282 Bob Charles (New Zealand)
     66-69-75-72
283 Peter Thomson (Australia)
     71-70-70-72
283 Roberto de Vicenzo (Argentina)
     72-73-66-72
284 Christy O'Connor (Ireland)
     71-65-74-74
285 Jack Nicklaus (USA)
     75-70-68-72
285 Davis Love Jr (USA)
     70-73-71-71

JACKLIN, Tony

LITTLE did he realize it at the time, but Tony Jacklin's momentous British Open win at Royal Lytham in 1969 was the stepping stone for the British golfing success stories that came in the eighties.

The son of a Scunthorpe steel-worker, Jacklin was identified as the 'ordinary' man who went out and became a champion. Consequently, his success led to a boom in the popularity of golf amongst everyday working-class people. That was good for the game and it helped inspire men like Sandy Lyle, Nick Faldo and Ian Woosnam who have since become great champions in their own right.

Although Jacklin started his working career in a local steelworks, he had decided on a golfing career and at the age of 17 turned professional and worked at the Potter's Bar club under the guidance of Bill Shankland.

Rookie of the Year for 1963, he won his first event, the GorRay Assistants Championship, two years later. Having tried his hand on the US circuit, he served notice that a great talent was about to emerge when he won the Jacksonville Open in 1968, the first win by a British golfer on US soil since Ted Ray in 1920.

His talent exploded that July day at Lytham in 1969 when he beat the left-handed New Zealander Bob Charles to become the first British winner of the Open since Max Faulkner in 1951. But to prove his win was no fluke he took the US Open a year later and by an amazing seven-stroke margin.

Although he came close to winning the British Open a couple more times in the early seventies, he never enjoyed that level of success again until he took charge of the European Ryder Cup team and steered them to a memorable victory over the Americans at the Belfry in 1985, the Americans' first defeat since 1957. But two years later Jacklin enjoyed an even greater moment when he led the team to its first win on US soil.

Sadly for Jacklin and his three children, his wife Vivien, the woman who was by his side when he enjoyed his moment of triumph at Lytham, died from a brain haemorrhage whilst driving near their Spanish home in 1988.

JOHNSON, Lyndon Baines

LBJ was sworn in as the 36th President of the United States aboard the Presidential jet on 22 November 1963, following the assassination of President Kennedy earlier that day.

Born at Stonewall, Texas, on 27 August 1908, he served in the US Navy which he joined immediately after Pearl Harbour. He had been involved with politics since 1937 when he was elected to the House of Representatives as a New Deal Democrat. His inspiration was his wife Claudia, better known as 'Ladybird', and in 1948 he was elected a Senator. He became Vice-President to Kennedy in 1960.

President Johnson (right) with former President Dwight D.Eisenhower.

The year after Kennedy's death, Johnson was returned as President with a huge majority and under his administration the Civil Rights Act and Voting Rights Act, which Kennedy had started, were passed and thus helped ease the racial problem.

However, public unrest over American involvement in Vietnam led to a decline in Johnson's popularity. On 31 March 1968 he announced that he would not stand at the next Presidential election.

He retired to his ranch near Johnson City (named after his grandfather) in Texas and wrote his memoirs before dying on 22 January 1973. His administration was not one of the most popular in American history, but it was certainly one of the most significant.

JONES, Tom

BORN as Thomas Jones Woodward in June 1942, Tom Jones hailed from the Welsh mining community of Treforrest. Like so many of his Welsh contempories he started his singing career in the local chapel choir.

Tom formed his own group The Playboys, and in 1962 they had their big break when invited to appear on BBC television's *Donald Peers Presents*. Tom made such an impact that he was offered a contract with Decca and his first disc, *Chills And Fever*, was cut shortly afterwards.

The record which set the Jones boy on a road to stardom which has since taken him to Las Vegas, was *It's Not Unusual* in 1965. Written by Les Reed and Gordon Mills (Tom Jones' manager), the record was a number-one hit in Britain and also did well in the States.

Songs like *Green, Green Grass Of Home* and *Delilah* further enhanced his reputation and by 1968 he was the first British artiste to have his own show on American network television. One of the highlights of his act was the removal of his bow-tie, normally after the first number. That alone was enough to get his many female fans going.

His great stage show, not to mention his great voice, helped make him one of the highest-paid entertainers in the United States where he has made his home.

Top Ten hits of Tom Jones in the 1960s:

Year	Record	Pos
1965	It's Not Unusual	1
1966	Green Green Grass of Home	1
1967	Detroit City	8
1967	Funny Familiar Forgotten Feelings	7
1967	I'll Never Fall In Love Again	2
1967	I'm Coming Home	2
1968	Delilah	2
1968	Help Yourself	5
1969	Love Me Tonight	9
1969	Without Love	10

JUKE BOX JURY

A POPULAR panel show, *Juke Box Jury* was first broadcast by the BBC on 1 June 1959 and ran until 27 December 1967.

The chairman was David Jacobs and each week four panellists from the world of entertainment would review a selection of new discs and would have to declare it a hit or a miss in their opinion. A separate panel from the audience would act as a tie-breaker. There was also a mystery guest lurking behind the curtain and he or she would have to listen to the panellists reviewing their record. Of course, they were quite often embarrassed when the mystery guest appeared after they had torn it to pieces.

The theme music for the programme was appropriately called *Hit And Miss* and was played by the John Barry Seven. It reached number ten in the British charts.

JUMBO JET

IN April 1966, the Boeing company announced plans for its new 747, the first of a new breed of airliner that would be labelled 'wide-bodied' because of the seating across the main deck for nine or ten passengers.

Pan Am immediately placed an order for 25 of the new aircraft which was nicknamed the 'Jumbo Jet' by the media, because of its size. The height of the 'plane from the ground to the top of the fin was 63ft 5in. There were two aisles on the main deck and first-class accommodation was situated above the flight deck on the upper level. It was capable of carrying in excess of 350 passengers.

The first Jumbos were fitted with four Pratt and Whitney 41,000lb thrust turbo-fan engines, each with a diameter of approximately 8ft. The maiden flight of the new aircraft was on 9 February 1969 over Puget Sound, Seattle, and the Pan Am service from New York to London started on 22 January 1970. It is now hard to imagine the aircraft industry without the Jumbo.

KEELER, Christine

IN 1963 Christine Keeler was Britain's most notorious woman when she was at the centre of the Profumo scandal which resulted in the War Minister resigning.

Born at Wraysbury, near Slough, in 1942, 'Chrissie', as she was known to her friends, was a former chorus-line girl at Murray's Club, London. But her notoriety stemmed from her relationship with minister John Profumo, who she met at the West End flat of osteopath Dr Stephen Ward, having earlier met him at Ward's Cliveden Cottage on Lord Astor's estate.

At the same time as the affair with Profumo, she was also having a similar relationship with the Russian diplomat Eugene Ivanov. He was purported to have asked Keeler to obtain information from Profumo about defence.

There was never any proof that such information was passed, but the situation was one of grave concern, and indeed embarrassment, to the Government, particularly after Profumo had initially denied any such relationship with Keeler.

In her biography, *Mandy*, Keeler's former flatmate, Mandy Rice-Davies, said that Christine was too patriotic to ask Profumo the questions Ivanov put to her.

In December 1963 Christine was jailed for nine months after pleading guilty to a charge of perjury and conspiracy to pervert the course of justice, involving her former boyfriend 'Lucky' Gordon. It was nothing to do with the Profumo affair.

Keeler was released from Holloway

prison in June 1964 and has since tried to pick up the pieces of her life. She ended up living in a high-rise flat in Chelsea, and amongst the jobs she tried her hand at was as an Agony Aunt for *Men Only* as she struggled to make ends meet.

Scandal, a film of the Profumo Affair, was released in 1989 amidst much publicity. It turned out to be a big box office success. Christine had earlier made a substantial sum of money from her biography.

KENNEDY, John Fitzgerald

JOHN Fitzgerald Kennedy, affectionately known as JFK, served as President of the United States for less than three years. But in that short period he became one of the most popular Presidents in US history.

The son of the wealthy Joseph Patrick Kennedy, JFK was born at Brookline, Massachusetts, in 1917. He was educated at Harvard and London, and stayed in London to work at the American Embassy after completing his education. Kennedy then served in the US Navy and won a Purple Heart before entering politics as a Democratic Representative in 1947. He became a Senator five years later. In 1953 he married Jacqueline Lee Bouvier, who was later to become America's 'First Lady'.

Jackie Kennedy on a visit to Greece in June 1961.

When he was elected the 35th President in 1960, Kennedy became, at 42, the youngest-ever President, and was also the country's first Roman Catholic leader.

During his short term of office he did much for the Civil Rights movement and averted possible nuclear warfare because of his handling of the Cuban missile crisis. It was also under Kennedy's tenure at the White House that American involvement in the space race was increased.

Kennedy died in Dallas on 22 November 1963, when he became the fourth reigning US President to lose his life at the hands of an assassin.

Assassinated US Presidents:
15 Apr 1865   ABRAHAM LINCOLN
Shot by James Wilkes Booth while watching a play at the Ford's Theatre, Washington, on 14 April.

19 Sep 1881   JAMES ABRAM GARFIELD
Shot by Charles Guiteau while entering a railroad station in Washington on 2 July 1881. Died ten weeks later.

14 Sep 1901   WILLIAM McKINLEY
Shot by anarchist Leon Czolgosz while welcoming citizens to the Pan-American exhibition at Buffalo, New York, on 6 September.

22 Nov 1963   JOHN FITZGERALD KENNEDY
Shot in motorcade at Dallas, Texas. Assassin believed to be Lee Harvey Oswald.

KENNEDY, Robert

THE YOUNGER brother of President John F. Kennedy, Bobby was born in 1925. Like his brother, he was to lose his life at the hands of an assassin.

Educated at Harvard and Virginia Universities, he was admitted to the Massachusetts State Bar in 1951 and to the US Supreme Court in 1955. He acted as the campaign manager for his brother in 1960 as he sought, and won, election to the White House.

Robert was given the post of Attorney General in his brother's administration and in 1964 promoted his Civil Rights Act. When he was overlooked in preference to Hubert Humphrey as Lyndon B.Johnson's vice-president nominee in 1964, he quit and became Senator for New York. He campaigned for the Presidency in 1968 but shortly after his victory in the Democratic nomination in California, his life was taken on 6 June that year when he was shot by a Jordanian-Arab, Sirhan Bissara Sirhan, at the Ambassador Hotel, Los Angeles.

After making a brief campaign speech in the hotel ballroom he left, accompanied by a bevy of aides, advisors and bodyguards, including ex-Olympic decathlon gold medallist, Rafer Johnson, and professional footballer Roosevelt Grier. Suddenly the assassin appeared and fired three .22 calibre bullets and Bobby Kennedy lay dying.

Robert Francis Kennedy was destined to follow in his brother's footsteps. He was a good politician and he was well liked. He was popular with the young and with opponents of the Vietnam war. Surely he was only one step away from becoming President of the United States when the assassin's bullet ended that dream and created more anguish for the Kennedy family.

KENYATTA, Jomo

JOMO Kenyatta was the assumed name of Kamua Ngengi, the son of a Kenyan farmer brought up at a Church of Scotland mission.

As a politician Kenyatta rose to fame shortly after the war as leader of the *Mau Mau*, who were fighting an armed struggle for their country's independence. He was elected president of the Kenyan African Union party in 1946 and in 1961 became an MP before assuming the role as Kenya's Prime Minister in June 1963. Six months later he led the country to independence and in 1964 became President of the Republic of Kenya.

In 1953 he was sentenced to seven years hard labour for his *Mau Mau* involvement and went into temporary exile after his release.

Jomo Kenyatta died in 1978 at the age of 89.

KHRUSHCHEV, Nikita

NIKITA Sergeyevich Khrushchev, along with President Kennedy, provided the bulk of interest in world politics in the early 1960s.

Nikita Khrushchev and President John F.Kennedy at the US Embassy in Vienna in June 1961.

Born near Kursk in 1894, he was reported to be almost illiterate until his mid-20s and his rise up the Communist Party ladder was a dramatic one.

He joined the Party in 1918 and

became a full member of the Politburo in 1939. After the war he announced plans for a massive reconstruction of the Soviet agricultural programme. In 1953, after the death of Stalin, he became leader of the All Union Party.

As the 1960s dawned, the arms and space races were well and truly on and, while Khrushchev was intent on projecting Russia's image outside the country, he still had arms at the forefront of his mind. When the Cuban crisis erupted in 1962, Khrushchev showed typical displays of anger, protest, and stubbornness. Nevertheless, he was forced to give way and President Kennedy gained a 'moral' victory.

He was deposed in 1964 and the one-time most powerful man behind the Iron Curtain went into retirement. When Nikita Khrushchev died in 1971 there was no official Soviet recognition of either his death or his achievements.

Johnny KIDD and The Pirates

JOHNNY Kidd and the Pirates enjoyed success at the beginning of the sixties just before the start of the Mersey boom. They had only two Top Ten hits but one of them, *Shakin' All Over* (co-written by Kidd), was one of the classics of the sixties.

Lead singer Kidd was born as Frederick Heath in London in 1939. On stage he used to dress in black leather and wear an eye patch. After having a minor solo hit with *Please Don't Touch* in 1959, he formed the Pirates which consisted of Mike Green (guitar), Johnny Spence (bass) and Frank Farley (drums). After another minor hit, *Shakin' All Over* then spent 19 weeks in the charts in 1960, and went to number one on 4 August.

The group's next three records were nowhere near as successful and it was not until 1963 that Kidd had a Top Ten hit again with *I'll Never Get Over You*. After that it was an uphill struggle against the new sounds which had emerged and the once-distinctive sound of Johnny Kidd was no longer required in the world of pop.

Johnny Kidd was killed in a car crash on 7 October 1966, and ten years later Mick Green re-formed the original Pirates, but the revival didn't last long.

KING, Billie Jean

LOOKING for the outstanding lawn tennis player of the sixties was an easy task. One has to go no further than the bespectacled Billy Jean King, the 'Queen' of Wimbledon.

Billie-Jean King during her Wimbledon Women's Singles Final against Britain's Ann Jones in 1967.

Martin Luther King Junior (centre) taking part in a Civil Rights march in 1965.

Born in Long Beach, California, in 1943, she appeared in 13 Wimbledon finals in the 1960s. She won nine titles, including the singles on three consecutive occasions.

Her first title was in 1961 when she played as Billie Jean Moffitt. With Karen Hantze she won the ladies doubles title, beating the Australian pair Jan Lehane and Margaret Smith. It was Smith who beat Billie Jean in her first singles final in 1963. But she eventually lifted the crown in 1966 when she beat the great Brazilian Maria Bueno 6-3, 3-6, 6-1.

Britain's Ann Jones lost to King in the final a year later and Billie Jean completed her hat-trick by beating Judy Tegart of Australia. A fourth consecutive title was thwarted when Ann Jones gained revenge for her 1967 defeat by winning the 1969 final 3-6, 6-3, 6-2.

Billie Jean, who married Californian lawyer Larry King in 1965, went on to win three more singles titles, the last in 1975. In 1979 she won her 20th and record-breaking Wimbledon title. Coincidentally, Elizabeth Ryan, the woman who previously held the record, died the day before Billie Jean's last triumph.

KING, Dr Martin Luther, Junior

DR MARTIN Luther King Junior was a fervent supporter of the American Civil Rights movement in the 1960s but he believed that improved rights for negroes could be obtained without violence. It is ironic, therefore, that he should die at the hands of an assassin.

King was born in 1929, at Atlanta, Georgia, scene of many race riots in the 1960s. His father was a Baptist pastor and Martin studied Theology at Boston University. He became a Civil Rights leader and for his efforts

> "I still have a dream. It is a dream chiefly rooted in the American dream. I have a dream that one day this nation will rise up and live out the true meaning of its creed. We hold these truths to be self-evident, that all men are created equal. I have a dream that the sons of former slaves and the former sons of slave owners would sit together at the table of brotherhood."
> Washington DC, 28 August 1963.

received the Kennedy Peace Prize and, in 1964, the Nobel Peace Prize.

In Washington, DC, in 1963, King had given his moving 'I have a dream' speech to 200,000 followers.

He was gunned down at Memphis, Tennessee, in 1968 (see ASSASSINATIONS). Blacks throughout America mourned a great man who had done much to unite black and white.

Since 1986, Martin Luther King Day on 15 January has been officially recognized throughout the United States. To mark the first celebration of the holiday, President Reagan unveiled a bust of King in the Great Rotunda at the Capitol. He was the first black person, amongst many notable leaders, to have a bust in the Rotunda.

KINKS, The

THE KINKS hailed from Muswell Hill, London, and were known as *The Muswell Hill Hippies* and also the *Muswell Hillbillies*. They formed their band in 1961 with the intention of raising enough money to survive

while they continued their studies at art college.

The group consisted of brothers Ray and Dave Davies, Peter Quaife and Michael Avory. Because of their way-out clothes they were described as 'kinky', hence the group's name. They became popular in the Muswell Hill area and received invitations to play at high-class parties and balls.

Their music was brought to the attention of Larry Page and he secured a contract with Pye. The Kinks' first record *Long Tall Sally* was not a chart-buster. Neither was their next. But record number three, *You Really Got Me*, written by Ray Davies, became a million seller and number one. It was one of the great records of the 1960s and is still regarded as a classic.

Ten more chart hits followed in the 1960s and they had a huge following of Mods, who identified themselves with the group. In addition to their successes, Dave Davies had a hit single with *Death Of A Clown* in 1967. It reached number three.

The group became largely anonymous in the 1970s, although Ray Davies enjoyed a brief flirtation on television. They returned to the studios in 1983 to record *Come Dancing* which made the Top Twenty reaching number 12. They also reissued *You Really Got Me* but it did not have the same impact the second time around.

Top Ten hits of The Kinks in the 1960s:

Year	Record	Pos
1964	You Really Got Me	1
1964	All Day And All Of The Night	2
1965	Tired Of Waiting For You	1
1965	Set Me Free	9
1965	See My Friend	10
1965	Till The End Of The Day	8
1966	Dedicated Follower Of Fashion	4
1966	Sunny Afternoon	1
1966	Dead End Street	5
1967	Waterloo Sunset	2
1967	Autumn Almanac	3

KOPECHNE, Mary Jo

TWENTY-seven-year-old Washington secretary Mary Jo Kopechne died when a black Oldsmobile driven by Senator Edward Kennedy plunged into Nantucket Sound from a bridge at Chappaquidick Island, New England, at approximately 11.15pm on 18 July 1969. At the same time astronauts Armstrong, Aldrin and Collins were hurtling through space towards an historic moon walk.

Mary Jo, a former secretary of Robert Kennedy, had attended a party at Joseph Gargan's house on the island of Martha's Vineyard. Gargan was a cousin of the Kennedys. It was nine hours before Edward Kennedy reported to the police.

The car was discovered by two boys fishing off the bridge. Police chief Dominic Arena arrived and dived into 8ft of water where he saw the body of Mary Jo lying face upwards. She was dressed in a white blouse, slacks and sandals. He radioed his station and told them to get hold of the Senator and advise him of the accident. At that moment Kennedy had walked into the Martha's Vineyard police station and reported the incident himself.

Five days later, Kennedy pleaded guilty to the charge of leaving the scene of an accident. He was given a suspended two-month prison sentence. He went on television and explained the incident, appealing to the American people to help him decide whether he should resign. On 30 July he announced he was dropping plans to run for President in 1972.

Because death was obviously due to drowning, no post-mortem was carried out. At the inquest in April 1970, the judge said he doubted the truth of Senator Kennedy's testimony. And in 1989, Leslie Leland, the foreman of the Grand Jury, spoke for the first time about the cover-up to try and protect Kennedy's political career.

Above: Mary Jo Kopechne. Below: A frogman recovers her body from the car in Nantucket Sound.

Billy J.Kramer and the Dakotas.

KRAMER, Billy J, and the Dakotas

BORN as William Ashton in the Bootle district of Liverpool in August 1943, Billy J.Kramer worked as an apprentice engineer with British Railways after leaving school. In his spare time he played the guitar and sang. It was after landing the job as lead singer with a group called The Coasters that he changed his name to Kramer.

He became very popular around the North-West clubs and the Beatles' manager, Brian Epstein, got word of this new sensation. Epstein liked what he saw and signed up Billy J., installing him as lead singer with one of Manchester's top bands, The Dakotas.

The group's first two singles, *Do You Want To Know A Secret?* and *Bad To Me* were both Lennon and McCartney compositions. *Bad To Me* went to number one as did *Little Children* in 1964.

Trains And Boats And Planes was the groups' last chart success in 1965 (number 12) but since then the group has continued working and in the '80s have been a popular part of the 'Nostalgic Back to the 1960s' concerts that have toured the country.

Top Ten hits of Billy J.Kramer and the Dakotas in the 1960s:

Year	Record	Pos
1963	Do You Want To Know A Secret?	2
1963	Bad To Me	1
1963	I'll Keep You Satisfied	4
1964	Little Children	1
1964	From A Window	10

KRAY BROTHERS

THE KRAY Brothers consisted of more than twins Ronnie and Reggie. There was also older brother Charles. But while all three have been in a bit of 'bower' over the years, it is Reggie and Ronnie who have claimed the greater notoriety.

Gangland bosses, they ran 'The Firm', and Scotland Yard were intent on closing down their operation. But like Elliot Ness and his ambitions to close down Al Capone, they were often beaten on technicalities. But, in the end, they got their men.

Reggie and Ronnie were born in 1934. They both enlisted in the army as 18-year-olds but both deserted six months later. They left the army with dishonourable records.

Ronnie's first conviction was in 1953 when he was given a one-month prison sentence for assaulting a police officer. Reggie, on the other

hand, had received his first sentence in 1950 when he was given two years probation for causing grievous bodily harm to a police officer.

In April 1965, the twins, plus Edward Smith, were cleared at the Old Bailey of obtaining protection money with menaces from the Hideaway Club, Gerrard Street, Soho. This was a retrial, and proceedings were halted by Mr Justice Lyell who directed the jury to return not guilty verdicts after the unreliability of the one witness upon whose case the prosecution was dependant. Two weeks after being cleared, Reggie got married in a show-business-style wedding.

Three months later, Charles Kray (born 1927) and Cornelius White-head, were cleared of the murder of Frank Mitchell, alias the 'Mad Axeman', who escaped from Dart-moor in December 1966. However, three others, including the Kray twins, were committed for trial charged with Mitchell's murder. They were also committed for trial charged with effecting his escape from prison and harbouring him.

In March 1969, Ronnie and Reggie (and others) appeared in the famous Number One Court at the Central Criminal Court, on a charge of murdering Jack 'The Hat' McVitie and George Cornell. Ronnie was found guilty of both murders while Reggie was convicted of the stabbing of McVitie. They received the longest sentences ever imposed for murder at the Old Bailey. Both men were jailed for life with a recommendation from Mr Justice Melford Stevenson that they serve at least 30 years. At the same time the Judge paid special tribute to the man who had brought the Krays to justice, Detective Superintendent Leonard 'Nipper' Read.

The Kray brothers. Left to right: Reggie, Charles and Ronnie.

Charles Kray received a ten-year sentence as an accessory to McVitie's murder and a further six men received sentences ranging from two years upwards. Leave to appeal by Reggie and Ronnie was refused and shortly after the trial they were split up as Reggie went to Parkhurst and Ronnie went to Durham Jail.

Two months after starting the sentences, the twins, plus Frederick Foreman, were back in court on the Mitchell murder charge. All three were acquitted of the murder but Reggie was found guilty of effecting his escape from prison and for harbouring him for which he received concurrent five-year and nine-month sentences. The other two were acquitted. As he left the dock Reggie bowed to the members of the jury and said: "God bless you, members of the jury."

LADY CHATTERLEY'S LOVER

AFTER being out for three hours, the jury at the Old Bailey trial ruled that *Lady Chatterley's Lover* by D.H. Lawrence was not an obscene publication and could go on general sale.

The book had been banned in Britain for 30 years because of its explicit love scenes and strong

language. But it was ruled in 1960 that the book could be released to the public. And what an impact it had. Like the *Spycatcher* case 20 years later, the six-day trial did much for advance sales. When the 3s 6d Penguin paperback hit the book-stands, the first 200,000 copies were sold in one day.

So, what was all the fuss about? Well, the story told the tale of the frustrated Lady Chatterley whose husband couldn't fulfil her sexual desires. She chose to seek 'comfort' from her gamekeeper Mellors . . .and they banned that for 30 years? It's the sort of thing kids watch on TV these days!

LANCASTER, Burt

BURT Lancaster started his show business career as a member of the circus acrobatic act Nick Cravat, Lang and Cravat. But his movie career took off after his performance with Deborah Kerr in *From Here To Eternity* in 1953, when he was involved in that romantic scene on the beach with his co-star. Despite calls of it being obscene and degenerate, the film won an Oscar.

Born as Burton Stephen Lancaster in New York City in 1913, he made his film debut playing the part of a Swede in *The Killers* in 1946. But since his appearance as Sgt Warden in *From Here To Eternity*, Lancaster went on to play some notable parts including Wyatt Earp in *Gunfight At The OK Corral* (1957), the title role in *Elmer Gantry* for which Lancaster won an Oscar, Ernst Jannings in *Judgement At Nuremberg* and, perhaps one of his best-known roles, Robert Stroud in *Birdman Of Alcatraz*, for which he received an Oscar nomination.

In 1970 he appeared in the first of the 'disaster' movies that hit the screens when he played Mel Bakersfield in *Airport*.

Films of Burt Lancaster in the 1960s:

The Unforgiven	(1960)
Elmer Gantry	(1960)
The Young Savages	(1961)
Judgement At Nuremberg	(1961)
Birdman Of Alcatraz	(1962)
A Child Is Waiting	(1963)
The List Of Adrian Messenger	(1963)
The Leopard	(1963)
Seven Days In May	(1964)
The Train	(1965)
The Hallelujah Trail	(1965)
The Professionals	(1966)
The Scalphunters	(1968)
The Swimmer	(1968)
Castle Keep	(1969)
The Gypsy Moths	(1967)

LAVER, Rod

ROD Laver, the 'Rockhampton Rocket', was the most outstanding male tennis player of the sixties, and one of the finest produced by Australia.

Born in Langdale, Queensland, in 1938, he won successive men's singles titles at Wimbledon in 1961 and 1962. He then turned professional but returned to the sport's top event after it went open in 1968 and won his third title. He followed that a year later by beating fellow Aussie John Newcombe to win title number four.

But it was not just at Wimbledon that Laver was outstanding. The left-hander with the lethal serve was equally at home in the other leading tournaments and in 1962 became the second man, after Donald Budge, to perform the Grand Slam. He went on, in 1969, to become the first man to twice achieve tennis' ultimate

Australian tennis star Rod Laver holds up the Wimbledon Men's Singles trophy which he has just won by beating fellow Australian Tony Roche, 6-3, 6-4, 6-2 in July 1968. It was Laver's third title.

success when he won all four major tournaments again.

In the 1970s, and with youth starting to dominate the game, Laver slipped away and into the over-35s veteran events that were established and today is still a very active member of that circuit.

LEMMON, Jack

JACK Lemmon was born as John Uhler Lemmon in Boston on 8 February 1925. He was educated at Harvard and later served as a communications officer in the Naval Reserve before embarking on a career in the world of entertainment where he started life as a piano player.

He made his film debut in the 1954 movie *It Should Happen To You* opposite Judy Holliday. A year later he won the best supporting actor Oscar for his role in *Mister Roberts*. And in 1959 he won a British Academy Award for his performance alongside Tony Curtis and Marilyn Monroe in the classic Hollywood comedy *Some Like It Hot*.

As the sixties approached, Lemmon was becoming a big box office hit in the United States and during the decade most of his films saw him cast in a comedy role and one of his best performances was Baxter in *The Apartment*. As the alcoholic Joe Clay in *Days Of Wine And Roses*, he showed how underestimated he was as a straight actor.

His other leading sixties films included *The Odd Couple*, *The Fortune Cookie* and *Irma La Douce*.

After receiving Oscar nominations for his roles in *Some Like It Hot*, *The Apartment* and *Days Of Wine And Roses*, he eventually won the elusive award for his part in *Save The Tiger* in 1973. He nearly repeated the feat at the 1983 awards ceremony following his part in *Missing*, but was beaten by Ben Kingsley for *Gandhi*.

Films of Jack Lemmon in the 1960s:

The Apartment	(1960)
Pepe	(1960)
The Wackiest Ship In The Army	(1961)
The Notorious Landlady	(1962)
Days Of Wine And Roses	(1962)
Irma La Douce	(1963)
Under The Yum-Yum Tree	(1963)
Good Neighbour Sam	(1964)
How To Murder Your Wife	(1965)
The Great Race	(1965)
The Fortune Cookie	(1966)
Luv	(1967)
The Odd Couple	(1968)

LONG-DISTANCE WALKING

IAN Botham hit the headlines in the 1980s for his much publicised John O'Groats to Land's End and 'Elephant' walks. But the Test cricketer's ideas were far from new. Had he been old enough in the early 1960s he would have been just one of many people trekking up and down Britain.

Fifty-six-year-old Dr Barbara Moore was responsible for the craze of long-distance walking in 1960. Having set a new time for the 373-mile walk from Edinburgh to London, she then set her sights on Britain's longest walk, from John O'Groats (the northern tip of Scotland) to Land's End (the south-western tip of England).

In January 1960 she set off on the trek that was to take her through snow, floods and gales. But she was not the only one to make the trip. Liverpool hairdressing sisters Joy (22) and Wendy (19) Lewis were in pursuit of the Doctor and making the trip in the opposite direction was Julian Nielson. Britain was inundated with people walking the length of the country!

Dr Barbara Moore, aged 56, after being fined £25 for speeding in a bubble-car in 1960.

Moore completed the journey on 4 February 1960 and was followed home by Wendy Lewis. Joy Lewis was forced to pull out at Okehampton, Devon, with a septic foot. Moore and Nielson passed each other going in opposite directions near Bridgwater.

These treks spurred Billy Butlin into setting up a John O'Groats to Land's End walking race. More than 700 entrants took part hoping to lift the two £1,000 first prizes on offer; one for men and the other for women. The men's prize went to Doncaster glassworker James Musgrave while Wendy Lewis was the first woman home in only 17 days.

Other long-distance walks were planned and attempted. Dr Moore walked across the United States, as did two British soldiers, while all sorts of people were hoping to grab attention by doing the John O'Groats to Land's End trip (or vice versa) including several grandfathers and grandmothers.

LOREN, Sophia

SOPHIA Loren was undoubtedly one of the most glamorous film stars of the sixties. Today, more than 20 years later, she still looks pretty good.

Born into poverty in 1934, her real name is Sophia Villani Scioloni, and she is the illegitimate sister of Mussolini's daughter-in-law. She won the 'Princess of the Sea' beauty contest in her home town, Naples, in 1948, and two years later was voted 'Miss Elegance'. That same year her

Sophia Loren in typically sexy pose.

mother took her to Rome to try and find work in the film industry. After both appeared as extras in *Quo Vadis* they met Carlo Ponti and he gave Sophia a small role in the film *Anna*. Ponti changed Sophia's surname to Loren, became her manager, and subsequently her husband (the lucky man!).

In 1961 she won the best actress Oscar for her performance in *Two Women*, making her the first person to win an Oscar for a performance in a foreign language film. It was made in Italy and directed by Vittorio de Sica.

Other films for which she received acclaim in the sixties included *El Cid*, *Judith* and the Peter Sellers comedy classic *The Millionairess* from which the duo had a number-four British Top Ten hit with *Goodness Gracious Me*. Her first American-made film was *The Pride And The Passion* in which she starred opposite Cary Grant and Frank Sinatra.

For income tax irregularities Sophia Loren served 17 days of a month's prison sentence in a Rome jail in 1982. What a way to treat one of the great sex symbols of the silver screen, and probably the best looking of them all.

Films of Sophia Loren in the 1960s:

Pink Tights	(1960)
It Started In Naples	(1960)
A Breath Of Scandal	(1960)
The Millionairess	(1960)
Two Women	(1961)
El Cid	(1961)
Madame	(1961)
Five Miles To Midnight	(1962)
The Condemned Of Altaria	(1962)
Yesterday, Today And Tomorrow	(1963)
The Fall Of The Roman Empire	(1964)
Marriage Italian Style	(1964)
Judith	(1965)
Operation Crossbow	(1965)
Lady L	(1965)
Arabesque	(1966)
A Countess From Hong Kong	(1966)
More Than A Miracle	(1967)
Cinderella Italian Style	(1967)
Happily Ever After	(1967)
Ghosts Italian Style	(1967)

LULU

LULU made a dramatic entrance on to the pop scene with *Shout*, one of the liveliest records of 1964. She was hailed as the 'British Brenda Lee' but unlike her American mentor, Lulu has survived the test of time.

Born in Glasgow in 1948, her full name is Marie McDonald McLaughlin Lawrie. She was singing by the time she could walk and at the age of six won a talent contest in Blackpool.

In 1963 she was singing with a group called the Gleneagles. She was recommended to London impres-sario Marian Massey, who arranged a recording contract for the group, whose name was then changed to Lulu and the Luvvers. Their first record, *Shout*, which was a cover version of an old Isley Brothers hit, was released in 1964 and reached number seven. Remarkably when the record was re-released in 1986 it reached only one place lower in the charts, number eight.

The lively act of Lulu became much sought after and in 1966 she became the first British female pop singer to appear behind the Iron Curtain when she performed in Poland. The following year she appeared with Sidney Poitier in the film *To Sir With Love*. The title song gave her a number-one hit in the States. Surprisingly, it never charted in Britain.

Lula married Maurice Gibb of the Bee Gees in 1969 but the marriage lasted only four years. Since then, although she has made too few visits to the recording studios, Lulu has been kept busy by hosting television programmes, having her own show on Capitol Radio and appearing on the West End stage and in pantomime. She also played the part of Adrian Mole's mum in the popular television series.

Lulu is now married to top hairdresser John Freida and lives a millionairess's lifestyle in Mayfair.

Top Ten hits of Lulu in the 1960s:

Year	Record	Pos
1964	Shout	7
1965	Leave A Little Love	8
1967	The Boat That I Row	6
1968	Me The Peaceful Heart	9
1968	I'm A Tiger	9
1969	Boom Bang-a-Bang	2

MacLAINE, Shirley

IF EVER there was a classic case of being 'in the right place at the right time', then Shirley MacLaine is that example.

Born as Shirley MacLean Beaty in 1934, she is the older sister of Warren Beatty (he changed his name from Beaty to Beatty). Having appeared in the chorus line of *Oklahoma* she was Carol Haney's understudy in the stage production of *The Pyjama Game*. When Haney hurt her ankle Shirley stepped in, and in the audience that night was film producer Hal Wallis. He was so impressed he gave her a contract and the following year she made her screen debut in Hitchcock's *The Trouble With Harry*.

Since then she has become one of the most versatile of all Hollywood performers as a singer, dancer and actress. She has also tried her hand at writing and wrote a book about travel in China entitled *You Can't Get There From Here*. She also wrote several popular autobiographies.

Her best known film in the sixties was *The Apartment* in which she played the part of the mistress, Fran Kubelik and, along with co-star Jack Lemmon, won an Oscar nomination. She also received an Oscar nomination in 1963 for the title role in *Irma La Douce*. Her portrayal of Charity Hope Valentine in *Sweet Charity* in 1968 gave her the chance to display her dancing talents as well as her acting skills.

Having also received two other unsuccessful Oscar nominations (*Some Came Running* in 1958 and *The Turning Point* in 1977) Shirley eventually got her just rewards when she received the best actress award at the 1983 ceremony following her portrayal of the slightly eccentric Aurora Greenway in *Terms Of Endearment*.

Films of Shirley MacLaine in the 1960s:

Can-Can	(1960)
The Apartment	(1960)
Ocean's Eleven	(1960)
Two Loves	(1961)
My Geisha	(1962)
The Children's Hour	(1962)
Two For The Seesaw	(1962)
Irma La Douce	(1963)
What A Way To Go!	(1964)
John Goldfarb Please Come Home	(1964)
The Yellow Rolls Royce	(1965)
Gambit	(1966)
Woman Times Seven	(1967)
Sweet Charity	(1968)
The Bliss Of Mrs Blossom	(1968)

MACMILLAN, Harold

HAROLD Macmillan was the Prime Minister who told us in 1957: "You've never had it so good!" And how right he proved to be, especially in the 1960s.

Educated at Eton and Oxford, Macmillan joined the family publi-

> "The wind of change is blowing through this continent and, whether we like it or not, this growth of national consciousness is a positive fact."
> Harold Macmillan, Cape Town, 3 February 1960.

shing business before successfully standing as the Conservative candidate for Stockton-on-Tees in 1924. He lost his seat in 1929 but was re-elected in 1940. He lost the seat again in the Labour Party landslide of 1945, but returned to the Commons a few months later as MP for Bromley, which remained his constituency until his retirement in 1964.

He held a series of Cabinet positions as Minister of Housing, Defence, Foreign Secretary and Chancellor of the Exchequer before, in 1957, succeeding Anthony Eden as Prime Minister. One of his first aims was to restore the friendship between Britain and the United States which had been soured following the Suez crisis of 1956. Initially, he was viewed with scepticism but he soon became popular and led the Tories back to power at the 1959 General Election.

Set-backs like the continued refusal of entry into the Common Market, the Vassall spy affair and the Profumo affair rocked the Govern-

Sir Harold Macmillan (right) and Lord Hailsham emerge from Holy Communion, in 1963.

ment and in October 1963, following a prostrate gland operation, Macmillan retired.

'Supermac', as he was nicknamed, later became the First Earl of Stockton and on his maiden speech in the House of Lords, his colleagues were reminded of his wit and political brain. Lord Stockton died on 29 December 1986 at the age of 92.

MAGIC ROUNDABOUT

THE *Magic Roundabout* was launched by the BBC in 1964. Now, 25 years later, it has returned with a cult following as the BBC has put out video copies of the wonderful children's programme which ran until 1977.

How will we ever forget the mop-head look-alike Dougal and of course Florence? There was also Zebedee who was forever bouncing around the set going 'Boing'! Other members of the Roundabout included Brian the snail, Ermintrude the cow, and the rabbit, Dylan.

MAKARIOS III, Archbishop

THE Archbishop and Primate of the Orthodox Church in Cyprus, Makarios III became deeply involved in politics as leader of the *Enosis* (Union with Greece) movement. With Cyprus still under British rule, and Makarios' apparent condoning of *Enosis'* violent tactics, the island was not top of the conscripts' list of places to visit.

Makarios was deported to the Seychelles in 1956 by the British Governor but was released after the terrorism of 1955-59 and was elected President of the Republic of Cyprus in August 1960. In 1964 British troops were flown into the island after fighting broke out between Turks and Greek Cypriots. It was six months before a cease-fire was achieved.

Archbishop Makarios was twice re-elected, in 1968 and 1973. In 1970, he escaped an assassination attempt. He was overthrown by a coup in July 1974 and was air-lifted to England in a Hercules transport 'plane. Reinstated after the Turkish invasion in 1975, he remained in office until his death in 1977, at the age of 64.

MALCOLM X

BORN as Malcolm Little in Omaha, Nebraska, on 19 May 1925, he had a tough upbringing. His father was a Nationalist minister who was murdered by whites and his mother spent 26 years in a mental institution.

Although he came from a middle-class family, he chose to live in the Boston ghetto where he became known as 'Big Red' and once served a ten-year prison sentence as the leader of a gang of armed robbers. It was during his time at the Norfolk prison colony that he found his new identity — Malcolm X.

On his release he joined the Black

Police flank the stretcher bearing the body of Malcolm X, who was felled by a barrage of bullets as he addressed a Harlem, New York, rally.

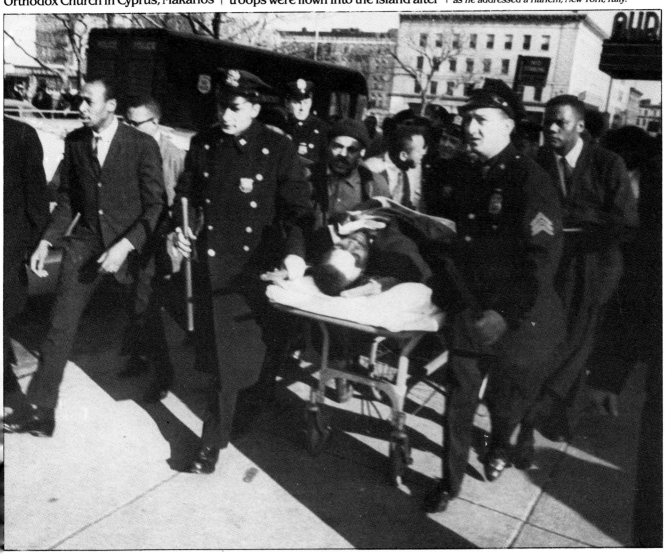

Muslim movement and instead of reverting to crime, turned his attentions to helping the blacks in the ghettos form themselves into a self-help group.

He made known publically his hatred of whites and by 1964 was such a powerful figure in the Black Muslim movement that he was second only to Elijah Mohammed.

After a pilgrimage to Mecca in 1964 he assumed the name El-Hajj El-Shabazz and announced that he was leaving the Black Muslims and forming his own group. During his trip to Mecca he had become more aware that Islam was not limited by colour or race and he turned his attentions towards multi-racial protest and harmony. Nevertheless, he was still regarded as a trouble-maker and racist in the United States.

Malcolm X was assassinated on 21 February 1965 by Black Muslims who could not accept his rejection of their movement.

MAN FROM U.N.C.L.E.

THE EXPLOITS of Napoleon Solo (Robert Vaughn) and Illya Kuryakin (David McCallum) certainly made compulsive viewing in the 1960s as the men from U.N.C.L.E. (The United Network Command for Law Enforcement) tried to stop T.H.R.U.S.H. (Technological Hierarchy for the Removal of Undesirables and the Subjucation of Humanity) from dominating the world.

U.N.C.L.E.'s headquarters were based behind Del Floria's dry cleaning and tailoring repair shop in Manhattan, New York. U.N.C.L.E.'s boss was Alexander Waverly, played by the veteran actor Leo G.Carroll.

A man largely responsible for the series was Ian Fleming, author of the James Bond books, and his influence is obvious when you look at the 007-type gadgetry that the two heroes used.

Some of the well-known names who appeared as guests in the series:
Robert Culp, Cesar Romero, Sharon Tate, Dorothy Provine, Vincent Price, Jill Ireland (McCallum's then real-life wife), Juliet Mills, Joan Collins, Janet Leigh, Jack Pallance, Nancy Sinatra, Victor Borge, Sonny and Cher, Joan Crawford, Telly Savalas, Terry Thomas, Broderick Crawford, Michael Rennie.

The series ended in 1968 after 99 recordings, but those of us who were gullible enough firmly believed the world was a safer place with Solo and Kuryakin around!

Eight feature films of the tremendously popular TV series were made and a television spin-off, *The Girl From U.N.C.L.E.*, featuring Stephanie Powers as Agent April Dancer, and Noel Harrison (son of Rex) as her accomplice Mark Slade, was first seen in 1966.

MANDELA, Nelson

MOST people who lived through the 1960s will have heard more about Nelson Rolihlala Mandela and the ANC in the 1980s than they did 20 years ago. The campaign to free him from his life sentence has been a fervent one in recent years. But in the 1960s he was a strong campaigner against the South African Government's apartheid policies.

Born into the Royal Family of the Tembu tribe in 1918, he was a Johannesburg lawyer before joining the African National Congress (ANC) in 1944 and that was to herald the start of a 20-year campaign against the Government and its policies.

In 1961, Mandela was responsible for a three-day national strike and the following year he was sentenced to a five-year prison term for incitement and for leaving South Africa illegally. During his gaol term he was, in 1964, sentenced to life imprisonment for various political offences including treason. He gave a memorable four-hour speech in his defence at his trial but it did not affect the outcome of his sentence.

Nelson Mandela, known as 'The Black Pimpernel', remains a prisoner despite the efforts of his wife Winnie, and other ANC members, to obtain his release. The Nelson Mandela 70th birthday concert at Wembley Stadium in 1988 attracted thousands of fans and highlighted the strength of feeling for his cause throughout Britain and the rest of the world.

MANFRED MANN

MANFRED Mann was no ordinary pop singer. Just look at this pedigree. Born as Michael Lubowitz in Johannesburg in 1941, he studied at the Vienna Academy and then the Juilliard School of Music in New York. In 1961 he came to Britain, where his love of music saw him team up with drummer Mike Hugg and guitarist Mike Vickers to form the Mann-Hugg Blues Brothers. They played mostly in the coffee bars and clubs in the south of England and specialized in jazz and rhythm and blues.

In 1963, after securing a contract with EMI and having recruited Paul Jones and Tom McGuinness, they started playing under the name of Manfred Mann and the Manfreds, but soon dropped the Manfreds (wouldn't you?)

Their first British hit single, *5-4-3-2-1*, reached number five. The record was used as the theme music for the television pop programme *Ready, Steady, Go*. Despite personnel changes over the next five years (Mike d'Abo in for Paul Jones, and Jack Bruce, later of *Cream* fame, in for Mike Vickers) the group continued with its chart successes and had three number ones.

The band finally split up in 1969, but in 1971 Manfred Mann formed a new band, Manfred Mann's Earth

Manfred Mann.

Band. Six years later they topped the US charts with *Blinded By The Light*. Paul Jones went on to enjoy a solo career as a singer and on stage and television. Tom McGuinness teamed up with Hughie Flint to form McGuinness Flint. They had a monster hit with *When I'm Dead And Gone* in 1970. They were a talented bunch of lads, those early members of Manfred Mann.

> *Jack Bruce was replaced by Klaus Voorman who was responsible for designing the cover illustrations on the Beatles'* Revolver *Album.*

Top Ten hits of Manfred Mann in the 1960s:

Year	Record	Pos
1964	5-4-3-2-1	5
1964	Do Wah Diddy Diddy	1
1964	Sha La La	3
1965	Come Tomorrow	4
1965	If You Gotta Go Go Now	2
1966	Pretty Flamingo	1
1966	Just Like A Woman	10
1966	Semi-detached Suburban Mr.James	2
1967	Ha Ha Said The Clown	4
1968	Mighty Quinn	1
1968	My Name Is Jack	8
1968	Fox On The Run	5
1969	Ragamuffin Man	8

MANSON, Charles

CHARLES Manson was born in 1935. He was the illegitimate son of a prostitute and spent much of his life from the age of 11 in one penal institution or another.

In 1967 he boarded a long-distance bus — destination unknown.

The long-haired, bearded, guitar-playing Manson alighted in the Haight-Ashbury district of San Francisco, the centre of flower power and the hippie movement. He soon established a following and set up his own commune in nearby Hollywood Hills. His following was to develop into a bloodthirsty Satanic cult who would steal, maim and murder to satisfy the demands of their leader, Manson.

On 8 August 1969, the 'Manson family' carried out an horrific crime that was to shock the American nation.

They entered the Beverly Hills home of actress Sharon Tate, wife of Roman Polanski, and savagely murdered her, three of her friends and a passer-by. Sharon was eight months pregnant at the time and was stabbed 16 times by members of the Manson family. The word 'pig' was daubed in Sharon's blood over the front door of the house.

Sharon Tate at the age of 22.

Charles Manson leaves a Los Angeles courthouse after being found guilty of the first-degree murders of seven people, including Sharon Tate.

These five murders were not the only ones perpetrated by the 'family'. Other victims were supermarket owner Leon LaBianca and his wife Rosemary.

For the crimes mentioned, Manson and three female accomplices, Leslie van Houten, Susan Atkins and Patricia Krenwinkel, were found guilty on 29 March 1971 after a 121-day trial which cost over $1 million. On 19 April sentence was officially passed and all four were sentenced to death in the gas chamber. After being found guilty Manson was allowed to address the court. He said: "I have always lived in the truth of this courtroom. I have always done what I was told. Sir, I invented this courtroom — I accept this court as my father."

Charles Manson.

A week later Manson and Atkins faced further charges of murder. Both were charged with murdering musician Gary Hinman in July 1969, and Manson alone was charged with the murder of stuntman Donald 'Shorty' O'Shea. They were both found guilty of their respective charges in November 1971.

However, two months earlier, Charles 'Tex' Watson admitted to killing Sharon Tate and was found guilty of her murder on 13 October. He maintained he did the killings under the orders of Manson, and at the end of the trial pleaded insanity but was, nevertheless, sentenced to death for the murder of Tate and six others.

None of the 'family' went to the gas chamber because on 18 February 1972 the Californian Supreme Court declared the death penalty unconstitutional. Manson's death penalty was commuted to nine life sentences and he was taken off Death Row at San Quentin.

Manson remains incarcerated but is unrepentant about the misery and anguish he caused.

MARTIN, Millicent

BORN in 1934, Millicent Martin gained fame as the TW3 girl in the satirical *That Was The Week That Was* as she sang the introduction to the programme with a montage of the week's news in song form.

Born in Romford, Essex, her first acting role was at the age of 16 when she appeared in *Blue For A Boy*. She followed that with an appearance in *South Pacific* and between 1954 and 1957 toured the United States in a production of *The Boyfriend*.

Millicent later had her own TV series, *The Millicent Martin Show* and *From A Bird's Eye View,* in which she played an air hostess. It ran only for a brief spell in 1970.

Other films of hers included *Alfie* in which she appeared in the opening scene in a car with Michael Caine, and again in the closing scene. She also appeared in *Stop The World I Want To Get Off.*

Millicent was once married to singer Ronnie Carroll.

McQUEEN, Steve

STEVE McQueen received much acclaim following his performance as Vin in *The Magnificent Seven,* one of the best films of the 1960s. He followed that with a great performance in *Bullitt,* in which he did a lot of his own stunt work during the memorable car chase.

McQueen gained a reputation for playing tough guys and this was displayed to its fullest in *The Great Escape,* yet another great film of the '60s. Again he did his own stunt work during the motor-cycle chase.

McQueen was born at Indianapolis on 24 March 1930. It was hardly surprising therefore that later in life

After starring in Getaway in 1972 McQueen married his co-star, Ali McGraw, the following year.

he enjoyed the thrills and spills of motor-racing. His early childhood saw him as a rebel and at 14 he was sent to a reform school. He later joined the Marines and then had a succession of jobs, ranging from encyclopaedia salesman, barman, taxi mechanic and poker player. He decided on an acting career and went to drama school.

After minor success in television, McQueen appeared in such low-budget movies as *The Blob* and *Never Love A Stranger,* but his big break came when he appeared in *The Magnificent Seven.* Thereafter, he enjoyed success with almost every film in which he appeared and in 1967 he received an Oscar nomination for *The Sand Pebbles.*

McQueen contracted a rare form of lung cancer and while undergoing surgery in Mexico on 7 November 1980, he suffered a heart attack which claimed his life.

The films of Steve McQueen in the 1960s:

The Magnificent Seven	(1960)
The Honeymoon Machine	(1961)
Hell Is For Heroes	(1962)
The War Lover	(1962)
Love With The Proper Stranger	(1963)
Soldier In The Rain	(1963)
The Great Escape	(1963)
Baby, The Rain Must Fall	(1965)
The Cincinatti Kid	(1965)
Nevada Smith	(1966)
The Sand Pebbles	(1966)
Bullitt	(1968)
The Thomas Crown Affair	(1968)
The Reivers	(1969)

MICHELMORE, Cliff, CBE

THE genial front man of a variety of television shows over the years, Cliff Michelmore was born in Cowes, Isle of Wight, on 11 December 1919 and worked for the British Forces Network while serving in the RAF. His first job with the BBC was as a writer of children's stories before becoming a sports commentator and interviewer.

Between 1957 and 1964 he fronted the *Tonight* programme, and between 1964 and 1968 worked on *24 Hours*. In 1969 he started work on the first of the holiday programmes for which he has been better known in recent years.

Cliff helped present the popular *Two Way Family Favourites* on BBC Radio on Sunday lunchtimes and he would often link up from his Hamburg base with the London presenter, Jean Metcalfe, whom he eventually married. Cliff was awarded the CBE for his services to radio and television.

MILES, Michael

NEW Zealander Michael Miles was the host of one of television's most popular quiz shows of the 1960s, *Take Your Pick*. It was so successful that at its peak it spent more weeks in the Top Ten ratings than any other programme except *Coronation Street*.

Born in 1920, Miles worked in New Zealand and Australia before getting a job as a newsreader in Singapore. He came to Britain and became host of *Take Your Pick* in 1955 and was its 'quiz inquisitor' until its last showing in 1968, when Rediffusion dropped the programme after they merged with ABC. It was one of the

forerunners of the many quiz programmes which now crowd British TV screens. Miles was not off the screens for long because he returned the following year as host of *Wheel of Fortune*.

Take Your Pick and Hughie Green's *Double Your Money*, were rivals for the top TV quiz programme in the 1960s and both were popular. Mind you, there wasn't much opposition.

Michael Miles died while on business in Spain in 1971. He was 51 and left a widow and two children.

MILLS, Hayley

BORN in 1946, Hayley Mills is the daughter of Sir John Mills, one of Britain's top actors. Her sister Juliet is also an actress and their aunt, Annette Mills, fronted *Muffin The Mule*, one of the great TV characters of the fifties.

Hayley was a child star and shot to stardom in *Tiger Bay* in 1958 when she appeared alongside her father. One of her best performances was in the classic black and white film *Whistle Down The Wind* when a group of Lancashire children thought they had found Jesus (played by Alan Bates) living in a barn. Hayley and the other kids gave great performances.

Other Hayley Mills films of the sixties included *That Darn Cat, The Chalk Garden* and *Pollyanna,* for which she won a special Oscar.

Hayley married producer/director John Boulting in 1966 but the marriage has since been dissolved.

In recent times she has appeared in the television blockbuster *The Flame Trees Of Thika*.

The films of Hayley Mills in the 1960s:

Pollyanna	(1960)
Whistle Down The Wind	(1961)
The Parent Trap	(1961)
In Search Of The Castaways	(1962)
Summer Magic	(1962)
The Chalk Garden	(1963)
The Moonspinners	(1963)
The Truth About Spring	(1964)
That Darn Cat!	(1965)
Sky West And Crooked	(1965)
The Trouble With Angels	(1965)
The Family Way	(1966)
Pretty Polly	(1967)
Africa — Texas Style!	(1967)
Twisted Nerve	(1968)
Take A Girl Like You	(1969)

MINI CAR

WHEN Alex Issigonis designed the Mini he added a new word to our vocabulary. It became one of *the* words of the sixties.

The Mini made its debut on 26 August 1959. Less than six years later, in 1965, the millionth model rolled off the production line.

Because of the Suez crisis in 1956 there was a need to develop smaller, more economical cars. The bubble cars had made their appearance on British roads in the late 1950s and these were eventually superceded by the Mini.

The first BMC Minis were cheap to buy and economical to run. They brought new car ownership within the reach of many who had given up hope of owning a new car. A Mini cost around £500 to put on the road.

While the interior was basic, Issigonis cleverly designed the transverse mounted engine which drove the front wheels. He also placed the four small 10in wheels, each independently suspended, one at each corner of the car to allow for more room inside. The controls were basic; the front windows were sliding rather than winding, the gear lever was massive, and pull strings were used to open the door. But for £500 you couldn't have expected much more.

The cars were available under both the Morris and Austin names as the Austin Seven and Morris Mini-Minor. It was not long before 'new' minis, like the Riley Elf and Wolseley Hornet were on the market. Rootes also developed their own 'mini', the Hillman Imp, but none ever matched the popularity of the Mini and today, while it has had to make way for its slightly bigger

Austin Mini Super de luxe Saloon.

brother, the Metro, the Mini remains a good seller.

In the early days the most popular colours for the Mini were light blue and dark green and youngsters of the day started a craze of packing as many bodies as they could into a Mini!

Alexander Arnold Constantine Issigonis died in 1988 at the age of 82.

The following chart shows how production of the Mini increased throughout the 1960s. The figures on the right indicate the cost of the basic Mini, including car tax and purchase tax.

1959	19,749	£495 19s 0d
1960	116,677	£495 19s 0d
1961	157,059	£495 19s 0d
1962	216,087	£526 5s 0d
1963	236,713	£447 13s 0d
1964	244,359	£469 16s 0d
1965	221,974	£469 16s 0d
1966	213,694	£478 0s 0d
1967	237,227	£508 15s 0d
1968	246,066	£561 2s 0d
1969	254,957	£595 10s 0d

The car peaked in 1971 when 318,475 were produced. The cost of the basic Mini City in 1989 would set you back £4,554, but in real terms it is not much different to the price back in 1959.

MINISKIRT

UNQUESTIONABLY the biggest happening in the fashion world in the sixties was the birth of the miniskirt.

Nobody is quite sure who was responsible for its design, but Mary Quant is regarded as the woman who helped popularize it through her famous *Bazaar* boutique. Paris designer André Courreges should also receive some credit for the miniskirt because of his designs

A great comment from John V. Lindsay, the Mayor of New York City, about the miniskirt: "It will enable young girls to run faster, and because of it, they may have to!"

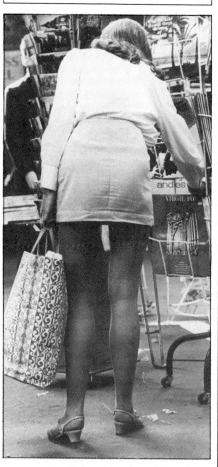

which appeared in an edition of *Vogue* early in 1964.

It was not long before girls all over Britain, and later the United States and the rest of the world, were donning the mini. Hemlines started just above the knee around 1963 but gradually got higher and higher until they were well up the thighs. By December 1965 skirts six inches above the knee were commonplace

in Chelsea and they still kept going up and up and up.

Predictably, the mini brought a temporary end to the days of stockings and suspenders, and made way for the boom in tights, and from the miniskirt came, inevitably, the minidress.

Eric Morley with the Miss World contestants of 1967.

ten years later Rosemarie Frankland became the first United Kingdom winner. Her win heralded the start of a good run for the UK, with two more successes in the 1960s.

One of the most popular winners in the '60s was the Indian girl Reita Faria, the 1966 winner.

1960s winners:

Year	Winner	Country
1960	Norma Cappegli	(Argentina)
1961	Rosemarie Frankland	(UK)
1962	Rina Lodders	(Holland)
1963	Carole Crawford	(Jamaica)
1964	Ann Sidney	(UK)
1965	Lesley Langley	(UK)
1966	Reita Faria	(India)
1967	Madeleine Hartog-Bel	(Peru)
1968	Penny Plummer	(Australia)
1969	Eva Rueber-Staier	(Austria)

MISTER ED

A TELEVISION series about a talking horse — have you ever heard anything so absurd? But as crazy as it sounds, *Mister Ed* was one of the top American television shows of the sixties which gained popularity this side of the Atlantic. Furthermore, it has enjoyed a second successful life in the 1980s just like its contemporaries of 25 years ago: *Bewitched, Beverly Hillbillies, The Munsters* and so on.

Mister Ed was played by a horse called Bamboo Harvester (who couldn't really talk!) In the series Ed is owned by architect Wilbur Post (played by Alan Young) who is the only person who knows that Ed can talk. Wilbur is married to Carol and she, like their neighbours, the Addisons, thinks her husband is a bit eccentric. Mind you, Ed wasn't that far behind. He was a big fan of Leonard Bernstein and insisted on his stable being modernized in Chinese decor!

Mister Ed's voice was supplied by the former cowboy star Allan 'Rocky' Lane. The show ran from 1961-65 and Bamboo Harvester died on 28 February 1979.

MODS AND ROCKERS

THE BATTLES between the mods and rockers became something of a weekend ritual in the 1960s, particularly over Bank Holiday weekends. The first major tussle between the two groups was at Margate on 18 May 1964.

Youths had converged on the town late on Whit Saturday by public transport and on a procession of scooters and motorbikes. Scuffles started at around 7am on the Sunday and the first arrests were made. By lunchtime there had been 11 arrests after the youths had been on a rampage of destruction, breaking shop windows and causing havoc in the Dreamland amusement centre.

MISS WORLD

THE ANNUAL beauty contest to find the world's most glamorous woman and thus earn the title 'Miss World', this event was launched in 1951. It was sponsored by Eric Morley's Mecca empire. Morley's wife, Julia, helped with the organization each year.

The first winner of the title in 1951 was Kiki Haakonson (Sweden) and

The Battle of Hastings 1964. Police take time off from dealing with Mods and Rockers to separate two men who are having their own private argument.

Police reinforcements were brought in and the violence was quelled for a while, but further fighting broke out on the beach in the afternoon. There were more arrests. In the evening a further wave of violence brought yet more arrests as about 100 mods attacked 30 rockers with a wide variety of weapons, mostly broken bottles. Two youths were treated for stab wounds following the skirmishes.

It is reported that approximately 400 youths were involved in the fighting, although police estimated a presence of around one thousand. The number of arrests was 51. Fines totalling £1,900 were imposed and three youths were each sentenced to three months' imprisonment, while another six were sent to detention centres for up to six months. The chairman of the magistrates described the hooligans as 'these long-haired, mentally unstable, petty little sawdust Caesars who seem to find courage like rats by hunting only in packs'.

> 'Mods' was short for Modernists.

Margate was not the only town to feel the force of violence that weekend. A large crowd of mods gathered in Brighton, and there was fighting at Southend, Bournemouth and Clacton. Two months after the Margate clashes police were drafted into Hastings to break up another battle between the factions.

The situation seems to have changed very little some 25 years later. But for 'mods and rockers' read 'lager louts'.

MONKEES, The

IN SEPTEMBER 1965 an advertisement appeared in the *Hollywood Reporter*. It read: 'MADNESS AUDITIONS. Four insane boys aged 17 to 21 required to form a group for a TV show'. There were over 400 applicants, out of which were selected Mickey Dolenz, Mike Nesmith, Peter Tork and the Manchester-born Davy Jones.

The television series was born in 1966 and showed the crazy adventures of the four lads. The story-line of each show was virtually non-existent, but it was good clean fun and appealed to the pop fans of the day. A highlight of each programme was an interlude when the group performed one of their many hit records. The series lasted nearly two years during which time 59 programmes were recorded.

Although it was admitted that they did not play their respective instruments on early recordings, their personality, and the recruitment of such top songwriters as Goffin and King and Neil Diamond ensured the group's phenomenal chart success. Glen Campbell was one of the musicians who played on their early recordings.

In Britain only *I'm A Believer* made it to number one while in the States

Above: Monkees' fans protest about the proposed call-up of Davy Jones to the US Army. Below: The Monkees on stage.

Last Train To Clarksville, I'm A Believer and Daydream Believer all topped the charts.

By 1969, Monkee-mania had gone and the members all went their own way. Davy Jones went back to acting and starred in Godspell for a while and in the 1980s Mickey Dolenz is one of the leading producers of children's television programmes, responsible for Metal Mickey, Murphy's Mob, amongst others, and lives in a country mansion in Nottinghamshire.

Top Ten hits of The Monkees in the 1960s:

Year	Record	Pos
1967	I'm A Believer	1
1967	A Little Bit Me A Little Bit You	3
1967	Alternative Title	2
1967	Daydream Believer	5

MONRO, Matt

MATT Monro's rise to the top was a long, hard road. He was born as Terry Parsons in the Shoreditch district of London in 1930. He completed his National Service as a tank instructor in Hong Kong in 1953 and while serving abroad he had ambitions to become a professional singer. But the breaks were not forthcoming and he had a variety of jobs while waiting for that break.

He was a long distance lorry driver, electrician, milkman, baker and a London bus driver on the No. 27 run from Highgate to Teddington. Monro also dovetailed his activities with singing semi-professionally with the Harry Leader Orchestra. But it was after being spotted by Winifred Atwell that his singing career took steps forward.

Atwell helped promote him, and it was her suggestion that he change his name. The Matt came from a journalist who once interviewed him and Monro from Atwell's father. Monro got a series on Radio Luxembourg in the late-1950s but his real big break came when he met record producer George Martin. In 1960 he had his first big hit under Martin's direction when Portrait Of My Love went to number three in the charts.

After that, the delightfully smooth voice of Matt Monro became a firm favourite with the ladies and, despite the pop boom, he managed to hold his own in the world of groups until the mid-sixties. Despite his lack of chart success, he remained a great favourite and his concerts were often sell-outs.

Runner-up in the Eurovision Song Contest in 1964 with *I Love The Little Things,* he was voted Male Singer of the Year in 1965.

A popular singer with members of the Royal Family, Matt had two homes, one in Ealing and the other in Florida. He died of cancer on 7 February 1985 at the age of 54.

Top Ten hits of Matt Monro in the 1960s:

Year	Record	Pos
1960	Portrait Of My Love	3
1961	My Kind Of Girl	5
1962	Softly As I Leave You	10
1964	Walk Away	4
1965	Yesterday	8

MONROE, Marilyn

ALTHOUGH Marilyn Monroe 'belongs' to the 1950s, and possibly the '80s, it was in 1962 that she died so tragically. And it was a death that shocked millions of fans.

She was born Norma Jean Baker (or Mortenson) on 1 June 1926 and was brought up in a variety of different homes and orphanages because her mother, Gladys, spent a great deal of time in mental institutions. Marilyn claimed she was a descendant of former US President James Monroe.

Despite becoming one of the greatest-ever sex symbols, Marilyn's life was shrouded by anguish and tragedy. She was first married to an aircraft worker at the age of 16; it lasted four years. When she was 20 she got a job as a photographic model and in 1948 was a stripper at the Mayan Burlesque House in Los Angeles. She got her first minor film role that year in the 'B' movie *Ladies Of The Chorus.*

A series of other 'bit' parts followed, but in 1952 she had her first major role in *Don't Bother To Knock* followed by the successful *Niagara.* After that it was one box office success after the other: *Gentlemen Prefer Blondes, How To Marry A Millionaire, Seven Year Itch* and *Some Like It Hot.*

Monroe's talent lay in her brilliant comic timing and, of course, sex appeal.

A marriage to New York Yankees

> *Marilyn Monroe's sexy wiggle was not deliberate. She walked like that because she had weak ankles.*

baseball star, Joe Di Maggio, was dissolved in 1954 after only nine months. In 1956 she married Arthur Miller, who wrote the film in which she gave her finest ever performance, *The Misfits.* But, despite the success, their marriage went the way of Marilyn's other two and was dissolved in 1961, shortly after the completion of the film. It was her last completed film.

Just before her death Marilyn was sacked from the film *Something's Got To Give* for continued absence. The film was later remade with Doris Day in the lead, and it was renamed *Move Over Darling.*

Marilyn Monroe's career was aided by a massive publicity drive which sought to project the greatest sex symbol Hollywood had ever seen. In the end it meant she could not lead a private life and stories abounded about affairs with the Kennedys, secret diaries, and investigations by the FBI and CIA. On the morning of 5 August 1962 she lay naked in her bed at her Mexican-style ranch at Brentwood, Los Angeles. She had a telephone in her hand and by her side lay an empty bottle of barbiturates. Her death was recorded as suicide but there are many who still have their doubts.

Her death at 36 left behind a legend. Today, Marilyn Monroe is idolized by millions, many of whom were not even born when she died.

> *Marilyn Monroe made only two films in the 1960s:* Let's Make Love *(1960) and* The Misfits *(1961).*

Marilyn Monroe wears a smile as she leaves hospital in 1961, after four weeks' psychiatric care.

MONTY PYTHON'S FLYING CIRCUS

WHEN it came to zany comedy and outright lunacy in the sixties, you had to look no further than *Monty Python.*

The series was the idea of Cambridge graduates Graham Chapman, John Cleese, Eric Idle, Terry Jones, Michael Palin and Terry Gillam, who was the programme's animator.

Python used a combination of live and animated sketches. The result — some classics like the 'dead parrot' sketch and, of course, John Cleese's famous 'Ministry of Silly Walks' routine.

Python was first broadcast on 5 October 1969. It started life on BBC2 and was hailed as television's answer to *The Goon Show.* Because of its popularity it was moved from BBC2 to BBC1 and brought forward from its late-night slot. Within 12 months of making its debut, Python was a cult and in 1972 won a BAFTA award as the Best Light Entertainment Programme.

The last series was recorded in 1974 and then sold to America but whenever repeats are shown the programme still gets good audience figures.

MOODY BLUES

THE Birmingham-based Moody Blues were founded by Denny Laine in the early '60s. Laine was to later become an important member of the Paul and Linda McCartney band, Wings.

The five-man Moody Blues soon established themselves as the leading Midlands band of the 1960s. They attracted a bigger audience after appearing at London's famous Marquee Club and were then in big demand on the club circuit and also by radio and television producers.

They signed their first recording contract, with Decca, in the summer of 1964. Their first record for the label, *Lose Your Money*, did not chart but their next became one of pop

The Moody Blues.

music's all-time classics. It was, of course *Go Now*. Written by Larry Banks and Milton Bennett, it was a million seller and topped the British charts.

While *Go Now* was the only top ten entry for the group in the 1960s, it would be wrong to say they were not a success. Their *Nights In White Satin*, while only reaching number 19 in Britain in 1967, was a big hit on the Continent and sold over a million copies after two chart re-entries which reached nine and 14. They also had huge success with their 1969 LP *On The Threshold Of A Dream*. It remained in the album charts for 73 weeks. By this time John Lodge and Justin Hayward had replaced Laine and another founder member, Clint Warwick.

The Moody Blues were regarded as one of the best live bands in the 1960s. Those who saw them will rightly agree. Those who did not missed a treat.

MOON LANDING

THE 1960s was certainly a decade of space exploration. At the start of the decade man made the first space flight. By the end of the '60s Moon walks were almost part of our lives. But the first historic landing on the

Moon by man is the one we all remember as we were kept on tenterhooks waiting for Neil Armstrong to leave the lunar module and take those first steps into the unknown.

Apollo 11 blasted off from Cape Kennedy on 16 July 1969. On board were the commander, 38-year-old Neil Armstrong, Edwin 'Buzz' Aldrin and Michael Collins. Four days later the *Eagle* module landed on the Moon's surface in the Sea of Tranquility. As hundreds of millions sat glued to their television sets for hours, the seemingly never-ending wait for Armstrong to appear ended at 3.56am BST on 21 July when he climbed down the ladder and became the first human to set foot on the Moon. His first words: "That's one small step for a man, one giant leap for mankind" echoed around the world and became one of the great quotes of the century.

Buzz Aldrin climbs down from the lunar module. Neil Armstrong took the picture.

Armstrong was joined on the Moon's surface by Aldrin, while Collins remained in the command module, *Columbia*. An hour and five minutes after man first set foot on the Moon's surface, the United States Stars and Stripes flag was implanted.

Eagle remained on the lunar surface for just under a day. The two astronauts carried out a series of experiments and gathered as much information about the Moon as they could. Two hours before they set off to rejoin *Columbia* an unmanned Russian craft, *Luna 15*, landed on the

Moon about 500 miles from Tranquility base.

Armstrong and Aldrin returned *Eagle* to the command module before splashing down in the Pacific on 24 July, only one mile away from their target. The *Apollo 11* mission lasted 195 hours 18 minutes and 21 seconds. But that second when Neil Armstrong touched his left foot on to the Moon's surface for the first time was the most important moment in space exploration history — not only of the 1960s, but of all time.

Neil Armstrong salutes the Stars and Stripes on the surface of the Moon.

MOORE, Dr Barbara

LONG-DISTANCE walking was the craze in 1960 and the woman who helped popularize it was Dr Barbara Moore, the 56-year-old Russian-born scientist/dietician wife of sculptor Henry Moore.

Having completed three long-distance walks, twice from Birmingham to London and once from Edinburgh to London in a record time of seven days, she embarked on the trek from John O'Groats to Land's End, which she completed in February 1960 in 23 days.

After that she set off for the United States to walk the width of the country. Despite being hit by a motor car on the way she completed the 3,307 mile journey at New York. And all she could say was: "Well, that's that."

Other walks, like the one from Rome to London, followed, and Dr Moore was certainly a lot safer walking than she was behind the wheel of her bubble car . . .in January 1960 she was fined £2 for speeding in Hyde Park and in December 1960 she was involved in an accident with another car at Prees Heath, Shropshire.
(See also LONG-DISTANCE WALKING)

MOORS MURDERS

THE memory of the Moors Murders lingers on more than 20 years after the horrendous crimes of Myra Hindley and Ian Brady. The anguish for the parents will never fade, and the nation's sympathies have constantly gone out to them every time the name of Hindley or Brady is flashed across the front page of the daily newspapers.

On 21 October 1965, Brady, a 27-year-old stock clerk, and 23-year-old Hindley, a typist, both of Wardle Brook Avenue, Hattersley, Hyde, Cheshire, appeared at Hyde Magistrates Court, charged with the murder of ten-year-old Lesley Ann Downey. The youngster disappeared the previous Boxing Day when she left her Ancoats home to visit a local fair. Her body was found 1,400ft up on Saddleworth Moor in the Pennines and three miles away from Greenfield in the West Riding.

At the time of their appearance before Hyde magistrates, Brady was on remand on a charge of murdering 17-year-old Edward Evans on 6 October. Hindley was also on remand on a charge of harbouring Brady. They were reported to the police by Hindley's brother-in-law David Smith on 7 October.

On the same day that Brady and Hindley appeared in court, the body of 12-year-old John Kilbride, who had been missing since leaving his Ashton-under-Lyne home in November 1963 to attend the matinée at a local cinema, was also discovered following a search of the Moors. Brady and Hindley were subsequently charged with his murder.

Myra Hindley.

Ian Brady.

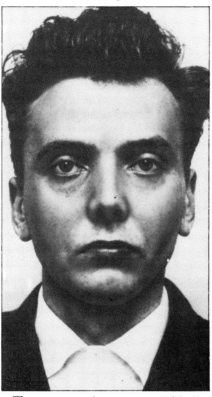

There were ugly scenes outside the courthouse every time Hindley and Brady appeared as the local community built up hatred for the killers.

They were eventually brought to trial at Chester Assizes in the spring of 1966 and on Friday, 6 May the jury returned guilty verdicts on both of the accused. They took two hours 14 minutes to reach their decision.

Brady was found guilty of the murder of Evans, Downey and Kilbride while Hindley was found guilty of the murder of Evans and

Downey, but not of Kilbride. The Judge, Mr Justice Fenton Atkinson, saying their killings were the most cold-blooded of the century, sentenced Brady to three concurrent life sentences while Hindley received two. Hindley appealed two weeks later but the appeal was turned down. The death penalty had been abolished in November 1965, barely two weeks after Hindley and Brady were charged.

They were believed to have committed at least two other murders on the moors and police continued their search for the bodies.

In May 1987, after Myra Hindley broke her silence, the body of one more victim was discovered. Ian Brady allegedly admitted to five more killings as the nightmare of the Moors Murders continues more than 20 years on.

MORECAMBE & WISE

UNQUESTIONABLY the finest double act in the 1960s, Morecambe and Wise paved the way for other double acts in the two decades since then.

However, Eric (the one with the glasses) and Ernie (the one with the short fat hairy legs) had been treading the boards long before they gained popularity via the medium of television in the sixties and learned their trade through the music hall, having formed their partnership in 1940.

While they would openly admit to admiring the work of such greats as Laurel and Hardy, and Abbott and Costello, Eric and Ernie had their own distinctive styles.

Their television series was one of the great comedy shows of the decade and such was their popularity that they had no problem enticing top stars like Glenda Jackson, Sir Ralph Richardson and André Previn on to their show. But when they appeared, they knew they would be brought down to earth by Eric who had a habit of not recognizing these famous people. Ernie, on the other hand, spent time grovelling to them.

The duo also appeared in some films, notably *The Intelligence Men* and *The Riviera Touch* but their brand of humour never came across in the same way on the big screen as it did on the little screen.

Eric was born Eric Bartholomew in Morecambe on 14 May 1926. He entered show business at the age of 13 as one of *Brian Michies Discoveries.* In 1956 he married Joan Bartlett, the 1951 Miss Kent. Sadly the world of entertainment was shocked when Eric died in the summer of 1984, having already survived a heart attack some years earlier. Ernie was born as Ernest Wiseman in Leeds on 27 November 1925. He still appears on television in the likes of *What's My Line* but without Eric he has lost half of him, not just half of his act.

MOTORING

AS 1960 rolled in, two of the most popular cars in Britain at the time were the Alex Issigonis designed Mini, which had been launched in 1959, and the Triumph Herald, as BMC and Triumph stood out as two outstanding British manufacturers. The Morris Minor, of course, was still a big seller despite the birth of the Mini. And, of course, we had the Bubble Car. But, by the end of the decade, the Minor could not withstand the competition from its 'baby brother' and production stopped in 1970.

There were two major mergers within the car industry in 1960 when Jaguar took over Daimler and Leyland took over Standard-Triumph. The first thing they did was to reduce the price of the Herald and bring out the new Triumph TR4 sports car. BMC, on the other hand, started production of the slightly bigger and modified Mini under the Wolseley (Kestrel) and Riley (Elf) names. They were launched in 1961, as was the powerful Mini-Cooper. But a lot of the limelight was taken away from the Mini by the Morris Minor when model number 1,000,000 rolled off the BMC production line.

In 1961 there were 38 British car manufacturers, not including the small firms making specialist cars. But the American influence was apparent at Fords where the new Consul Classic and original Ford Capri (different from the second version some years later) took on the looks of their American counterparts. The first Capri was, as Fords said: 'The car you always promised yourself'. Unfortunately not enough people had made that promise! However, one car that did prove to be a success in 1961 was Jaguar's brand new sports car, the 'E'-Type. They also launched their Mark X saloon in the same year.

Purchase tax on cars was brought down to a post-war record low of 25% in 1962 and this helped curtail the price of the classy Rover 3-litre Coupé which made its debut, as did the Issigonis-designed Morris 1100 — the bigger Mini. Ford's opened their new £50 million Halewood plant on Merseyside in 1962 and set about producing their own small car, the Anglia. But the success of Fords hinged on the popularity of the Cortina 1200cc saloon; the car with the comfort of a larger car and economy of a smaller car. The Cortina was very popular and indeed, was one of the big success stories of the sixties, along with the Mini.

Also from Ford in 1962 came the Zodiac III, a de luxe version of the

Consul Cortina, September 1962.

Zephyr Six, and over at Triumph they launched the Spitfire, a sports car to rival BMC's Midget and Sprite. All three are now collectors' items. At the top of the sports car range Aston Martin brought out the 266bhp DB4 Vantage.

The cost of a car in 1962? Well, a Mini would cost you a touch under £500; the Cortina was not much more than £500 while the Hillman Super Minx ranged from £805 to £846.

The first Ford Anglia came off the Halewood production line on 8 March 1963 and was presented to a Mr N.Taylor who won it in a local competition. Coincidentally, it was 52 years to the day that Ford first established their company in England. It was quite a significant year in the car industry because manufacturers started adding extras to their cars, thus making them look that little bit more attractive. Today extras are standard!

Apart from the Anglia, the other new cars of 1963 were the rear-engined Hillman Imp, the car designed to rival the Mini. But oh what problems they had to begin with. In September 1963 there came the most significant newcomer of the year: the Vauxhall Viva.

The DB4 Vantage, manufactured by Aston Martin Lagonda Ltd in 1962. List price was £2,900 plus £1,330 purchase tax.

There were no major newcomers in 1964. The 'E'-Type became available with a 4.2 litre engine, manufacturers started adding more extras to their ranges and called their cars standard, super, de luxe, GT etc. and made the same models with different sized engines. The car boom was well and truly on its way.

Again there was little in the way of new cars in 1965, although it was an historic year for the Mini as the 1,000,000th was produced. There were a couple of mergers: Rover with

Avus and BMC with the Pressed Steel Company. In 1966 there came the new style Vauxhall Viva, and a six-cylinder Triumph Spitfire was announced. Ford launched their Executive, with a sliding roof. And for those with more than a few bob to spare there was the new Jensen FF and Interceptor. Once more there were a couple of mergers: BMC with Jaguar and across the Channel, Peugeot and Renault got together. Rootes launched their new Hillman Hunter at the end of 1966 and a couple of months later the company was taken over by the US firm Chrysler and their new car for 1967 was the Sunbeam Rapier. The Leyland Motor Corporation announced on 12 December 1966 that it was paying £25 million for the Rover Company, the last of the big British independent manufacturers.

Vauxhall launched their OHC (overhead cam) engine in 1967 and

the introduction of the twin rotor Wankel engines by NSU (RO80) and Mazda (Cosmo) were revolutionary developments. Over at BMC there were a few developments. They announced a new 3-litre Austin and introduced the MG 'C' sports car. They also announced the Mark II series of Minis with bigger and more powerful engines up to 1300cc. Automatic and semi-automatic transmission on smaller cars, like the Viva, became very popular in 1967.

In an otherwise poor year for new British cars, in 1968 there were two outstanding new 'arrivals', the Jaguar XJ6 and the Ford Escort which was launched as a replacement for the previous best seller, the Anglia. On the merger front, British Leyland Motor Corporation was formed out of the merger of Leyland and British Motor Holdings.

And so to the close of the decade. British Leyland brought out their

Austin Maxi in 1969 with its five-door body, and Fords had another go with 'The car you always promised yourself', the Capri. This time there were enough people who had promised themselves this new car. Aimed at the sporty-minded driver, it was an instant success and remained a big seller until its demise in the 1980s. Fords also brought out the big selling Corsair shortly before the Capri.

Twin Cam Ford Escort pictured in January 1968.

In the United States the 'car of the decade' was the Ford Mustang...ideal for cruising and 'pulling' the females. Between its launch in April 1964 and January 1965 it sold nearly 700,000, a then US record for first-year sales of any new car.

The car industry came a long way in the 1960s. The number of vehicles registered in Britain at the start of the decade was approximately 9.5 million. Ten years later it was 15 million. This was despite the industry being severely crippled at times by industrial disputes. The car industry felt the full force of the unions in the 1960s, probably more than any other industry. But it survived and gave us some great sixties cars. But my word! What a long way it has come in the 20 years since then.

'Flower Power' Mini parked off the King's Road, Chelsea.

The bubble car which was a feature of the early 1960s.

Apart from getting new cars, what else did the motorist of the sixties have? Well, there was the introduction of traffic wardens, parking meters (and parking tickets!) and the breathalyser. There was also the imposing of the 70mph speed limit in 1965 and that, of course, is still with us. Panda Cars were also launched in 1965.

The MOT test was introduced on 12 September 1960, and the first urban motorway in Britain, the M62 Stretford-Eccles by-pass, was opened on 28 October 1960. Even travel across level crossings was made easier with the introduction of the automatic half-barrier which was first seen at a crossing at Spath, near Uttoxeter, Staffordshire, on 5 February 1961. The new registration system was introduced by certain counties in 1963 when cars were suffixed with the letter 'A' and adopted throughout two years later.

The largest underground car park (capacity 1,000 cars) was opened at Hyde Park by the Prime Minister in 1962 and that same year the first British self-service filling station was opened on London's Southwark Bridge. Still with petrol, the star grading system was introduced in March 1967.

For those who didn't want to drive there was always the cab. On 6 March 1961 the first mini-cabs were introduced by Carline of Wimbledon.

All in all, it was quite an eventful time for the motorist in the 1960s.

Some car prices in the 1960s:
1965
New Austin Mini Super de luxe
£515 2s 1d
New Austin Mini basic   £469 16s 0d
New Austin Healey Sprite
£611 15s 5d

1968
New Sunbeam Rapier from £1,323
New Ford Corsair £1,290
Second-hand Rolls-Royce
Silver Shadow £7,750

MOULTON FOLD-UP BICYCLE

IN 1958 Alex Moulton of Bradford-on-Avon designed the fold-up bicycle. He put the idea to *Raleigh* but they knocked him back, saying they thought the small wheels and low

New-style 1960s bicycle.

centre of gravity would never make it popular.

Unperturbed, Moulton carried on and started making and selling his bike. Surprisingly, it did catch on — and with a market not previously identified as bike-buyers, the city gent, who would park his car on the outskirts of the city, take his bike out of the boot and ride the remainder of the way to work. Amongst such notable Moulton-riders was Lord Hailsham, who used to cycle to the House of Commons.

In 1967 *Raleigh* held up their hands, admitted their mistake and took over Alex Moulton's company.

MUNSTERS, The

THE MUNSTERS is another of the black and white sixties television programmes that has found a whole new audience in the 1980s.

Like *The Addams Family* and *Bewitched*, it was pure fantasy and was about a family of 'odd-ball' ghouls who firmly believed there was nothing wrong with them. It was the rest of civilization that was barmy.

The Munster family consisted of: Herman, a Frankenstein-type monster with a bolt through his neck. He worked in a local funeral parlour and was played by the 6ft 7in tall Fred Gwynne who had previously been seen in the comedy programme *Car 54 Where Are You?* Herman's wife was Lily (Yvonne de Carlo) , a white-faced vampire, and they had a werewolf son, Eddie (Butch Patrick). Finally, there was Grandpa, brilliantly played by Al Lewis. He reckoned he was 378 years old (Grandpa that is, not Lewis) and was a close friend of Count Dracula. If the mood took him he could turn himself into a bat, and for transport he used a coffin on wheels called 'Dragula'.

There was one other member of the family, Marilyn (Pat Priest), who was the only one to appear as a normal sane person, completely adverse to the mayhem surrounding her.

To confuse the issue even further, the family had three pets: Igor the Bat, Spot, a prehistoric beast, and a raven that was constantly quoting the works of Edgar Allan Poe. The family lived at 1313 Mockingbird Lane, Mockingbird Heights.

President Nasser addressing a peasant rally at Mansoura, a provincial capital in the Nile delta, in April 1968.

NASSER, Gamal Abdul

IN 1956 the name of Colonel Nasser was rarely out of the news. Born in 1918, the son of a postal clerk, he was first Prime Minister and then President of Egypt at the time of the Suez crisis which attracted worldwide attention and affected many nations, including Great Britain.

One of the great world leaders, he was responsible for the growth of not only Egypt as a nation, but also of the entire Arab world. Relying heavily on the Eastern Bloc for support, Nasser was made a Hero of the Soviet Union by Khrushchev in 1964. The same year, Nasser and the Soviet leader pushed a button which altered the course of the Nile. It activated a sand barrage which changed the course of the great river as part of the next phase of the building of the Aswan High Dam.

As well as being President of Egypt, Nasser was President of the United Arab Republic from 1958. He died of a heart attack on 28 July 1970. Some say he died of a broken heart at the non-unified state of the Arab nations. He was succeeded as UAR President by Anwar Sadat, the man who helped him with his 1952 coup which ousted King Farouk.

NATIONAL SERVICE

THE compulsory calling up of men on their 18th birthday to do National Service ended in 1960 after 21 years. Since its introduction at the outbreak of the war in 1939, a total of 5.3 million men had been called up. Since the end of the war, the number that entered the scheme was 2.3 million.

The period of National Service was two years and the last men to join did so on 17 November 1960, when a total of 2,049 were called up. The last recruits were scheduled for the end of the year but the final date was brought forward.

Since the abolition of National Service the three services have had to rely on recruitment campaigns to encourage volunteers.

NEWMAN, Paul

IT IS hard to imagine that Paul Newman is 65 years of age. But the ever-youthful star of the movies was born in Cleveland, Ohio, on 25 January 1925.

He studied drama at both Kenyon College and Yale and after appearing in New York stage productions, was given a Hollywood contract which led

The last National Service man. Private R.J.O'Hara

to his first film *The Silver Chalice* in 1954. But the big breakthrough came in 1956 when he played the part of Rocky Graziano in the film *Somebody Up There Likes Me.* It told the rags-to-riches tale of a boxer who over-came the depression to become a 'somebody'. Two years later he received his first Oscar nomination for his part in *Cat On A Hot Tin Roof.*

In the sixties he played such roles as Eddie Felson in *The Hustler,* Hud Bannen in *Hud* and Luke Jackson in *Cool Hand Luke,* all of which won him Oscar nominations. But perhaps his finest performance during the decade was as Butch Cassidy in *Butch Cassidy And The Sundance Kid.*

Newman married his second wife, Joanne Woodward, in 1958 and she appeared in *Rachel Rachel,* the first feature film directed by her husband. For her performance Woodward received an Oscar nomination.

Amongst Newman's films of the seventies were *The Sting, The Life And Times Of Judge Roy Bean* and *Towering Inferno* when he, and the other movie heart-throb and box-office rival, Steve McQueen, appeared in a film together for the one and only time.

Paul Newman eventually won an Oscar in 1986 for his portrayal of Eddie Felson (again) in *The Colour Of Money,* the sequel to *The Hustler.*

Films of Paul Newman in the 1960s:

From The Terrace	(1960)
Exodus	(1960)
Paris Blues	(1961)
The Hustler	(1961)
Sweet Bird Of Youth	(1961)
Adventures Of A Young Man	(1962)
A New Kind Of Love	(1963)
What A Way To Go!	(1963)
The Outrage	(1964)
Lady L	(1965)
Harper (The Moving Target)	(1966)
Torn Curtain	(1966)
Hombre	(1966)
Cool Hand Luke	(1967)
The Secret War Of Harry Frigg	(1967)
Winning	(1969)
Butch Cassidy And The Sundance Kid	(1969)

Paul Newman and Joanne Woodward.

NEWSPAPERS

LIKE other apsects of the sixties, the world of newspapers saw some comings and goings as well as technological advances.

New papers hit the bookstands in the sixties and the very first, on 15 January 1960, was the *National Christian News.* But that same year two popular papers, the *News Chronicle* and *The Star* disappeared. The 'Chron' was incorporated into the *Daily Mail* while *The Star* went in with the *London Evening News.* The saddest demise of them all was that of the *Sunday Empire News.* Predomi-nantly a northern paper, it had been established since 1884 but in 1960 it was absorbed by the *News of the World.* Another popular paper to disappear was the *Sunday Graphic* which closed on 10 December, to make 1960 a bad year for the news-paper business.

On the technical side, the *Sunday Dispatch* and *Daily Herald* became the first British newspapers to carry colour pictures of a national event when they carried pictures of Princess Margaret's wedding.

The first *Sunday Telegraph* was launched in 1961, and it was priced at 4d. But it was goodbye to another old favourite as the 160-year-old *Sunday Dispatch* merged with the *Sunday Express.* Elsewhere there was speculation over the *Daily Sketch's* future and the Mirror Group won control of Odhams. In 1961 there were 133 daily newspapers in the United Kingdom and Eire (morning and evening) and 1,310 weeklies. Most national dailies went up from 2½d to 3d in March 1961, and that same year *The Guardian* began simultaneous printing in Manchester and London.

On 4 February 1962 the *Sunday Times* became the first British news-paper to issue a colour supplement with Lord Snowdon as its artistic adviser. Its first front cover contained 11 pictures of model Jean Shrimpton taken by David Bailey, and one of Ireland international soccer player Jimmy McIlroy. The rest of Fleet Street frowned upon the *Sunday Times* innovation. Just look at the number of colour supplements now!

It looked as though the *Daily Herald* would be the next paper to fold when it was announced in 1963 that it was running at a substantial loss. And indeed its end came in September 1964. The next day, the first new national daily for 34 years, *The Sun,* was launched. By 1964 *The Observer* had followed the *Sunday Times* lead and had issued a colour supplement and the *Daily Telegraph* started issuing a colour magazine with its Friday edition.

The SUN newspaper front page reproduced here.

Lord Thompson launched 'the world's most modern newspaper' in September 1965 when the *Evening Post* was seen for the first time, and in October 1965, after a 25-day strike, the *New York Times* came back to the stands with a monster 946-page Sunday edition. It contained 1.2 million lines of advertising!

For the first time in 181 years (emergencies excepted) *The Times* carried news stories on its front page in 1966. That same year the *Daily Worker* became the *Morning Star* and in Bristol the *Evening Post* was making a bit of history when it changed its typesetting methods to a computer-controlled system — now very much part of the newspaper business.

In 1967 William Rees-Mogg became editor of *The Times* and the 100-year-old *Sunday Citizen* and *Reynolds News* closed.

As the decade came to a close, two men who made newspaper news were two men who are still doing so in the 1980s — Rupert Murdoch and Robert Maxwell.

Murdoch gained control of the *News of the World* for which Maxwell had put in a bid the previous year. The two men have since been two of the most powerful in the world of newspapers.

NEW TOWNS

SINCE 1946 a total of 28 new towns have been created in Britain. Nearly half of them were established in the 1960s. This is the full list of the sixties new towns:

1962	Skelmersdale
1962	Livingston (Lothian)
1963	Telford
1964	Runcorn
1964	Washington (Tyne & Wear)
1964	Redditch
1966	Irvine (Strathclyde)
1967	Milton Keynes
1967	Newtown (Powys)
1968	Northampton
1968	Warrington
1968	Peterborough

NICKLAUS, Jack

APART from Tony Jacklin's great achievement at Lytham in 1969, golf was dominated by the 'big three' — Jack Nicklaus, Arnold Palmer and Gary Player in the 1960s. The most successful of that threesome was undoubtedly 'The Golden Bear', Jack Nicklaus.

Born in Columbus, Ohio, in 1940, he won the 1959 US Amateur Championship, finished second to Palmer while an amateur in the US Open a year later, and in 1961 won his second Amateur title. He then turned professional and won his first US Tour event in 1962 when he turned the tables on Palmer to win the Open at Oakmont.

Jack Nicklaus, winner of the 1966 British Open Golf Championship.

Since then Nicklaus has won a record 18 majors, culminating in his sixth US Masters success at Augusta in 1986 when he was 46 years of age, thus defying the host of youngsters that have come into golf in recent years.

While Nicklaus' golden years were in the seventies, his triumphs in the sixties were a springboard for his later success.

He won both the US Masters and PGA Championship in 1963, the Masters again in 1965 and 1966, the year of his first British Open success at his favourite British course, Muirfield. He named his own course in the United States after it.

His final major success of the 1960s was at Baltusrol in 1967 when he won his second US Open. He has since won the British Open on two more occasions and has amassed worldwide earnings in excess of five million dollars.

NIXON, Richard

RICHARD Milhous Nixon was the 37th President of the United States. He could well have been the 35th, but for losing to John F.Kennedy by just over 100,000 votes in a close-fought election in 1960.

Born in California on 9 January 1913, Nixon practiced as a lawyer in Whittier for five years before joining the US Navy in 1942. His career in politics saw him elected as a Republican to the House of Representatives in 1946 and in 1950 he became a Senator. He was Vice-President to Eisenhower in 1952 and was Ike's Vice-President during his second term.

Nixon had a clever political mind, but was often outspoken and on a tour of the Soviet Union in 1959 he was engaged in some heated exchanges with Khrushchev.

After his defeat by Kennedy in the Presidential election, Nixon was then defeated in the election for Governorship of California two years later. In 1968 however he defeated Hubert Humphrey by a small margin (510,000 votes) and became President. He was returned with a large majority (18 million) four years later and he looked set to become the first President since Eisenhower to complete two terms of office when the Government was rocked with the Watergate scandal which led, on 9 August 1974, to Nixon's resignation. It was the first time a President had resigned during a term of office.

NORTHERN IRELAND

CONFLICT amongst Catholics and Protestants in Ireland is nothing new, but in the late 1960s the wave of violence reached new peaks of ferocity. It proved to be the springboard for a renewed confrontation that has grown more savage and bitter every year since then.

In October 1968, police broke up two days of battles in the streets of Londonderry after approximately 800 Roman Catholics marched on the town in protest at the sectarian discrimination against them.

The scene was repeated three months later when Catholic civil rights campaigners marched into the town once more. This time they trapped the Rev Ian Paisley in the Guildhall. Paisley was a bitter opponent of the Catholics who were demanding equal voting rights and equal housing opportunities which many Protestant-controlled councils were not giving them.

The Royal Ulster Constabulary

A rioter fires a catapault during the 1969 Londonderry riots.

113

Street of fire in Londonderry.

received the aid of the largely Protestant 'B Specials'. However, their role was, a few months later, seen to be a partisan one and they had their weapons withdrawn. The 'B' Specials were eventually disbanded and replaced by the Ulster Defence Regiment.

Within a couple of months of each other, two of the central characters in the conflicts at the time, Paisley and Bernadette Devlin, both made headline news. Paisley was arrested and imprisoned for three months in January 1969 for unlawful assembly. And on 18 April, civil-rights worker Devlin was elected to Westminster as the MP for Mid-Ulster. She was only 21.

As the troubles spread, British troops were called in to guard key areas around Belfast as Post Offices, the bus station and the main reservoir were attacked. Within five days, another 500 troops were sent in as reinforcements.

Terence O'Neill quit as leader of the Unionists and also as Prime Minister shortly after the troops were brought into the province. He was replaced by Major James Chichester-Clark.

On 12 August 1969, troubles reached a peak when 112 people were treated for injuries following a night of rioting. The fighting lasted a week and five people died. British troops were called in to patrol the streets of Londonderry and Belfast after gun battles in the Protestant Shankhill Road and Catholic Falls Road areas. Within a month, the total number of British soldiers in Northern Ireland was 7,000.

Reverend Ian Paisley leaves prison in January 1969.

As the 1960s came to a close, Bernadette Devlin, like Ian Paisley, was sentenced to a prison term. On 22 December 1969 she was sentenced to six months for inciting a riot in the Bogside. Devlin and Paisley both continued to make Northern Ireland news in the years to follow. So too has the bloodshed.

BP drilling rig Sea Gem *which capsized in December 1965.*

Nationalist Chinese team march around the Olympic Stadium in Rome in 1960. They objected at having to compete under the title of 'Taiwan'.

NORTH SEA GAS AND OIL

ON 17 September 1964, the Minister of Power, Frederick Erroll, announced in Parliament that licences had been granted to 22 applicants to drill for oil and gas in the North Sea as Britain became the first nation bordering the sea to issue licences for the full scale search for natural resources.

The 22 applications represented 48 groups, individual companies, or individuals and the Government allocated 34,100 square miles of sea, stretching from northern Scotland to the Suffolk coast. The area was divided into 341 one-hundred square-mile blocks and the Shell-Esso consortium were allocated the most; they received 75 blocks.

BP, however, was the first company to pipe gas ashore when they began their flow along the 16in diameter, 45-mile pipeline from the West Sole field on 7 March 1967. The first gas to be piped to the mainland arrived at Easington, Humberside. The West Sole field was discovered 18 months earlier and was the first commercial find in the British part of the North Sea.

Since then many more fields have been established as North Sea Gas and Oil have become very much part of our lives. The cost has been high, and sadly that cost has at times been measured in terms of human life.

OLYMPIC GAMES

THERE were three Olympic celebrations during the 1960s — at Rome in 1960, Tokyo in 1964 and at Mexico City in 1968. The respective Winter Games were at Squaw Valley, Innsbruck and Grenoble.

The first Olympic Games of the 1960s was the VIIIth Winter Olympics at Squaw Valley, USA, the first purpose-built Winter Games venue. They were officially opened by US Vice-President Richard Nixon, and the opening ceremony was directed by Walt Disney.

The divided German nation agreed to compete as one and further agreed that *Beethoven's Ninth Symphony* should be played at any medal ceremony. It was played four times.

South Africa appeared in the Winter Olympics for the first and only time, but they did not get amongst the medals. Top honours went to the Soviet Union with 21 medals, including seven golds.

Six months later the competition moved on to Rome for the Summer Games; the XVIIth Olympics.

Held in extreme heat they were the first Games to receive global television coverage and the world saw some great champions. There was the barefooted Ethiopian Abebe Bikila, who won the marathon. There was also the American sprinter Wilma Rudolph, who won three golds. Her triumph was a remarkable one because she overcame polio to become an Olympic champion. She was also one of 19 children! The men's 1,500 metres, the 'Blue Riband' of the track, went to Australian Herb Elliot.

Australia and the United States dominated the swimming events although that domination was broken once, by Huddersfield's Anita Lonsborough. It was in the boxing arena, though, that one of the biggest names in the sport was to emerge as Cassius Marcellus Clay, won the light-heavyweight title.

The Rome Games saw the death of Danish cyclist Knut Jensen, who became the first man since Portuguese runner Francisco Lazaro, in the

Dawn Fraser (centre) displays her Olympic gold medal at Tokyo in 1964 after coming first in the women's 100 meteres free-style. At right is silver medallist S.M.Stouder and at left is bronze medallist Kathleen Ellis.

to win the same event at three successive Games. In the boxing ring the heavyweight title went to Joe Frazier, the man who later became heavyweight champion of the world.

Mary Rand pictured making her World and Olympic record long jump at Tokyo.

Medallists in the light-heavyweight boxing division at the Rome Olympics.

1912 marathon, to lose his life during Olympic competition.

Four years later the Winter Games were held at Innsbruck. Due to 'good' weather, snow had to be transported into the area. The Soviets again dominated the Games, but Britain had a rare moment of glory when Tony Nash and Robin Dixon took the gold medal in the two-man bobsleigh competition. It was the first-ever victory by a 'lowland' country in the event.

In Tokyo for Asia's first Games during the summer, Britain did not have much more to cheer, collecting only four gold medals, all in track and field events. Mary Rand became the first British girl to win an athletics gold medal when she took the long jump, and her Tokyo roommate, Anne Packer, won gold in the 800 metres shortly afterwards. Lynn Davies made it a remarkable long-jump double for Britain by winning the men's event. Britain's other champion was walker Ken Matthews.

Ethiopia's Bikila became the first man to retain the marathon title, but this time he wore shoes. And New Zealand's Peter Snell completed a rare 800 and 1500 metres double. For Ron Clarke there was not to be the Olympic gold so widely predicted.

Again the pool was dominated by the Australians and Americans. Don Schollander became the first swimmer to win four golds at one Games. The controversial Australian girl Dawn Fraser won the 100 metres freestyle for the third consecutive time and became the first swimmer

After the euphoria of winning gold at Innsbruck in 1964, the British team came away from the Xth Winter Olympics at Grenoble in 1968 without a single medal. Norway, on the other hand, upstaged the Soviets by winning six golds to the Russians' five.

But the star of the Games was the Frenchman Jean-Claude Killy. Regarded as one of the finest skiers of all time, he emulated Tony Sailer's feat and won all three Alpine events.

If Killy was the star of the 1968 Winter Olympics, then Bob Beamon was the star of the Summer Games at Mexico City eight months later when he destroyed the world long-jump record and improved it from 27ft 4¾in to 29ft 2½in, an amazing increase of 1ft 9¾in. Between 1935 and 1968 the record had increased by a mere 8½in.

The rarified atmosphere certainly helped Beamon, just as it helped the other jumpers; but none of them could manage 27ft . . .let alone 28 or 29! Beamon's leap is still in the record books and still no other man has leapt 29 feet.

Bob Beamon's world-shattering long jump in Mexico.

The men's high-jump also saw the emergence of a new hero, Dick Fosbury. He was the man who threw himself over the bar backwards. How strange everyone thought at the time. But try and find somebody going over the bar forwards in the old-fashioned straddle these days. They are nearly all 'floppers'.

Still with the men's field events, American Al Oerter won the discus for the fourth time, the only person to win the same track and field event on four occasions.

However, the track events were clouded by the Black Power salute given by the Americans Tommy Smith and John Carlos during the US National Anthem after they had received their respective gold and bronze medals in the 200 metres. Australian silver medallist Peter Norman was the man who stood,

David Hemery (402) is congratulated by John Sherwood after they finished first and third in the men's 400-metre hurdles in Mexico.

embarrassed, alongside the two demonstrating athletes.

Czech gymnast Vera Caslavska won four gold medals and her *Mexican Hat Dance* routine was one of the highlights of the Games. While in Mexico she married fellow athlete Josef Odlozil and when she returned to Czechoslovakia gave one medal each to the four Czech leaders who were deposed during the Soviet invasion that year.

Gymnast Vera Caslavska of Czechoslovakia in action at the Mexico Olympics in 1968.

Britain's medal tally was up to five in 1968. This was aided by Chris Finnegan's gold in the boxing competition. The heavyweight gold medallist was once again another man who went on to win the world heavyweight title, George Foreman. He is still fighting today.

Black power salute by American athletes Tommy Smith (centre) and John Carlos at the Mexico Olympics.

The Mexico Olympics were the first to be seriously affected by politics. The Black Power demonstration was one example. But, even before the Games started there was a threatened boycott by Black African nations after the International Olympic Committee were going to readmit South Africa into the Games. They were forced to reverse their

119

decision. Politics have since been a common feature of the Olympic Games as sport often has to take second place.

Britain's Olympic gold medallists in the 1960s:

1960	ROME
Don Thompson	50 km walk
Anita Lonsborough	200 metres breaststroke

1964	INNSBRUCK
Tony Nash & Robin Dixon	Two-man bobsleigh

	TOKYO
Lynn Davies	Long jump
Mary Rand	Long jump
Anne Packer	800 metres
Ken Matthews	20km walk

1968	MEXICO CITY
David Hemery	400 metres hurdles
Chris Finnegan	Middleweight boxing
Rodney Pattison & Ian Macdonald-Smith	Flying Dutchman yachting
Derek Alhusen, Richard Meade & Reuben Jones	Three Day Event team
Bob Braithwaite	Clay Pigeon Shooting

ORBISON, Roy

ROY Kelton Orbison was born in Vernon, Texas, on 23 April 1936, but was brought up in nearby Wink. And it was after the town that he named his first group, the Wink Westerners, which he formed when he was 13.

Orbison attended the North Texas University where Pat Boone was also a student. Inspired by Boone's subsequent success in the music world, Orbison cut his first record *Ooby Dooby*, with his new group, the Teen Kings.

After three changes of record company he eventually had his first big hit with *Only The Lonely*, a record which was intended for Elvis Presley and then the Everly Brothers. The record made number one in Britain and number two in the States.

Orbison became popular in Britain at a time when few American artistes were having big successes this side of the Atlantic. In the 48 weeks from 8 August 1963 he was the only American to have a British number one.

Famous for wearing sunglasses on stage, a feature which came about only by accident after he once left his normal glasses on a plane, Roy Orbison's life was clouded with tragedy. His wife Claudette died following a motor-cycle accident in 1966 and two years later, two of his sons, Roy and Tony, lost their lives in a fire at the family home.

Despite trying to carry on with his career, it had virtually come to a standstill by the late 1960s. He toured the US again in 1977 and in the late-1980s was part of the all-star Travelling Wilburys. In December 1988, Orbison died of a heart attack. A song he recorded just before he died, *You Got It*, became a big hit to put Roy Orbison back into the British charts, albeit posthumously. Subsequently the album and single *Mystery Girl* became chart hits after Orbison's death, as did the LP *The Legendary Roy Orbison*.

Top Ten hits of Roy Orbison in the 1960s:

Year	Record	Pos
1960	Only The Lonely	1
1961	Running Scared	9
1962	Dream Baby	2
1963	In Dreams	6
1963	Falling	9
1963	Blue Bayou/Mean Woman Blues	3
1964	It's Over	1
1964	Oh Pretty Woman	1
1964	Pretty Paper	6
1966	Too Soon To Know	3

OSCARS

THE following won the two main Oscars at the Academy of Motion Picture Arts and Sciences during the 1960s.

Best Actor

1960	Burt Lancaster	*Elmer Gentry*
1961	Maximilian Schell	*Judgement At Nuremberg*
1962	Gregory Peck	*To Kill A Mockingbird*
1963	Sidney Poitier	*Lillies Of The Field*
1964	Rex Harrison	*My Fair Lady*
1965	Lee Marvin	*Cat Ballou*
1966	Paul Schofield	*A Man For All Seasons*
1967	Rod Steiger	*In The Heat Of The Night*
1968	Cliff Robertson	*Charly*
1969	John Wayne	*True Grit*

> *The 1962 winner Gregory Peck, and 1968 winner Cliff Robertson both hail from La Jolla, California.*

BEST ACTRESS

1960	Elizabeth Taylor	*Butterfield 8*
1961	Sophia Loren	*Two Women*
1962	Anne Bancroft	*The Miracle Worker*
1963	Patricia Neal	*Hud*
1964	Julie Andrews	*Mary Poppins*
1965	Julie Christie	*Darling*
1966	Elizabeth Taylor	*Who's Afraid Of Virginia Woolf?*
1967	Katharine Hepburn	*Guess Who's Coming To Dinner?*
1968	Katharine Hepburn	*The Lion In Winter*
&	Barbra Streisand	*Funny Girl*
1969	Maggie Smith	*The Prime Of Miss Jean Brodie*

The Oscar-winning films of the 1960s were:

1960: THE APARTMENT
A comedy starring Fred MacMurray, Jack Lemmon and Shirley MacLaine. Lemmon plays the part of C.C.Baxter, a junior executive trying to make his way to the top. However, when senior bosses, including J.D.Sheldrake (played by MacMurray) discover he has his own apartment they offer him a quick way to promotion. Naturally they want the flat for a bit of 'nookie' and Sheldrake's girlfriend is Miss Kubelik (Shirley MacLaine). However, Baxter's plans go all wrong when he falls in love with Miss Kubelik. Directed by Billy Wilder.

1961: WEST SIDE STORY
Based on Shakespeare's Romeo and Juliet it is the story about rival American white and Puerto Rican gangs, the Sharks and the Jets, and is set in New York's West Side. Originally a stage musical, it contains some fine songs and great dance routines. Most of the principal characters were new to the movie business and specially cast, while others had starred in the New York and London stage productions. George Chakiris and Natalie Wood were two notable exceptions. The music was by Leonard Bernstein and

Yul Brynner presents Elizabeth Taylor with her Oscar which she won for best actress in her role in the film Butterfield 8.

lyrics by Stephen Sondheim. Some of the better known scores were: *America, Tonight, I Feel Pretty* and *Somewhere*. Natalie Wood's voice was dubbed by Marni Nixon who also dubbed for Audrey Hepburn in *My Fair Lady* and Deborah Kerr in *The King And I*.

1962:   LAWRENCE OF ARABIA
The 3¾ hour David Lean epic saw Peter O'Toole give a stunning performance in the role of T.E.Lawrence. Remarkably, O'Toole had a striking resemblance to the character he portrayed. It told the story of Lawrence's life and was set around World War One. The rest of the cast contained such notables as Alex Guinness, Anthony Quinn, Jack Hawkins, Anthony Quayle, Claude Rains, and Omar Sharif. The film won seven Oscars and in 1989 was re-released and contained some 20 minutes which had originally been edited out. No sound-track from the missing portion survived and the original actors were recalled to dub their lines after lip-reading experts had established the dialogue.

1963:   TOM JONES
Based on Henry Fielding's classic novel of the same name, it was an hilarious account of life in the 18th century. Albert Finney was brilliantly cast as the title character, a country lad without a care in the world, who spent all his time with local wenches, casually making his way through life. Producer Tony Richardson had problems getting finance for the film in the first place and at £500,000 it was one of the most expensive British films ever made at the time. Its worldwide popularity helped recoup that money, and much more, for the investors.

1964:   MY FAIR LADY
Based on George Bernard Shaw's play *Pygmalion*, *My Fair Lady* was a musical with lyrics by Alan Jay Lerner and music by Frederick Loewe. The most expensive musical and studio film set of all time (at that time) it cost $17 million to make but it grossed more than $30 million in its first year. The story is about professor Higgins (Rex Harrison) and Pickering (Wilfred Hyde-White) who have a bet as to whether Higgins could educate and completely change the character of a typical market girl. That girl is Eliza Doolittle played by Audrey Hepburn.

(Julie Andrews played Eliza on the stage). Higgins won his bet because 'e taught 'er 'ow to talk proper' in the end. Some of the great songs from the film include: *I Could Have Danced All Night, The Rain In Spain, On The Street Where You Live* and *Get Me To The Church On Time*. The film won eight Oscars.

1965:   THE SOUND OF MUSIC
After her blockbuster as the magical Mary Poppins in 1964, Julie Andrews was back with another big money-earner a year later when *The Sound Of Music* won the Oscar for best film. But more than that, it became the biggest box office success of the 1960s. The LP of the sound-track sold in excess of 14 million which was an all-time record and by 1 January 1969 the film had grossed around $42½ million and surpassed *Gone With The Wind's* record of $41 million. Originally a stage play, it is based on the true story of Maria (played by Andrews) who quits her life in a convent to become governess to Captain Von Trapp's seven children. Inevitably she falls in love with the Captain, played by Christopher Plummer whose voice was dubbed over for his singing part. Some of the Rodgers and Hammerstein songs became hits. Who will ever forget: *Sixteen, Going On Seventeen, My Favourite Things, Climb Every Mountain, Doh-Ray-Me* and of course, *Edelweiss* ?

1966:   A MAN FOR ALL SEASONS
Another film that made the successful journey from the stage, it was about the conflict between Henry VIII and Sir Thomas More. For his powerful portrayal of More, Paul Schofield won the Best Actor Oscar. Robert Shaw played the part of Henry and other such notables as Orson Welles, as Cardinal Wolsey, and Vanessa Redgrave, as Anne Boleyn, helped the film to the Oscar. Directed by Fred Zimmermann it was, in contrast to other recent winners of the best film Oscar, a powerful drama.

1967: IN THE HEAT OF THE NIGHT
The first thriller for some time to win the best film Oscar. It was set in a small Mississippi town in which police chief Bill Gillespie, played by Rod Steiger, arrests negro Virgil Tibbs (Sidney Poitier) on suspicion of murder. Tibbs is a stranger in the area but turns out to be a Philadelphia detective. The film brings together two powerful actors who activate the feeling of prejudice and morals that existed at the time. Steiger won an Oscar for his portral of Gillespie. It was one of three Oscars for the film.

1968: OLIVER!

It was back to the musicals in 1968 as *Oliver!* swept the awards with five Oscars. Based on Charles Dickens' *Oliver Twist* and with songs from Lionel Bart, it sees the young Mark Lester's charming portrayal of Oliver while Ron Moody is excellent in his role of Fagin. The re-creation of London in the early 19th century is clever and some of the songs, like *Pick A Pocket Or Two* were brilliantly choreographed.

1969: MIDNIGHT COWBOY

A John Schlesinger film, it is the tale of Joe Buck (Jon Voigt) who comes from Texas to New York to make a living as a stud. He refuses to wear anything but his cowboy clothes and that, together with his failure to produce the goods in his 'business', soon see him on the downward slide. Then he meets con-man Ratso Rizzo (Dustin Hoffman) and things get worse. They struggle through hard times but Ratso's health gives out and Joe steals to buy food and to get a bus ticket to take them to a new life in Florida. But just before they reach their destination Ratso dies on the bus.

OSWALD, Lee Harvey

BORN in New Orleans on 18 October 1939, Lee Harvey Oswald enlisted in the US Marines at the age of 17. He was not popular and was nicknamed 'Ozzie Rabbit'. At the age of 19 he was

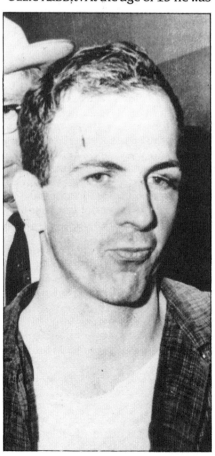

transferred to the inactive reservists and promptly emigrated to Russia but failed to get Soviet citizenship. He returned to America in 1961 with a Russian wife and daughter. Upon his return he became chairman of the pro-Castro group, 'Fair Play for Cuba'.

He gained worldwide notoriety in November 1963 when he was charged with killing President Kennedy.

He was captured at the Texas Theatre, Dallas, on the evening of the assassination after the murder of a policeman. He was originally charged with the murder of the officer, J.Tippit, but was later also charged with the President's murder.

Lee Harvey Oswald was gunned down in Dallas on 24 November 1963, two days after the assassination of JFK. But his 24 hours of 'fame' has seen his name indellibly printed in the minds of millions as the man who killed President Kennedy.

Police at the time reported that Oswald worked in the building from where shots were fired, but now, more than a quarter of a century later, there is doubt as to exactly who was the killer and where all the shots came from.

O'TOOLE, Peter

ALTHOUGH born in Connemara, Ireland, Peter O'Toole was brought up in Leeds and worked as a journalist for the *Yorkshire Evening News* in the early fifties. He later studied at RADA in London where Albert Finney and Alan Bates were classmates. O'Toole then toured with the Bristol Old Vic Theatre Company before making his film debut in the Walt Disney production *Kidnapped* in 1959.

After a brief return to the theatre he was, in 1962, cast in the role that would turn him into a movie superstar when he played the part of T.E.Lawrence in the epic *Lawrence Of Arabia*, one of David Lean's finest films. Lean won the best director Oscar, while the film won the top film Oscar. O'Toole also received a nomination but was unsuccessful.

After that success he played the part of Henry II in *Becket*, Michael James in *What's New Pussycat?* and Arthur Chipping in the remake of the 1939 classic *Goodbye Mr Chips*, to name but a few.

He has been nominated for an Oscar no fewer than six times: *Lawrence Of Arabia* (1962), *Becket* (1964), *The Lion In Winter* (1968), *Goodbye Mr Chips* (1969), *The Ruling Class* (1972) and *The Stunt Man* (1980) but the coveted award still eludes him.

O'Toole has continued to enjoy the stage and in recent years has appeared in *Macbeth* and *Man And Superman*. He has also appeared in television mini-series like *Masada*.

Films of Peter O'Toole in the 1960s:

Savage Innocents	(1960)
The Day They Robbed The Bank Of England	(1960)
Lawrence Of Arabia	(1962)
Becket	(1964)
What's New Pussycat?	(1965)
Lord Jim	(1965)
The Bible	(1966)
How To Steal A Million	(1966)
Night Of The Generals	(1967)
Casino Royale	(1967)
Great Catherine	(1968)
The Lion In Winter	(1968)

Goodbye Mr Chips	(1969)
Country Dance	(1969)

PALMER, Arnold

THE current crop of golf professionals owe a huge debt to Arnold Palmer. He was the man who played a big role, together with his business partner, Mark McCormack, in bringing sponsors into golf which has made it one of the 'big bucks' sports of the eighties.

Palmer hails from Latrobe, Pennsylvania, where he was born in 1929. He was the US amateur champion in 1954 and turned professional the following year. He won his first pro event, the Canadian Open and then took the US Masters in 1958. After winning the US Open in 1960, he ventured across the Atlantic to compete in the British Open at a time when American interest in the great tournament was declining. Palmer took the title at Birkdale and returned the following year to win again, this time at Troon.

But he did more than capture the British Open twice. He revived US interest in the tournament and with his exciting brand of golf, the likes of which Seve Ballesteros brought with him into the sport nearly 20 years later, he aroused interest amongst the 'ordinary' people.

Arnold Palmer Driving Ranges sprang up all over the world as thousands of people wanted to go out and hit a golf ball. Palmer became very rich, not only from his on-course earnings, but also from endorsements which he and McCormack arranged.

Palmer, together with his vast following of fans known as 'Arnie's Army', is as popular as ever and can be found playing in the competitive world of Seniors Golf in the United States. He is still a most welcome visitor to these shores.

PATTERSON, Floyd

BETWEEN the end of Rocky Marciano's reign as world heavyweight boxing champion and the arrival of Cassius Clay, the boxing world was treated to the delightful skills of Floyd Patterson.

The Olympic middleweight champion in 1952, he became the youngest person to win the world heavyweight title when he beat Archie Moore in 1956 for the vacant title

following Marciano's retirement. After four successful defences he lost his crown to the Swede Ingemar Johansson in 1959, but the following year created history by becoming the first man to regain the heavyweight crown when he beat Johansson in five rounds.

He lost his title in the first round to Sonny Liston in September 1962

From left: British heavyweight champion Henry Cooper, former world champion Floyd Patterson and British heavyweight Billy Walker pictured at a Soho restaurant in September 1966.

Referee Billy Regan seems to be on the end of a punch from heavyweight champion Floyd Patterson. Challenger Ingemar Johansson looks on after being knocked to the canvas at Miami Beach in 1961.

and the following year suffered another first-round defeat at the hands of Liston. He had a crack at Muhammad Ali's title in 1965 but lost in 12 rounds, and in 1968 he fought Jimmy Ellis in Stockholm for the WBA title. He lost on points over 15 rounds.

Patterson's last fight was against Ali for the US heavyweight title in 1972. He was 37 at the time.

Floyd Patterson's manager was Cus D'Amato, and he was the man who set Mike Tyson on the road to success. Coincidentally, it was Tyson who stripped Patterson of the 'Youngest Heavyweight Champion of the World' tag.

PECK, Gregory

GREGORY Peck was born in La Jolla, California, in 1916 and in 1963 he had the distinction of becoming the first Californian-born actor to win an Oscar for his performance in *To Kill A Mockingbird*. When you consider most major US film studios were based in California, it was quite a record.

Peck made his film debut in the RKO production *Days Of Glory* in 1943. The film was made up entirely of actors and actresses making their screen debuts. Peck, of course, went on to become a silver screen legend.

Within five years of making his screen debut, the former Radio City guide had received four Oscar nominations as best actor for *The Keys Of The Kingdom* (1945), *The Yearling* (1946), *Gentleman's Agreement* (1947) and *Twelve O'Clock High* (1949).

Before the arrival of the sixties he had starred in other such films as *Duel In The Sun, Moby Dick, Captain Horatio Hornblower* and many more. In the sixties, apart from his Oscar-winning performance as the southern lawyer, Atticus Finch, in *To Kill A Mockingbird*, he played the part of Mallory in *The Guns Of Navarone*, David Pollock in *Arabesque* and Mackenna in *Mackenna's Gold*.

Now in his seventies, Gregory Peck remains one of Hollywood's best loved and respected personalities.

Films of Gregory Peck in the 1960s:

The Guns Of Navarone	(1961)
Fear	(1962)
To Kill A Mockingbird	(1962)
How The West Was Won	(1962)
Captain Newman MD	(1063)
Behold A Pale Horse	(1964)
Mirage	(1965)
Arabesque	(1966)
The Stalking Moon	(1968)
Mackenna's Gold	(1969)
The Most Dangerous Man In The World	(1969)
Marooned	(1969)

PEYTON PLACE

PEYTON PLACE was America's answer to *Coronation Street* but, despite its popularity during the five years from 1964 to 1969, it did not stand the test of time like 'Corro'.

Unlike its British counterpart, the plots were often complex and difficult to understand and that led to a decline in the ratings in 1969.

Set in New England, the main storylines concerned the love affair between Alison Mackenzie and Rodney Harrington, played respectively by two up-and-coming stars, Mia Farrow and Ryan O'Neal.

Alison was born as the result of the affair between Constance (Dorothy Malone), the owner of the town's bookstore, and Elliot Carson (Tim O'Connor) who was a local publisher. Carson eventually went to gaol during which time Constance had an affair with doctor Mike Rossi (Ed Nelson). When Carson was free he had another affair with Constance and they eventually married! Other characters included Rodney's bitchy ex-wife, Betty (Barbara Parkins), his goody-goody younger brother, Norman (Christopher Connelly) and his wife Rita (Patricia Morrow). The town's principal benefactor, and Rodney's grandfather, was Martin Peyton...hence the series' name.

When the series ended in 1969, there were many unanswered questions but a follow-up series, *Return to Peyton Place* in 1972 failed to unravel the web of intrigue that had been left in Elm Street.

PHILBY, Kim

In 1963, Kim Philby, who had been highly-placed in the British intelligence service, admitted that he was a Russian spy. The revelation shook Government circles because, eight years earlier, Philby had been cleared by a Foreign Office inquiry. Born

Kim Philby

Harold Adrian Russell Kilby in 1911, he was recruited by the Russians as early as 1933 and worked for them whilst setting up and running the British anti-Russian counter-intelligence network between 1944 and 1946. From 1949 to 1951 he worked closely with the CIA and was able to inform the Soviets of almost every Western counter-espionage operation. He also warned other double-agents Burgess and MacLean and assisted their escape in 1951, when he first came under suspicion. Philby

Lester Piggott on Nijinsky.

was asked to leave the Foreign Service but was 'rehabilitated' in 1955. After admitting that the allegations were true, he fled to the Soviet Union and was granted Russian citizenship. The Queen withdrew Philby's OBE in 1965.

Donald MacLean (above) and Guy Burgess (below) pictured in Moscow after their defection.

PICKLES

WHILST on display at the Central Hall, Westminster, soccer's most famous trophy, the Jules Rimet Trophy, better known as the World Cup, was stolen on Sunday, 20 March 1966.

The 12-inch high solid gold trophy was taken from its locked cabinet amidst immediate fears that it had been melted down. With England staging the World Cup for the first time, the footballing authorities were faced with the possible embarrassment of seeing the tournament get under way with no trophy. But to the rescue came a mongrel called Pickles.

He gained worldwide fame by finding the coveted trophy wrapped in newspaper in the garden of a house at Beulah Hill, Norwood, South London, on 27 March. Pickles managed to do what Scotland Yard's best had failed to do. For his find Pickles received a £6,000 reward via his owner David Corbell, a Thames lighterman.

During its period of absence from its display cabinet, the trophy was replaced by a rare Swiss stamp.

PIGGOTT, Lester

LESTER Piggott was a dedicated professional and possessed that

Pickles wearing his National Canine Defence League medal awarded 'for playing an important part in the recovery of the World Cup'.

quality required to make a good sportsman into a champion; the sole desire to win. Second best was never good enough for Piggott. It had to be the winner's enclosure or nothing.

Piggott was born into a racing family at Wantage, Berkshire, on 5 November 1935. He had his first winner aboard *The Chase* at Haydock Park on 18 August 1948. Between then and his retirement from the saddle in 1985, he rode 4,349 winners in Britain; a figure bettered only by Sir Gordon Richards.

Included in Piggott's total was a record 29 English Classic successes, and of course he won the word's top races in the other leading racing countries — Ireland, France and the United States.

He was associated with some great horses over the years and in the sixties was to partner the likes of *St Paddy* and *Sir Ivor* who both provided him with Derby success. *St Paddy* also won the St Leger in 1960, and *Sir Ivor* won the Two Thousand Guineas in 1968.

Piggott was champion jockey 11 times throughout his career, including seven times in the 1960s. His 191 winners in 1966 was a personal best.

In 1969 Piggott partnered *Nijinsky* for the first time in the Dewhurst Stakes at Newmarket. The following year the pair of them landed the Triple Crown. He was the best horse Piggott ever rode.

After retiring from the saddle, Piggott took up training, but his world was shattered in 1987 when he was sentenced to a three-year prison term for tax evasion totalling £3.1 million. He served 12 months before his release in 1988.

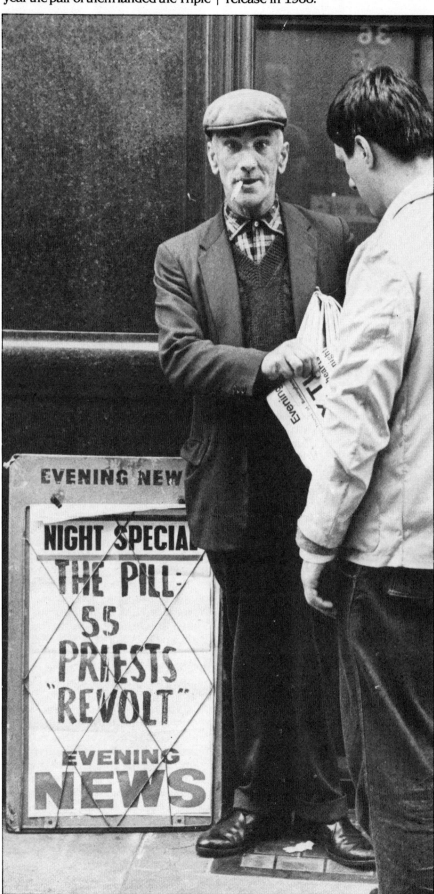

PILL, The

THE first oral contraceptive was produced by Dr Gregory Pincus of Shrewsbury, Massachusetts, in 1954. And after full-scale tests the first 'Pill' was commercially produced in the United States in August 1960.

The first Pill to be made available in the United Kingdom was on 30 January 1961 after a trial period involving 50 Birmingham women. The first Pill, *Conovid*, was a progesterone-oestrogen mixture and was reported to have side effects which were said to wear off after its first few months of use.

Understandably, the introduction of the Pill caused much controversy amongst the Roman Catholic Church and in 1968 Pope Paul published *Humanae Vitae (Of Human Life)*, condemning its use as acting against the will of God. Society was becoming more permissive and the Church, and many others, saw the Pill as an encouragement for even more immoral behaviour.

The Pill became available on prescription in June 1963.

The Pill made headline news. Opposite: Newspaper seller on London's Ludgate Hill does a brisk trade in October 1968.

'PIRATE' RADIO STATIONS

THE 'pirate' radio explosion started with *Radio Caroline* in 1964. But by the end of that year there were many more illegal stations dotted around the coastline of Britain.

Caroline was the brainchild of Rohan O'Rahilly. It was a 763-ton, 188ft vessel, and was moored five miles off the coast from Harwich. It dropped anchor on 27 March 1964 and the following day, Easter Saturday, the station went over the airwaves on 199 metres when Simon Dee started proceedings by announcing: "Good morning ladies and gentlemen. This is Radio Caroline. Your all-day music station." Three weeks after its launch, Caroline had captured seven million listeners.

Within a week of Caroline's 'birth', the GPO took steps to bring an end to offshore commercial radio.

The second 'pirate' station, *Radio Atlanta* (200.6m) was anchored 14 miles from Caroline and first broadcast on 9 May 1964. But in July the two stations merged to become Caroline North and Caroline South. The Atlanta ship was used for the southern operation while the original Caroline moved to a new base off the Isle of Man.

Caroline and Atlanta were soon followed by Radio King, Radio England, Britain Radio, Cheetah II,

Coastguards stand by as Radio Caroline *is pounded by heavy seas off Frinton Beach in January 1966.*

Radio Invicta, Sutch Radio, Radio London, *Radio 270* (moored off Scarborough), *Radio Scotland* (five miles out from Troon) and the disused forts of Radio Essex, Radio 390 and Radio City.

The new stations had become a serious threat to the BBC's Light Programme and were soon attracting big-name sponsors and advertisers. The disc jockeys also showed a more lively approach to their job than their BBC counterparts.

However, after the BBC announced its plans in December 1966 for a reorganization of its stations, and following the introduction of the Marine Broadcasting (Offences) Bill in August 1967, many 'pirate' stations folded, despite teenager protests outside Downing Street. Storms at sea in the early part of 1967 also rocked a few stations, in more ways than one, including Caroline. But the 'pioneers' decided to carry on until it played its last disc in March 1968.

Caroline may have gone but was certainly not forgotten. The station was the breeding ground for many of the top disc jockeys of the decade. It also spurred the BBC into doing something. Their response was Radio One.

PLAYER, Gary

SOUTH African Gary Player was the man who made up golf's 'Big Three' in the sixties along with Arnold Palmer and Jack Nicklaus. And their made-for-television matches were popular with golf fans. Gary was readily identifiable as the one who always wore the black trousers and black polo-neck sweater.

Born in Johannesburg in 1935, he first attracted the attention of the British fans in 1959 when he won the Open at Muirfield. He has since won the title on two more occasions, and in two different decades — at Carnoustie in 1968 and at Lytham in 1974, when he beat Peter Oosterhuis into second place.

Player was one of the most consistent golfers during the 1960s and won all the world's majors — the Masters in 1961, US PGA in 1962 and US Open in 1965. He was also the supremo at match-play golf and won the World Match-Play title at Wentworth in 1965, 1966 and 1968. He also won it twice in the seventies.

One of the finest bunker players of the modern era, Gary Player still enjoys the game he has graced for more than 30 years and is an active member of the US Seniors Tour.

POLITICS IN THE 1960s

AS THE 1960s dawned, the man who led Britain into the new decade was Harold Macmillan, the Prime Minister since 1957 when he replaced Anthony Eden in the wake of the Suez Crisis. But politics in the 1960s are best remembered for the confrontations between Harold Wilson, the pipe-smoking, Gannex-wearing Labour leader, and the 'ho-ho-ho-ing' shoulder-jerking leader of the Conservatives, Ted Heath.

Wilson took over as leader of the Labour party following the death of Hugh Gaitskell in 1963, when he beat George Brown for the leadership. And in 1964 he became Prime Minister

President John F.Kennedy and Prime Minister Harold Macmillan pictured in London in June 1963.

after the Conservatives went to the polls following 13 consecutive years of rule. Harold Macmillan had stood down as Tory leader in October 1963 as a result of ill health. But his departure came shortly after the Profumo affair, which rocked the Government, and was 12 months after a major reshuffle of the Cabinet which resulted in Selwyn Lloyd being replaced as Chancellor by Reginald Maudling. Macmillan was succeeded as Tory leader by Lord Home, who, when he took over, was not even a Member of Parliament. He immediately renounced his peerage and became Alec Douglas-Home, and a month after his appointment was elected to the Commons after winning the Kinross by-election. Because they felt he was not strong enough, Ministers Enoch Powell and Iain Macleod refused to serve under the new PM.

Home Secretary 'Rab' Butler seems a little sleepy at the 1960 Tory Party Conference at Scarborough.

However, by the time the 1964 General Election came round, the nation was ready for a change and they gave Harold Wilson and the

Liberal leaders take a stroll on the beach at Llandudno before their 1962 Conference. From left: Jeremy Thorpe, Emlyn Hoosen QC, Arthur Holt, Jo Grimond, Donald Wade, Eric Lubbock and Roderick Bowen QC.

Labour party a chance. They were duly elected, but only just, by a majority of four. Their vote was actually down from the last General Election in 1959 but the big swing to the Liberals took votes away from the Tories.

One of Wilson's Ministers in his new Government was Patrick Gordon-Walker, who was appointed Foreign Secretary. However, the appointment caused a stir because Gordon-Walker lost his Smethwick seat at the General Election. In order to get back into Parliament he stood at the Leyton by-election, created especially for him in January 1965. He was defeated again. Amidst embarrassment for Harold Wilson, Gordon-Walker handed in his resignation the following day. He later

returned to the Cabinet in 1967 as a Minister without portfolio. This time he was an MP after winning the Leyton seat at the 1966 General Election. Later in 1967 he was appointed Secretary for Education and in 1968 he was made a Life Peer.

After 20 months of struggling to rule with such a thin majority, Harold Wilson was forced to go back to the electorate in 1966. By now the Tories had a new leader, Ted Heath, who had been elected in July 1965.

The Labour party fought the election campaign with the slogan 'You Know Labour Government Works' while the Conservatives used Common Market entry and Union

Harold Wilson addresses the 1966 Labour Party Conference. George Brown is to Wilson's left and James Callaghan is next to him.

reforms as two major issues. But it was Wilson who won the day and with an increased majority of 97. Harold Wilson and the Labour party stayed in power for the rest of the decade, while Heath remained the leader of the opposition.

He had doubled his majority in the Bristol south-east by-election in 1961, but the High Court subsequently quashed his victory and awarded the seat to the runner-up. However, after much campaigning by Stansgate, the Peerage Bill was published in 1963. It gave the opportunity for peers to renounce their titles. Benn was the first person to take advantage of the new law. He reverted to Anthony Wedgwood Benn and resumed his career as an MP. The new Bill also allowed Lord Home to renounce his title and in 1963 Viscount Hailsham also renounced his title to become Quintin Hogg and a very important political figure of the sixties. He was made a life peer in 1970 and became Lord Chancellor.

The leadership of the Liberal party, who promised so much in the mid-

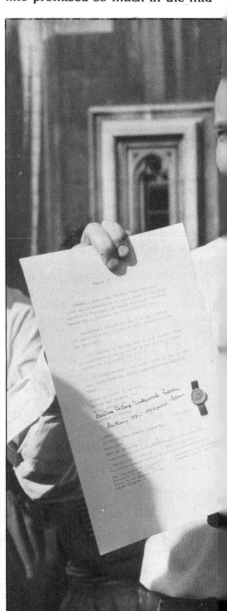

sixties, changed hands when Joe Grimmond resigned on 17 January 1967. He was replaced by Old Etonian and television personality Jeremy Thorpe.

In 1961 the start of a great political career was being furthered when Margaret Thatcher, the youngest Tory woman MP at the time, was appointed to her first government job when she was made joint Parliamentary Secretary to the Ministry of Pensions. Some election results of note from the 1960s — Michael Foot won the Ebbw Vale seat vacated following the death of Nye Bevan, and when David Steel won the Roxburgh, Selkirk and Peebles by-election for the Liberals in 1965 he became, at 26, the youngest MP in Britain. Gynfor Evans was sworn in as MP for Carmarthen in July 1966 as the first Welsh Nationalist Member of Parliament, and in November 1967

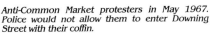

Call me Mister. Anthony Wedgwood Benn, pictured with his American wife Carlone, holds up the piece of paper which proclaims that he has successfully renounced his peerage in August 1963. Nowadays, the former Viscount Stansgate would rather be known as plan Tony Benn.

Winifred Ewing became the first Scottish Nationalist MP since 1945 when she won the Hamilton by-election.

Entry into the Common Market was

Anti-Common Market protesters in May 1967. Police would not allow them to enter Downing Street with their coffin.

one of the big issues of the decade. Ted Heath was the man who the Tories sent to do the negotiating on our behalf. But often his efforts were thwarted by General De Gaulle who was against our entry. Heath vowed that if he took control of the country he would take Britain into the Common Market, and he did.

Other major issues of the sixties were the devaluation of the pound in November 1967 which eventually led to the resignation of James Callaghan as Chancellor. And some important Bills which made their appearance during the decade were the Race Relations Bill which was published in 1968, and the Trade Description Act which became law the same year. Capital punishment was abolished in 1965 and that year Capital Gains Tax was introduced. The following year saw the introduction of Corporation Tax.

Prices and wages were constantly hitting the headlines in the sixties and in 1966 there was a freeze on both. And one of the biggest issues that all Governments faced in the sixties was that of immigration, a subject which has been covered in greater detail elsewhere in this book. Strikes, also mentioned elsewhere, were prevalent in the sixties, notably in the motor-car industry, as the 1960s became a strong era for the unions. A State of Emergency was called during the dock strike of 1966.

Towards the end of the decade, Northern Ireland became a major political issue as British troops were sent into the province. All subsequent Governments have found the Northern Ireland problem a major issue. At the start of the decade, however, the Tory Government's big

US Presidential elections of the 1960s:

Year	Candidates	Electoral Vote	Popular Vote	Vice-President
1960	John F.Kennedy (D)	303	34,226,731	Lyndon B.Johnson
	Richard M.Nixon (R)	219	34,108,157	Henry Cabot Lodge
1964	Lyndon B.Johnson (D)	486	43,129,484	Hubert H.Humphrey
	Barry M.Goldwater (R)	52	27,178,188	William E.Milller
1968	Richard M.Nixon (R)	301	31,785,480	Spiro T.Agnew
	Hubert H.Humphrey (D)	191	31,275,166	Edmund S.Muskie
	George C.Wallace (AI)	46	9,906,473	Curtis F.LeMay

(D) Democrat (R) Republican (AI) American Independent

concern was the 'wind of change' that was sweeping through the African continent as the Commonwealth was continually shrinking as a result of many nations gaining their independence. The Ian Smith Rhodesian UDI affair of the mid-sixties proved to be a difficult time for Harold Wilson.

In the United States John F.Kennedy was sworn in as President in 1961 after beating Republican candidate Richard Nixon in the race to the White House. Kennedy took over from Dwight D.Eisenhower who had completed his maximum two terms of office. Sadly, despite doing so much in such a short period of time, Kennedy was assassinated on 22 November 1963 and was succeeded by his Vice President, Lyndon Baines Johnson, who was sworn in while aboard the Presidential jet at Love Fields, Dallas.

Johnson easily won the 1964 election but decided not to stand in 1968 in the wake of the Vietnam War, and Richard Nixon had a narrow win for the Republicans over Hubert Humphrey.

A lot was happening in world politics in the 1960s, as it does in every decade. But in a decade filled with so much more going on, it didn't seem to have the importance it should have.

General Elections of the 1960s:
Seats won

Date	Lab	Con	Lib	Maj
15 Oct 1964	317	303	9	4
31 Mar 1966	363	253	12	97

NB. The Speaker reduces the majority by one.

POP ART

A DECADE during which a lot of people took very little seriously gave rise to a new period in the world of art. But how revolutionary the world of *Pop Art* was as it gave the opportunity to the new breed of artist to depict almost anything, so long as it had the artist's own individual style.

Anything from *Brillo* pads to baked bean tins found their way on to canvas, and of course the use of psychedelic colours played an important part in this new style of painting. Life-sized pictures of pop stars and other heroes and heroines also adorned living room and bedroom walls up and down the country. Marilyn Monroe and Che Guevara were two firm favourites in the sixties. Marilyn is, of course, still popular today.

Andy Warhol and David Hockney were exponents of *Pop Art* which can best be described as a way of looking at life around you. It provided the likes of Warhol and Hockney with the freedom of expression, use of colour and a means of escape from reality. It worked wonderfully well.

POP MUSIC

SOME say that Pop Music **was** the sixties. Well, a quick look through this book will reveal that other things were happening around us in those ten glorious years between 1960 and 1969. But my word! What an influence pop music had on our lives during that decade.

The 3rd of February 1959 is often referred to as 'the day the music died'. It was, of course, the day in which the great Buddy Holly — together with the Big Bopper and Richie Valens — was killed in a plane crash. But, on the contrary, their music certainly never died and probably never will. It was the end of the great rock'n'roll era certainly, but about to dawn was a new decade of pop music that was going to change the lives of not only people who lived in the sixties, but of generations to come.

One wonders how bored the children of today must get as we constantly tell them about the 'great days' of the sixties. And how they must get sick and tired of hearing about pop stars like the Beatles, the Stones, the Hollies, Gerry and the Pace-

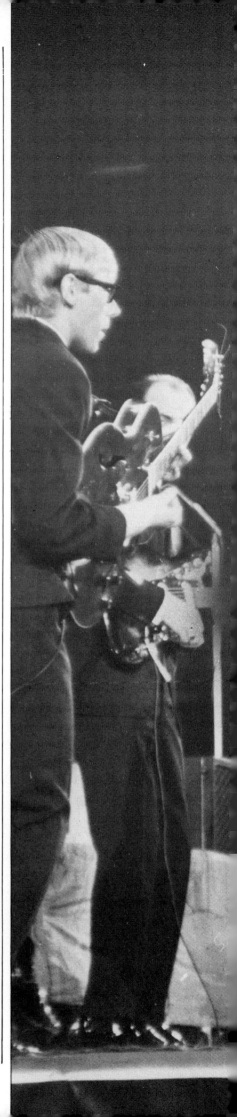

makers and so on, and so on. But the stark reality is these people changed our lives so much with their new style of music. So how can we ever forget them?

With the exception of the likes of Elvis, Cliff Richard and a few others, the music of the late-fifties and early-sixties had become tedious and, to a certain extent, boring. The music industry had developed technically, but little had been done to develop new sounds. Perhaps if they had made a steady progression then us '60s freaks' wouldn't keep going on about the wonderful world of pop music that existed in those days.

Standing on top of the charts on 1 January 1960 was Emile Ford and the Checkmates with *What Do You Want To Make Those Eyes At Me For.* But a new sound was needed. The early years, 1960, '61 and '62, were hangover years from the fifties, and it was during this time that Elvis, Cliff, and the Shadows ruled the charts. Record collections were further boosted by the sounds of Shirley Bassey, Anthony Newley and Adam Faith. But it was also a time when fresh new young musicians were learning their trade and getting ready for the explosion which was about to happen. And in 1963 it happened.

It was then that the so-called 'Swinging Sixties' began and it was Liverpool that became the 'centre of the universe' when it came to pop music.

Liverpool FC had just got back into the First Division and the whole city was reverberating. Not just to the echoes of *You'll Never Walk Alone* on the Kop, but to the sounds of 'Yeah yeah yeah' from the Cavern Club. By the end of 1963, the Beatles, Gerry and the Pacemakers, Billy J.Kramer and the Searchers had all come out of Liverpool and gone to the top of the charts.

The new type of music had a knock-on effect around Britain. Other groups sprang up. By 1964 the reputation of the British groups spread worldwide and the American Press cried 'The British are coming'. Furthermore, the top groups like the Beatles not only went to the States, but they also saw and conquered. The Beatles no longer belonged to Liverpool — they belonged to the world.

As the Stones emerged on the scene as rivals to Liverpool's Fab Four, there were cries of 'Rubbish', 'Disgusting' and 'Look at the length of their hair!' from parents up and down the country. But the groups and singers overcame all such objections and became superstars. But, in retrospect, what was all the fuss about?

Freddie and the Dreamers on stage at the Empire Pool, Wembley, at a gala concert held on Sunday, 26 April 1964.

While the Beatles were winning over the Americans, back home the charts started to take on a different look. No longer was it Mersey-dominated as many other leading groups, equally as talented, emerged and remained at the top for many years. There were, of course, the Stones. But there were also the Kinks, the Hollies, Freddie and the Dreamers, Manfred Mann and the founder of the Tottenham Sound, the Dave Clark Five, to name but a very small number. Dusty Springfield, Sandie Shaw and Tom Jones kept the flag flying for the solo artistes and what about the 'one hit wonders'? Who can say that *Juliet* by the Four Pennies was not one of the best records of its time or that *Have I The Right* by the Honeycombs would not have been a big hit in any other era?

Whilst it is nice to bang the patriotic drum, it is also fair to state that during the great days of pop on these shores, the Americans made a significant contribution. Motown was of course on the up-and-up and they gave us such wonderful evergreen stars as Diana Ross and the Supremes, Stevie Wonder, the Temptations, the Four Tops, the Miracles and so on. They became big favourites this side of the 'pond' as did Tamla Motown music in general. Motown's first number one in the States was *Please Mr Postman* by the Marvellettes in 1961. And this side of the Atlantic their first number one was *Baby Love* by the Supremes in 1964.

The Big 'O', Roy Orbison, was another American who had a big influence this side of the Atlantic, as did Sonny and Cher, Simon and Garfunkel and of course the King was still the King. Would all this have happened in the first place if it had not been for Elvis?

The awe-inspiring Beatles guided us through the middle years of the sixties. They had changed the face of pop music in 1963 and they did it again in 1967 with the album *Sergeant Pepper's Lonely Hearts Club Band*.

They had already brought us

Three records went straight into the British charts at number one in the 1960s:
It's Now Or Never, *Elvis Presley, 1960.*
The Young Ones, *Cliff Richard and the Shadows, 1962.*
Get Back, *The Beatles and Billy Preston, 1969.*

different hairstyles and fashions. Now they were to be trendsetters again in a world that was ready to be led. Their

From left: Paul McCartney, Dusty Springfield, Tom Jones and Ringo Starr at the 1965 Melody Maker Awards.

The One-Hit Wonders of the 1960s were:
(i.e. only chart success was a number-one hit.)
Tell Laura I Love Her, *Ricky Valance, 1960*
Nut Rocker, *B.Bumble and the Stingers, 1962*
Michelle, *The Overlanders, 1966*
Fire, *Crazy World of Arthur Brown, 1968*
In The Year 2525 (Exordium And Terminus), *Zager and Evans, 1969*
Je T'Aime. . . Moi Non Plus, *Jane Birkin and Serge Gainsbourg, 1969*
Sugar Sugar, *The Archies, 1969*

album was described as the 'total' album as the 'new' Beatles emerged. Gone were the 'Yeah yeah yeahs' of the early days. Now their music and lyrics had undertones of drugs and mysticism as the Beatles themselves turned into hippies. They, like other groups of the day, turned to transcendental meditation, and the guru to many groups was the Maharishi Maresh Yogi.

As the second half of the decade unfolded we were treated to flower power, folk rock, early punk and heavy metal. Such acts as The Who, Pink Floyd, Led Zeppelin, Elton John, Rod Stewart, David Bowie, the Bee Gees and Fleetwood Mac were establishing themselves as stars of the future.

Bob Dylan, Joan Baez and Barry Maguire all warned us of the dangers of war or, in Dylan's case, the dangers of almost everything! But despite the birth of the new breed of rock musician at the end of the decade, the last number one record of the 1960s belonged to, believe it or not, Rolf Harris with his monster hit *Two Little Boys.*

As the decade came to a close the youth of the world had gained their freedom and independence. They had a bigger say in what they wanted and were freer to do what they wanted. What had started as rock'n'roll music at the start of the decade had turned into pure rock. A lot happened musically in between. But what an influence the music of the day had on our lives. We have never looked back, although it is terrific to keep going back and listening to those sounds of the 1960s.

In 1968, at the age of 68, Louis Armstrong became the oldest person to top the British charts when What a Wonderful World *went to number one.*

Christmas number ones of the 1960s:

Year	Title	Artiste(s)
1960	It's Now Or Never	Elvis Presley
1961	Tower Of Strength	Frankie Vaughan
1962	Return To Sender	Elvis Presley
1963	I Want To Hold Your Hand	The Beatles
1964	I Feel Fine	The Beatles
1965	Day Tripper/We Can Work It Out	The Beatles
1966	Green, Green Grass Of Home	Tom Jones
1967	Hello Goodbye	The Beatles
1968	Lily The Pink	Scaffold
1969	Two Little Boys	Rolf Harris

Engelbert Humperdinck's Release Me *spent a record 56 consecutive weeks in the charts between January 1967 and March 1968. Acker Bilk's* Stranger on the Shore *spent 55 consecutive weeks in the charts, the most by a record which never reached number one.*

The following had the most number ones in the 1960s:

Total	Artiste(s)
17	The Beatles (including one with Billy Preston)
11	Elvis Presley
8	The Rolling Stones
7	Cliff Richard
5	The Shadows
4	Frank Ifield
3	Everly Brothers, Roy Orbison, Gerry and the Pacemakers, The Searchers, Manfred Mann, The Kinks, Sandie Shaw, Georgie Fame (including two with the Blue Flames).

The following spent the most weeks at number one in the British charts in the 1960s:

Total Wks	Artiste(s)
69	The Beatles (including six weeks with Billy Preston)
44	Elvis Presley
20	Cliff Richard
18	The Rolling Stones
17	Frank Ifield
16	The Shadows
12	The Everly Brothers
11	Gerry and the Pacemakers, Engelbert Humperdinck
9	Sandie Shaw
8	The Archies, Tom Jones
7	Roy Orbison, Cilla Black, Manfred Mann, The Searchers
6	Helen Shapiro, The Tremeloes (including three with Brian Poole), Procol Harum, Mary Hopkin, Nancy Sinatra (including two weeks with her dad)

POPE JOHN XXIII

POPE John XXIII was one of the most popular Popes of recent years and his views made him especially popular with young people as he sought to bring the Roman Catholic religion in line with the 20th century.

A peasant's son from Bergamo, he was born Angelo Giuseppe Roncalli in 1881. He was ordained as a priest in 1904 and in 1920 worked in the Vatican. He was made a Cardinal in 1956 and appointed the Archbishop of Venice.

He succeeded Pius XII as Pope in 1958 when 77 years of age and surprised many when, in 1959, he announced the Second Vatican Council, nearly 100 years after the first. More than 2,000 Bishops gathered to discuss the way the church should fit in with the modern age.

Peace on earth was also one of Pope John's tasks and he met with many political and religious leaders of other denominations. In 1960 he had a meeting with Dr Fisher, the Archbishop of Canterbury. Also in 1960 he named the first black African, Japanese and Filipino cardinals.

Pope John died of cancer on 3 June 1963 but in his short reign did much for world peace and unity. He was succeeded by Giovanni Montini (Pope Paul VI) who had been made a Cardinal by Pope John in one of his first acts as Pope in 1958.

POST OFFICE TOWER

THE first announcement of the building of the Post Office Tower came in February 1961 when it was announced it would be 507 feet tall. It was later increased to 603 feet and when it opened had increased to 619 feet, the tallest building in Britain.

Towering above Bloomsbury and with magnificent views across London it was opened on 8 October 1965 by the Prime Minister, Harold Wilson. He

The following records spent the most weeks at number one in the 1960s:

Wks	Title	Year	Artiste(s)
8	It's Now Or Never	1960	Elvis Presley
8	Wonderful Land	1962	The Shadows
8	Sugar Sugar	1969	The Archies
7	Cathy's Clown	1960	Everly Brothers
7	I Remember You	1962	Frank Ifield
7	From Me To You	1963	The Beatles
7	Green, Green Grass Of Home	1966-7	Tom Jones
7	Hello Goodbye	1967-8	The Beatles
6	Wooden Heart	1961	Elvis Presley
6	The Young Ones	1962	Cliff Richard and the Shadows
6	Release Me	1967	Engelbert Humperdinck
6	A Whiter Shade Of Pale	1967	Procol Harum
6	Those Were The Days	1968	Mary Hopkin
6	Get Back	1969	The Beatles with Billy Preston

did not perform the opening ceremony by cutting the traditional piece of tape, but declared it open by talking down the first microwave to leave the tower when he engaged in a conversation with the Lord Mayor of Birmingham. The Postmaster General at the time of the opening was Anthony Wedgwood Benn.

The 30-storey tower had a capacity to handle 150,000 telephone calls simultaneously and cope with 40 television channels — it needs to these days! The rotating restaurant and viewing galleries were opened to the public on 19 May 1966.

POSTAGE

AT the start of the decade the cost of posting a standard 1oz letter was 3d and had remained unaltered since 1957. The next change was in 1965. This is how the cost altered during 1960s:

	Cost	Weight of Std Letter
1960	3d	1oz
1961	3d	1oz
1962	3d	1oz
1963	3d	1oz
1964	3d	1oz
1965	4d	2oz
1966	4d	2oz
1967	4d	2oz
1968	4d	4oz, 2nd Class
	5d	4oz, 1st Class
1969	4d	4oz, 2nd Class
	5d	4oz, 1st Class

The two-tier system came into force on 16 September 1968. The cost as at 1 June 1989 was 14p for 2nd Class and 19p for 1st Class. They are equivalent to 2s 10d and 3s 11d respectively.

POWELL, Enoch

BORN at Stechford, Birmingham, in 1912, Enoch John Powell rose to become one of the most controversial Tory MP's in the 1960s particularly with his open views on racial problems and immigration.

He was educated at Cambridge and at the age of 25 became a professor of Greek at Sydney University. He was one of the youngest professors in the Commonwealth.

During the war he joined the army as a private and reached the rank of brigadier in less than six years. After the war he had ambitions of becoming a politician and in 1950 became the Conservative MP for Wolverhampton.

Powell quickly rose to senior Governmental positions and in 1960 was appointed Minister of Health. However, he resigned three years later after Alec Douglas-Home became Prime Minister. Two years later Powell stood for the Party leadership.

Above: Enoch Powell greets a black passer-by after leaving a television studio in June 1969.

"As I look ahead I am filled with foreboding. Like the Roman, I see the River Tiber flowing with much blood."
Enoch Powell, Birmingham, 21 April 1968.

Immigration was his big issue of the 1960s and his 'Rivers of Blood' speech at Birmingham in April 1968 was one of the biggest political controversies of the era. It led to Ted Heath dismissing him from the Shadow Cabinet.

Powell, however, was prepared to take a stand on any issue that he felt was not in line with true Tory policies. Consequently, because he was against Britain's entry into the Common Market, he did not stand at the February 1974 General Election, even advising Britain to vote Labour as they would at least place the issue of EEC membership before a referendum. Eight months later he returned to Westminster as an Ulster Unionist MP representing his new constituency of South Down. He lost his seat at the 1987 General Election.

POWERS, Gary

IF it hadn't been for Gary Powers, then top Irish band U2 would never have got their name. Powers was the pilot

of the American U2 bomber which was shot down by the Russians in 1960.

Francis Gary Powers was born in 1929 and served with the US Air Force. He was piloting the high altitude U2 plane when he was shot down on 1 May 1960 over Sverdlovsk. Found guilty of spying, he was sentenced to ten years loss of liberty, with the first three years to be spent in prison. He was released in 1962 in exchange for a soviet spy.

Upon his return to the United States, Powers worked as a civilian helicopter pilot in later life and was killed while reporting for Los Angeles television in 1977 when his helicopter crashed.

PRESLEY, Elvis

ELVIS Aaron Presley changed the whole face of rock and roll music with his new exciting style in the 1950s. The Beatles did the same in the sixties. But it would be impossible to write a book about any of the last four decades without mention of Elvis, the undisputed 'King of Rock and Roll'.

It is impossible to do justice to the achievements of Elvis in a few lines. Seldom have they been fully catalogued despite the many volumes written about him. So what chance have we got?

Born in Tupelo, Mississippi, on 8 January 1935, Elvis sang from an early age in the church choir and also took part in talent contests. For his 12th birthday he was given a guitar and taught himself to play. Throughout his entire career he played the instrument from memory — he never learned to read music.

On his graduation from Memphis High School in 1953, Elvis studied as an electrician whilst earning money in his spare time as a truck driver. As a surprise for his mother in 1954 he recorded two songs at the private studio of the Sun Record Company. The president of the company accidentally overheard the youngster singing and his recordings, *That's All Right Momma* and *Blue Moon Over Kentucky* received some air space on local radio. This brought him limited success and he toured the southern states of America under the name of 'The Hillbilly Cat'.

After singing at a disc jockey's convention at Nashville in 1955, Elvis was signed by RCA-Victor Records and he gained media attention when they released five Elvis Presley records on one day!

He received nationwide attention when he appeared on the *Jackie Gleason Show*. Other television appearances followed, but, following cries of 'disgusting' from outraged parents of teenage fans, he was often seen only from the waist upwards. His sensual gyrating hips were obliterated from the camera shots. Television viewers had certainly never seen anything like it before, certainly not from a music star.

An appearance on the *Ed Sullivan Show* enhanced his career further and in 1956 he signed a seven-year film contract. His first movie was *Love Me Tender*. Suddenly the Elvis Presley industry was well and truly on its way under the guidance of his shrewd manager, Colonel Parker.

Elvis then took the pop charts by storm when *Heartbreak Hotel*, backed by *I Was The One,* spent eight weeks at number one in the US charts in 1956 and earned him two gold discs, one for each side!

The record reached number two in the British charts, and that year he had no fewer than 11 British chart successes. His first British number one came the following year when a re-entry of *All Shook Up* went to the top of the charts.

His greatest era, as far as British chart success was concerned, was in the sixties when he had 11 chart-topping hits this side of the Atlantic. When *It's Now Or Never, Are You Lonesome Tonight?* and *Wooden Heart* all went to number one, it was the first time any artiste had enjoyed three successive number-one hits. But not content with that, Elvis's next record, *Surrender,* went on to make it four in a row.

Despite serving two years in the Army between 1958 and 1960, he never lost his band of faithful fans. The hysteria Presley generated was something only repeated by the arrival of the Beatles some years later, as people sought to see Elvis both live and on the silver screen. He appeared in 34 films portraying everything from an Indian to a boxer, a cowboy to a lifeguard. But invariably he ended up with a beautiful girl in his arms. Some of his best-known films of the sixties included: *Flaming Star, GI Blues, Wild In The Country, Blue Hawaii, Follow That Dream, Kid Galahad, Girls Girls Girls,* and *It Happened At The World's Fair.*

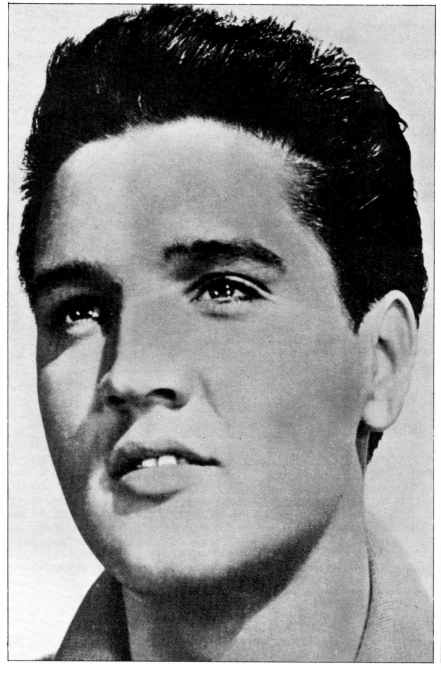

Elvis' biggest-selling record was It's Now Or Never. *World sales were in excess of 20 million, five million of which were in the United States. It was originally written by Caupurro and Di Capua in 1901 under the title* O Sole Mio. *The 'B' side of Presley's version in the States was* A Mess Of Blues *while the 'B' side in Britain was* Make Me Know It.

In the 1970s he wound down his recording and film commitments and devoted more time to night club appearances but the once slimline 'King' had substantially increased his waistline. Despite the change of appearance, he was as electric and charismatic as ever. Never one for touring abroad (he never played in Britain), he became a virtual recluse at his Graceland home at 3764 Elvis Presley Boulevard, Memphis, and despite rumours of Elvis suffering a drink and drugs problem, his millions of loyal fans never deserted him.

On 16 August 1977, Elvis was found unconscious in the bathroom of his home. He was rushed to the Baptist Memorial Hospital, Memphis, but nothing could be done. At the age of 42, Elvis Aaron Presley was dead.

He has left us with the legacy of his music and, whatever a minority of people who take pleasure in degrading him might say, the point is simple: without Elvis Presley there would be an awful lot of blank spaces in this book. We owe him an unrepayable debt.

Elvis' Army serial number was: 553310761.

Top Ten hits of Elvis Presley in the 1960s:

Year	Record	Pos
1960	Stuck On You	3
1960	A Mess Of Blues	2
1960	It's Now Or Never	1
1961	Are You Lonesome Tonight?	1
1961	Wooden Heart	1
1961	Surrender	1
1961	Wild In The Country/I Feel So Bad	4
1961	His Latest Flame/Little Sister	1
1962	Rock A Hula Baby/Can't Help Falling In Love	1
1962	Good Luck Charm	1
1962	She's Not You	1
1962	Return to Sender	1
1963	Devil In Disguise	1
1964	Kissin' Cousins	10
1965	Crying In The Chapel	1
1966	Love Letters	6
1969	In The Ghetto	2
1969	Suspicious Minds	2

His other British number-one hits were:

1957	All Shook Up
1958	Jailhouse Rock
1959	One Night/I Got Stung
1959	A Fool Such As I/I Need Your Love Tonight
1970	The Wonder Of You
1977	Way Down

Elvis' last performance was at Indianapolis on 26 June 1977.

PRICES

BECAUSE prices of goods and services varied and changed so much throughout the decade, and in different parts of the country, the following is just a random selection of prices in the sixties:

In 1960 Littlewoods department store advertised for Junior Management Trainees, aged 16-20. The starting salary was £250 per annum. Ten years later the National Giro Bank were offering 16-year-old Clerical Officers a starting salary of £420 a year. The salary of a Clerical Assistant ranged between £5 19s 6d per week at 15 to £14 15s 0d at 25.

The cost of a modern three-bedroomed semi-detached house in a good class area in the north of England was around £3,000 in 1960, while the 1969 price of the same house would have been in the region of £4,150. A comparable house in London would have cost about £6,250. It was possible in 1960 to buy a brand new two-bedroomed semi for under £2,000.

A 15-day holiday at Lloret de Mar in 1960 would have cost you a mere 42 guineas. For £59 you could have spent Christmas or New Year 1963 aboard the Queen Mary on a six-day cruise from Southampton to Las Palmas, but you would have needed to go to Burtons to get a new hand-made suit for the trip. That would have cost a further nine guineas. Mind you, for 3d you could have bought a copy of the *Daily Mirror* and stayed at home!

In 1964 you could have enjoyed a 17-day cruise around the Greek Islands for only 49½gns, the same price you would have paid for a fully automatic washing machine.

A look at some other prices at the start of the decade shows that a pound of New Zealand butter cost 3s 11d. A brand new kitchen table, made of a tubular frame and *Formica* top (of course!) and complete with four chairs cost 10gns. A 21-piece bone china tea set would have set you back 59s 11d and a *Parker Knoll* fireside chair cost around £8 10s.

In 1963 you could have bought a *Ewbank* carpet sweeper for anything between 45s 6d and 85s 6d. A packet of *Beechams* powders cost 2s 0d, a packet of *Zip* firelighters cost 1s 6d for 12 and a mink-dyed musquash coat would have knocked a 69-guinea dent in the bank balance.

At the end of the decade, when the average wage for male manual workers over 21 was £24 16s 5d, a sliced loaf cost 1s 8d, 20 tipped cigarettes cost 5s 2d and untipped cost 6s 1d (Capstan full strength cost 3s 11d for 20 in 1960). Council rents were an average of £3 15s per week and the mortgage rate was 8½%. Perhaps surprisingly a 19in colour television set in 1969 cost £290…considerably more than today. But a bottle of Scotch cost only 49s 11d…considerably less than today.

In the grocer's shop in 1969 a 16oz tin of *Heinz* beans would have cost 1s 0d and an 8oz jar of *Nescafé* coffee was 7s 11d, whereas a packet of *Jacobs* cream crackers was 10d.

Holidays were still cheap at the end of the decade. A fortnight in two of the newest resorts, the Costa Brava and Majorca, would have cost less than £40 while two weeks in Tenerife would have cost £70, quite high in comparison, but cheap compared to 1989. However, you must never lose sight of the fact that the average weekly wage was only around £20 at the end of the decade. That made many items a lot dearer than they are today in real terms.

PRINCE CHARLES' INVESTITURE

JULY 1969 was quite a memorable month. Ann Jones won Wimbledon, Tony Jacklin won the British Open, man landed on the Moon and Prince Charles was invested as the Prince of Wales.

From the moment Her Majesty the Queen announced, during the closing ceremony of the 1958 Commonwealth Games in Cardiff, that she would make Prince Charles the Prince of Wales, the majority of the Welsh people looked forward to the big day, although many nationalists had reservations and a minority actually saw the Investiture as an insult to the Welsh nation.

Security for the Investiture on 1 July 1969 was tight. There was cause for concern when a 'bomb' was found on a railway bridge over the River Dee

The Queen presents her son to the people of Wales at Caernarfon Castle.

at Chester. The Royal train was scheduled to travel over the bridge during the Royal Family's trip to Caernarfon. The train was held up at Crewe while the suspect packet was removed and found to be a dummy.

Every precaution was taken to make sure the Investiture passed without incident, but there was an egg-throwing incident, a banana skin thrown under one of the royal horses and some booing amongst the crowd. Happily those incidents were in the minority and for 250,000 crowded into the North Wales town it was a day of pageantry and splendour.

Prince Charles became the 19th Prince of Wales since 1301 and the first since 1911. Millions watched the occasion on television, not only in

---

In his speech, the Prince made reference to Harry Secombe, the Welsh Goon. Secombe was driving along in his car when he heard the speech; he couldn't believe his ears when he got a mention. The Goons, of course, was one of the Prince's favourite radio programmes.

Britain but also in the United States, Australia and Canada, as well as other countries. They saw the Queen place the jewelled coronet on the Prince's head as he assumed the titles of Prince of Wales and Earl of Chester. The coronet was made by Louis Osman at a cost of £3,600 and was given to Her Majesty by the Goldsmith's Company.

After the official part of the ceremony the Queen then escorted the new Prince of Wales to the Queen Eleanor's Gate where he was presented to the Welsh people for the first time.

After the ceremony the Queen, Duke and other members of the Royal Family returned to their train which had been waiting for them at the private sidings of the Ferodo company. The new Prince of Wales then headed for the Royal Yacht Britannia which was berthed off Anglesey. The next day he started a four-day tour of Wales.

PRINCESS MARGARET'S WEDDING

FROM the moment Princess Margaret's engagement to Mr Anthony Armstrong-Jones was announced on

26 February 1960, virtually the whole nation awaited the big day. And on Friday, 6 May they were treated to the most glittering event since the Coronation seven years earlier. It was certainly the great Royal occasion of the 1960s.

The crowds which packed London's streets were the biggest since the Coronation, but millions more watched the event on television as schoolchildren were given a day off school.

Westminster Abbey was decorated in gladioli, roses and tulips in yellow, blue and red. Two thousand privileged guests were allowed inside the Abbey but outside, lining every street on the route, the adoring British public tried to get a glimpse of the Princess, who became the first of royal blood to marry a commoner for 450 years.

The Princess looked radiant in her Norman Hartnell-designed dress made of white silk organza with a high 'V' neck and full-length tight sleeves. Thirty yards of fabric were used in the top layer alone.

The Duke of Edinburgh gave away the 29-year-old Princess, the best man was Dr Roger Gilliatt and there were eight bridesmaids, including Princess Anne.

THIS popular 1967 British series starring Patrick McGoohan became something of a cult in the sixties, and again in later years.

Set in the beautiful Portmeirion village in North Wales, it featured McGoohan playing the part of a former secret agent who was captured and held prisoner in a mystery high-security village.

There were only 17 episodes filmed, and each told the story of McGoohan, known simply as *Number Six*, trying unsuccessfully to escape his captors. The main obstacles in his way were *Rovers*, giant plastic bouncing balloons, which had the power to swallow up anybody trying to abscond from the village.

The series was full of gimmicks as the enemy tried to brainwash our hero, but he remained resilient to the end. When the series finished, the viewer was left wondering what it had all been about and the eventual fate of *Number Six* was never known.

Some of the well-known stars who appeared in the series included: Leo McKern, Nigel Stock, Patrick Cargill, Finlay Currie, Peter Wyngarde, Donald Sinden and Paul Eddington of The Good Life *and* Yes Minister/Yes Prime Minister *fame.*

PROCOL HARUM

ALTHOUGH Procol Harum had only two Top Ten hits in their career, both in 1967, one of them, *A Whiter Shade Of Pale*, was one of the biggest and quickest-selling singles of the decade.

Procol Harum is the name of a breed of Burmese Cat.

A Whiter Shade Of Pale spent 11 weeks at number one in France and in Switzerland it was the fastest selling single of all time.

It was released on Decca's new Deram label on 12 May 1967. Within days it was number one in Britain and became a sensation across Europe and in the United States. It stayed in the British charts for 15 weeks and was at number one for six of them. It sold 350,000 copies in its first 16 days of release in Britain and soon went past the half-million mark. Global sales exceeded six million copies.

The song is based on a poem by Keith Reid, who was responsible for forming the group, although he did not play in it. The meaning of the lyrics

An estimated 300 million people sat glued to their television sets to watch the last spectacular Royal Wedding until that of Princess Anne and Mark Phillips in the 1970s.

The newlyweds honeymooned on the Royal Yacht Britannia in the Caribbean and when they returned on 18 June, moved into their new home at Kensington Palace.

The marriage was dissolved in 1978.

The eight bridesmaids at the wedding of Princess Margaret and Anthony Armstrong-Jones were:
Princess Anne
Miss Catherine Vesey
Miss Annabel Rhodes
Miss Sarah Lowther
Lady Virginia FitzRoy
Lady Rose Nevill
Miss Marilyn Wills
Miss Angela Nevill

have never been fully explained. It probably refers to what the subconscious undergoes when under the influence of drugs. Nevertheless, the combination of the lyrics and music based on Bach's *Air On A G String* were enough to make it one of the most distinctive singles of 1967, possibly of the decade.

Top Ten hits of Procol Harum in the 1960s:

Year	Record	Pos
1967	A Whiter Shade Of Pale	1
1967	Homburg	6

PROFUMO, John, OBE, CBE

ON 22 March 1963 John Profumo, the Secretary of State for War, made a personal statement to the House of Commons in which he said there had been: "no impropriety whatsoever" between him and Christine Keeler. This statement was made after the rumours of his affair with Miss Keeler, who was also acquainted with a Russian diplomat.

Ten weeks later, on 5 June, John Profumo resigned from the Government and from Parliament after he admitted that he had lied when he said there had been no impropriety. He did emphasize, however, that there had been no breach of national security.

Profumo was forced to make this latter statement after Dr Stephen Ward, at whose flat Profumo and Miss Keeler met, challenged the original statement. Ward wrote privately to both the Prime Minister, Harold Macmillan, and the leader of the opposition, Harold Wilson.

Educated at Harrow and Oxford, Profumo first became an MP in 1940 and was awarded the OBE in 1944. He held several Government posts before becoming Secretary of State for War in 1960.

John Profumo had been a one-time friend of the Royal Family, and it was not until 1971 that Her Majesty the Queen met him again for the first time since his fall from grace. But in the 1975 Birthday Honours list, he was made a CBE in recognition of his charity work.

PROFUMO AFFAIR

OVER the years various Governments have had to sustain scandals. Mrs Thatcher has had a few in her reign as Premier and has come through most of them unscathed. But in Harold Macmillan's case the Profumo affair was just another burden for the government and a few months after the scandal the Premier resigned due to ill health.

John Profumo was the Secretary of State for War in Macmillan's Government. In March 1963 it was alleged that he had an acquaintanceship with Christine Keeler, who also had a relationship with Soviet naval attaché, Eugene Ivanov. On 22 March, in a personal statement, Profumo told MPs that there was no impropriety whatsoever. Prime Minister Macmillan was reported to have regarded the matter as closed.

Ten weeks later, however, Profumo admitted he had lied to the Commons when he said there was no impropriety. However, he denied any breach of security.

Profumo was forced to admit his relationship with Keeler after pressure was put on the Prime Minister and opposition leader Harold Wilson by Dr Stephen Ward, a West End osteopath, at whose flat Profumo met Keeler. Ward was regarded as the man who brought together high-class girls and men of high-ranking positions.

Five days after Profumo's admission, Ward appeared in court charged with living off immoral earnings.

Keeler was just one of Ward's girls. Another was Mandy Rice-Davies, the 18-year-old mistress of Ward, and

Russian naval attaché Eugene Ivanov.

Dr Stephen Ward.

former girlfriend of racketeer Peter Rachman. Davies and Keeler were two of the key figures in the scandal.

The trial of Stephen Ward began on 22 July and on the morning of the final day he was found unconscious at a Chelsea flat. He had taken an overdose of sleeping pills.

In his absence the jury found him guilty on two charges of living off immoral earnings, but the judge deferred passing sentence and Ward died on 3 August.

Two months later Harold Macmillan resigned as Prime Minister. John Profumo resigned his post. Christine Keeler was jailed for nine months in December 1963 after pleading guilty to perjury and conspiracy to pervert the course of justice in a case that had nothing to do with Profumo. She returned to the limelight in 1989 when a film of the

Christine Keeler pays a London taxi driver who has just dropped her off in Soho in July 1963.

affair was made. Profumo dedicates his life to charity work and was awarded the CBE in 1975.

PSYCHO

ALTHOUGH *Psycho* was not one of the Oscar-winning films of the 1960s, it was still one of the classics of the era and brought out the best in its director/producer, Alfred Hitchcock.

Based on the book by Robert Bloch, it tells the chilling tale of Marion Crane, played by Janet Leigh, who absconds with $40,000. Instead of banking her company's cash she leaves town and, during an overnight stay at a motel, is brutally murdered in the now famous shower scene.

From then on Hitchcock takes the audience down a series of paths, misleading or otherwise, in an attempt to find the killer, which you are led to believe is the aged hotel-owner Mrs Bates. Anthony Perkins, who plays Norman Bates, the owner's son, gives a great performance. When *Psycho II* was made in 1983, Perkins was chosen to play the same role.

Hitchcock used string instrument accompaniment to the film. That way he got a chilling effect which left his audiences gripping the edge of their seats throughout the film. It was also a stipulation of Paramount films' contracts with exhibitors that they had to refuse admission after the film had started. Out of curiosity people had to go and watch the film to see why.

QE II

THE Cunard luxury liner *Queen Elizabeth II* was launched on 20 September 1967 when her Majesty the Queen performed the ceremony at the Clydebank shipyard in front of a 100,000 cheering crowd. However, the vessel would not be ready for her maiden voyage for more than 18 months. More than 2,000 men still had to fit her out.

The QE II during her trials off the coast of Scotland.

The *QEII* was scheduled to set sail during the Christmas-New Year period in 1968 but troubles with her turbines led to the first voyage being delayed by four months. Her first trip was in November 1968 when she made the 13-mile trip from Clydebank to Greenock with Prince Charles on the bridge with captain William Warwick. She eventually set sail from Southampton on 22 April 1969 on her maiden voyage. When she arrived at New York she was greeted by hundreds of wellwishers and a flotilla of small boats followed her into New York harbour.

Built at a cost of £29 million she has certainly lived up to her reputation as one of the world's great luxury liners. In 1982 she also played her part when she acted as a hospital ship during the Falklands War.

QUANT, Mary, OBE

MARY Quant's name is synonymous with the fashion boom of the 1960s. She may not have been responsible for the making of the first miniskirt, but she certainly played a big role in popularizing it during a period when she designed clothes for the new breed of teenage girls who she felt 'no longer wanted to wear the same clothes as their mothers'.

Born in London in 1934, she met her business partner and future husband, Alexander Plunket-Greene, during her time as an art student at Goldsmith's in London. Together with Archie McNair, they opened their first *Bazaar* boutique in the King's Road. Their modern designs, aimed at the teenage market, helped make the King's Road one of the fashion centres of Europe as Mary proclaimed the Paris fashion show as 'out of date'.

The second *Bazaar* was opened at Knightsbridge in 1961 and two years later their Ginger Group was exporting their own mass-produced designs to the United States.

Mary was awarded the OBE in 1966 and that same year she diversified into the world of cosmetics. From there she lent her name to a wide

range of leisure goods like jewellery, sunglasses, ties and so on.

In the 1980s the name of Mary Quant is as big as ever, but more for her range of cosmetics and textile design. In the 1960s however, there was no bigger name in the fashion world than that of Mary Quant. She was the woman who knew what clothes girls wanted to wear. She fulfilled their needs.

RADIO LUXEMBOURG

BEFORE the advent of the 'pirate' radio stations and BBC Radio One, the pop music fans of the sixties had to content themselves with listening to Radio Luxembourg, affectionately known as *Luxy*.

The station was founded in 1930 and had its studios at the palace-like Villa Louvigny in the Grand Duchey of Luxembourg. Many of the programmes, however, were recorded at their London studios at Hertford Street.

Broadcasting on 208 metres, Luxembourg, known as 'The Station of the Stars', was one of the pioneering commercial radio stations in Europe. And many big name sponsors added their names to programmes.

Luxy only went over the air in the evening, from 7.30pm to 3am weekdays and 7.00pm to 3am on Sundays. They were their summer broadcasting hours. In winter the times were brought forward by one hour. The highlight of the week was the Top Twenty show on a Sunday night when your DJ, 'BA' Barry Aldis took you through the hit parade.

The *Music In The Night* programme came on the air at 12 o'clock each night and it catered for a wide range of musical tastes. The first half-hour was devoted to chart music, the next 30 minutes to LPs, and the remainder to the easy-listening sounds that sent you to sleep. And how often did you fall asleep with your earplug in only to wake up in the early hours listening to somebody babbling away in a foreign language?

Jimmy Savile was one of the station's top DJs in the early sixties, as was Jimmy Young, and they both featured in Luxy's own weekly magazine, *Fabulous 208*.

RADIO ONE

IT WAS goodbye to the old BBC Light

Radio One disc jockeys pictured outside Broadcasting House on the day the new station opened in September 1967.

and Third Programmes, and the Home Service on 29 September 1967. The following day it was 'hello' to the new Radio One, Two, Three and Four.

Each station was designed for a specific type of listener, just as it is today, and the station given over to pop music was Radio One.

The presenter who had the honour of hosting the new station's first show was Tony Blackburn. He greeted the listeners with the opening words: "Welcome to the exciting sounds of Radio One." He then proceeded to play the new station's first record which was *Flowers In The Rain* by The Move.

Other Radio One DJs in those early days included Bob Holness, now of *Blockbusters* fame, Kenny Everett, Jimmy Young, Pete Murray, Ed 'Stewpot' Stewart and the only survivor of the first 20 years of Radio One, John Peel.

RAMSEY, Sir Alf

ALF Ramsey was the man who guided England soccer to its finest hour when, in July 1966, they beat West Germany 4-2 after extra-time to win the World Cup.

Ramsey was born in 1922 and made his name as a full-back first with Southampton and then with the push-and-run Spurs team of the early fifties. An England international, he was capped 32 times before eventually retiring in 1955. He became manager of Third Division Ipswich Town and steered them into the top division and eventually to the Championship of the Football League in 1962. It was a remarkable achievement and he was the obvious successor to Walter Winterbottom as England team boss when a new manager was sought in October 1962.

His first game officially in charge was the 5-2 defeat by France in the European Championship. But from there Ramsey set about bringing in new talent and developing 'his' team. One of his first moves was to promote Bobby Moore to captain. And it was under Moore's leadership that England won the World Cup.

Ramsey introduced such great individual players as Alan Ball, Martin Peters, Geoff Hurst, Gordon Banks, Nobby Stiles and Jackie Charlton to the team. But, more importantly, he brought them together as a team and not just as 11 individuals. They justly rewarded him with the World Cup triumph.

After failing to qualify for the 1974 World Cup, Ramsey was relieved of his job and he later had a spell back in club management with Birmingham City.

RAY, James Earl

JAMES Earl Ray, the man who assassinated Martin Luther King Junior, was born in Alton, Illinois, on 10 March 1928. His real name was Eric Starvo Galt and his upbringing was not one of the soundest. His father was an habitual criminal and his mother was an alcoholic and part-time streetwalker.

Ray served in the US Army but later followed the same path as his father and found himself in the Missouri penitentiary from where he escaped in April 1967.

His freedom lasted for more than a year, during which time he murdered Dr King at Memphis. He was arrested at London Airport on Saturday, 6 June 1968, two months after King's assassination.

He was travelling under the name of Raymond George Sneyd and is believed to have arrived at Heathrow from Lisbon. He was scheduled to fly on to Belgium but was arrested by Chief Superintendent Tom Butler, head of the Flying Squad, at 11.15am as he tried to pass through immigration.

Ray was taken to Cannon Street police station where he was questioned. He was later extradited to the United States under heavy guard and on 7 May, a first degree murder indictment was made against him by the Grand Jury in Memphis. On 10 March 1969 he was sentenced to a 99-year term of imprisonment.

READY, STEADY, GO

A POP music programme hosted by Keith Fordyce and Cathy McGowan, it was broadcast on a Friday night and, as the programme said, 'The Weekend Starts Here'.

The first programme went out live from TV House, Kingsway, London, on Friday, 9 August 1963 between 7.00 and 7.30pm (it was later moved to a late-evening slot), when the first live artistes were Billy Fury and Brian Poole and the Tremeloes, who

Cathy McGowan pictured with the very latest record-player in August 1966.

performed in front of an audience of around 200 enthusiastic teenagers.

It was compulsive viewing for the pop fans of the day and was the most influential live pop show of the decade. There had been nothing like it since the days of *Oh Boy!* in the fifties.

Affectionately known simply as RSG, it featured the top bands of the day and also gave the opportunity to new up-and-coming bands to get their first big television break. RSG helped launch the careers of the Stones, the Animals, Manfred Mann and many more.

The groups that appeared on the programme were chosen simply because the producers and presenters 'liked them'. Chart position at the time was irrelevant.

The theme music to the programme was Manfred Mann's first big hit, *5-4-3-2-1* and other RSG presenters included David Gell and Michael Aldred. In 1964 the *Ready, Steady, Go* magazine was launched; it cost 2s 0d. In 1965 the miming to records ended and groups in the studio sang live.

One of the great pop shows of the sixties finally came to an end on 23 December 1966.

The film clips from the series are now collectors items and widely used whenever there is a programme or film about the decade. The tapes of the series were acquired, wisely, by Dave Clark (of Dave Clark Five fame) in the 1980s.

REEVES, Jim

THERE is some music that will never die. The music of the late Jim Reeves falls into that category.

Whilst his style of music was not 'the vogue' in the 1960s, he still managed to sell millions of copies of his records, and would still get amongst the likes of the Beatles and Stones at the top of the singles and LP charts.

Born in Texas in 1924, he was an excellent sportsman as a youngster and joined the Houston Buffaloes baseball team as a pitcher. He was forced to quit the sport early because of a leg injury, but that gave him time to concentrate on his second love, singing.

Inspired by the great Hank Williams, Jim's early recording successes were with such songs as *Mexican Joe, Bimbo* and *Four Walls* in the 1950s. His first British success was *He'll Have To Go* in 1960.

He was in the British charts with *I Won't Forget You*, when the music world was stunned on 31 July 1964 by the announcement of Jim Reeves' death following a plane crash. He continued to have posthumous hits and in 1966 *Distant Drums* became

his first and only British number one.

His only film appearance was in *Kimberley Jim*, released in 1965 after his death. He was elected to the Country and Western Hall of Fame in 1967.

Top Ten hits of Jim Reeves in the 1960s:

Year	Record	Pos
1963	Welcome To My World	6
1964	I Love You Because	5
1964	I Won't Forget You	3
1964	There's A Heartache Following Me	6
1965	It Hurts So Much	8
1966	Distant Drums	1

RHODES, Zandra

WHILE Mary Quant and Biba are associated with the early and mid-1960s, then Zandra Rhodes is associated with the latter part of the decade, the psychedelic era.

She was born at Chatham in 1942 and her mother was a lecturer at Medway College of Art where Zandra studied textile design and lithography. She completed her education at the Royal College of Art before designing and selling her own clothes.

She opened the *Fulham Road Clothes Shop* where her unmistakable designs, with a touch of romanticism, became very popular. As the 1960s were coming to a close, she moved towards the trend for brightly coloured patterns, not only for clothes, but also for other furnishings and her designs fitted nicely into the psychedelic part of the decade.

RHODESIAN UDI

IAN Smith declared a Unilateral Declaration of Independence for Rhodesia in 1965, much against the will of the British Government.

Having threatened to declare independence since he came to

Demonstrators outside Rhodesia House, London, in March 1968.

power in 1964, Smith had engaged in talks with the Conservatives. While they were against such moves they never made any public attack on the situation.

When Harold Wilson came to power, he announced that UDI was in effect treason by the white Rhodesians. A referendum amongst the whites a few weeks later revealed that they were fully behind Ian Smith and wanted independence.

In 1965, on the 11th day of the 11th month at 11am, Smith eventually issued Rhodesia's Unilateral Declaration of Independence. He chose that date and time because it coincided with Armistice Day 1918.

The British Government refused to accept the legal validity of the independence on the grounds that it was unconstitutional. Other countries also failed to recognize the territory's independence. Harold Wilson immediately announced the breaking of ties with Rhodesia and imposed economic sanctions on the rebel nation. Wilson was in a difficult situation. He was called upon by the heads of Black African nations to take action, forceful or otherwise, to end the Smith rebellion. At the same time many British people had close relatives living in Rhodesia. One could not risk bloodshed of that kind.

The Government decided against using force but chose to impose stricter sanctions. Smith did not give in and 13 months later, after a series of talks with Wilson, he rejected the British premier's plan to end UDI. Two weeks later Rhodesia left the Commonwealth.

A new constitution was adopted in 1969 and Rhodesia became a republic. It was only after Harold Wilson was replaced by Ted Heath as Prime Minister that Ian Smith signed a treaty with Britain to restore links between the two countries.

RICE-DAVIES, Mandy

THE attractive blonde Mandy (real name Marilyn) Rice-Davies was one of the characters in the Profumo scandal of 1963 which resulted in the eventual downfall of the Government.

Rice-Davies was born in Solihull in 1943 and left home for London at the age of 15. She met Christine Keeler (who was then 17) and they became flatmates. At the age of 16 Mandy was the lover of landlord racketeer Peter Rachman.

She later met Dr Stephen Ward and became his lover. And it was at his Cliveden cottage that she participated in sex romps with the rich and famous. Because of her involvement with Ward and Keeler, she had to give evidence in the John Profumo affair.

After the scandal she tried to

Top: Mandy Rice-Davies. Below: Peter Rachman, the country's most notorious landlord and one-time 'protector' of Rice-Davies.

launch herself into a showbusiness career and, as Christine Keeler was starting her prison sentence in the winter of 1963, Mandy was embarking on her new career at Eve's Bar, Munich. She then got small parts in a couple of plays, including a West End farce. She also ran night clubs and a garment factory, and had a couple of marriages.

Despite the stories about her and her sexual prowess, she always maintained that she never took part in orgies because, as she said, she never had the 'team spirit'. In her autobiography Mandy (Michael Joseph), published in 1980, she said she could never understand why she was constantly labelled a call-girl. "Promiscuous, perhaps, but not a call-girl" she said.

RICHARD, Cliff, MBE

BY THE time the Beatles had their first chart success, Cliff Richard had enjoyed 17 Top Ten hits. Since the Fab Four had their last number one in 1969, Cliff has gone on to have 13 more Top Ten hits. Even during the days of the Beatles and the other groups of the mid-1960s, Cliff was still a regular amongst the Top Twenty each week. It didn't seem to matter what new sounds came in, Cliff Richard was a top-selling recording star.

His success has been phenomenal and he remains one of, if not THE, most popular solo singer in Britain.

Born in Lucknow, India, on 14 October 1940, his real name is Harry Rodger Webb. The family moved to England when Cliff was eight and they settled at Cheshunt. And it was during his spell at Cheshunt Secondary Modern School that Cliff started singing in a group called the Quin-tones, made up of two boys and three girls.

Cliff became an office clerk after leaving school. But it was after seeing Bill Haley in 1957 that he decided skiffle was for him and he joined a group run by Dick Teague. Cliff started playing guitar during his time with Teague's skiffle group before he quit and formed his own group, the Drifters, with Terry Smart and Ken Pavey.

They took their sound around the local clubs and occasionally into the famous Two Is coffee bar in London, and it was while playing there one night that they met up with Sammy Samwell, who joined the group. Upon the suggestion of London booking agent John Foster the group changed its name to Cliff Richard (without the 's') and the Drifters.

Cliff and his group became even more popular and agent George Canjou spotted them playing at the Shepherd's Bush Gaumont in 1958. He secured a four-week contract for them at Butlins, Clacton. Canjou also arranged a demo disc to be cut which he duly sent to Norrie Paramor, the Columbia (EMI) boss. This led to their first record, *Move It.* After they had performed the song on *Oh Boy!* on 15 September 1958, the record became a big hit and within two weeks was in the charts and on its way to the number-two position. The Cliff Richard story was on its way.

The group went on their first major British tour in October 1958 when they were a support act for the Kalin Twins. Within a year the Drifters had become the Shadows and the line-up was completely different. It now consisted of the recognized first four Shadows members, Hank Marvin, Bruce Welch, Tony Meehan and Jet Harris.

Having been given a part in the film *Serious Charge,* Cliff released one of the records from the film and it became his first million seller. The record was the Lionel Bart composition, *Living Doll.* It was, of course, to spend a further spell at number one in 1986 when Cliff re-recorded the song with the comedy team, the Young Ones.

Other records like *Dynamite* confirmed Cliff as a top rock'n'roller and he was often described as the British Elvis Presley, which was totally unfair because Cliff's unmistakable sound made him the English Cliff Richard.

But Cliff soon showed that he was versatile and sang some great ballads like *Voice In The Wilderness, Theme For A Dream* and *When The Girl In Your Arms Is The Girl In Your Heart.*

As a film star, Cliff starred in *The Young Ones, Wonderful Life* and one of the great early-1960s pop films, *Summer Holiday.* But, despite his diversion into the world of films and television, Cliff still maintained his hold on the charts and carried on having chart-topping hits until 1968 when his Eurovision Song Contest entry, *Congratulations,* topped the hit parade. It was to be his last number one for more than ten years when *We Don't Talk Anymore* went to number one in 1979.

But don't think that because he wasn't having number-one hits he wasn't active. Far from it. Cliff appeared on a lot of television shows and involved himself with religion, having become a born-again Christian. He also did concerts and today

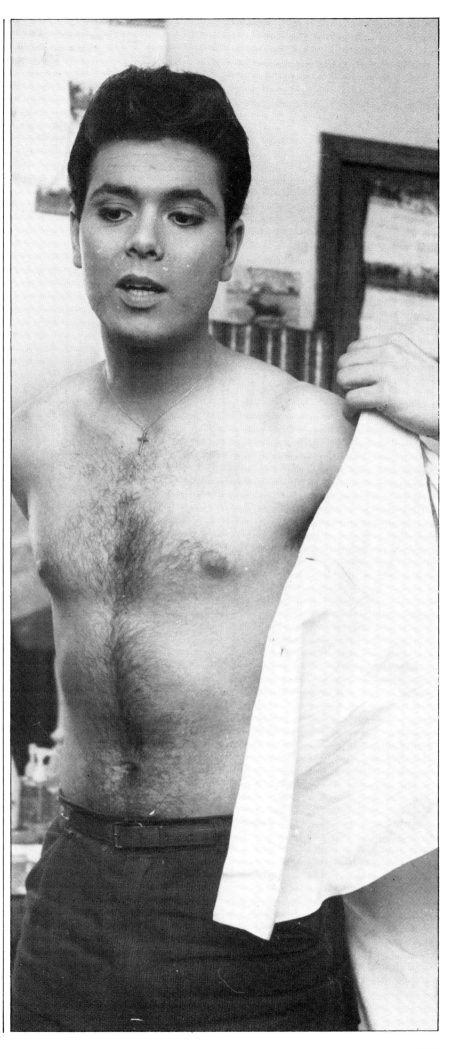

a Cliff Richard concert is as big a sell-out as it was in the 1960s. The only difference is, they have to book Wembley Stadium for him these days.

Cliff has never married but there have been three 'loves' of his life which have been well documented over the years. Firstly there was his co-star on *Summer Holiday*, Una Stubbs. Then there was Jackie Irvine who later married Cliff's big rival of the early-1960s, Adam Faith. And more recently there was the former international tennis player, Sue Barker.

Cliff Richard was a superstar in the 60s, the 70s and the 80s. So, what do the 90s have in store? Probably more hits and more sell-out concerts.

Top Ten hits of Cliff Richard in the 1960s:

Year	Record	Pos
1960	Voice In The Wilderness	2
1960	Fall In Love With You	2
1960	Please Don't Tease	1
1960	Nine Times Out Of Ten	3
1960	I Love You	1
1961	Theme For A Dream	3
1961	Gee Whiz It's You	4
1961	A Girl Like You	3
1961	When The girl In Your Arms Is The Girl In Your Heart	3
1962	The Young Ones	1
1962	I'm Looking Out The Window/Do You Wanna Dance	2
1962	It'll Be Me	2
1962	The Next Time/Bachelor Boy	1
1963	Summer Holiday	1
1963	Lucky Lips	4
1963	It's All In The Game	2
1963	Don't Talk To Him	2
1964	I'm The Lonely One	8
1964	Constantly	4
1964	On The Beach	7
1964	The Twelfth Of Never	8
1964	I Could Easily Fall	9
1965	The Minute You're Gone	1
1965	Wind Me Up (Let Me Go)	2
1966	Visions	7
1966	Time Drags By	10
1966	In The Country	6
1967	It's All Over	9
1967	The Day I Met Marie	10
1967	All My Love	6
1968	Congratulations	1
1969	Big Ship	8
1969	Throw Down A Line	7

Cliff's other number ones:

1959	Living Doll	
1959	Travellin' Light	
1979	We Don't Talk Anymore	
1986	Living Doll (with the Young Ones)	
1988	Mistletoe And Wine	

ROE, Tommy

TOMMY Roe was a welcome visitor to Britain in the 1960s and would often tour with the likes of Chris Montez

and the Beatles. In his own right, Roe was a distinctive songwriter and vocalist, with a style not unlike that of Buddy Holly. His first British hit *Sheila* in 1962, was similar to Buddy Holly's *Peggy Sue*.

He followed up his first hit with *The Folk Singer* and *Everybody*, but his musical career came to a halt in 1964 when he enlisted in the US Army for two years. It was not until 1969 that he found his way back into the British charts when *Dizzy* provided him with his only number one. It also topped the American charts.

Since the 1970s Tommy Roe has not recorded any records of note but back home in Georgia he still appears on the cabaret circuit and writes songs for other performers.

Top Ten hits of Tommy Roe in the 1960s:

Year	Record	Pos
1962	Sheila	3
1963	The Folk Singer	4
1963	Everybody	9
1969	Dizzy	1

ROLLING STONES, The

IN MANY people's eyes the Rolling Stones are the greatest band of the modern rock era, let alone that of more than 20 years ago.

They were brought together after watching a show at London's Marquee Club and the six-man group made their debut late in 1962. The original six members were Mick Jagger, Brian Jones, Keith Richard, Dick Taylor, Mick Avory and Ian Stewart, who soon quit the group to become their road manager. They took their name from an old Muddy Waters song. Avory and Taylor went their own ways and were replaced by Bill Wyman and drummer Tony Chapman, who was replaced by Charlie Watts in January 1963.

Their dress and approach to rhythm and blues music was exciting and very different to the style of their contemporaries of the day. You were either a Beatles fan or a Stones fan. There was no in between.

Initially, they had a huge following in London, but after signing up with

The Rolling Stones on stage with Mick Jagger in typical pose.

Decca and reaching number 21 with their first record, *Come On,* there were signs that the Stones were starting to roll.

The Lennon/McCartney composition, *I Wanna Be Your Man,* reached number 12 in 1964. *Not Fade Away* reached number three and later that year *It's All Over Now* started a run of five consecutive number-one hits for the Stones. They had eight

149

number ones during the 1960s, four top-selling albums and topped the US charts no less than five times (that figure was to rise to eight by 1978).

They became acknowledged as the best live band in the world and mass hysteria would be commonplace at their concerts, so much so that they sometimes had to be cancelled or abandoned.

Most parents of the day thought that Mick Jagger's gyrating antics and pouting lips were disgusting and distasteful. They implored their children not to be influenced by such outrageous performances. But no matter what parents thought of the Stones there was no denying their extraordinary talent.

Mick Jagger and Keith Richard leave a Chichester court in May 1967 after facing drugs charges.

The Stones were often in the news for the wrong reasons and in June 1967, Richard was sentenced to one-year's imprisonment on a drugs charge, and Jagger received a three-month sentence. However, both walked free after appeal judges quashed the sentences. Later that year, lead guitarist Brian Jones received a nine-month sentence. Like the others the sentence was quashed.

On 2 July 1969, Jones was found dead in a swimming pool at Hartfield, Essex. A coroner ruled that death was due to drugs and alcohol. Three days after Jones' death, and with Mick Taylor in as his replacement, the group played for free to over a quarter of a million people in London's Hyde Park in what became known as the 'Stones in the Park' concert. That, more or less, brought about the end

The flamboyant Brian Jones arrives in New York.

of the decade. But the Stones have carried on and constantly remained in the public eye for whatever reason, whether it be controversial or otherwise. But if you describe them as controversial, you must also dovetail that with the adjective 'brilliant'.

Top Ten hits of the Rolling Stones in the 1960s:

Year	Record	Pos
1964	Not Fade Away	3
1964	It's All Over Now	1
1964	Little Red Rooster	1
1965	The Last Time	1
1965	(I Can't Get No) Satisfaction	1
1965	Get Off My Cloud	1
1966	Nineteenth Nervous Breakdown	2
1966	Paint It Black	1
1966	Have You Seen Your Mother Baby Standing In The Shadow	5
1967	Let's Spend The Night Together/Ruby Tuesday	3
1967	We Love You/Dandelion	8
1968	Jumping Jack Flash	1
1969	Honky Tonk Women	1

RONAN POINT COLLAPSE

SHORTLY before 6am on 16 May 1968, one entire corner of a new 23-storey block of flats collapsed like a deck of cards. Three people were killed immediately and 80 families were forced to flee their homes.

The flats, at Custom House, E, Butchers Road in the heart of London's Docklands, was one of four blocks in a £2.1 million slum-clearance contract awarded to Taylor Woodrow-Anglian. The flats had been occupied for only two months at the time of the collapse which was as a result of a gas explosion on the 18th floor. Of the 110 flats in the block, only 80 were occupied at the time but it resulted in 260 people being forced to leave their new homes.

The three people who died were two men and a woman. A fourth victim, an 80-year-old woman, died two weeks later.

ROSE, Sir Alec

AFTER the exploits of Sir Francis Chichester, Britain's next famous solo round-the-world yachtsman was Alec Rose.

A 58-year-old greengrocer from

Sir Alec Rose.

Ronan Point after its collapse.

Portsmouth, he set off on his epic voyage from his home town aboard *Lively Lady* on 16 July 1967, and on 17 December he sailed into Melbourne harbour at the end of the 14,500-mile journey which completed the first leg of his trip. He returned to Portsmouth on 4 July 1968 to learn that the next day he was, like Chichester, to be knighted. A quarter of a million people greeted him on the quayside at the end of his 28,500-mile journey which had taken 354 days to complete.

ROYALS

ROYALTY is best remembered in the 1960s for the glittering wedding of Princess Margaret to commoner Anthony Armstrong-Jones. It was one of several Royal marriages that took place during the decade but by far the most spectacular. It is widely remembered because we all had a day off school to watch the great occasion; the girls *did* sit glued to the television all day, while the boys went to play football. After all, it was another day off school!

Amongst the other Royals to 'tie the knot' in the 1960s were the Duke of Kent to Katherine Worsley in 1961; Princess Alexandra of Kent and the Honourable Angus Ogilvy in 1963 and the Queen's cousin, the Earl of Harwood, married Miss Patricia Tuckwell in 1967, only four months after his divorce.

Weddings were plentiful amongst members of overseas Royal Families. Don Juan Carlos of Spain married Princess Sophia of Greece in 1962 and one of the bridesmaids was Princess Alexandra, herself a bride less than a year later. Princess Anne was a bridesmaid at the wedding of King Constantine of the Hellenes in 1966 and when Princess Ann-Marie of Denmark married Herr Claus von Amsberg in the same year, the British Royal Family was represented by Princess Marina, the Duchess of Kent, Princess Alexandra, Angus Ogilvy and Princess Michael of Kent.

There were few deaths amongst members of the Royal Family in the 1960s. The Princess Royal died at her home in 1965. Two years later the Duke of Westminster died at the age of 60 and in 1968 Princess Marina, Duchess of Gloucester, died at the age of 61.

In contrast, there were certainly plenty of arrivals.

The Queen gave birth to her last two children in the 1960s, Prince Andrew (Albert Christian Edward) was born on 19 February 1960 and Prince Edward (Antony Richard Louis) was born on 10 March 1964.

Princess Margaret gave birth to her first child, David Albert Charles, better

Prince Edward pictured in June 1965.

known as Viscount Linley, in 1961. The following year the Duchess of Kent gave birth to her first son, George Phillip Nicholas, who later became the Earl of St Andrew's. But what a busy time 1964 was for Royal births . . .

Within the space of nine weeks the number of Royals had increased by four. First, on 29 February, Princess Alexandra gave birth to her first son at Richmond. He was christened James Robert Bruce Ogilvy. The Queen had Prince Edward on 10 March. On 28 April the Duchess of Kent gave birth to a daughter, Lady Helen Marina Lucy Windsor. And completing the quartet, Princess Margaret gave birth to Lady Sarah Frances Elizabeth Armstrong-Jones on 1 May. The final Royal of the 1960s was born to Princess Alexandra on 31 July 1966, when she gave birth to a daughter, Marina Victoria Alexandra.

One other 'Royal' birth of the 1960s attracted little publicity at the time; Diana Frances Spencer was born on 1 July 1961. She later became wife of the heir to the throne.

Members of the Royal Family did a lot of globetrotting during the 1960s, largely due to the number of Independence celebrations that required official attendance.

And what else happened to the Royals in the 1960s apart from getting married, having babies and globetrotting?

Well, Prince Charles hit the headlines quite a lot but, after all, he was heir to the throne, and was going through his teenage years.

In 1962 he underwent an appendix operation at the Hospital for Sick Children at Great Ormond Street. In May that same year he attracted a lot of media attention as he started his first day at his father's old school, Gordonstoun. The biggest 'scandal' to rock the Royal Family in the 1960s was on 17 June 1963 when Buckingham Palace announced that

Opposite top: No worries about security in 1962. Lord Mountbatten, Princess Anne and the Queen watch the Badminton horse trials. Bottom: Prince Charles enters Gordonstoun in May 1962.

153

The Royal Family at Balmoral in September 1960. The Queen and Prince Philip with Princess Anne, Prince Andrew and Prince Charles.

Prince Charles had bought a *Cherry B* in a hotel bar. And he was only 14 at the time.

Charles was back in hospital in 1964, this time in Aberdeen after he contracted pneumonia while on a camping holiday. He spent ten days in hospital.

After two terms at Geelong Grammar School in Australia in 1966, Charles started at Trinity College, Cambridge, in October 1967 where he was to read archaelogy and anthropology. In 1969, Prince Charles started a nine-week term at the University College of Wales.

Of the numerous duties and tasks Her Majesty The Queen had to perform in the 1960s, one of the most pleasant was her investing Prince Charles as the Prince of Wales at Caernarfon Castle in 1969.

Among the other pleasant duties performed by the Queen in the 1960s were the following:

1962 — Attending the consecration of the new Coventry Cathedral.

1965 — dedicating a piece of land at Runnymede to the late President Kennedy.

1966 — Opening the Severn Road Bridge.

1966 — granting a posthumous free pardon to Timothy Evans.

1967 — bestowing a knighthood on yachtsman Francis Chichester.

1967 — launching the *QE II*.

And among the not-so-pleasant duties were the attending of Sir Winston Churchill's funeral in 1965 and, later the same year, withdrawing spy Kim Philby's OBE.

Princess Anne was too young to attract a lot of attention in the 1960s, although she stole a piece of the limelight when she attended her first

The 1st Marylebone Cub Scout pack's newest recruit, Prince Andrew, salutes for the camera.

Prince Philip was the 'champion' when it came to making overseas tours as the following shows:

Jan 1961	Tour of India . . .shot a 9ft tiger!
Feb-Apr 1962	Started two-month tour of South America.
May 1962	Flew to Amsterdam with the Queen for silver wedding.
May-June 1962	Visited United States and Canada.
Nov 1962	Opened Commonwealth Games in Australia (went via San Francisco).
Jan-Mar 1963	Toured Australia and New Zealand with the Queen.
June 1964	Visited Iceland on Royal Yacht *Britannia*.
Sept 1964	Attended wedding of King Constantine in Athens.
Oct-Nov 1964	Week-long tour of Canada with the Queen, then visited West Indies, Central America and Galapagos Islands on his own.
Feb-Mar 1965	Eight-day State visit of Ethiopia with the Queen followed by a four-day visit to the Sudan. Duke then went on a six-week tour of Australia and south-east Asia on his own.
May 1965	Ten-day visit to Germany with the Queen, which included a visit to West Berlin.
Feb-Mar 1966	Five-week Caribbean tour with the Queen.
Mar 1966	Ten thousand mile tour of the United States started in Miami.
May 1966	Attended a British Trade Fair in Oslo.
May 1966	On a five-day State visit to Belgium with the Queen.
Aug 1966	Opened the Commonwealth Games in Kingston, Jamaica.
Sep-Oct 1966	Three-week visit to Argentina as part of the republic's 150th anniversary celebration. The Argentinians were not too friendly in 1966 . . .shots were fired at the British Embassy where the Duke was staying.
Feb-Mar 1967	Visited Greece, Jordan, Pakistan, Singapore and Australia.
June-July 1967	Accompanied the Queen to Canada for their centenary celebrations.
Nov 1967	One-week visit to Toronto.
Nov 1967	Accompanied Queen on a three-day State visit to Malta.
May 1968	Went to Australia for the 3rd Commonwealth Study Conference.
Oct-Nov 1968	Attended Olympic Games in Mexico and then joined the Queen at Recife during her 18-day State visit to Brazil.
May 1969	Accompanied the Queen on a five-day State visit to Austria.

Seventeen-year-old Princess Anne arrives at the Aldwych Theatre, London, in April 1967.

day at Benenden School, Kent, in 1963. In 1969 she embarked on her first public engagement alone when she presented leeks to the Welsh Guards during a St David's Day ceremony at Pirbright, Surrey.

And finally, the Queen Mother. She was as popular in the 1960s as she is today. She was idolized and adored wherever she went. And she fulfilled many Royal duties. Times have certainly not changed as far as the most popular member of the Royal Family is concerned, even though the number of appointments is considerably less.

RUBY, Jack

Jack Ruby was the 52-year-old Dallas striptease club owner who took the law into his own hands because of 'a deep sense of sympathy' for Mrs Jacqueline Kennedy, and shot Lee Harvey Oswald, the man charged with the assassination of her husband, President Kennedy. Ruby said the President's wife should be spared the ordeal of Oswald's trial.

He shot Oswald as he was being moved from the City Hall to the County jail a mile away on 24 November 1963. Ruby was dressed in a grey suit and grey hat and looked like a Dallas plain-clothes policeman. But suddeny he burst through a crowd of police and photographers surrounding Oswald and shot him from less than a foot away. Someone in the crowd said: "They ought to give this guy a medal."

Born as Jacob Rubenstein, he was a Jew born in Chicago on 19 April 1911. The son of a carpenter, he was one of eight children and was raised in the ghetto area of the city. He served in the US Air Force during the war and after his discharge he moved to Dallas where he ran his sister's night club. He eventually became quite wealthy.

The trial of Jack Ruby opened on 17 February 1964 and he was subsequently found guilty of Oswald's murder and was sentenced to death. However, in October 1966, the Texas Court of Criminal Appeal annulled the conviction and sent the case back for retrial in any county other than Dallas. However, Ruby was never to stand

also played by Moore. Templar's pride and joy was his yellow Volvo two-seater sports car with the registration plate ST1.

The series was first seen in 1963 and was made in black and white. By the time the 114th and last episode was filmed in 1968 it was in colour. It was sold to more than 100 countries and the part played by Moore somewhat typecast him, but it later made him an ideal candidate for the part of Bond.

Simon Templar returned to the small screen in 1978 when Ian Ogilvy, this time driving a Jaguar XJS, played the part of Simon Templar in *The Return Of The Saint*.

Opposite: Roger Moore and actress Jan Walters, who also starred in The Saint.

SASSOON, Vidal

THE MOST celebrated hairdresser of the 1960s, Vidal Sassoon was the only stylist to visit if you were one of the top fashion-conscious stars of the day and the likes of Mary Quant and Jean Shrimpton were regular customers at his Bond Street salon.

Born in the East End in 1928, he started work for the top hairdresser of the fifties, 'Teazy Weazy' Raymond and in 1955 Vidal opened his first salon. The media attention he attracted in the 1960s with his creations like the geometric cut, the 'One-Eyed Girl' cut and the Greek goddess style, saw him gain popularity in the United States and his Vidal Sassoon products sold in their millions on both sides of the Atlantic.

further trial. On 3 January 1967 he died in the same hospital where the President and Oswald had been taken three years earlier. Ruby had been admitted on 10 December 1966 with advanced cancer.

The case against him was officially closed on 30 January 1967 and District Judge, Louis Olland said: "The Good Lord saw fit to bring his trial to a close."

SAINT, The

ALTHOUGH *The Saint* had been seen on the movies, heard on the radio and read in comic strips since 1938, it was not until 1963 that Leslie Charteris' character, Simon Templar, appeared on television.

The man chosen to play the smooth-talking character was Roger Moore, whose previous television roles had included *Ivanhoe* and as cousin Beau in the popular western series *Maverick*.

Simon Templar was a private detective and his exploits were often to the annoyance of Scotland Yard's Superintendent Claude Teal because *The Saint* solved mysteries before Teal's men could get to the bottom of them.

The world of *The Saint* was filled with attractive girls and beautiful locations; just as that of James Bond,

When one of his customers, Mia Farrow, was filming *Rosemary's Baby*, Sassoon was flown from London to Hollywood just to cut her hair. For that one cut he was paid $5,000! The talents of Vidal Sassoon were also used at the 1984 Los Angeles Olympics; he was the hair-care consultant.

SAVILE, Jimmy, OBE

JIMMY Savile was the son of a bookie's clerk. He was born in Leeds, purportedly in 1926, and was a former 'Bevin boy' (miner). But after an accident that nearly left him paralysed from the waist down, he quit the colliery life for a show-business career and started as the manager of the Locarno in Leeds. He began disc jockeying in the late-fifties and landed a job with Radio Luxembourg where he hosted the *Warner Bros Record Show* and later *The Teen And Twenty Disc Club* and *Guys, Gals And Groups* shows.

He was very much part of the pop boom of the 1960s and became one of the top DJs. He had the honour of hosting the first *Top Of The Pops* programme from Manchester on 1 January 1964.

The silver-haired Savile became one of Radio One's top disc jockeys. But in recent years he is best remembered for his *Jim'll Fix It* television series which has brought delight to hundreds all over the country.

He has maintained his connections with his home town and enjoys nothing more than helping out at the Leeds Infirmary where he gives his time free. But far more than that, his mere presence acts as a tonic for the many patients. He is noted for his charity work and devotes a lot of time to the Stoke Mandeville hospital. In particular, he has raised money for the spinal injuries unit, perhaps a

desire created by his own accident when working down the mines. His long-distance walks have only been a part of his money-raising activities which have yielded millions of pounds over the years.

Jimmy has a single-minded desire to make people happy, and he succeeds. The tabloid Press have tried over the years to dig up dirt about Jimmy Savile, but have failed. The man is sincere, honest and a real gem. His only indulgences are driving the best car, a Rolls Royce, and smoking the best cigars.

SAVUNDRA, Emil

THE former chairman of the Fire, Auto and Marine Insurance Company, Dr Emil Savundra was arrested and charged with fraud on 10 February 1967, just seven days after receiving a grilling from David Frost on his television programme.

Savundra's insurance company collapsed in 1966 with losses estimated at £1.4 million. He was invited to be questioned in front of a television audience by Frost on *The Frost Programme* for Independent Television.

Some members of the audience were FAM customers who had lost money or been unable to get claims settled. Some of the exchanges were heated and Savundra was often interrupted by the audience, particu-

larly when he tried to convince them a £300,000 loan never found its way to him personally. He also said: "I am not going to cross swords with peasants." At the end of the 20-minute interview, the audience shouted 'Good Old Frostie' to the interviewer.

At the time of his arrest, 43-year-old Savundra had recently moved from his Hampstead mansion, 'White-walls', to a four-bedroomed house at 12 Ouseley Road, Old Windsor, Berks. He was 'signing-on' at the Finchley unemployment exchange. Charged on two counts of intent to defraud, Savundra was initially remanded in custody, but a week later was allowed bail subject to a £42,000 surety being paid.

On 7 March 1968 at the Old Bailey, Savundra was sentenced to eight years imprisonment and fined £50,000. The former managing director of Fire, Auto and Marine, Stuart de Quincy Walker, was given five years and a £30,000 fine. The judge described their crime as a 'gigantic swindle'.

SEARCHERS, The

ANOTHER of the many talented groups to come from Liverpool in the days of the pop boom of the early 1960s, the Searchers were orginally the backing group for one of Merseyside's top vocalists, Johnny Sandon. Consisting of founder

The Searchers (from left): John McNally, Chris Curtis, Tony Jackson and Mike Pender, pictured in New York.

members John McNally, Chris Curtis, Tony Jackson and Mike Pender, they eventually branched out on their own. They took their name from the John Ford film *The Searchers*, starring John Wayne.

While the Beatles wooed their fans at The Cavern, the Searchers did the same at Liverpool's Iron Door Club. After doing the rounds of the Merseyside pubs and clubs and making the 'statutory' trip to Hamburg's Star Club, the boys were recommended to Tony Hatch, recording manager of Pye Records, and in July 1963 they released *Sweets For My Sweet*. It turned out to be the first of three number-one hits for the popular group.

During 1964 they were rarely out of the public eye, both in Britain where they embarked on a nationwide tour, and in Australia, Hong Kong and the United States were they also appeared.

In 1965, with Frank Allen in the group as a replacement for Tony Jackson, they found it increasingly hard to maintain their chart success.

The group has stuck together, despite several changes of personnel, and their interpretation of their old hits like *Sugar And Spice* and *Needles And Pins* still brings back memories as they continue to do the rounds.

Now billed as Mike Pender's Searchers, they still sound great.

Top Ten hits of The Searchers in the 1960s:

Year	Record	Pos
1963	Sweets For My Sweet	1
1963	Sugar And Spice	2
1964	Needles And Pins	1
1964	Don't Throw Your Love Away	1
1964	When You Walk In The Room	3
1965	Goodbye My Love	4

SEEKERS, The

THE SEEKERS were a folk group formed in 1964 by four Melbourne, Australia, friends who wanted to do something with their spare time. Little did they realize at the time that less than 12 months later they would be performing at the London Palladium singing their chart-topping hit *I'll Never Find Another You*, written by Tom Springfield.

Their next two records, again inspired by Springfield, were also gold discs as the Seekers, with female singer Judith Durham, became one of the most popular visitors to British shores.

When they returned to their homeland in 1967, they appeared in front of an estimated 200,000 people at the Myer Music Bowl in Melbourne. Such was their popularity.

The group split up in 1968. Judith Durham embarked on a solo career, while Keith Potger founded the New Seekers with completely new members. Within the space of three years the original Seekers had come, seen and conquered the pop world. Their album *Best Of The Seekers* spent an incredible 125 weeks in the LP charts, including six weeks at number one.

Top Ten hits of The Seekers in the 1960s:

Year	Record	Pos
1965	I'll Never Find Another You	1
1965	A World Of Our Own	3
1965	The Carnival Is Over	1
1966	Walk With Me	10
1966	Morningtown Ride	2
1967	Georgie Girl	3

SELLERS, Peter

PETER Sellers was one of the finest British comedy actors ever to grace the big screen. His sense of fun, devilment and impeccable timing combined to produce sheer brilliance and every role he played seemed to bring out a new aspect of his great talent.

Born in Southsea on 8 September 1925, Sellers served in the RAF during the war and soon found himself involved with forces entertainment. After the war he worked at the Windmill Theatre before moving into radio and, in 1951, formed the Goons with Spike Milligan, Harry Secombe and Michael Bentine. The radio series ran for seven years and became a cult.

Having made his film debut in *The Ladykillers* in 1955, he made his first impact on the movie world with *I'm All Right Jack* in 1959.

Success followed in *The Millionairess*, *Lolita* and *Dr Strangelove*. But it was in 1963 that he played the part of his best-known character, Inspector Clouseau in *The Pink Panther*, a character who Sellers was to play

Peter Sellers and Britt Ekland attending the premier of the film Dr Strangelove.

again in the mid-seventies. His last film was *The Fiendish Plot Of Fu Man Chu* in 1980.

Sellers was married four times — to Anne Howe, Britt Ekland, Miranda Quarry and Lynne Frederick, whom he married in 1977. A heart attack in 1964 nearly killed him. Sixteen years later a second one did claim the life of one of Britain's most versatile and funniest comedy actors as Peter Sellers died in London on 24 July 1980.

The films of Peter Sellers in the 1960s:

Two Way Stretch	(1960)
The Millionairess	(1960)
Never Let Go	(1960)
Mr Topaze	(1961)
Lolita	(1962)
The Dock Brief	(1962)
Only Two Can Play	(1962)
The Road To Hong Kong	(1962)
Waltz Of The Toreadors	(1962)
The Wrong Arm Of The Law	(1962)
Heavens Above	(1963)
Dr Strangelove	(1963)
The World Of Henry Orient	(1964)
The Pink Panther	(1964)
A Shot In The Dark	(1964)
What's New Pussycat?	(1965)
The Wrong Box	(1966)
After The Fox	(1966)
Casino Royale	(1967)
The Bobo	(1967)
Woman Times Seven	(1967)
I Love You, Alice B.Toklas	(1968)
The Party	(1968)
The Magic Christian	(1969)

SHADOWS, The

BEFORE the formation of the Shadows, lead guitarist Hank Marvin, and rhythm guitarist Bruce Welch became pals while studying at college together.

Marvin, born in Newcastle-upon-Tyne as Brian Rankin in 1941, was originally a banjo player before turning to the guitar. He and Bruce (born in Bognor Regis in 1941) joined the Railroaders skiffle group and in 1958 set off for London where they played in the capital's top coffee bars, including the famous 2 I's.

It was after appearing at the 2 I's that Bruce and Hank were paired up

Cliff Richard, flanked by Bruce Welch (left) and Hank Marvin.

with bass guitarist Jet Harris and drummer Tony Meehan (both born in London) as the backing group to a new young up-and-coming singer by the name of Cliff Richard. Cliff was booked for a tour of Britain as a support for the Kalin Twins and a music impressario got the new band together which was named the Drifters.

The new group was given its own recording contract in 1959 and released two vocal singles and an instrumental, *Jet Black*. They had very limited success in their own right, but after changing their name to The Shadows, so as not to be confused with the American group called the Drifters, the career of the 'Shads' really took off.

They recorded the instrumental *Apache*, which was written by Jerry Lordan, a singer who appeared on tour with Cliff and the Shadows. The record went to number one and was one of the biggest selling singles of 1960.

During the next five years the Shadows gained international popularity as Cliff's backing group, as a leading instrumental group, and as film stars alongside Cliff in such popular films of the day as *Summer Holiday*. They enjoyed five chart-topping singles and two top LPs during the decade.

The Shadows had to overcome changes in personnel in the early days, but this did not affect their popularity. Tony Meehan left in September 1961 and was replaced by Brian Bennett, while bass guitarist Harris was replaced by Brian 'Liquorice' Locking in 1962 and he, in turn, was replaced by John Rostill in 1963. Harris and Meehan teamed up and had three big hits in 1963; *Applejack*, *Scarlett O'Hara* and their only number one, *Diamonds*. Both also had individual successes, the biggest hit being Harris's theme from *The Man With The Golden Arm* which reached number 12 in 1962.

The last number one for the Shadows was *Foot Tapper* in 1963 and their last hit before the group officially disbanded in 1968 was *Maroc 7* a year earlier. It reached number 24.

The Shadows re-formed in 1972 with the line-up of Welch, Marvin, Bennett and newcomer John Farrar on bass. Since then they have enjoyed further chart success and have had two more chart-topping albums. They have also regularly appeared on television, and even came second in the 1975 Eurovision Song Contest with *Let Me Be The One*. They have also teamed up with Cliff for the occasional nostalgic appearance — for example the anniversary reunion concert to celebrate 25 years in the music business.

Top Ten hits of the Shadows in the 1960s:

Year	Record	Pos
1960	Apache	1
1960	Man Of Mystery/The Stranger	5
1961	F.B.I.	6
1961	Frightened City	3
1961	Kon-Tiki	1
1961	The Savage	10
1962	Wonderful Land	1
1962	Guitar Tango	4
1962	Dance On	1
1963	Foot Tapper	1
1963	Atlantis	2
1963	Shindig	6
1964	The Rise & Fall Of Flingel Bunt	5
1965	Don't Make My Baby Blue	10

> *Cliff Richard played the bongos on the Shadows' first big hit* Apache.

SHANNON, Del

DEL SHANNON was the American singer with the falsetto voice who shot to fame in 1961 with *Runaway* which topped the charts on both sides of the Atlantic. Although he never attained such success again, he still had other Top Ten hits, more in Britain than in the United States, as he became a popular visitor to these shores.

Born as Charles Westover at Grand Rapids, Michigan, on 30 December 1939, he was a keen musician from an early age. After leaving school he was drafted into the Army where he entertained the troops. After leaving the Army he became a carpet salesman and in his spare time played with Charlie Johnson and the Big Little Show Band. It was with a fellow member of the band, Max Crook, that Del wrote his smash hit *Runaway*.

Del Shannon is still involved in music although the shift from those pop days has been towards country and western and he spends a great deal of his time in Nashville, the capital city of country music.

Top Ten hits of Del Shannon in the 1960s:

Year	Record	Pos
1961	Runaway	1
1961	Hats Off To Larry	6
1961	So Long Baby	10
1962	Hey Little Girl	2

1962	Swiss Maid	2
1963	Little Town Flirt	4
1963	Two Kinds Of Teardrops	5
1965	Keep Searchin' (We'll Follow The Sun)	3

SHAPIRO, Helen

BEFORE she had reached her 15th birthday, Helen Shapiro had achieved enormous success, including a number one hit record with *You Don't Know,* and being voted Best British Female Singer of the Year for 1961.

She was still attending the Clapton Girls School at the time. It was while at that school that she decided to take singing lessons at the Maurice Berman Singing School where, by chance, she was heard by John Schroeder of EMI. He secured her a recording contract and also wrote her first record *Don't Treat Me Like A Child,* which went to number three.

Schroeder also wrote her second number one, *Walkin' Back To Happiness* as she became the first female artist to have back-to-back number ones. She could not maintain her run of success once the new wave of groups hit the pop scene and her last Top 20 success was in 1962 with *Little Miss Lonely.*

Helen remained popular on the cabaret circuit and today still pulls them in whenever she performs.

Top Ten hits of Helen Shapiro in the 1960s:

Year	Record	Pos
1961	Don't Treat Me Like A Child	3
1961	You Don't Know	1
1961	Walkin' Back To Happiness	1
1962	Tell Me What He Said	2
1962	Little Miss Lonely	8

SHARPEVILLE MASSACRE

THE NEW South African pass laws, requiring Africans to carry identity cards, came into force on 21 March 1960. Instead of accepting the new law the Africans rebelled in their thousands and at Sharpeville, near Vereeniging, Witwatersrand (where the treaty to end the Boer War was signed), approximately 15,000 converged on the local police station to protest.

The Sharpeville protest was only one of many campaigns of disobedience across the townships of South Africa that day, but it was by far the bloodiest.

As the police station was stormed, the 75 white police officers inside opened fire and within minutes 56 blacks lay dead and another 162 were injured.

The police alleged that the first shots came from the Africans, who also stoned the police. Police Commander Colonel Pienaar said afterwards: "If they do these things, they must learn their lesson the hard way."

Rioting broke out in other townships and at Langa, near Cape Town, there were seven more deaths. A state of emergency was declared just over a week later and it was not officially removed until August 1960.

There has been much bloodshed in South Africa since then, but none as horrific as that day at Sharpeville on 21 March 1960.

Heavily-armed South African police move amongst the bodies of dead Africans at Sharpeville.

SHAW, Sandie

AT VIENNA in 1967 the barefoot Sandie Shaw had the distinction of becoming the first United Kingdom representative to win the Eurovision Song Contest. Her entry, *Puppet On A String,* also topped the British charts and was the third number one for Essex-born Sandie, who became the first female singer to have three British number ones. Only Madonna in the 1980s has surpassed that achievement.

She was born as Sandra Goodrich in Dagenham on 26 February 1947. At the age of 17 she had decided on a singing career and after an Adam Faith concert, cheekily went back stage and sang for him. Adam was impressed, as was his manager Eve Taylor. Sandie was signed by Pye records and cut her first disc, *As Long As You're Happy, Baby*. It never charted but her next record, *(There's) Always Something There To Remind Me* spent three weeks at number one.

Sandie epitomized the 1960s fashion — casual dress, slim figure, long-flowing straight hair and knee-length white boots except on stage, where she always performed barefoot. Her looks captured many a man's heart during the swinging era.

After an absence of 15 years, Sandie Shaw returned to the charts in 1984 with *Hand In Glove*, a duet with Morrissey, lead singer of The Smiths.

Top Ten hits of Sandie Shaw in the 1960s:

Year	Record	Pos
1964	(There's) Always Something There To Remind Me	1
1964	Girl Don't Come	3
1965	I'll Stop At Nothing	4
1965	Long Live Love	1
1965	Message Understood	6
1966	Tomorrow	9
1967	Puppet On A String	1
1969	Monsieur Dupont	6

SHRIMPTON, Jean

JEAN Shrimpton was the girl with the international face and, as such, became one of the leading models in the 1960s at the time of the miniskirt boom. Although she admitted that she occasionally got bored with being photographed, she never gave that impression as she became 'the most beautiful girl in the world'.

Born on 16 November 1942, she never changed her name from Jean Shrimpton and became known as 'The Shrimp'. Brought up on her parents' farm at Burnham, Bucks, she

had a great love of horses and after finding fame had a mania for collecting antique rocking horses.

Along with Twiggy, she became one of the most sought-after models by the leading designers of the day like Mary Quant and with the leading magazines *Vogue, Elle* and others.

Wherever she went, 'The Shrimp' turned heads and at Flemington Park racetrack on Melbourne Cup day in 1966 she appeared clad in a miniskirt and was gloveless, hatless and stockingless — something of a 'crime' at the Melbourne Cup. After that she went on television and said: "Surely people are more important than clothes?"

While she was one of the best-known faces of the 1960s, Jean Shrimpton was very much a private person and never regarded herself as part of the 'swinging scene' in the 1960s. She was linked romantically with actor Terence Stamp for a while, but nothing developed, despite their three-year affair.

In the early 1960s, whilst still a teenager, she was capable of earning £20 an hour modelling as she helped popularize the miniskirt and sell magazines. She ventured into the world of films in 1966 and made the transition from modelling to acting without too much difficulty. Her screen debut was alongside singer Paul Jones in *Privilege*.

Today Jean Shrimpton, the 'Face of the 1960s', enjoys life running a Penzance hotel.

SIDNEY, Ann

THE second United Kingdom winner of the Miss World title, Ann Sidney was 20 when she won the coveted crown in 1964. A hairstylist from Parkstone, Dorset, she went from being Miss United Kingdom to Miss World within a few months.

Ann was 5ft 8in tall and weighed

9st 6lb. She was the first winner with the classic 36-24-36 measurements.

She wanted to pursue an acting career after winning the title but was only offered 'walk-on' parts which she refused. However, after serving her time in 'rep', she got a part in one of the James Bond movies in 1967.

SIMON AND GARFUNKEL

PAUL Simon and Art Garfunkel met whilst appearing in a production of *Alice In Wonderland* during their schooldays in Forest Hills. Paul played the White Rabbit while Art played the Cheshire Cat.

They started their singing career under the unimaginative name of Tom and Jerry. After they finished their schooling they headed for Greenwich Village, that great training ground for many singers of the sixties. Their big breakthrough came on New Year's Day 1966 when Paul's composition *The Sound Of Silence* went to the top of the US charts.

It heralded the start of a career that is still going on, albeit in different directions.

They enjoyed chart success on both sides of the Atlantic as well as recording the marvellous album *Bookends* which was surpassed by their million-selling *Bridge Over Troubled Water* album in 1970 from which the title song became a monster hit worldwide.

> Homeward Bound *is reputed to have been written by Paul Simon on Widnes railway station. If you've ever been to Widnes railway station you'll appreciate there isn't much more to do there other than write songs!*

One of their best singles in the 1960s was their rendering of *Mrs Robinson* which came from the Dustin Hoffman movie *The Graduate*. Paul Simon wrote most of the music for the film.

The duo eventually split up in 1970 after earlier rumblings that all was not well, and the two men went their own ways. Paul had an American number one with *50 Ways To Leave Your Lover* in 1974, made his acting debut in Woody Allen's award-winning *Annie Hall*, married actress Carrie Fisher in 1983, and in 1986 recorded one of the best albums of recent times, *Gracelands*.

Art Garfunkel, on the other hand, had two British chart-toppers: *I Only Have Eyes For You* in 1975 and *Bright Eyes* from the movie *Watership Down* in 1979.

In 1981 more than half a million people converged on New York's Central Park for a reunion concert. The turnout was a fitting tribute to one of the best singer/songwriting teams of the sixties.

Top Ten hits of Simon and Garfunkel in the 1960s:

Year	Record	Pos
1966	Homeward Bound	9
1968	Mrs Robinson	4
1969	Mrs Robinson (EP)	9
1969	The Boxer	6

SIRHAN SIRHAN

SIRHAN Sirhan was the man who claimed the life of Robert Kennedy in 1968. He was a Jordanian nationalist and sought revenge for Kennedy's support of Israel. His full name is Sirhan Bashara Sirhan; Sirhan means 'wanderer'.

He was born in Jerusalem on 19

Paul Simon (at back) and Art Garfunkel.

March 1944. His parents were Jordanian Christians but they split up and on 12 January 1957 Sirhan, along with his mother, three brothers and a sister, emigrated to the United States where they settled in an ethnic neighbourhood of Los Angeles. His father stayed in Jerusalem where he worked as a plumber in the British public works department.

At the time of the Senator's assassination, Sirhan worked as a track exerciser at the Hollywood Park race track in Los Angeles, and lived in a wooden house on Howard Street, Pasadena. He constantly boasted of being Jordanian and had ideas of returning to his home country a hero.

Sirhan Sirhan.

Sirhan Sirhan took those steps towards gaining hero status in his homeland when he murdered Robert Kennedy in June 1968. As he fired three shots at the Senator, Sirhan said: "I am doing this for my country. I love my country." He was referring to Jordan, not America.

Initially sentenced to death he was on Death Row at San Quentin with Charles Manson, and others, when the death penalty in California was abolished in 1972. His sentence was commuted to life and in 1989 he was given permission to apply for parole.

SIX-DAY WAR

PRIOR to 1967 the last major clash between Israel and her Arab neighbours was in 1956, when Egypt closed the Suez Canal. On that occasion the Israelis seized the Gaza Strip and drove through the Sinai to the East Bank but withdrew under US and UN pressure. In 1967 the fighting started again in what became known as the Six-Day War.

Israel threatened retaliation against Syrian border raids. The Syrians called upon Egyptian aid, but on 5 June 1967, the Israelis mounted the first attack of the war with simultaneous air attacks on Syrian, Jordanian and Egyptian air bases, destroying more than 370 Arab aircraft. On the ground the Israelis captured Al 'Arish, the Sinai capital.

Despite a call for a cease-fire from the United Nations, the Israeli troops dominated the ground battles on the second day and took the Gaza Strip from Egypt and Bethlehem and Hebron from the Jordanians.

Day three was no different as the Israelis took Jerusalem, Jericho, most of the West Bank and the Egyptian fortress of Sharm ash Shaykh on the Suez Canal.

Jordan had accepted the UN cease-fire on day three and on the fourth day, the Egyptians also accepted it. As Israel bombed Damascus and went into the Golan Heights on the fifth day, so the Syrians accepted the cease-fire.

The war came to an end on 10 June, when Israel accepted the cease-fire. Israel had increased its territory size by more than 200% but the cost of doing so had resulted in the loss of approximately 100,000 lives. The Israeli army was led by general Moshe Dayan

SMITH, Ian

MEETINGS between Rhodesian Premier Ian Smith and Harold Wilson were common in the mid-1960s as Smith sought to gain independence for his country without majority African rule.

A former fighter pilot, Smith became an MP in 1948. A founder member of the Rhodesian Front in 1962, he succeeded Winston Field as

Captured Egyptian soldiers en route to a prisoner-of-war camp in June 1968, after the Israelis overran Al 'Arish. A column of Israeli armoured troop carriers passes them going towards the front line.

Prime Minister in 1964. Despite the lengthy talks with Wilson, Smith declared unilateral independence for Rhodesia in November 1965.

Britain and other nations imposed crippling economic sanctions on Rhodesia. Further meetings with Harold Wilson aboard *HMS Tiger* and *HMS Fearless* off the coast of Gibraltar, in 1966 and 1969 respectively, failed to resolve the situation.

Rhodesia (now called Zimbabwe) finally gained full independence on 18 April 1980 and Ian Smith continued to serve in the governments of Bishop Abel Muzorewa and Robert Mugabe.

SMOG

IN December 1962, most of Britain was covered with the worst fog for ten years. But in London the smog, as it was known, got hold of the capital and in five days claimed the lives of 60 people.

It started on 3 December and brought traffic to a standstill as visibility was down to nil on many main roads in the Metropolitan area. The Port of London also came to a standstill and approximately 60 ships were fog-bound in the Thames. London Airport at Heathrow was closed for four days and most rail

Ian Smith pictured in December 1966.

services were either cancelled or disrupted. But it was to human health that the smog posed the biggest hazard.

The amount of smoke in the London air was ten times higher than normal for the time of year and the sulphur dioxide content of the atmosphere was 14 times higher.

About 800 people were admitted to various London hospitals with chest and heart conditions. Some 60 people lost their lives, 28 of them in one day, 6 December.

The smog eventually cleared on 8 December and for the first time in five nights, the people of London could breathe cleaner air.

SOBERS, Sir Garfield

ALTHOUGH one of the finest all-round cricketers in Test history, Garfield Sobers will best be remembered for that day in August 1968 when he hit luckless Glamorgan bowler Malcolm Nash all over the Swansea ground as he became the first man to hit six sixes off one over in county cricket.

Born in Barbados, Sobers was only 17 when he made his Test debut against England in March 1954. In 1958 he set a Test record when he scored 365 not out against Pakistan. That record still stands today.

He succeeded Frank Worrell as West Indies captain in 1965 and in 1967 Sobers joined Nottinghamshire where he helped revive a club that had been struggling near the bottom of the County Championship.

Sobers was knighted for his services to cricket, and when he retired in 1974, he had appeared in 93 Test matches, and his statistics of 8,932 runs, 235 wickets and 109 catches made him the most prolific all-rounder in Test cricket history.

SONNY AND CHER

BEFORE achieving success in their own right, Sonny (Salvatore Phillip Bono) and Cher (Cherilyn La Pierre Sakisian) had worked together as backing singers at Phil Spector's studio. The best-selling discs they worked on included *Be My Baby* by the Ronettes and *You've Lost That Lovin' Feelin'* by the Righteous Brothers.

Sonny was also an accomplished writer and penned *Needles And Pins, Dream Baby, Baby Don't Go* and of course, their own monster hit *I Got You Babe* which reached number one on both sides of the Atlantic and was a multi-million seller worldwide.

They eventually became Mr and Mrs Bono and were established as one of the finest duos of the era. They also enjoyed individual successes — Sonny with *Laugh At Me* in 1965 and

Sonny and Cher in August 1965.

Cher with *All I Really Want To Do* the same year and *Bang Bang (My Baby Shot Me Down)* a year later. Their great cabaret routine made them much sought after and in the early '70s that act was transferred to the small screen where CBS television showed their *Sonny And Cher Comedy Hour.*

During the early '70s Cher became more independent and had three US number-one hits. Alas, it also heralded the start of the break-up of their marriage and they were divorced in 1974. Since then they have established themselves in other fields. In 1988, Sonny was elected Mayor of Palm Springs and in the same month Cher won an Oscar as best actress for her performance in the movie *Moonstruck.* The one-time hippies have certainly come a long way in 25 years.

Top Ten hits of Sonny & Cher in the 1960s:

Year	Record	Pos
1965	I Got You Babe	1
1966	Little Man	4

Top Ten hits of Sonny in the 1960s:

1965	Laugh At Me	9

Top Ten hits of Cher in the 1960s:

1965	All I Really Want To Do	9
1966	Bang Bang (My Baby Shot Me Down)	3

SPACE EXPLORATION

THE whole spectrum of space exploration was covered in the sixties. It started with Yuri Gagarin making the first manned space flight and ended with Neil Armstrong becoming the first man to set foot on the moon.

Space flight suddenly became reality in the 1960s. It was no longer restricted to comic strips and Jules Verne adventure stories. But space flight was not new. It just seemed to all happen in the sixties.

In preparation for manned space flight animals had been used for experiments, and as early as 1951 it is believed that the Americans sent four monkeys into space. All returned to earth safely but one subsequently died from his ordeal. In 1957 the Russians launched the dog *Laika* into space via their *Sputnik II* satellite. The dog subsequently died. But the Russians made a breakthrough in August 1960 when they sent two dogs, *Strelka* and *Belka* into space for 24 hours. This time they returned to earth safely and were proclaimed Soviet heroes.

The Russians are believed to have made four unsuccessful manned space flights between 1957-60 but the four cosmonauts, Alexis Ledovski, Serentsky Schiborin, Andrei Mitkov and Ivan Kachur all lost their lives.

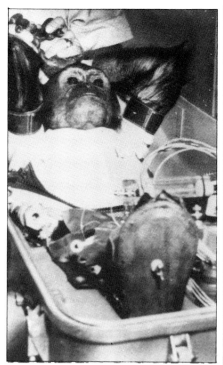

Enos, a five-year-old male chimpanzee, strapped into a Mercury Atlas spacecraft in November 1961. The unfortunate animal made a three-day orbit of Earth.

The Russians never admitted the fatalities. However, they did boast the first successful manned space flight on 12 April 1961 when Major Yuri Alekseyevich Gagarin was launched from Baikonur, Siberia, at 07.07 hrs. His flight aboard *Vostok 1* lasted 108 minutes before he landed safely at Smelovka, near Engels.

One of the great frontiers had at last been broken. Man could travel into space and return safely. Naturally the Americans were not too far behind the Russians and on 5 May 1961 Alan Shepard, aboard *Freedom 7*, went into space for a little over 15 minutes. Two weeks after Shepard's flight, President Kennedy announced that the Americans would aim to be the first to put a man on the moon.

Gus Grissom became the second American in space on 21 July, but he was up for only about 15 minutes. On 6 August Gherman Titov became the first cosmonaut to spend 24 hours in space when he went into orbit in *Vostok 2* and in February 1962 John Glenn became the first American to actually orbit the earth when he spent 4hr 55min aboard *Friendship 7*.

Having established manned space flights, it was time to experiment. The Russians launched *Vostok 3* on 11 August 1962 and the following day launched *Vostok 4*. The two craft came within four miles of each other during their three and two-day flights respectively. This was a pioneering flight for space docking, which was to come later.

Valentina Tereshkova made history by becoming the first woman in space in 1963 when she spent nearly three days in *Vostok 6* and the following year the cosmonauts Komarov, Yegerov and Feoktistov made the first multi-manned space flight in *Voskhod 1*. In March 1965 Alexei Leonov got himself into the 'Space record book' when he became the first man to walk in space, and a week later Gus Grissom and John Young took off in *Gemini 3* in the first two-manned American space flight. Grissom became the first man to make two space flights. Later that same year Edward White became the first American to walk in space and on 21 August 1965 Gordon Cooper and Charles Conrad became the first astronauts to spend a week in space, aboard *Gemini 5*.

Two American crafts, *Gemini 6* and *Gemini 7*, met in space for the first rendezvous in December 1965 but with all this pioneering going on it was, perhaps, inevitable that tragedy would

From left: Neil Armstrong, Michael Collins and Edwin 'Buzz' Aldrin.

follow, and on 27 January 1967 Gus Grissom, Edward White and Roger Chaffee lost their lives when they were killed in a fire on board their *Apollo 1* spacecraft on the launch pad during a training schedule. Ironically, it was the first *Apollo* mission, the rocket that would eventually take man to the moon. Three months after the American tragedy Vladimir Komarov was killed when his parachute failed to open during the descent of *Soyuz 1*.

Despite the set-back, the Americans continued with their *Apollo* flights and the next manned flight, *Apollo 7*, was in October 1968. And when Frank Borman, James Lovell and William Anders set off in *Apollo 8* on 21 December 1968 they spent Christmas orbiting the moon. Man was not far away from setting foot on what was once the great unknown.

Tom Stafford, John Young and Eugene Cernan, in *Apollo 10* were the last American astronauts before the eventual historic moon landing. They went within nine miles of the moon's surface and tested the lunar module in lunar orbit. They set it all up for *Apollo 11* which contained crew members Neil Armstrong, Buzz Aldrin and Michael Collins.

Those three set off on their historic flight on 16 July 1969, and at 9.18 BST on 20 July, landed on the Sea of Tranquility on the moon's surface. At 3.56am BST the next day, Neil Armstrong set foot on the moon and those famous words: "that's one small step for a man, one giant leap for mankind" echoed across the world. Armstrong was joined by Aldrin on the moon while Collins remained in the command module. The two men spent nearly two hours walking on the moon's surface where they carried out a variety of exercises and manoeuvres. They also planted the US flag and unveiled a plaque which read: *'Here men from the planet Earth first set foot upon the Moon July 1969 AD. We came in peace for all mankind.'*

Charles Conrad, Richard Gordon and Alan Bean made the only other lunar flight of the sixties, when Conrad and Bean became the next two men to walk on the moon. But after the Armstrong, Aldrin and Collins mission, the rest seemed all a bit of an anti-climax. Since then man has benefited from the lunar missions. Communication satellites are commonplace and, of course, the setting up of space stations was the inevitable progression from landing on the moon, and indeed that is what has happened.

But while man was preparing himself for that first moon landing, other space exploits were being carried out.

The US craft *Mariner 11*, which was

The US flag 'flutters' on the Moon. In fact, the flag had to be supported because there is no atmosphere there.

Manned Space Flights of the 1960s

Start	Craft	Duration Day	Hrs	Min	Cosmonauts/Astronauts
12 Apr 1961	Vostok 1	-	1	48	Yuri Gagarin
5 May 1961	Freedom 7	-	-	15	Alan Shepard
21 Jul 1961	Liberty Bell 7	-	-	15	Gus Grissom
6 Aug 1961	Vostok 2	1	1	18	Gherman Titov
20 Feb 1962	Friendship 7	-	4	55	John Glenn
24 May 1962	Aurora 7	-	4	56	Scott Carpenter
11 Aug 1962	Vostok 3	3	22	22	Andrian Nikolyev
12 Aug 1962	Vostok 4	2	22	1	Pavel Popovich
3 Oct 1962	Sigma 7	-	9	13	Walter Schirra
15 May 1963	Faith 7	1	10	20	Gordon Cooper
14 June 1963	Vostok 5	4	23	6	Valeri Bykovsky
16 Jun 1963	Vostok 6	2	22	50	Valentina Tereshkova
12 Oct 1964	Voskhod 1	1	0	17	Vladimir Komarov, Konstantin Feoktistov, Boris Yegerov
18 Mar 1965	Voskhod 2	1	2	2	Pavel Belayev, Alexei Leonov
25 Mar 1965	Gemini 3	-	4	53	Gus Grissom, John Young
3 June 1965	Gemini 4	4	1	56	James McDevitt, Edward White
21 Aug 1965	Gemini 5	7	22	55	Gordon Cooper, Charles Conrad
4 Dec 1965	Gemini 7	13	18	35	Frank Borman, James Lovell
15 Dec 1965	Gemini 6	1	1	52	Walter Schirra, Tom Stafford
16 Mar 1966	Gemini 8	10	41	26	Neil Armstrong, David Scott
3 Jun 1966	Gemini 9	3	0	21	Tom Stafford, Eugene Cernan
18 Jul 1966	Gemini 10	2	22	47	John Young, Michael Collins
12 Sep 1966	Gemini 11	2	23	17	Charles Conrad, Richard Gordon
11 Nov 1966	Gemini 12	3	22	35	James Lovell, Buzz Aldrin
23 Apr 1967	Soyuz 1	1	2	48	Vladimir Komarov
11 Oct 1968	Apollo 7	10	20	9	Walter Schirra, Donn Eisele, Walt Cunningham
26 Oct 1968	Soyuz 3	3	22	51	Georgi Beregovoi
21 Dec 1968	Apollo 8	6	3	1	Frank Borman, James Lovell, William Anders
14 Jan 1969	Soyuz 4	2	23	21	Vladimir Shatalov
15 Jan 1969	Soyuz 5	3	0	54	Boris Volynov, Alexei Yeleseyev, Yevgeny Khrunhov
3 Mar 1969	Apollo 9	10	1	1	James McDevitt, David Scott, Russell Schweickart
18 May 1969	Apollo 10	8	0	3	Tom Stafford, John Young, Eugene Cernan
16 Jul 1969	Apollo 11	8	3	19	Neil Armstrong, Buzz Aldrin, Michael Collins
11 Oct 1969	Soyuz 6	4	22	43	Georgi Shonin, Valeri Kubasov
12 Oct 1969	Soyuz 7	4	22	40	Anatoli Filipchenko, Vladislav Volkov, Viktor Gorbatko
13 Oct 1969	Soyuz 8	4	22	51	Vladimir Shatalov, Alexei Yeliseyev
14 Nov 1969	Apollo 12	10	4	36	Charles Conrad, Richard Gordon, Alan Bean

launched on 27 August 1962, travelled within 21,500 miles of the planet Venus. It might not sound very close, but when you consider it had to travel 180 million miles in four months to get there, it wasn't a bad effort. The Russians also sent a spacecraft, *Venus III*, to, would you believe, Venus. It was launched in November 1965 and made a hard landing on 1 March 1966. It was the first spacecraft to land on another planet. In 1967 Britain had its share of glory when *Ariel 3*, the first satellite entirely designed and built in Britain, was launched from Vandenburg Air Force base, California.

In November 1960, an American rocket launched from Cape Canaveral, went off course and crashed in Cuba. It killed a cow. The Cuban Government gave the cow an official funeral because it was, in the eyes of Fidel Castro and his colleagues, a 'victim of imperialist aggression'.

SPENCER DAVIS GROUP

A LOVER of rhythm and blues music, Birmingham University student Spencer Davis was keen on forming his own group. After watching The Muff-Woody Quartet performing he asked them to join him and form a new group, which they did in 1961. Two members of the new band were the brothers Steve and Mervyn (Muff) Winwood.

After a couple of years playing clubs and pubs in the Birmingham area they signed a contract with Fontana Records in 1964. The band's first three records were all minor hits but then came *Keep On Running* in 1965. By the following January it was number one and their follow-up *Somebody Help Me* also went to the top of the charts.

Over the next couple of years they toured at home and abroad which enhanced their popularity. In the spring of 1967, the Winwoods left to follow individual careers. The Spencer Davis Group continued but the loss of such talented musicians was too big a burden to shoulder. By 1968 the chart career of the group was over.

Steve Winwood went on to form his own group, Traffic, and then joined Eric Clapton, Ginger Baker and Ric Grech in the supergroup, Blind Faith. He returned to the charts in the 1980s as a solo artist and had a US number one in 1986 with *Higher Love* and the successful single and album *'Roll With It'* in 1988.

Top Ten hits of the Spencer Davis Group in the 1960s:

Year	Record	Pos
1965	Keep On Running	1
1966	Somebody Help Me	1
1966	Gimme Some Loving	2
1967	I'm A Man	9

SPORT IN THE 1960s

UNLIKE the fifties when there was the first four-minute mile, the 'Matthews Cup Final' and an Ashes win over the Aussies, the 1960s were nowhere near as momentous; and there were certainly no Ashes successes.

Football, however, provided the bulk of the great sporting moments and within two years, 1966-68, British football was riding high in Europe and the rest of the world.

In July 1966 Alf Ramsey's England team proudly reached the World Cup Final on home soil against the West Germans, but Bobby Moore, Bobby Charlton and co, not to forget Geoff Hurst and his hat-trick of goals, saw off the Germans as England won the

Bobby Moore receives the World Cup from the Queen in 1966.

trophy for the first time by four goals to two.

A year later Glasgow Celtic made the breakthrough that British clubs had been attempting for more than ten years when they beat Inter-Milan of Italy 2-1 to win the European Cup in Lisbon, and so become the first British club to win the trophy. Celtic were guided by Jock Stein, one of the game's great managers, and 12 months later, at Wembley, another of the game's great bosses, Matt Busby, fulfilled a ten-year dream when he guided Manchester United to the trophy with a 4-1 extra-time win over Benfica.

British clubs had started to make the European breakthrough in 1963 when Spurs, complete with Jimmy Greaves, beat Atletico Madrid to win the European Cup-winners' Cup and become the first British club to make inroads into Europe.

By the end of the decade, West Ham United, Leeds United and Newcastle United had also become British winners of European trophies.

On the domestic scene, Liverpool returned to the First Division in 1962 after an absence of eight years, and their return to the top flight coincided with the arrival of the great Bill Shankly. Suddenly Liverpool was to have more than pop groups. They were about to have two of the most successful teams in England.

Liverpool won the Football League title in 1964 and since then have proved to be the most outstanding team in English League soccer and have won the title 11 more times since that 1963-4 season — a truly outstanding record. They won the FA Cup for the first time in 1965 and Everton won it the following year when they came from 2-0 down to beat Sheffield Wednesday 3-2 in the best Final of the decade.

Manchester United, apart from their great European triumph, won the FA Cup in 1963 and the League Championship in 1965 and 1967. But they will hardly want reminding that the 1967 success was their last Championship win.

But for one of the finest soccer achievements of the 1960s, the glory went to North London and to White Hart Lane, home of Tottenham Hotspur, in 1960-61 when they became the first 20th-century club to win the League and Cup double. Many great teams had come close in the fifties, but all had failed. Manager Bill Nicholson and his team, led by Irishman Danny Blanchflower, eventually pulled off what seemed like a modern-day impossibility.

The Football League Cup, since called the Milk Cup and the Littlewoods Cup, started its life in 1960 with Aston Villa beating Rotherham United in the first Final. But the competition was not supported by all League teams in those early days and many thought it too gimmicky. It's a different story today as it is another of Wembley's showpieces. The competition moved its Final to Wembley in 1967 when Third Division Queen's Park Rangers stunned First Division West Brom with a 3-2 win.

In Scotland, Glasgow certainly belonged to Celtic. They won the League title in 1966 and that was to herald the start of a run of nine successive League titles.

Stanley Matthews made a nostalgic return to Stoke City when well into his forties and he helped his home town back into the First Division. Remarkably, he played First Division soccer at the age of 50. Stoke paid a nominal fee to bring Matthews back to the Victoria Ground, but the 1960s was a decade of big transfer fees and spiralling wages after Johnny Haynes of Fulham paved the way in 1961 by becoming the first £100-a-week footballer.

Denis Law became Britain's costliest player when he moved from Huddersfield Town to Manchester City for £55,000 in 1960. And he further broke the record when he became the first British £100,000 player on his move to Torino of Italy the following year. By the end of the decade Leeds United had pushed the British record up to £165,000 when they bought Allan Clarke from Leicester City. The world record at the time stood at £675,000 which was the amount Juventus paid Verese for Pietro Anastase in 1968.

Sadly, violence at soccer grounds became prevalent and Glasgow Rangers and Everton were forced to take measures in an attempt to thwart such hooliganism. Unfortunately, their efforts have all been in vain as violence went on to become a sorry part of soccer.

One of the biggest scandals to hit soccer, however, was the football 'result fixing' affair which was brought to light in 1964 by the *Sunday People* newspaper. Ten current and former players were convicted at Nottingham assizes, including England internationals Peter Swan and Tony Kay.

While our footballers won the World Cup, the England cricketers gave us little to cheer in the 1960s. There were no Ashes wins over the old enemy despite the efforts of skippers Peter May, Ted Dexter, M.J.K.Smith and Colin Cowdrey. And, following the Basil D'Oliveira affair, when he was picked to tour South Africa in the winter of 1968-9, South Africa played its last Test match in 1969-70. Freddie Trueman remained one of England's best fast bowlers until his retirement from the Test arena in 1965 and on 15 August 1964 he became the first man to take 300 wickets in Test cricket when he dismissed Australia's Neil Hawke.

Trueman's Yorkshire dominated the County Championship throughout the 1960s and won the title six times. Amongst the other winners were Wales' surprise package, Glamorgan, who won the title in 1969. The one-day game emerged in the 1960s with the start of the Gillette Cup in 1963 and at the end of the decade, the John Player Sunday League started in 1969. It was good for the spectators and it helped bring sponsorship and money into cricket, but one can't help wondering whether its introduction into the game was the demise of the fast bowler in Britain.

One of the most outstanding individual cricketing achievements was at the St Helen's Ground, Swansea, on 31 August 1968 when Gary Sobers of Nottinghamshire hit Glamorgan bowler Malcolm Nash for six sixes in one over as he scattered balls all around Swansea — King Edward Road and all. It was the first time such a feat had been achieved in the first-class game.

Athletes were given plenty of opportunity to shine at three Olympic Games — Rome (1960), Tokyo (1964) and Mexico City (1968). There were also two Commonwealth Games, at Perth, Australia, in 1962 and Kingston, Jamaica, four years later. The one thing common to both championships in the latter half of the 1960s was the emergence of the black African athletes like Kip Keino and Naftali Temu of Kenya. But for outstanding achievements of the decade, the Mexico Olympics were the place to be as first Bob Beamon shattered the world record and Lee Evans did likewise in the 400 metres. Beamon's record still stands while Evans' survived until 1988. Both were remarkable achievements.

Britain produced its usual crop of fine athletes and at the Olympics, long-jumpers Lynn Davies and Mary Rand did us proud, as did Ann Packer, the golden girl of middle-distance running. And how close that other golden girl, Lilian Board, came to striking gold. Hurdler David Hemery was our star of the Mexico games.

The 1960s was not a golden age for British boxing. We produced just three world champions: Terry Downes (middleweight), Howard Winstone (featherweight) and Walter McGowan (flyweight). But the most popular and best known of British fighters of the 1960s, and probably since then, was

Opposite top: Cassius Clay, alias Muhammad Ali, bottom: Great Britain's Ann Packer storms home for Olympic gold in the 1964 women's 800 metres final.

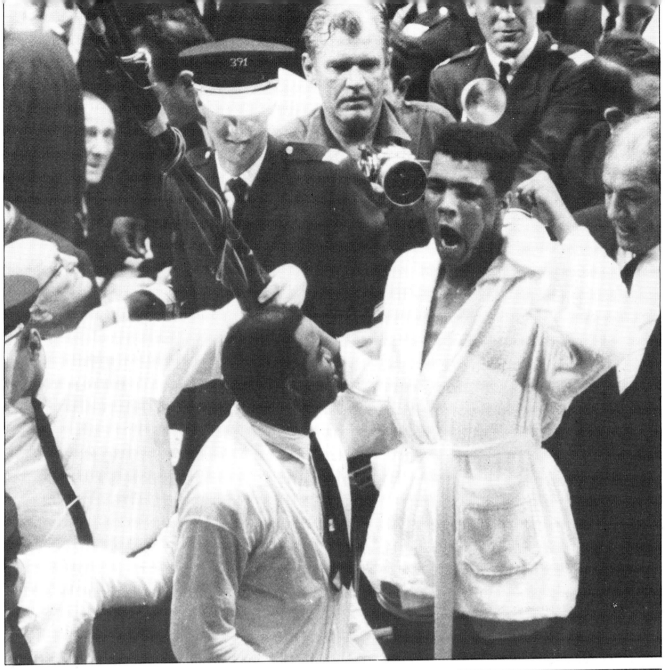

heavyweight Henry Cooper. But even 'Our 'Enery' was no match for the flamboyant and extrovert new heavyweight champion of the world who emerged in 1964, Cassius Clay, later to become Muhammad Ali.

The equestrian world saw Lester Piggott dominate the British flat racing scene as he partnered some of the great horses of the day, St Paddy, Sir Ivor, Ribero and Nijinsky. Noel Murless was the leading trainer of the 1960s and over the jumps the most outstanding name was that of Arkle, the greatest ever steeple-chaser.

Arkle never competed in the Grand National but the famous Aintree race produced some well-known winners like Merryman II in 1960, and Nicolaus Silver the following year. There was also Ayala (1963), Team Spirit (1964) and the 100-1 winner Foinavon who jumped through, when all around him were falling, to win the race in 1967.

In the world of high speed, Britain produced some great champions. John Surtees in 1964 added the world motor racing driver's title to his seven world motor cycling titles. To this day he remains the only man to win world titles on two and four wheels.

Graham Hill (1962 and 1968), Jim Clark (1963 and 1965) and Jackie Stewart (1969) were all British world motor racing champions during the 1960s, which was the golden era for both British drivers and manufacturers like Lotus, Tyrrell and Matra.

World Heavyweight Boxing Champions

26 Jun 1959 to 20 Jun 1960	Ingemar Johansson	Sweden
20 Jun 1960 to 25 Sep 1962	Floyd Patterson	United States
25 Sep 1962 to 25 Feb 1964	Sonny Liston	United States
25 Feb 1964 to 28 Apr 1967	Cassius Clay (Muhammad Ali)	United States
5 Mar 1965 to 6 Feb 1967	Ernie Terrell	United States, WBA title
4 Mar 1968 to 22 Jan 1973	Joe Frazier	United States, NY State title
27 Apr 1968 to 16 Feb 1970	Jimmy Ellis	United States, WBA title

World Mile Record Holders of the 1960s

3min 54.5sec Herb Elliott (Australia) set at Dublin 6 Aug 1958.
3min 54.4sec Peter Snell (New Zealand) set at Wanganui 27 Jan 1962.
3min 54.1sec Peter Snell (New Zealand) set at Auckland 17 Nov 1964
3min 53.6 sec Michel Jazy (France) set at Rennes 9 Jun 1965.
3min 51.3sec Jim Ryun (United States) set at Berkeley, USA, 17 Jul 1965.
3min 51.1sec Jim Ryun (United States) set at Bakersfield, USA, 23 Jun 1967.

Wimbledon Singles Champions

Year	Men	Women
1960	Neale Fraser (Australia)	Maria Bueno (Brazil)
1961	Rod Laver (Australia)	Angela Mortimer (Great Britain)
1962	Rod Laver (Australia)	Karen Susman (United States)
1963	Chuck McKinley (United States)	Margaret Smith (Australia)
1964	Roy Emerson (Australia)	Maria Bueno (Brazil)
1965	Roy Emerson (Australia)	Margaret Smith (Australia)
1966	Manuel Santana (Spain)	Billie Jean King (United States)
1967	John Newcombe (Australia)	Billie Jean King (United States)
1968	Rod Laver (Australia)	Billie Jean King (United States)
1969	Rod Laver (Australia)	Ann Jones (Great Britain)

On two wheels, the most outstanding rider of the decade was Mike Hailwood who, in addition to winning nine world titles, dominated the Isle of Man TT races and twice (1961 and 1967) won three races in one week.

Golf produced some great champions in the shape of the 'Big Three', Jack Nicklaus, Arnold Palmer and Gary Player. They dominated world golf but there was the occasional hiccup as far as British fans were concerned. The biggest thrill of the decade was seeing Tony Jacklin walk up the 18th fairway at Royal Lytham in 1969, knowing he was the first British winner of the Open since 1951.

Tennis also produced some great

Mike Hailwood.

Gary Player.

heroes. In the men's game there was the Australian trio of Rod Laver, Roy Emerson and John Newcombe. The Aussies had a useful woman player as well in the shape of Margaret Smith (later Margaret Court) but the 'queen' of tennis in the 1960s was unquestionably the fast emerging Billie Jean Moffitt (later Billie Jean King). Again though, the British fans had their rare moments of glory when Angela Mortimer won the Wimbledon title in 1961 and Ann Jones beat Billie Jean to win the title in 1969. The year before, Virginia Wade had become the first winner of the US Open title. As far as the British men were concerned, well, sadly there was little to

cheer. Mike Sangster and Roger Taylor each reached Wimbledon semi-finals. But that was about it.

Elsewhere in the world of sport in the 1960s the first US Super Bowl was contested in 1967. American football is now one of the sports of the eighties. *Pot Black,* the BBC television snooker programme was launched in 1969. Without it there is little doubt that snooker would not be perched on such a high pedestal as it is today.

Karen Muir of South Africa put herself into the sporting record books in 1965 when she broke the swimming 110 yards backstroke world record with a time of 1min 8.7sec and at the age of 12 became the youngest-ever world record holder for any sport.

And finally, for sheer agony and pity one has to look to the tough world of Rugby League. In the 1968 Challenge Cup Final at Wembley, Leeds were leading Wakefield Trinity 11-7 with seconds remaining. Keith Hirst then touched down under the posts for Trinity. It was 11-10 to Leeds but Don Fox had the easiest of kicks to secure the two points good enough to win the trophy. But what agony it was for Fox, his teammates and the Wakefield supporters as he sliced the kick inexplicably wide. It was truly the most agonizing of the many great sporting moments of the 1960s.

Some sporting winners of the 1960s:
FA Cup
1960 . . . . .Wolverhampton Wanderers
1961. . . . . .Tottenham Hotspur
1962. . . . . .Tottenham Hotspur
1963. . . . . .Manchester United
1964 . . . . .West Ham United
1965 .Liverpool
1966 . . . . .Everton
1967. . . . . .Tottenham Hotspur
1968 . . . . .West Bromwich Albion
1969 . . . . .Manchester City

Football League Champions
1960 . . . . .Burnley
1961. . . . . .Tottenham Hotspur
1962 . . . . .Ipswich Town
1963 . . . . .Everton
1964 .Liverpool
1965 . . . . .Manchester United
1966 .Liverpool
1967 . . . . .Manchester United
1968 . . . . .Manchester City
1969 . . . . .Leeds United

County Cricket Champions
1960 .Yorkshire
1961 . . . . .Hampshire
1962 .Yorkshire
1963 .Yorkshire
1964 . . . . .Worcestershire
1965 . . . . .Worcestershire
1966 .Yorkshire
1967 .Yorkshire
1968 .Yorkshire
1969 . . . . .Glamorgan

Derby Winners

Year	Horse	Jockey
1960	St Paddy	Lester Piggott
1961	Psidium	Roger Poincelet
1962	Larkspur	Neville Sellwood
1963	Relko	Yves Saint-Martin
1964	Santa Claus	Scobie Breasley
1965	Sea Bird II	Pat Glennon
1966	Charlottown	Scobie Breasley
1967	Royal Palace	George Moore
1968	Sir Ivor	Lester Piggott
1969	Blakeney	Ernie Johnson

Grand National Winners

1960	Merryman II	Gerry Scott
1961	Nicolaus Silver	Bobby Beasley
1962	Kilmore	Fred Winter
1963	Ayala	Pat Buckley
1964	Team Spirit	Willie Robinson
1965	Jay Trump	Tommy Smith
1966	Anglo	Tim Norman
1967	Foinavon	John Buckingham
1968	Red Alligator	Brian Fletcher
1969	Highland Wedding	Eddie Harty

World Motor Racing Champions

1960	Jack Brabham	Australia
1961	Phil Hill	United States
1962	Graham Hill	Great Britain
1963	Jim Clark	Great Britain
1964	John Surtees	Great Britain
1965	Jim Clark	Great Britain
1966	Jack Brabham	Australia
1967	Denny Hulme	New Zealand
1968	Graham Hill	Great Britain
1969	Jackie Stewart	Great Britain

British Open Golf Champions

1960	Kel Nagle	Australia
1961	Arnold Palmer	United States
1962	Arnold Palmer	United States
1963	Bob Charles	New Zealand
1964	Tony Lema	United States
1965	Peter Thomson	Australia
1966	Jack Nicklaus	United States
1967	Roberto de Vicenzo	Argentina
1968	Gary Player	South Africa
1969	Tony Jacklin	Great Britain

SPRINGFIELD, Dusty

BORN in Hampstead, London, as Mary O'Brien on 16 April 1939, Dusty Springfield was educated at a convent and on leaving school worked in a record store. At the time, her elder brother Tom was establishing himself as an entertainer and Dusty would often appear on stage with him. In 1960 a good friend of Tom's, Tim Field joined them and the threesome became known as The Springfields.

Voted the top British vocal group of 1961 and 1962, their hits included *Island Of Dreams* and *Say I Won't Be There.* The trio split up in 1963 and the members went their own way. Dusty followed a solo singing career. Her debut single *I Only Want To Be*

Steptoe and Son.

With You won a gold disc and after a succession of Top 20 hits she eventually enjoyed her first number one this side of the Atlantic when *You Don't Have To Say You Love Me* topped the charts in 1966.

For the three consecutive years 1965-67 she was voted top British female singer. Although she spent more time concentrating on her stage performances rather than cutting discs, she remained tremendously popular and her popularity amongst her fans never waned. She returned to the charts in 1987 when she teamed up with The Pet Shop Boys on their hit *What Have I Done To Deserve This?* and in March 1989 she had her first solo Top Ten hit for 23 years with *Nothing Has Been Proved* from the film *Scandal*.

The revival of the girl with the bouffant hairstyle and the darling of the eye-shadow manufacturers in the 1960s, has been a welcome bonus to the *aficianados* of 1960s music fans.

Top Ten hits of Dusty Springfield in the 1960s:

Year	Record	Pos
1963	I Only Want To Be With You	4
1964	I Just Don't Know What To Do With Myself	3
1964	Losing You	9
1965	In The Middle Of Nowhere	8
1965	Some Of Your Lovin'	8
1966	You Don't Have To Say You Love Me	1
1966	Going Back	10
1966	All I See Is You	9
1968	I Close My Eyes And Count To Ten	4
1968	Son Of A Preacher Man	9

STAR TREK

ONE OF the great television series of the 1960s, *Star Trek* became a cult in the 1970s and 1980s.

The series was first seen in 1966 and was the brainchild of Gene Roddenberry as it became the first science fiction programme to attract a large adult audience.

Set in the 23rd century, the series was about the starship *Enterprise* and its occupants, notably Captain James T.Kirk, First Officer Mr Spock, Dr Leonard 'Bones' McCoy, Engineering Officer Montgomery Scott (Scotty), Helmsman Sulu, Navigator Chekov and Communications Officer, Lieutenant Uhura. The main characters, Kirk and Spock, were played by William Shatner and Leonard Nimoy respectively.

The *Enterprise* had the identification number NCC1701 and was the largest starship in the Fleet of the United Federation of Planets. In the series it never landed; all occupants were 'beamed up' (or down) by Scotty.

Mr Spock was half Earthling and half Vulcan and was the one with the pointed ears, green blood and to whom everything had a logical explanation. He was also emotionless and telepathic.

Between 1966 and 1969 a total of 79 episodes were made and the series proved to be more successful on the re-run, largely because of the success of the US manned space-flights at the time.

Many *Star Trek* fan clubs were established and the followers of the series became known as *Trekkies*. As a tribute to the series, President Ford named the first US space shuttle craft *Enterprise*.

In the late '70s and through the '80s, a number of *Star Trek* movies were made, along with an all-new TV show: *Star Trek: The Next Generation* which featured a different cast.

STEPTOE AND SON

A BRITISH comedy series about a father and son who ran a scrap business. It was written by Ray Galton and Alan Simpson, who were also responsible for *Hancock's Half Hour*.

Albert Steptoe (Wilfred Brambell) and his son Harold (Harry H.Corbett) made their debuts in 1962 when an episode entitled 'The Offer' was shown as part of the *Comedy Playhouse* series. It was given its own slot in 1964 and soon became Britain's most popular television show. It graced the screen for nearly ten years, although the later episodes in colour lacked the humour of the original black and white recordings.

Albert and Harold ran their rag and bone business from Oil Drum Lane, Shepherd's Bush, but Harold constantly had ambitions of moving on to better things. Every time he looked like escaping the clutches of his father he was dragged back and never got away. The pair carried out their business with the aid of a cart pulled by their faithful old horse, Hercules.

The Americans copied the idea and their equivalent was *Sanford And Son* which used black actors.

Harry H.Corbett died in 1982 and Wilfred Brambell died three years later.

On election day 1964 Harold Wilson asked the BBC to delay the series by 90 minutes until after the polling stations had closed so as to give people the chance of voting and also seeing the programme!

STRIKES

STRIKES were plentiful in the 1960s, particularly amongst the car workers. But the worst strike during the decade was in 1966 when the seamen went on strike at midnight on 15 May after failing to get a cut in their working week from 56 hours (without overtime!) to 40. On 23 May, the Government declared a state of emergency and Harold Wilson announced that he felt that communists were behind the strike. The dispute eventually came to an end on 29 June after 44 days.

One of the first major strikes of the 1960s was the powerworkers' strike in 1963 which caused blackouts up and down the country. But that was only minor compared to their action in the early 1970s when strikes were even more common than they were in the '60s.

But it was the car industry that was hit with the bulk of the strikes in the 1960s. Approximately 11,000 BMC workers were idle in August 1965 following an unofficial strike by maintenance men. And in 1966 they were hit again after 7,000 workers were laid off in September and BMC announced plans for 11,000 redundancies. The work-force came out on strike and all BMC factories in England and Wales were closed. The stoppage was unofficial and ended on 11 November, the day of the wholesale redundancies. The car industry was in turmoil in general at that time and because of a delivery drivers' strike and cutbacks in production, 100,000 car industry workers were either idle or on short time during the period from September to November 1966. The following January saw BMC hit again when a strike by maintenance men at a components firm caused 20,000 workers to be laid off.

Ford's too were hit by disputes. A strike by 24,800 at the Dagenham plant brought the works to a standstill for three days in June 1961 and in 1968 women machinists at the same plant, and also at Halewood, went on strike for equal pay. The dispute cost the company £9 million in lost export orders. The following year, another dispute, this time lasting 3½ weeks in February and March, cost the company dearly.

Also in 1968, the National Union of Railwaymen played their part in causing chaos for rail users. They had, early in the decade, engaged in a series of lightning one-day strikes, just as the teachers had.

The airways were also affected by strikes. In fact, very little was strike-free in the 1960s; even Hollywood had its first-ever actors strike.

Striking dustmen outside Caxton Hall, Westminster, in October 1969.

Telegraph operators, on strike over pay, picket the Post Office's overseas cable 'nerve centre' at Electra House, London, in January 1969.

A selection of other strikes in the 1960s:

Feb 1960 — A 24-hour token strike by London Underground workers.

Aug 1960 — Unofficial strikes by seamen and dockers at selected ports.

Nov 1961-Apr 1962 — Dispute between Equity, the actors' union, and the Independent Television companies lasted five months.

Jan 1962 — London traffic at a standstill because of unofficial one-day strike by Underground workers again.

Feb 1962 — Three million members of the engineering workers union out on a one-day token strike.

Oct 1962 — One-day rail strike. It caused little chaos; most people stayed at home!

Jul 1964 — ITV was off the air for five days because of a strike by ACTAT technicians.

Jul 1964 — Unofficial strike by engineers and other workers at Heathrow caused cancellation of 275 BEA flights.

Jul 1964 — Postmen came out on an official 24-hour strike.

Postmen staged a one-day strike in June 1964. Photo shows them marching towards Speakers' Corner, Hyde Park.

Dec 1964 — An unofficial one-day strike by stewards and stewardesses grounded 100 BEA flights.

Jan 1965 — Poor old BEA were hit again by an engineers strike.

Apr 1965 — Some booking office clerks on the London Underground went on strike. Passengers were asked to put money in 'honesty boxes' . . .

June 1965 — BEA again — this time porters at Heathrow caused the grounding of their planes.

Dec 1965 — A two-day strike by bakery workers meant many people in England and Wales were without bread.

1966 — That belonged to the car workers (see previous page).

Sep 1967 — Liverpool dock workers started a six-week unofficial strike.

Their London counterparts were out at the same time. Their dispute lasted eight weeks.

Nov 1967 — The National Union of Bank Employees started a series of two-day strikes.

Nov 1967 — The National Union of Teachers called off a three-month ban on serving school dinners.

Dec 1967 — It was BOAC's turn to get hit as pilots began a 48-hour strike in support of a pay claim.

May 1968 — Post Office counter clerks at 1,800 offices went on a two-hour strike in protest at delays in their claims for increased pay.

Jun 1968 — BOAC pilots were out again. There were no BOAC flights out of Heathrow.

Jan 1969 — Main Post Offices in 19 major cities were closed by a one-day strike.

Mar 1969 — The BOAC pilots were out on strike yet again following a dispute over pay and productivity. All BOAC flights were grounded.

The above is only a sample of the many strikes and disputes that arose during the decade. Don't forget there were also the countless 'work-to-rules'. But spare a thought for the French. The whole country came to a near standstill in May 1968 when approximately ten million workers in all sorts of industries came out on strike.

Striking seamen outside NUS headquarters.

Six hundred nurses converge on Downing Street in August 1968.

SUN, The

SHORTLY after 10pm on Monday, 14 September 1964 the switch was thrown to start the presses running and so bring about the birth of *The Sun*, Britain's first new national daily newspaper for 34 years. The non-tabloid paper replaced the *Daily Herald* which was published for the last time that day.

The first edition of *The Sun* contained 24 pages and the front page showed Sir Alec Douglas-Home during his election campaign. The paper's editor was Sydney Jacobsen and its editorial director was Hugh Cudlipp. Sales on the first day exceeded 3.5 million. The *Herald* averaged 1.3 million at the time of it 'death'.

The Sun became a tabloid on 17 November 1969.

SUPREMES, The

DIANA Ross, Mary Wilson and Florence Ballard all attended the same Detroit school. They also shared the same ambition, to become singing stars.

During their school days they performed as The Primettes. It was after winning a talent contest that they gained a contract with Motown Records and it was chief executive Berry Gordy who suggested a change of name. Florence Ballard came up with the Supremes.

Between August 1964 and December 1969 the talented trio had no fewer than 12 US number ones, ten of them being written by that equally talented trio of Holland, Dozier and Holland. Despite their success in America they had only one British chart topper, *Baby Love*.

Ballard left the group in 1967 and was replaced by Cindy Birdsong. Florence Ballard died on 22 February 1976 of a cardiac arrest at the age of 32. Shortly after Birdsong's arrival, the group's name was changed to Diana Ross and the Supremes, on the instruction of Gordy. The intention was to elevate Diana Ross to star billing and that was certainly achieved.

She left the group to go solo in 1970 and had five number-one hits in America, two in Britain, and also received rave reviews for her performance as Billie Holiday in *Lady Sings The Blues*. Even today she is one of the most sought-after of super-stars.

The Supremes carried on for many years after Ross' departure. She was replaced by Jean Terrell. Other members of the Supremes in later years were Lynda Laurence and Scherrie Payne, sister of Freda who

From left: Florence Ballard, Diana Ross and Mary Wilson.

> *Jean Terrell's brother Ernie was WBA heavyweight boxing champion between 1965-67.*

had the 1970 hit *Band Of Gold*. They eventually called it a day in the early '80s and only Mary Wilson survived from those heady days of 20 years earlier.

In 1982, at the 25th anniversary of Motown Records, and after a break of 12 years, Diana, Mary and Cindy were reunited for the special occasion.

Top Ten hits of the Supremes in the 1960s:

Year	Record	Pos
1964	Where Did Our Love Go	3
1964	Baby Love	1
1965	Stop In The Name Of Love	7
1966	You Can't Hurry Love	3
1966	You Keep Me Hangin' On	8
1967	The Happening	6
1967	Reflections	5

> *Diana Ross has had 18 number-one hits in America — 12 with the Supremes, five as a solo artiste and one (Endless Love) with Lionel Richie.*

The 'Yes, No Interlude' with Michael Miles (right).

TAKE YOUR PICK

WHEN it came to quiz programmes in the 1960s your choice was limited. You could take your pick between *Take Your Pick* or *Double Your Money*. There were a few others, but these two were the most notable of the day.

How they would stand up in today's

world of a never-ending stream of quiz programmes is anybody's guess. But *Take Your Pick*, hosted by Michael Miles, was a big attraction.

It started in 1955 (the day after the start of Independent Television) and ran for 13 years. In order to get the chance to win one of the 'star' prizes, the contestants had to first endure the 'Yes-No' interlude where they could not answer either 'yes' or 'no' to a barrage of questions put to them by Miles. If successful, they then had to answer three questions and if all three were answered correctly they were given the chance to collect a key to one of the ten boxes which contained a variety of prizes. Three of the boxes, however, contained booby prizes and, of course, there was the mystery box 13 . . .exciting stuff, eh!

Contestants would then have the chance to 'take the money' or 'open the box'. Miles would bid to buy the key off the contestant who, if he or she did not sell it to the host, opened the box to see what thrilling prize had been won . . .anything from a holiday in Armenia to a stale kipper. It was that exciting.

When Miles was attempting to buy the key off contestants he would usually stop his bidding at between £10 and £20. But on one occasion a frail old lady said, after Miles had made a couple of low bids, 'I wouldn't sell it to you, not even for £100'. He immediately offered her the £100 — and she took it! That was *Take Your Pick*.

TARBUCK, Jimmy

THEY say that Liverpool is the home of comedy and in recent years there has been a constant stream of top class comedians from Merseyside. But to succeed at comedy in the early 1960s, when Liverpool was such a stronghold of the pop scene, took something special. Jimmy Tarbuck had the qualities necessary to make the breakthrough at that time.

Jimmy started his showbusiness career as a compere on a rock and roll show before becoming a Butlins redcoat. He turned professional in 1963 and made his television debut on *Comedy Bandbox* that same year. He was an instant success and was chosen as the next host of *Sunday Night At The London Palladium* where his brand of cheeky Liverpool humour, although hard to comprehend at first by some southerners, became very popular. He used to do his stand-up routine in front of the

Jimmy Tarbuck.

back-drop known as 'Tarby's Wall', complete with Liverpool-wit graffiti.

Since then the affable Tarbuck has made a name for himself on *It's Tarbuck, Live From Her Majesty's* and *Tarby And Friends*. He has also enjoyed success on the popular quiz show *Winner Takes All*.

A great lover of sport, Tarby is a keen Liverpool FC fan and an avid golfer. He also devotes a lot of his spare time to raising money for the underprivileged, via the Variety Club.

Tarbuck's daughter Lisa starred in the recent ITV comedy series *Watching*.

TAYLOR, Elizabeth

OFTEN referred to as 'the last of the old-fashioned movie queens', Elizabeth Taylor was born of American parents in London on 27 February 1932. Her father was a London art dealer and she spent the first seven years of her life in Hampstead. After that she was brought up in America

and graduated from the University High School, Hollywood, at 18.

She made her film debut at the age of 10 in *There's One Born Every Minute* and the following year, 1943, she was contracted to MGM where she starred in a series of films for them over the next ten years, including the children's favourites, *Lassie Come Home* and *National Velvet*. In the 1950s she starred in *Cat On A Hot Tin Roof* (1958) and *Suddenly Last Summer* (1959) amongst others. She was one of the world's most beautiful women and by the end of the 1950s she was a box office sensation as her roles saw her develop from being a child star into a serious and sensual actress.

The 1960s proved to be a golden age in the career of Elizabeth Taylor. She won the first of her two Oscars for her performance as Gloria in *Butterfield 8* in 1961 and five years later she collected her second award after playing the part of the gin-swigging Martha in *Who's Afraid Of Virginia Woolf?*

Her portrayal of Cleopatra in the

Elizabeth Taylor as Cleopatra.

film of the same name attracted a lot of attention and, while it was not the blockbuster as expected, during the filming one of the best-known romances of the decade was born — Elizabeth Taylor and Richard Burton.

Burton lavished expensive gifts on the new love of his life, including the 33-carat Krupp diamond. They were married in 1964 and it lasted until 1974. They remarried the following year before a second divorce in 1976. In the 1960s they were one of the most celebrated married couples in movie history.

> During the filming of Cleopatra, her then husband Eddie Fisher was paid $1,500 a day to make sure she got to work on time.

As the 1970s got under way, illness, drink and the stress of her marriage took its toll as Liz cut down on her movie appearances. She remains beautiful. She remains a headline maker. And there is constant talk amongst the gossip columnists that marriage number eight is on the horizon.

Films of Elizabeth Taylor in the 1960s:

Scent Of Mystery	(1960)
Butterfield 8	(1960)
Cleopatra	(1963)
The V.I.P.s	(1963)
The Sandpiper	(1965)
Who's Afraid Of Virginia Woolf?	(1966)
The Taming Of The Shrew	(1967)
Reflections In A Golden Eye	(1967)
The Comedians	(1967)
Doctor Faustus	(1968)
Boom!	(1968)
Sweet Ceremony	(1968)
Anne Of A Thousand Days	(1969)

(She appeared unbilled in a crowd scene, just as she had done in *Quo Vadis* in 1951.)

Elizabeth Taylor's husbands:

No 1	Nicky Hilton	1950-51
No 2	Michael Wilding	1952-57
No 3	Michael Todd	1957-58*
No 4	Eddie Fisher	1959-64
No 5	Richard Burton	1964-74
No 6	Richard Burton	1975-76
No 7	John Warner	1976-81

*Todd was killed in a plane crash (all the other marriages ended in divorce).

TELEVISION

TELEVISION in the 1960s saw a big advancement in technological terms. There was the launch of the Telstar satellite, which allowed pictures from all around the world to be beamed live into our living rooms. But perhaps the biggest breakthrough since John Logie Baird first invented the television was the introduction of the colour receiver in 1967.

The 1960s were very much a 'black and white' era as far as TV was concerned, but as the decade came to a close the first colour television programmes went out over the airwaves. That single development alone has been instrumental in a major change in many people's way of life as television (and of course the video) became a substitute for the cinema as people invested in colour televisions rather then spend money going to the pictures.

But long before colour television arrived, the TV screens had been filled with some great programmes. There was plenty of drama, comedy, light entertainment, political programmes and, of course, there was sport.

Outside broadcasting became very popular in the 1960s and it started with BBC's coverage of the Royal Wedding and Rome Olympics, the two biggest OB events of 1960. It was also in 1960 that the BBC announced that it wanted a second channel.

However, BBC2 was not launched until 21 April 1964 when *Play School* became the new station's first programme. It should have been launched the previous night, but a fire at Battersea Power Station, which blacked out most of London, caused the delay in its launch.

The new station aimed its programmes at the wrong class of viewer and it got off to a bad start. It was not until David Attenborough took charge at the beginning of 1965 that BBC2 started to win over the ordinary television viewers. Many popular series, later transferred to BBC1, started life on BBC2. There was the *Morecambe And Wise Show, Match Of The Day, Fawlty Towers* and *The Likely Lads* to name but a few. One of their early programmes which is still going was *Horizon.* And of course BBC2

179

gave us the *Forsyte Saga* and *Pot Black*.

But what about the programmes of the 1960s? Well, there were too many great ones to name them all. But of course there was the launch of *Coronation Street* which brought real-life northern drama into homes up and down the country. *Armchair Theatre* also did that with a variety of cleverly-written plays. It was also the programme that launched many acting careers. For heart-rending down-to-earth viewing you had to look no further than the controversial and disturbing *Cathy Come Home* in 1966 which showed the plight of the homeless in the 1960s.

'Corro' was not the only soap opera of the 1960s. There was also *Compact, Emergency Ward Ten* and *Crossroads.* And of course there was *The Forsyte Saga,* the last BBC series made entirely in black and white. British screens were also graced with that genial threesome, Doctors Finlay, Cameron and the delightful Janet in the 1960s as *Dr Finlay's Casebook* became very popular.

Lady Penelope from the puppet show Thunderbirds.

Comedy series were plentiful in the 1960s and *Steptoe And Son* was one of the top programmes in the middle of the decade. They were succeeded

by Alf Garnett in the equally popular *Till Death Us Do Part*. Morecambe and Wise also contributed a lot to comedy on television in the 1960s, as did the ever-popular Benny Hill and his bevy of beauties. Michael Bentine and his *It's A Square World* was innovative in its day and won a prize at the 1963 Montreux Television Festival. There

Opposite: Dr Finlay's Casebook.
Below: Characters of Coronation Street. From left: Len Fairclough, Ena Sharples, Annie Walker and Elsie Tanner.

Patrick Whymark, Peter Barkworth and Jack Watling in The Power Game.

Above: Billy Cotton and Adam Faith. Below: Sooty and Sweep with their creator Harry Corbett, who died in 1989.

was also that great comedy series, *The Rag Trade* starring Peter Jones and Miriam Karlin. And of course there was *Bootsie And Snudge*, a spin-off from *The Army Game*, starring Alfie Bass and Bill Fraser.

Satire became prevalent in the 1960s and *That Was The Week That Was* launched David Frost, Millicent Martin, Lance Percival, Willie Rushton, Ned Sherrin and others on the road to stardom. The programme got into hot water with the Government for 'having a go' at politicians. It resulted in the BBC temporarily banning mention of religion, sex, royalty and politics in its comedy shows.

Light entertainment shows were very popular in the 1960s and leading the way was the *Black And White Minstrel Show* which seemed to run on and on and on. Close behind came *Sunday Night At The London Palladium* with its ever-popular Beat the Clock feature as such men as Tommy Trinder, Bruce Forsyth and Norman Vaughan hosted the programme.

The Good Old Days from the Leeds City Variety Theatre was another long-running variety show which enjoyed its peak popularity in the 1960s, and the *Billy Cotton Band Show* was popular in the early 1960s. But as the world of pop music took a grip on the nation there became a demand for the teenagers to have their own programmes and *Thank Your Lucky Stars, Juke Box Jury, Ready Steady Go* and *Top Of The Pops* brought the top pop stars and sounds of the day to the television screens.

At the start of the 1960s cowboy programmes were popular and the likes of *Wagon Train* and *Bonanza* became firm favourites with British fans. But they gave way to the thriller series like *Danger Man, The Avengers, The Prisoner, Man From U.N.C.L.E., The Saint, The Protectors, Secret Agent* and so on, which all became the vogue at the time of the James Bond movies. Sci-fi programmes like *Star Trek* also became popular. Its particular popularity stemmed from the successful lunar space missions of the Americans at the time. Britain had its own fantasy programme, *Doctor Who* which was launched in 1965. It is still going strong nearly 25 years later.

Cops remained viewers favourites whether they be from Dock Green, Newtown *(Z Cars)*, Hawaii *(Five-O)* or Sunset Strip (No 77). The French also had their own top cop: *Inspector Maigret*, played by the pipe-smoking Rupert Davies.

British series like *The Power Game, The Trouble Shooters* and *This Man*

Opposite: The Black and White Minstrel Show. This type of entertainment — white people dressing up as black characters — would not be tolerated today, yet it seemed harmless enough in the 1960s.

Crane were all launched in the mid-1960s.

American comedy shows became increasingly popular as the fantasy world of *Bewitched, The Munsters, Batman, The Addams Family* and the talking horse, *Mr Ed,* all became favourites, initially with kids and now, second time around, with adults. The Americans also gave us the *Beverly Hillbillies,* and there were also the puppet programmes.

Long gone was *Muffin The Mule.* In his place came the adventure puppet programmes like *Supercar, Fireball XL5, Stingray,* and of course the delectable Lady Penelope in *Thunderbirds.*

Sport, more than any other field, benefited from the advancement of colour television. But even before colour TV arrived, Kenneth Wolstenholme had the privilege of commentating from Anfield for the first ever *Match Of The Day* on 22 August 1964 and he greeted the viewers by saying: "Welcome to Beatleville". As a matter of interest Liverpool beat Arsenal 3-2 and the honour of scoring *Match Of The Day's* first goal fell to Roger Hunt.

World Of Sport was launched on 2 January 1965 with Eamonn Andrews as its host, and the following year 32 million viewers saw England win the World Cup Final. By then the instant replay was very much an integral part of sports coverage and had first been used at the 1964 Grand National.

World In Action, This Week and *Tonight* (later *24 hours*) led the way in current affairs programmes, and on 3 July 1967, ITN launched *News At Ten.*

When it came to quiz programmes in the 1960s there was a very limited choice, unlike today when you can pick up a quiz on one channel or the other at most times during the day. *Take Your Pick* and *Double Your Money* were the two top programmes but in 1962 there was the launch of *University Challenge.* It is currently the longest-running quiz show in Britain.

TELEVISION LICENCE

THE cost of the television licence during the 1960s was:

1960-64 ... £4
1965 ...... £5
1967 ...... £5
(plus £5 supplement for colour television)
1968 ...... £5 black & white; £10 colour
1969 ...... £6 black & white; £11 colour

From 1960-63 the £4 cost included £1 excise duty. Throughout the 1960s if you did not have a television set, but did have a radio, you had to have a separate licence. The cost was £1 (1960-64), and £1 5s (1966-69). If you had a radio-receiving licence, either on its own or as part of the television licence, you still had to have a separate radio licence for a car radio!

The cost of a television licence in 1989 was: £22 for black & white; £66 for colour. The radio licence was abolished in 1971.

The total number of licences issued for television sets in the 1960s was:
1960-10,646,938   1965-13,253,045
1961-11,267,741   1966-13,567,090
1962-11,833,712   1967-14,267,271
1963-12,442,806   1968-15,068,079
1964-12,885,331   1969-15,496,061
                              (99,419 colour)
(Figures as at 31 March each year)
In 1988 there were 19,354,442 licences issued of which 2,220,482 were for black and white sets and 17,133,960 for colour receivers.
(Source: *Daily Mail Yearbook*)

TELSTAR

THE TELSTAR communications satellite, built by the American Telephone and Telegraph Company, was launched in 1962 and on 11 July that year the first transatlantic television pictures were beamed from the United States to France. In return the French sent pictures of singer Yves Montand to the States. But the big breakthrough in live transatlantic television came at 8pm (BST) on 23 July 1962 when 200 million viewers in 16 European countries shared 18 minutes of history with the Americans.

In Britain we saw live pictures of President Kennedy talking about not devaluing the dollar and we were then taken on a whistle-stop tour of the United States including a baseball game from Chicago. The viewers in North America were treated to a quick jaunt around Europe during the 18 minutes that Telstar was available for transmission. And they were to witness scenes like reindeer being cared for in Sweden, fishermen in Sicily, then on to Vienna and to Cornwall where they were fortunate enough to get a shot of the Lizard lifeboat being launched. Within no time American viewers found themselves in Belgrade, Rome, Geneva, at a steel mill in the Ruhr, at the Champs-Elysées and back to England where they saw a hovercraft at Southampton.

The subject matter may not sound all that exciting, but as an experiment in 1960s technology it was a wonder of the modern world that these pictures could be seen, not only live across Europe, but live in the United States.

Following the success, a second Telstar satellite was launched in 1963. Other satellites soon followed and these have all contributed to making live transatlantic broadcasting commonplace these days.

Inspired by the achievement, record producer Joe Meek wrote an instrumental entitled Telstar *which the Tornadoes recorded, and within a month of the historic transatlantic transmission the record was in the charts where it reached number one and stayed for five weeks.*

TENPIN BOWLING

TENPIN bowling, or just bowling as the Americans prefer to call it, has been popular in the United States for nearly 100 years. But its popularity as a mass-media sport grew in the 1950s with the invention of the automatic pin-spotters. The first of these was brought to Britain in 1960 and soon bowling became one of the fastest growing participant sports as cinemas were converted into bowling alleys.

The alleys were not just places to go and play this 'new' sport. They were also meeting places, like the coffee bars of the 1950s.

Suddenly leagues sprang up for those wishing to play competitively and soon the bowling centres up and down Britain were filled most nights of the week. The boom did not last and by the end of the 1960s most bowling alleys had been turned into bingo halls. Happily though, the sport is popular again and more people are currently registered as members of the British Tenpin Bowling Association than there were in the 1960s. Unfortunately there are only half the centres available than when the game was at its peak, when there were 125 centres providing 2,500 lanes.

TERESHKOVA, Valentina

VALENTINA Tereshkova made history on 16 June 1963 when she became the first woman in space.

She was born on a farm in Maslennikovo in 1937, the daughter of a tractor driver who was killed during the war. Valentina started work in a local tyre factory then went into the textile business. She took up parachuting as a hobby in 1959 and after Yuri Gagarin's epic space flight in 1961, she wrote to the space centre asking to be considered as a cosmonaut. She was accepted and in 1963, aboard *Vostok VI,* she spent two days 22hr 50min in space and orbited the earth 48 times.

She was named a Heroine of the

Soviet Union and received numerous awards and medals.

Valentina married fellow cosmonaut Andrian Nikolayev shortly after her historic flight and after the birth of their daughter continued working on the Soviet space programme as an engineer.

THANK YOUR LUCKY STARS

ONE of the first new ITV pop programmes of the 1960s, *Thank Your Lucky Stars* followed the success of the fifties programmes *Cool For Cats, Oh Boy!, Boy Meets Girl* and *Wham.*

Thank Your Lucky Stars was launched by ABC in 1961 and a feature of the programme was the audience participation slot when members of the audience used to give their opinions on new releases and mark them out of five. One such participant was the Birmingham girl Janice Nicholls who became well known for her 'Oi'll give it foive' phrase. She was so popular she was retained and became one of the show's presenters.

During the summer months the programe was renamed *Lucky Stars.*

THAT WAS THE WEEK THAT WAS

THAT *Was The Week That Was,* known affectionately as TW3, sent rumblings through Parliament and the 'Beeb' as the Government, sex and religion became the brunt of the satire that presenter David Frost and the rest of the team threw at the British public on Saturday nights, using the week's news as the basis for the programme's material.

The first programme went out over the air in front of a studio audience on 24 November 1962 and assisting Frost were Lance Percival, Millicent Martin, Roy Kinnear, Willie Rushton, Kenneth Cope, David Kernan, Timothy Birdsall and Ned Sherrin, the former *Tonight* producer who was TW3's director. Bernard Levin also lent a hand as the political journalist.

Each programme opened with the TW3 girl, Millicent Martin, going through the week's news in song form. Lance Pervical also made a musical contribution with his calypsos.

The programme soon got into bother for poking fun at politicians and religion — so much so that the Postmaster General asked to see the scripts in advance. The BBC was then forced to ban all mention of sex, royalty, religion and politics in comedy shows. But this ban was short-lived and was lifted in January 1963.

The first series of TW3 ran until 27 April 1963 and a second series started on 28 September that same year. However, Timothy Birdsall was missing from the line-up. Sadly he died of leukaemia during the summer. The series should have run into the spring of 1964 but was brought to an end on 28 December 1963 because 1964 was General Election year and the programme could (and probably would) have played a significant role in it if allowed to continue. The decision to end it came from the BBC governors but it was, as they say in boxing terms, a 'split decision'. Some wanted it to remain, because it was attracting audiences of over 12 million and men were even coming home from the pub early on Saturday nights to watch it!

The spin-off programme, *Not So Much A Programme, More A Way Of Life,* was launched on Friday, 13 May 1964, shortly after the election, and

Stars of That Was The Week That Was. *David Frost is the man on his knees.*

that same year David Frost made the first of his many jaunts across the Atlantic to appear on the American version of TW3, which was hosted by Elliott Reid.

THATCHER, Margaret

SINCE becoming leader of the Conservatives in 1975 and Britain's first woman Prime Minister four years later, the career of Margaret Thatcher has been well documented. But what about her days leading up to her becoming the Tory leader?

Born as Margaret Hilda Roberts in Grantham, Lincolnshire, on 13 October 1925, her father was a local grocer who became mayor. She was educated at Kesteven & Grantham Girls School and Somerville College, Oxford, from where she graduated in chemistry. During her time at University, she was elected president of the Oxford University Conservatives.

She stood as a Conservative Party candidate for Dartford in 1950 and at the 1951 General Election was the youngest Tory candidate at 26. However, she was unsuccessful on each occasion but, to make amends for the second disappointment, she married husband Dennis on 13 December 1951.

Mrs T studied law, specializing in taxation, and was called to the bar in 1953. However, she had another attempt at getting into Parliament in 1959 when she stood and won the Finchley seat. She has been their MP ever since.

She was given her first government job in Harold Macmillan's administration in 1961 when she was made a parliamentary secretary to the Ministry of Pensions and National Insurance. In 1968 she joined Ted Heath's shadow cabinet as the shadow Transport Minister and the following year was appointed the Shadow Education spokeswoman, becoming the Education Minister when the Tories came to power in 1970. The following year she announced plans to abolish free school milk, thus gaining the nickname 'Thatcher the milk snatcher.'

Since then Margaret Thatcher has gone on to become a leading politician and world leader.

THORPE, Jeremy

JEREMY THORPE was the man who succeeded Jo Grimmond as leader of the Liberal Party in 1967. Like his father and grandfather before him, he became a Member of Parliament, but

he did not follow in their footsteps completely, because they were Conservatives.

Educated at Eton and Trinity College, Oxford, he was a qualified barrister and in 1959 became the Liberal MP for North Devon.

He held the Party leadership until 1976 when he was forced to resign after allegations of a homosexual relationship with Norman Scott some years earlier. It resulted in charges being brought against Thorpe, who was charged with inciting a murder attempt on Scott's life. Thorpe was cleared of this charge in 1979 just a few months after losing his Devon seat at the General Election.

THUNDERBIRDS

THUNDERBIRDS hit the British television screens in 1966 and what a smash hit the spoof puppet series proved to be — and not only with children.

The central characters of the series were Jeff Tracey and Lady Penelope, the lovely but occasionally lethal London agent for International Rescue, the organization which resolved to fight worldwide crime.

Lady Penelope lived a life of luxury and her ladyship was served by her loyal butler-cum-chauffeur, Parker, an ex-safe blower and London criminal. She was driven around in a pink futuristic Rolls-Royce car with the registration number of FAB 1. It was equipped with an in-car phone, machine guns and closed-circuit television.

The head of IR was Jeff Tracey and he was assisted by his five sons; Scott, Virgil, Alan, Gordon and John — named after the first five Americans in space. Also in the team was 'Brains', the whiz-kid who took care of the technical side of the operation.

The puppet of Lady Penelope stood 22 inches tall and came with five interchangeable heads. Her television voice was provided by Sylvia Anderson, while David Graham was the voice behind Parker.

Two full-length feature films, Thunderbirds Are Go (1966) and Thunderbird Six (1968) were spawned from the series.

TIED TEST MATCH

NEVER before in the 80 years of Test cricket had a match resulted in a tie. But on 14 December 1960 the Australians and West Indians rewrote the record books in the First Test at Brisbane's Gabba Ground.

West Indies won the toss and elected to bat. They made 453 in their first innings, thanks to a fine 132 from

One of Margaret Thatcher's first public appearances after she became a member of the Cabinet in 1961.

Gary Sobers, who passed 3,000 runs in Test cricket during the innings. Norman O'Neill, however, went better in the game with 181 as Australia gained a first-innings lead of 52 after scoring 505.

Alan Davidson, who took five West Indian wickets in the first innings, collected six more in the second as the tourists were dismissed for 284 which left Australia needing 233 to win.

However, at 92-6, a win seemed impossible. They would have been grateful for a draw at that stage of the proceedings, but even that seemed unlikely.

Davidson and Benaud then pushed things along and when the seventh wicket had gone down, Australia had scored 226 runs. Suddenly the win was now realistic. As the final eight-ball over approached, Australia needed six runs to win and had three wickets intact. But what drama there was in store . . .this is how the final over by fast bowler Wes Hall went.

1st ball: Wally Grout acquired a leg bye.
2nd ball: Benaud was out, caught behind for 52.
3rd ball: New batsman Meckiff did not score.
4th ball: Meckiff and Grout ran a bye.
5th ball: Grout hit a single.
6th ball: Meckiff hit the ball towards the boundary, the batsmen had run two and were on the third run which would have given Australia the match, but a perfect throw from Conrad Hunte ran out Grout and the scores were level with nine wickets down.
7th ball: New batsman Kline hit the ball towards square-leg. Meckiff had started to run but seeing the pace of fielder Solomon, he went back. Solomon, able to see only one stump, scored a direct hit and Meckiff was run out. And so ended the first ever tied Test Match in cricket history.

Ball	Runs reqd.	Wkts left	Balls left
1st	5	3	7
2nd	5	2	6
3rd	5	2	5
4th	4	2	4
5th	3	2	3
6th	1	1	2
7th	1	0	1

Since then only one other Test match has resulted in a tie and again Australia were involved. It was against India at Madras in 1986-7.

Warren Mitchell (alias Alf Garnett).

TILL DEATH US DO PART

TILL Death Us Do Part was first seen as a *Comedy Playhouse* production on 22 July 1965.

Written by Johnny Speight, it centres around the loud, foul-mouthed Alf Garnett (Warren Mitchell) who constantly puts the world to rights and bickers with his long-haired 'Scouse git' son-in-law Mike (Anthony Booth).

Mike was married to Alf's daughter Rita (Una Stubbs) while his long-suffering wife Else was more often than not referred to as 'The silly old moo'. She was played by Dandy Nichols in the series but in the *Comedy Playhouse* version was played by Gretchen Franklin, now known for her portrayal of Ethel in *Eastenders*.

Apart from the Queen, Winston Churchill and his beloved West Ham United, no person or institution was safe from Alf's tongue. As for Harold Wilson, well, the stick he got was unbelievable.

Understandably, the series brought floods of complaints from viewers about the bad language and blasphemy. But to the majority, it was nothing more than a comedy series with a difference — but what a difference!

It is one of the few comedy shows which the Americans copied from us (it was normally the other way around) and their series *All In The Family* featured Archie Bunker as the Alf Garnett of American TV.

The last episode of *Till Death Us Do Part* was recorded in 1974. However, a sequel, *In Sickness And In Health* was launched in 1985 but it had to be cut short due to the death of Dandy Nichols. However, a further series followed with Mitchell being the only member of the original cast.

After watching the Comedy Playhouse *production in 1965 the* Daily Mirror *TV critic Kenneth Eastaugh had very little good to say about the programme and concluded by saying: "It was a non-starter."*

TILLOTSON, Johnny

BORN in Jacksonville, Florida, on 20 April 1939, Johnny Tillotson had a love of country music from an early age. As a teenager he built up a reputation as a fine singer and was eventually given a three-year stint on the local television variety show, *The Tom Dowdy Show*. If ever there was a claim to fame, that's it...three years on *The Tom Dowdy Show!*

In 1958, Tillotson signed a contract with Cadence/London records and in December 1960 released the record for which he is most famous, and probably the reason why he finds himself in this book. The song was, of course, *Poetry In Motion* which, along with Del Shannon's *Runaway*, was one of the American classics of the pre-Beatles era.

It reached number one in Britain and only Ray Charles' *Georgia On My Mind* prevented a double and stopped him topping the US charts.

Although he had some minor hits thereafter, Johnny Tillotson was basically a 'one-hit wonder'.

TINY TIM

TINY Tim was one for the eccentrics. The guy with the long hair, hooked nose, falsetto voice and ukulele certainly added a new dimension to the world of pop with his record *Tiptoe Through The Tulips*. Unfortunately, there weren't enough eccentrics in Britain at the time prepared to buy the record and put it into the British charts. However, he had one minor hit this side of the Atlantic with *Great Balls Of Fire* which reached number 45 in 1969.

Born as Herbert Buckingham Khaury, he shot to fame after an appearance on the popular American comedy show, *Rowan And Martin's Laugh-In* in 1968 when he spent most of his time blowing kisses to the audience.

Confirming his eccentricity, he married 17-year-old Vicki Budinger in front of a nationwide audience on the American TV programme *The Tonight Show* on 17 December 1969. Together they produced a daughter called Tulip but the marriage broke up in 1972 and they were eventually divorced in 1977. Tiny Tim slipped out of the limelight as quickly as he came. But what an impact he had during his brief spell at the top.

TOP OF THE POPS

TOP Of The Pops was first shown on BBC television on Wednesday, 1 January 1964. The programme came from a disused church in Manchester and was given only a six-week run by the 'Beeb' — it's still around 25 years later!

The first show went on the air at 6.36pm and the show's first presenter, Jimmy Savile, introduced the first group, the Rolling Stones, who mimed to *I Wanna Be Your Man*. Miming was a departure from normal BBC policy. However, the Beeb felt it was best for the viewers to hear the discs exactly as they were.

The number-one record at the time was the Beatles' *I Want To Hold My Hand*. They were not live in the studio but a film (not a video!) of them singing the number was shown. One reviewer said of the programme: 'A tatty poor-man's *Thank Your Lucky Stars*'.

At the time of the first *Top Of The Pops* a single cost 6s 5d (32p) and an album was £1 15s 0d (£1.75).

Cliff Richard has made the most guest appearances on the programme, with 80-plus and he is still adding to that total. Second to him is Shakin' Stevens.

Three records have been banned by *Top Of The Pops: Je T'Aime... Moi Non Plus* by Jane Birkin and Serge Gainsbourg in 1969, Chuck Berry's *My Ding-a-Ling* and recently, *Relax* by Frankie Goes to Hollywood, in 1984.

TORREY CANYON DISASTER

THE Torrey Canyon Disaster in 1967 threatened the beautiful Devon and Cornwall coastlines as thousands of gallons of oil spilled from the stricken vessel.

A 61,000-ton tanker carrying over 100,000 tons of crude oil, the *Torrey Canyon* ran aground on the Seven Stones reef between Land's End and the Scilly Isles on 18 March. Eight days later heavy seas resulted in her breaking her back. Consequently thousands of gallons of oil poured from the vessel. Strong westerly winds took the spill towards Land's End and within 24 hours an estimated 70 miles of coastline was polluted.

As the ship broke up, urgent action was needed to prevent a major disaster to one of the finest coastlines around Britain. Mr Foley, Under-Secretary for the Navy, described the disaster as 'the greatest peacetime menace to Britain's shores'.

A flotilla of little ships involving 4,000 men helped in a detergent spraying exercise. Navy Buccaneer jets were called in to bomb the vessel

Part of the broken Torrey Canyon.

and 54 planes attacked the ship which was bombarded with 62,000lb of high explosives. Despite the bombardment, including the dropping of 54 100-gallon tanks of kerosene and eight napalm bombs, the two sections still refused to stay alight.

The end eventually came when eight Sea Vixens dropped 16, 1,000lb bombs on the partly submerged wreck. Eight Buccaneers then chipped in with another 48 bombs and finally six Hunters covered the target area with 1,200 gallons of napalm . . .the end of one *Torrey Canyon!* Damage to the coastline was kept to a minimum.

Barracuda Tankers, owners of the *Torrey Canyon,* paid £3 million compensation to England and France in November 1969.

TOTTENHAM'S DOUBLE

PRESTON North End did it in 1888-89 and Aston Villa did it in 1896-97. But for any 20th century team to complete the Football League Championship and FA Cup double in one season was the ultimate dream.

The longer the century went on, the harder the task seemed. Eventually,

in 1960-61, Tottenham Hotspur paved the way for the other clubs as they became the first 20th century club to win the English game's two toughest competitions in one season.

Guided by that shrewd manager Bill Nicholson, and led by their Northern Ireland international skipper Danny Blanchflower, Spurs won the League title by eight points from Sheffield Wednesday and beat Leicester City 2-0 in the FA Cup Final at Wembley.

Spurs won their first 11 League games before being held to a 1-1 draw at home to Manchester City. Their first defeat came on 12 November when they went down 2-1 at Sheffield Wednesday. They lost seven League games all season, two of them after the League title had been clinched. Spurs scored 115 goals in the League and Bobby Smith was top scorer with 28.

In the Cup the only slight hiccup was in the 6th round when they were held to a 1-1 draw at Sunderland before winning the replay 5-0.

The team who represented Spurs in most matches during the season was: Bill Brown; Peter Baker, Ron Henry, Danny Blanchflower, Maurice Norman, Dave Mackay, Cliff Jones (or Terry Medwin), John White, Bobby Smith, Les Allen (father of Clive, who later played for Spurs and England), Terry Dyson.

John White tragically lost his life when he was struck by lightning while sheltering under a tree at Crew Hill golf course, Enfield, in July 1964.

Spurs retained the FA Cup in 1962 and since their great triumph, Arsenal in 1970-71 and Liverpool in 1985-86 have become 20th century winners of the double.

TRAFFIC WARDENS

TRAFFIC Wardens and their parking tickets were first seen in Westminster on 19 September 1960 and came about as a result of the Road Traffic Act 1960. The first shift of the 39 wardens started at 8am and a total of 344 tickets were issued on the first day.

The first person to fall foul of the new law was Dr Thomas Creighton, who was given a ticket after parking his Ford Popular outside a West End hotel while he treated a patient suffering from a heart attack. The ticket was issued by warden Frank Shaw, who was unaware the car belonged to a doctor. Because of the outcry it caused, Dr Creighton did not have to pay his £2 fixed penalty.

By 1961 wardens had spread throughout London and into the provinces where the streets of Blackpool and Leicester were patrolled by wardens issuing their fixed penalty tickets.

TRAGEDIES & DISASTERS

SADLY, tragedy is very much a part of our lives. It always has been and always will be. The 1960s, like any other decade, had its fair share of disasters. The following are the major ones of the decade.

1960

Jan 21 PIT DISASTER at Coalbrook, Orange Free State, South Africa killed 437.

Feb 27 CYCLONE at Mauritius. Ten killed.

Mar 4 EXPLOSION aboard a Belgian munitions ship at Havana killed 100.

Mar 12 A FIRE at a chemical plant at Pusan, South Korea, killed 68.

Mar 14 TRAIN CRASH at Bakersfield, California, killed 14.

Mar 28 FIRE at whisky warehouse in Glasgow killed 19 firemen.

Apr 25- EARTHQUAKES in Iran killed
28 approximately 4,000.

May 5-6 TORNADO in south-east Oklahoma, Arkansas, killed 30.

May 21- EARTHQUAKE in Southern
30 Chile killed 5,000

May 24 TIDAL WAVE in Japan (triggered by Chilean earthquake) killed 96.

Jun 22 FIRE at Henderson's store, Liverpool, killed 11.

Jun 28 PIT DISASTER at Six Bells, Monmouthshire, killed 45.

Jul 14 FIRE at a mental hospital in Guatemala City killed 225.

Jul 25 PIT DISASTER at Cardowan, Lanarkshire, killed 3.

Sep 4- HURRICANE Donna killed
12 148 in the Caribbean.

Oct 10 TIDAL WAVE AND FLOODS in East Pakistan. Death toll around 6,000.

Oct 31 Further TIDAL WAVE AND FLOODS hit East Pakistan and a further 4,000 lost their lives.

Nov 13 FIRE at a cinema in Amude, Syria, killed 152 children.

Nov 14 TRAIN CRASH at Pardubice, Czechoslovakia claimed 110 lives when two trains collided.

Dec 19 FIRE aboard the US aircraft carrier *Constellation* at Brooklyn Navy Yard killed 42.

1961

Jan 6 FIRE at the Thomas Hotel, San Francisco, claimed the lives of 20 people.

Jan 16 GALES caused a US Air Force radar base to collapse, killing 28.

Mar 13 DAM BURST near Kiev, USSR, 145 dead.

Apr 9 FIRE tragedy on board British liner *Dara* in Persian Gulf, 236 killed.

Jul 8 SHIP DISASTER at Save, off Mozambique, Portuguese ship ran aground, killing 259.

Jul 16 TRAIN CRASH near Blackpool, full of holidaymakers. Six dead and 116 injured.

Aug 29 CABLE CAR DISASTER when a French jet fighter cut the cables of cars across the High Alps. Six people were killed and dozens left stranded for up to 16 hours.

Sep 10 CAR CRASH at Monza during the Italian Grand Prix killed 13 spectators.

Sep 11-14 HURRICANE Carla killed 46 in Texas.

Oct 31 HURRICANE Hattie was responsible for over 400 deaths in British Honduras.

Nov 6 SHIP DISASTER off North West Tunisia when the British steamer *Clan Keith* sank after an explosion. 60 killed.

Dec 8 FIRE at a hospital at Hartford, Connecticut, killed 16 people.

Dec 17 FIRE at a circus at Niteroi, Brazil, killed 323.

Dec 23 RAIL CRASH in Southern Italy. 70 killed.

1962

Jan 8 RAILWAY CRASH at Haarlem, Holland, 91 killed.

Jan 11 AVALANCHE in Northern Peru. Approximately 3,000 killed.

Feb 7 PIT DISASTER at Saar, West Germany, 298 killed.

Feb 16 GALES all over Britain killed 11.

Feb 18-21 HURRICANE AND FLOODING in Hamburg killed 278.

Mar 22 PIT DISASTER at Hapton Valley, Burnley. 16 killed.

Apr 12 PIT DISASTER at Tower Colliery, Aberdare. 9 killed.

May 3 TRAIN CRASH killed 163 near Tokyo when a train crashed into the wreckage of two other trains that had been involved in an accident.

Jul 23 RAIL CRASH at Dijon, France. 42 killed.

Aug 21 EARTH TREMORS in Southern Italy. 16 killed.

Sep 2 EARTH TREMORS in Western Iran. 11,000 killed or injured.

Sep 17 BUILDING COLLAPSE in Brussels killed 16.

Sep 26 FLOODS in Barcelona. At least 323 killed and many more missing.

Nov 17 STORMS caused Seaham (County Durham) lifeboat to capsize while going to the rescue of a fishing boat. Nine men drowned.

Dec 4-6 SMOG killed 60 people in London.

Dec 26 TRAIN CRASH at Minshull Vernon, Cheshire. 18 killed.

1963

Feb 22 EARTHQUAKE at Barce, Libya, claimed over 300 lives.

Mar 17 VOLCANO at Mount Agung, Bali, erupted. 11,000 killed.

Apr 10 SHIP DISASTER when US atomic powered submarine *Thresher* sank in the North Atlantic claiming the lives of 129.

May 4 SHIP DISASTER in the Upper Nile when over 200 were killed after a ferry sank.

May 28-29 CYCLONE on East Coast of Pakistan killed approximately 22,000.

Jul 7 COACH CRASH near Stuttgart. Seven killed.

Jul 26 EARTHQUAKE at Skopje, Yugoslavia, killed 1,011.

Sep 3 EARTHQUAKE at Srinagar, Kashmir. More than 100 killed.

Oct 2-7 HURRICANE at Haiti and Cuba killed more than 6,500.

Oct 9 LANDSLIDE into the Vaiont Dam caused a FLOOD in the Belluno area of Italy. Approximately 2,500 killed.

Oct 31 EXPLOSION in Indianapolis. 60 killed.

Nov 9 COALMINE explosion at Omuta, Japan, killed 447.

Nov 9 TRAIN CRASH near Yokohoma, Japan, killed 162 people when a passenger train crashed into a derailed freight train.

Nov 19 FLOODS AND LANDSLIDES in Haiti left over 500 dead.

Dec 23 FIRE on board the cruise liner *Lakonia* in the Atlantic killed 117. More than 900 were rescued.

1964

Feb 10 SHIP DISASTER when the Destroyer *Voyager* sank off Australia with the loss of 85 lives.

Mar 27 EARTHQUAKE in Alaska, the strongest ever recorded in North America, killed 117 people.

May 11-12, Jun 1-2 CYCLONES in East Pakistan killed approximately 47,000.

May 24 RIOT at football match in Lima, Peru. 318 killed.

May 28 TRAIN CRASH at Cheadle Hulme, Cheshire, killed three.

May 28 FIRE in coalmine at Bihar, India, killed 375.

Jun 20 CRANE MAST CRASHED on to coach at Brent Cross, Middlesex, killing seven.

Jun 1 COALMINE disaster near Fukuaka, Japan, claimed 236 lives.

Jul 26 TRAIN CRASH near Custoias, Portugal, killed 94.

Aug 16 COACH CRASH in France killed 13 children when coach crashed over ravine at St Bernard Pass.

Sep 29 FLOODS in India killed 1,000 when a reservoir burst.

Dec 15 CYCLONE killed around 10,000 in Karachi, Pakistan.

Dec 24 HURRICANE in Ceylon and Madras (India) killed 7,000.

1965

Mar 29 TRAIN CRASH killed two when the Fenchurch Street to Shoeburyness train was derailed.

Apr 11 TORNADOES in mid-western America, more than 200 killed.

May 12 CYCLONE in East Pakistan killed approximately 10,000.

May 17 PIT DISASTER at Cambrian Colliery, Rhondda. 31 killed after explosion.

Jun 1 PIT DISASTER in Japan killed approximately 250.

Jul 8 COACH CRASH near Lille, France. Four killed.

Nov 1 GALES across Britain killed seven.

Dec 27 OIL RIG collapsed in North Sea. 13 killed when the *Sea Gem*, the top rig in the BP fleet, collapsed.

Dec 31 STAMPEDE at a dance in Nuneaton. Four killed.

1966

Jan 4 EXPLOSION of liquid gas at Lyons, France. 12 killed.

Part of the shattered city of Skopje in Yugoslavia, shortly after the earthquake which killed over 1,000 people in 1963.

Feb 3   PIT DISASTER at Silverwood Colliery, Rotherham. Two trains collided underground. Nine killed.

Mar 20   EARTHQUAKE in Uganda. More than 100 people killed.

Apr 3   SEA DISASTER off the Lincolnshire coast when the pleasure ship *Anzio* sank with the loss of 12 lives.

Jun 16   SEA DISASTER in New York Harbour when American and British tankers collided and caught fire. 32 died.

Jul 22   SHIP CAPSIZED at Merioneth. 15 killed.

Jul 25   COACH CRASH on Frankfurt-Cologne autobahn. 33 killed.

Jul 31   SEA DISASTER when a pleasure boat was lost between Fowey and Falmouth. 31 killed.

Aug 19   EARTHQUAKE in Eastern Turkey. More than 2,000 reported killed.

Sep 25   TYPHOON in Japan killed 174.

Oct 21   AVALANCHE of coal, waste, mud and rocks on to school at Aberfan killed 144, including 116 children.

The freighter Magdeburg *which sank in the River Thames in October 1964 after colliding with the Japanese cargo boat* Yamashro Maru.

BOAC Boeing 707 which crash-landed at London Airport in April 1968, killing five people.

Nov 1 BUILDING COLLAPSED at Aberdeen University. Five killed.

Dec 8 SEA DISASTER when the car ferry *Heraklion* sank while on a voyage from Crete to Pireaus. More than 250 were killed.

1967

Jan 16 FIRE at oil refinery at Billingham-on-Tees. Two killed, one missing.

Jan 27 SPACE TRAGEDY when Gus Grissom, Roger Chaffee and Ed White were killed when fire swept through *Apollo 1* on launch pad at Cape Kennedy.

Feb 7 BUSH FIRES in South Tasmania. At least 60 killed.

Feb 28 TRAIN CRASH near Birmingham. Nine killed.

Mar 5 TRAIN CRASH near Huntingdon. Five killed when train derailed.

Apr 23-24 SPACE TRAGEDY when Vladimir Komorov was killed when *Soyez 1* failed to land safely.

May 22 FIRE at a Brussels department store killed 322.

May 31 COACH CRASH on Stuttgart to Munich autobahn killed 12 pensioners from Lincoln.

Jun 25 FLOOD at Mossdale Caverns, Yorkshire. Six pot-holers killed.

Jul 22 FIRE aboard the US aircraft carrier *Forrestal* killed 134.

Aug 12 COACH CRASH in Majorca. Nine killed.

Sep 5 GALES swept across Britain, killing seven.

Sep 9 PIT DISASTER at East Wemyss, Fife. Underground fire killed nine.

Sep 30 COACH CRASH near Zagreb, Yugoslavia. 14 students killed.

Nov 4 FLOODS in Northern Italy killed 100.

Nov 5 TRAIN derailed at Hither Green, London. 49 killed.

Nov 26 FLOODS in Lisbon. More than 400 killed.

Dec 11 EARTHQUAKE in Western India. More than 100 killed.

Dec 15 BRIDGE COLLAPSE over Ohio River, USA. 13 known dead, 26 missing.

1968

Jan 6 TRAIN CRASH at level crossing at Hixon, Staffordshire. 11 killed.

Jan 15 GALES across Britain killed 20 people in Scotland.

Jan 15 EARTHQUAKE in Sicily. 500 killed.

Feb 5 SHIP SINKING: The Hull trawler *Ross Cleveland* sank in Icelandic waters during severe weather. 18 killed. Two other trawlers, *St Romanus* and *Kingston Peridot*, which left Hull on 10 January, both vanished in the same area with the loss of 40 more lives.

Feb 26 FIRE at Shelton Mental Hospital, Shrewsbury. 24 killed.

Apr 10 SHIP DISASTER in Wellington Harbour, New Zealand. the car ferry *Wahine* sank when lashed by 120mph gales. 46 killed, but 744 were rescued.

May 16 BUILDING COLLAPSE in London Dockland (Ronan Point). Four killed.

Jun 23 RIOT at a football match in Buenos Aries killed 74.

Aug 10 COACH CRASH in Austrian Tyrol. Five killed.

Aug 31-Sep 2 EARTHQUAKES in north-east Iran. Over 20,000 reported killed.

Oct 31 SHIPWRECK of the nuclear submarine *Scorpion* was found 400 miles south west of the Azores. It sank in late-May and claimed 99 lives.

Nov 15 SHIP CAPSIZED near North Sea drilling rig. Three killed.

Nov 18 FIRE at Glasgow warehouse. 22 killed.

1969

Jan 4 TRAIN CRASH at Marden, Kent. Four killed.

Jan 14 FIRE aboard the nuclear aircraft carrier *Enterprise* in Pearl Harbor killed 27.

Jan 18-26 FLOODS AND LANDSLIDES in Southern California caused the death of at least 100 people. Further rain a month later caused more floods and 18 more deaths.

Mar 17 LIFEBOAT CAPSIZED off Orkney. Eight killed when the Longhope lifeboat sank in heavy seas.

Apr 8 TRAIN CRASH near Wolverhampton. Both drivers killed when a passenger and a goods train collided.

May 7 TRAIN DERAILED near Morpeth, Northumberland. Six killed.

Jun 2 SHIP DISASTER in South China Sea when an Australian aircraft carrier cut a US destroyer in two. 56 US sailors died.

Jun 15 RESTAURANT COLLAPSE in Los Angeles de Raphael, Spain. 53 killed.

Aug 14 COACH CRASH near Stanhope, County Durham. 16 killed.

Nov 7 PIT DISASTER. 64 died in South African tragedy.

You will probably have noticed that airplane crashes are missing from the foregoing list. That is deliberate.

There has been much talk in recent years about how unsafe flying is. But when you look at this lengthy list of air disasters in the 1960s, you will appreciate how safe it is today compared to then. You must also bear in mind that there is considerably more air traffic in the skies now than there was in the 1960s.

TRAGEDY IN THE AIR

1960

Date	Dead	Details
Feb 25	61	Navy plane carrying musicians to dinner attended by President Eisenhower collided with Brazilian airliner at Rio de Janeiro.
Aug 29	63	Air France plane crashed into the sea off Dakar, Senegal.
Dec 16	134	United DC-8 and TWA Super-Constellation collided over New York City during snowstorm. Death toll included six on the ground.
Dec 18	49	US Air Force Convair crashed at Munich.

1961

Date	Dead	Details
Feb 15	73	US Skating team among dead when Sabena Boeing 707 crashed near Brussels.
Mar 28	52	Russian-built Ilyushin 18 of Czech airlines crashed at Nuremberg, Germany.
May 10	78	Air France Superstarliner crashed in Sahara desert.
Jul 12	73	Another Czech Ilyushin crashed, this time near Casablanca.
Sep 10	86	American DC-6 of President Airlines crashed after taking off from Shannon Airport.
Sep 12	77	Caravelle crashed near Rabat, Morocco.
Oct 7	34	British DC3 carrying

holidaymakers crashed into the Pyrenees.

Dec 21   26   BEA Comet 4B crashed at Ankara, Turkey.

1962

Mar 1   98   American Airlines Boeing 707 crashed at Long Island shortly after take-off from Idlewild Airport.

Mar 4   110   Caledonian DC-7 crashed at Douala, Cameroon.

May 6   10   East Anglia Flying Services Dakota crashed on the Isle of Wight on flight from Jersey to Portsmouth.

Jun 3   130   Air France Boeing 707 bound for Atlanta, USA, crashed on take-off from Orly Airport, France.

Jun 22   111   Air France Boeing 707 crashed into a mountainside at Guadeloupe.

Jul 7   94   Alitalia DC-8 from Australia to Rome crashed when about to land at Bombay, India.

Sep 23   28   American Super-Constellation came down in the Atlantic. There were 48 survivors.

1963

Feb 1   91   Two planes collided over Ankara. One was a Middle East Airlines Viscount and the other a Turkish Air Force C47.

Aug 13   16   French Viscount crashed at Lyons, France.

Sep 4   80   Swissair Caravelle crashed five minutes after taking off from Zurich.

Sep 12   40   Viking from Gatwick to Perpignan carrying holidaymakers crashed into the Pyrenees.

Oct 22   7   BAC One-Eleven crashed in Wiltshire while on a test flight. It had only made its maiden flight two months earlier.

Nov 29   118   Trans-Canada Airlines DC-8 crashed north of Montreal.

1964

Feb 29   83   British Eagle Britannia crashed into the Glunzeger mountain on its way to Innsbruck.

Mar 1   85   American Constellation

crashed into a mountain near Lake Tahoe on the California-Nevada border.

Mar 29   45   Alitalia Viscount crashed before landing at Naples.

May 11   74   US military plane crashed in the Philippines.

Jun 21   1   DC-3 carrying British holidaymakers from Palma to Ibiza crashed into the sea shortly after taking off. Thankfully the plane took five minutes to sink and 24 passengers and the crew were rescued by fishermen.

Nov 23   44   Trans-World Boeing 707 crashed on take-off from Rome Airport. There were 29 survivors.

1965

Jan 16   30   US Air Force jet crashed into a house at Wichita, Kansas.

Apr 14   26   Dakota on flight to Paris crashed near Jersey airport. The air hostess was the sole survivor.

Jun 20   121   Pakistan Airlines Boeing 720B crashed at Cairo airport.

Jul 6   41   RAF Hastings transport plane crashed near Dorchester, Oxfordshire.

Aug 17   30   United Airlines Boeing 727 on flight from New York to Chicago exploded and crashed into Lake Michigan.

Aug 24   58   US Marine Corps transport aircraft on flight to Vietnam crashed into Hong Kong harbour.

Oct 26   36   BEA Vanguard from Edinburgh crashed on landing at Heathrow.

Nov 8   58   American Boeing 727 from New York crashed near Cincinnati.

Nov 11   40   Boeing 727 from New York crashed at Salt Lake City airport.

1966

Jan 24   117   Air-India Boeing 707 from Bombay to New York crashed near the summit of Mont Blanc.

Jan 28   46   Lufthansa Convair crashed at Bremen airport.

Feb 4   133   Japanese Boeing 727 crashed into Tokyo Bay.

Mar 4   64   Canadian Pacific DC-8 crashed on landing at Tokyo airport.

Mar 5   124   BOAC Boeing 707 crashed into Mount Fuji shortly after take-off from Tokyo.

Sep 1   92   Turbo-prop Bristol Britannia carrying holidaymakers crashed in northern Yugoslavia near Ljubljana airport.

Dec 24   129   Chartered military plane crashed into village of Binh Thai, South Vietnam.

1967

Mar 30   18   DC-8 on training flight crashed into a New Orleans motel.

Apr 20   126   Swiss Britannia turbo-prop crashed at Nicosia, Cyprus.

May 3   2   Viscount airliner crashed on take-off at Southend. The two killed were airport workers.

Jun 3   88   DC-4 from Manston to the Costa Brava crashed into a mountainside near Perpignan.

Jun 4   72   Argonaut returning from Majorca crashed on to Stockport town centre.

Jul 19   82   Boeing 727 collided with a Cessna light aircraft near Hendersonville, North Carolina.

Oct 12   66   BEA Comet on flight to Nicosia crashed into the Mediterranean 170 miles west of Cyprus.

Nov 4   37   Iberia Caravelle *en route* from Malaga to Heathrow crashed at Fernhurst, Sussex.

1968

Mar 24   61   Aer Lingus Viscount on flight from Cork to London crashed into the Irish Sea.

Apr 8   5   BOAC Boeing 707 crashed a few minutes after taking off on a flight from Heathrow for Australia. Mercifully, 121 lives were saved.

Apr 20   122   South African Airways Boeing 707 from

A chance in a million brought this twin-engined Varsity plane down on top of a house at Gloucester in March 1963. The aircraft was on a single-engine test flight when the engine failed. The pilot and assistant were killed but they avoided a school containing 1,000 children, and three women in the house escaped unharmed.

Johannesburg to London crashed near Windhoek.

Jul 3	6	BKS air freighter crashed on landing at London airport. Eight horses aboard the freighter were also killed.
Aug 2	13	Alitalia DC-8 crashed near Milan. There were 82 survivors.
Aug 9	48	British Eagle Viscount crashed on to a West German autobahn.
Sep 11	95	Air France Caravelle from Ajaccio to Nice crashed into the Mediterranean.
Sep 29	55	Red Cross DC-4 crashed in Nigeria killing Nigerian troops.
Dec 13	51	Pan American Boeing 707 from New York to Venezuela crashed into the Caribbean.

1969

Jan 5	50	Afghanistan Airlines Boeing 727 crashed while trying to land in thick fog at Gatwick. Two of the dead were in a house hit by the plane.
Mar 16	155	Venezuelan DC-9 crashed on take-off at Maracaibo. Some of the dead were on the ground.
Nov 20	87	Nigeria Airways VC-10 crashed in jungle.

TRIVIA

AN assortment of Sixties trivia items:

The first £25,000 Premium Bond winner was Norman Jepson of Sandbach, Cheshire, on 1 February 1966.

The Richard Nixon-Hubert Humphrey US Presidential election campaign of 1968 was the first of the razzamatazz elections which are now commonplace in the multi-million dollar race for the White House.

British Mini-Coopers finished 1st, 2nd and 3rd in the Monte Carlo Rally in 1966 but were all disqualified for having illegal light-dipping systems.

One of the most successful books of the decade was *Sex And The Single Girl* by Helen Gurley Brown. It was a bestseller in 28 countries and was printed in 17 languages. Mrs Brown later became editor of *Cosmopolitan*.

L.K.O'Brien, the man who signed the £1 note (and others) between 1955 and 1962, was appointed Governor of the Bank of England in succession to the Earl of Cromer on 26 April 1966.

England's mascot for the 1966 World Cup was 'World Cup Willie'.

Alcatraz Prison in San Francisco harbour was closed on 21 March 1963.

After spending 12 years on death row at San Quentin, Caryl Chessman was executed on 1 May 1960.

Apart from the independencies gained across Africa in the 1960s, the most significant other one of the decade was that gained by Malta in September 1964.

The Pope travelled by train to Loreto and Assisi in October 1962. It was the first train journey by a Pope for 99 years.

In April 1967 Mrs Shirley Preston had the distinction of becoming the first woman to drive a London taxi.

In 1969 Glasgow Rangers FC announced plans to combat football hooliganism, the most serious problem facing football management at the time. Rangers announced that they were to ban fans convicted of bad behaviour and stewards were to be on the lookout for spectators arriving at the ground under the influence of drink and/or carrying drink into the ground, and a klaxon was to be sounded to drown the singing of obscene sounds — we would have thought the sounding of a klaxon for 90 minutes would have been worse than the obscene songs!

On 4 October 1965 Paul VI became the first Pope to set foot on US soil when he arrived in America to address the United Nations.

New £10 notes were issued on 21 February 1964. It was the first time since 1943 there had been notes of this denomination.

One of the candidates for the run-in to the White House in 1968 was Louis Abolafia. He was campaigning for 'Love and Peace' and posed nude on his advertising posters saying he had nothing to hide. He wasn't elected. Shame, he sounded as though he would have made a great President!

Sheila Scott landed at London Airport on 20 June 1966 in her Piper Commanche after her 33-day solo flight around the world; the first British woman to do so.

Brighton was the first English town to have Yellow Pages. They were introduced in July 1966.

Reading taught by the ITA (Initial Teaching Alphabet) system was first seen at 19 English schools on 4 September 1961.

Author Ernest Hemingway committed suicide on 2 July 1961.

The last trolley bus ran in London on 8 May 1962.

The Ministry of Pensions and National Insurance became the Ministry of Social Security on 6 August 1966.

Guildford Cathedral was consecrated on 17 May 1961. It was the first cathedral to be erected on a new site in the south of England since the Middle Ages.

Carol Doda is believed to have made history at the Condor Beach Club, San Francisco, in 1964 when she became the world's first topless waitress.

On 10 June 1965, Mrs C.V.Ward made history by becoming the first female member of the Stock Exchange.

Another first for women — on 12 August 1965 Elizabeth Lane was appointed the first woman High Court Judge in Britain.

HMS Resolution, Britain's first Polaris submarine, was launched by the Queen Mother at Barrow on 15 September 1966.

Kenyan-born Mohamet Yusuf Daar became Britain's first coloured policeman when he joined the Coventry force on 20 June 1966. He became PC492.

Mrs Sislin Fay Allen (born in Jamaica) beame Britain's first coloured policewoman after enrolled at the Metropolitan Police Training Centre at Westminster on 1 January 1968.

From 1965 the August Bank Holiday was moved from the first to the last Monday of the month.

Capt John Ridgway and Sgt Chay Blyth arrived at Kilronan on 3 September 1966 after their 92-day row across the Atlantic.

The new Euston Station was opened by Her Majesty the Queen on 14 October 1968.

There's no keeping those Reagans out of the spotlight. Maureen, the 21-year-old daughter of Ronnie, made her film debut in *Hootenanny Hoot* in 1963.

In 1960 Mrs Sirimavo Bandaranaike of Ceylon became the world's first woman Prime Minister.

The first British Christmas postage stamp was launched on 1 December 1966.

The last 10ft of the 7½-mile tunnel underneath Mont Blanc between France and Italy was completed on 14 August 1962.

On 12 February 1967 Dougal Haston of Edinburgh and Mike Burke of Wigan became the first Britons to climb the north face of the Matterhorn.

The first *Mothercare* store opened at Kingston, Surrey, on 14 September 1961.

English Electric and GEC announced plans to merge on 6 September 1968.

The book *The Feminine Mystique*, written by American authoress and feminist Betty Friedan in 1963, gave rise to female equality groups in the 1960s.

The Windmill Theatre closed its doors on 31 October 1964 after 32 years.

Her Majesty the Queen opened the Severn Road Bridge on 8 September 1966; the Queen Mother had opened the Tay Road Bridge three weeks earlier on 18 August.

Postcodes were launched in the W1 district of London on 5 June 1968.

The National Giro Bank at Bootle, Liverpool, was opened on 18 October 1968.

Stamford, Lincolnshire, was designated Britain's first conservation area on 3 October 1967.

OPEC (Organization of Petroleum Exporting Countries) was set up in November 1960 to control world prices.

Banks opened on a Saturday for the last time on 28 June 1969.

The old halfpennies were withdrawn from circulation on 1 August 1969.

The Duke of Bedford hosted the hippies' 'Festival of Flower Children' at Woburn Abbey over the August Bank Holiday weekend in 1969.

On 18 October 1966 the Queen granted a free pardon to Timothy Evans, the 25-year-old lorry driver hanged in 1950 for the murder of his wife and daughter. The murders were later found to have been committed by John Christie.

The liner *Queen Mary* was sold to the town of Long Beach, California, on 18 August 1967. She docked at Southampton on 27 September 1967 after making her final voyage across the Atlantic.

On 2 October 1968 Sheila Thorns gave birth to sextuplets at Birmingham. They were Britain's first live sextuplets. Sadly three died within the first three weeks of their life.

The first British commercial radio station was launched on 23 November 1964 when Radio Manx went on the air.

Jackie Kennedy married Aristotle Onassis on the Greek Island of Skorpios on 20 October 1968.

Princess Anne carried out her first public engagement on her own on 1 March 1969 when she presented leeks to the Welsh Guards at Pirbright in a St David's Day celebration.

On 24 October 1966 Spain closed its frontier with Gibraltar to all but pedestrians. A referendum by the Gibraltar people on 10 September 1967 showed that 12,138 inhabitants were in favour of remaining under British rule. Only 44 wanted Spanish rule!

Radio Nottingham launched the first radio phone-in programme, *What Are They Up To Now?* on 4 February 1968.

The first North Sea oilfields were discovered by BP in 1966 off the coast of Norfolk. The first three fields were called *Hewell, Leman Bank* and *Indefatigable*.

Mrs Dale's Diary ended its run on BBC radio on 25 April 1969. The first of nearly 5,500 episodes was broadcast on 5 January 1948. Three days after it went off the air, BBC listeners were given a new daily serial, *Waggoner's Walk*. It lasted until 1980.

Spy George Blake, who was serving 42 years imprisonment, was 'sprung' from Wormwood Scrubs on 22 October 1966. He turned up in East Berlin a month later.

Her Majesty the Queen had an acute attack of gastro-enteritis on 21 February 1967 and for the first time, the Duke of Kent carried out an investiture on her behalf.

The English Mass was introduced in all British Roman Catholic churches on 3 December 1967.

A merger between the National Provincial and Westminster banks was announced on 26 January 1968.

British international athlete Bruce Tulloh completed the 2,830-mile run across the United States from Los Angeles to New York on 25 June 1969. It had taken him 64 days 22 hours and he clipped a staggering eight days off the old record.

Police Five was seen on British television for the first time on 30 June 1962.

Permanent British Summer Time (BST) was adopted on 18 February 1968.

In May 1969, St George, the patron Saint of England, was demoted by order of the Vatican. His feast day of 23 April was no longer a compulsory day of devotion.

The World Wildlife Fund was started in 1961.

Brasília succeeded Rio de Janeiro as Brazil's capital on 21 April 1960.

London Bridge was sold to the McCulloch Oil Corporation of California for £1,015,000 on 18 February 1968. It was dismantled and re-erected at Lake Havasu City, Arizona.

The RAF got its first Harrier vertical take-off 'Jump Jet' in 1969.

In 1961 the Museum of Modern Art in New York displayed *Le Bateau* by French artist Henri Matisse. The painting was hung upside down — the mistake went unnoticed for 47 days!

Cigarette advertising was banned from the British TV screens in August 1965.

Footballer Danny Blanchflower, in February 1961, became the first person to refuse to appear on *This Is Your Life*.

BBC Radio Leicester, the first local BBC radio station, opened on 8 November 1967.

Britain's first legal casino was the Metropole, Brighton. It was opened on 2 June 1962.

Oxo's Katie between 1957 and 1976 was Mary Holland. But so many people called her Katie that she changed her name to Katie Holland.

Prescription charges were reintroduced on 10 June 1968. The charge was 2s 6d per item.

Dr Michael Ramsey was enthroned as the 100th Archbishop of Canterbury on 27 June 1961.

Majority jury verdicts in Britain were introduced at Brighton Quarter Session on 5 October 1967. The first person to be found guilty by a majority verdict was Saleh Kassem, a professional wrestler known as 'The Terrible Turk'. He was found guilty of stealing a handbag by a 10-2 majority.

TRISTAN DA CUNHA

TRISTAN Da Cunha is a group of small islands in the Atlantic ocean midway between South Africa and South America. It consists of the main island of Tristan da Cunha, (where the principal settlement is Edinburgh), Gough Island, Inaccessible Island, and the three Nightingale Islands (Nightingale Island, Middle Island and Stoltenhoff Island). All the islands are dependencies of St Helena which, in turn, is a United Kingdom dependancy.

The main island is volcanic and was believed to be extinct, but on 9 October 1961 it started to erupt about 300 yards east of Edinburgh. The inhabitants moved to the potato fields three miles away and, after spending the night in the open, left the main island and set sail for Nightingale Island the next day.

The Dutch liner *Tjisadane* picked up the refugees and took them to Cape Town where they were transported to Britain aboard *HMS Leopard*. They arrived at Southampton on 3 November and were taken to the Pendell Camp at Mertsham, Surrey, where they got accustomed to their new way of life which kept them in Britain for over 18 months.

When it was believed to be safe for them to return home, the refugees voted unanimously to return to their homeland and by November 1963, most of the island's 300 inhabitants had done so.

TUSHINGHAM, Rita

RITA Tushingham was born in Garston, Liverpool, in 1942. She was working at the Liverpool Repertory as an 18-year-old odd-job girl when she answered an advert in a local paper asking for a northern working class girl to play a leading role in the 1961 film *A Taste Of Honey*. She applied and was cast as Jo, the girl who gets pregnant and is befriended by Geoffrey, the homosexual played by Murray Melvin, in what became one of the best and most moving British films of the decade. Like Coronation Street it was set in Salford.

Considering it was her first film, Rita gave an outstanding performance which won her much praise as well as the best actress award at the Cannes Film Festival.

That success was followed by *The Leather Boys, The Girl With Green Eyes, The Knack* (she appeared in the stage production at Liverpool's Royal Court in 1960) and in 1966 *Doctor Zhivago*.

She slipped out of the limelight in the 1970s and went to live in Canada in 1980 after her second marriage to Ossie Rawi. She also became a Muslim. Tushingham continued to make regular trips to her home town and in the 1980s was cast in the popular television series *Bread* which was set only a couple of miles away from her Garston birthplace.

TWIGGY

ELFIN-like, with no bust and a male hair-style, Lesley Hornby was the least likely candidate for a top fashion model's job. But in the 1960s this frail-looking teenager became the biggest thing to hit the fashion world. Her working name was Twiggy.

At the peak of her career she was capable of earning £80 an hour modelling in New York. That was at a time when the average weekly wage was about £15.

Born in 1949, the girl from Kilburn with the 'Cockney' accent and giggly laugh became 'The Image of the 1960s'. Known as 'Sticks' at school she was dating 25-year-old hairdresser Justin de Villeneuve when she was 15 and he arranged her first photographic session. It was Justin who changed her name to Twiggy, supposedly because her legs were so skinny and looked like twigs!

The girl with the uninspiring 32-22-32 figure suddenly became a cult and her face appeared in all the leading fashion magazines. The cropped hair became the vogue and, of course, she did much to popularize the miniskirt.

By the time the 1960s came to a close, Twiggy was finished with modelling and had turned to acting. She received rave reviews for her performance in Ken Russell's *The Boyfriend* and later played the part of Eliza Doolittle in *Pygmalion*. With her accent she was a natural for the part. She was also involved in the popmusic business and her record *Here I Go Again* reached number 17 in the British charts in 1976.

In 1977 she married actor Michael Whitney. They produced a daughter, Carly. Michael died suddenly in 1983, shortly after the couple had split up. Twiggy subsequently married another actor, Leigh Lawson, star of the TV series, *The Travelling Man*.

The films of Rita Tushingham in the 1960s:

A Taste Of Honey	(1961)
The Leather Boys	(1963)
A Place To Go	(1963)
The Girl With Green Eyes	(1964)
The Knack	(1965)
Doctor Zhivago	(1966)
The Trap	(1966)
Smashing Time	(1967)
Diamonds For Breakfast	(1968)
The Guru	(1968)
The Bed-sitting Room	(1969)

TWIST, The

THE biggest dance craze of the 1960s was the Twist. The record *The Twist* was originally a hit for Hank Ballard and the Midnighters in 1960 and they are supposed to have devised dance steps to the music to be used by the group members as part of their stage routine. However, it was only after the more commercial verson of the same record by Chubby Checker later in the year sold over three million copies that the Twist became a worldwide craze.

People tried to add variety to the dance and the more athletic could get up to all sorts of things while 'twisting'. Naturally, it was also *Guinness Book Of Records* material, as youngsters twisted away non-stop for days on end.

But it was not only the youngsters who did this new dance; their parents were at it as well. In America the marketing men were quick to latch on as special Twist clothing was on offer, special Twist hairstyles were made available, so the hair would rotate and bounce with the twisting action, and of course special Twist shoes were in the shops.

A host of Twist records were recorded but Chubby Checker remained the 'master'. Even Hollywood went mad and brought out a couple of films about the Twist like, *Hey Let's Twist* and *Don't Knock The Twist* but there weren't too many Oscar nominations flying around.

Despite other dance crazes like the Mashed Potato, the Hully-Gully and the Fly, the Twist remained the dance of the decade, and today it is the one

Danny and the Juniors were the first choice to sing the commercial version of The Twist in 1960 but weren't available.

dance that is guaranteed to get the 40-year-olds up on the dance floor — hearts permitting that is!

Instructions for the Twist as given out with the original record:
Imagine you are stubbing out a cigarette with both feet, whilst drying your back with a towel...have you ever tried stubbing out one cigarette with both feet?

UNEMPLOYMENT FIGURES

THE following is the number of people registered unemployed in Britain as at April each year during the 1960s. The 1963 figure was high because of the bad weather which caused many agriculture-allied businesses to close. The unemployment figure in February 1963 was an all-time 1960s high of 878,400.

      1960 — 355,000
      1961 — 300,000
      1962 — 403,000
      1963 — 604,600
      1964 — 405,000
      1965 — 326,000
      1966 — 328,000 *
      1967 — 567,400
      1968 — 578,400
      1969 — 557,700

*Figure taken in February, not April.

UNIVERSITIES

TWENTY-TWO new universities were established in the 1960s:
1961   University of Sussex in
            Brighton
1962   University of Keele
1963   University of East Anglia in
            Norwich
         University of York
1964   University of Essex in
            Colchester
         University of Lancaster
         University of Strathclyde
1965   New University of Ulster in
            Coleraine, Co Londonderry
         University of Kent in
            Canterbury
         University of Warwick
1966   University of Aston in
            Birmingham
         Brunel University in Uxbridge
         Heriot-Watt University in
            Edinburgh
         Loughborough University of
            Technology
         The City University in London

The University of Sussex in October 1962.

VASSALL, William

WILLIAM Vassall was the £14-a-week Admiralty clerk who was sentenced to 18 years imprisonment in 1962 for passing information on to the Soviets.

He had been passing information since 1955 but it was not until 13 September 1962 that he was charged with offences under the Official Secrets Act.

On 22 October the 38-year-old vicar's son was sentenced after it was revealed his spying missions had started after he was posted to Russia in the mid-1950s. He was lured into a homosexual party and was threatened with blackmail after photographs of him in compromising positions had been secretly taken. The Soviets were doubling his £14-a-week wage with regular payments to him.

An enquiry into the scandal exonerated from blame Lord Carrington and Mr Thomas Galbraith, who resigned from the Government in November 1962, but stated that the method for selecting Vassall as naval attaché in Moscow was far from adequate.

VAUGHAN, Norman

THE ONE thing Norman Vaughan will be best remembered for in the 1960s was for giving us the sayings 'Swinging' and 'Dodgy' as we went around sticking thumbs up, or down, at each other. My word, did we enjoy ourselves in those days?

Vaughan was born in Liverpool in 1927 and started his stage career in a boy's troupe at the age of 14. The following year he formed his own trio known as The Dancing Aces and they toured until Vaughan joined the army where he appeared with such people as Harry Secombe and Spike Milligan.

He appeared in many stage shows, including *Boeing-Boeing, Play It Again Sam, No No Nanette* and *The Wizard*

Of Oz. He also appeared in pantomimes and summer seasons. His English television debut was in *New Faces* before he became a regular on *Saturday Showtime.* It was after touring with Cliff Richard that he got his big break in 1962 when he took over from Bruce Forsyth as compère of *Sunday Night At The London Palladium.* After that he had his own show, *A Touch Of Norman Vaughan* and also hosted *The Golden Shot* but since then very little was heard of the often nervous looking Vaughan.

VIETNAM WAR

THE Vietnam War was the longest war in US history. American involvement started in 1950 when President Truman sent a 35-man military advisory group to aid the French who were attempting to regain colonial power.

The French had lost administrative control to the Japanese in March 1945. However, the Japanese subsequently surrendered to the Communist coup led by Ho Chi Minh who proclaimed the new state of the Democratic Republic of Vietnam. The following year French forces re-entered Vietnam and an agreement was reached for the new state to become a 'free' state within the French Union but Minh pressed for complete independence and talks broke down. Consequently full-scale hostilities started on 19 December 1946. This war continued until a cease-fire agreement on 20-21 July 1954. One of the clauses of the agreement was that the DRV should

South Vietnamese girl, carrying her baby brother, arrives in Long Hai after being evacuated from their village in September 1969.

South Vietnamese marines capture a Vietcong guerrilla in March 1965.

re-form within a geographical location north of latitude 17°N. This subsequently became known as North Vietnam with Hanoi as its capital. The Republic of Vietnam, the area south of latitude 17°N, was proclaimed on 26 October 1955 with Saigon as the capital.

In 1959 guerrillas from the north attacked the Republicans in the south and it was from 1961 that intense US involvement started when they sent troops in to help the Republic (South Vietnam). From then on it became a battle between the United States, South Vietnamese, and their allies against the North Vietnamese and the

202

National Liberation Front (Vietcong).

Between 1961 and 1963 the number of US Military personnel in Vietnam rose from 2,000 to 15,000. In 1964 North Vietnamese torpedo boats attacked US destroyers in the Gulf of Tonkin and President Johnson ordered air strikes as a retaliatory measure. And the following year American involvement in the war escalated.

US planes began aerial combat and by June 1965 the total number of Americans actively involved in the war was 23,000. Before the year was out that figure was up to 184,000.

> *The largest ever demonstration to be seen in Washington DC was in November 1969 when 300,000 protested against the war in Vietnam.*

By 1968 the number of American servicemen under the command of General William Westmoreland was 525,000 and in April 1969 reached a peak of 543,400. However, shortly

British housewives and teenage girls march to the American Embassy in February 1968.

> *Anti-war campaigners in the States were known as 'Doves' while supporters of the war were known as 'Hawks'.*

afterwards the new President, Nixon, announced a peace offer and started withdrawing US troops. He had used the promise to quit 'Nam as part of

Peace demonstrator taunts military police outside the Pentagon in October 1967.

On 22 December 1961, James Davis became the first US soldier to be killed by the Vietcong.

his election campaign. On the other hand, one of the reasons Johnson did not re-stand was because of the escalation of American involvement during his term of office.

As the stories of one attrocity after another unfolded, there came the news in November 1969 that a lieutenant in the US Army, William Calley, was to be tried by Court Martial for his part in the killing of over 100 Vietnamese civilians in the My Lai massacre in 1968. On 29 March 1971 he was found guilty of murdering 20 civilians at My Lai and subsequently given a death sentence, later commuted to 20 years imprisonment.

Details of this attrocity were brought to light when a young soldier wrote to President Nixon and other members of Congress advising of what had happened.

The bombing of Vietcong bases in Cambodia in 1970 heralded the end of major US participation in the war. A peace settlement was signed on 27 January 1973 and agreement was made for the release of US prisoners. Within 60 days of signing the agreement, all US prisoners were returned and the US withdrew all military forces from South Vietnam.

There were a few skirmishes after that without US involvement but on 30 April 1975 the war officially came to an end. The cost in terms of dollars to the American people was $141 billion. In terms of lives 1.3 million Vietnamese were killed and 58,000 Americans. But for many who returned there still remains a bitter and everlasting memory of their time spent fighting the Vietcong.

WALKER BROTHERS

FIRST of all, let's dispel a myth; the Walker Brothers weren't brothers. The trio consisted of Gary Leeds, John Maus, and Scott Engel, although they called themselves Gary, Scott and John Walker. They chose the name Walker for no other reason than 'they liked it'.

Although talented musicians, they were not recognized in the United States and so, in 1965, they made the journey across the Atlantic and 'gate crashed' the party British pop music was enjoying.

They had all the ingredients for success — good looks, long hair, and they could sing. They signed a recording contract with Phillips and by the spring of 1966 had enjoyed two number-one hits in Britain. Their first, *Make It Easy On Yourself*, written by Hal David and Burt Bacharach, was a worldwide million seller.

Apart from working together, each of the trio had individual hits. Scott was the most successful of the three and his *Joanna* reached number seven in 1968.

The Walker Brothers' chart decline coincided with the close of the decade, but they made a startling comeback in 1976 when *No Regrets* reached number seven. It revived memories of one of the most popular American groups to come to Britain in the mid-1960s.

Top Ten hits of the Walker Brothers in the 1960s:

Year	Record	Pos
1965	Make It Easy On Yourself	1
1965	My Ship Is Coming In	3
1966	The Sun Ain't Gonna Shine Anymore	1

WARHOL, Andy

ONE OF the pioneers of 'Pop Art', Andy Warhol became famous after his *Campbells Soup* painting.

His real name was Andrew Warhola, and he was the son of a working class Czech immigrant family. He was brought up in Pittsburgh and graduated from college in 1949. He soon became one of the most sought after commercial artists in New York.

In the early-1960s he switched from drawing to painting, and in addition to his famous soup tin, his paintings of dollar bills and *Coca Cola* bottles, and other household goods, became distinctive. He then switched his attention to silk-screening techniques and transferred his paintings to canvas. His portrayal of Marilyn Monroe was one of his best works.

He also ventured into the world of films and one of his first was the three-hour silent film of a man sleeping entitled *Sleep* of course! There were other films, all of which seemed to have little story and often no ending, like an eight-hour view of the Empire State Building called *Empire*. There was also *Kiss, Blow Job, Flesh* and *Trash* (his title, not ours!)

In June 1968 Warhol was seriously injured when shot by actress Valeria Solania, who was appearing in one of his films.

Although he was an attention-seeker, Warhol was a very private man and never married. He died of a heart attack on 22 February 1987 while recovering from a gall bladder operation in a New York hospital. He was reputed to be 55 at the time, but nobody was quite sure.

WAYNE, John

COWBOY films are enjoying a mini-revival in the 1980s, but in the 1960s you couldn't beat a good western. And when it came to playing the part of the cowboy there was no bigger name than that of John Wayne.

Born as Marion Michael Morrison (no relation to the authors) at Winterset, Iowa, on 26 May 1907, he attended the University of California after being awarded a football scholarship. During his free time at university he worked on location as a props man for 20th Century Fox. When an injury forced him out of university he worked full time at the studio.

Wayne had his first film part as an extra in *Brown Of Harvard* in 1926 and as Duke Morrison, he appeared in the 1931 western *The Big Trail*. It was a 'B' movie and they were typical of the roles Wayne got over the next ten years. It was in the western *Stagecoach* in 1939 that his career took off. In the first western to be given 'A' movie status, Wayne played the part of the Ringo Kid.

After that he was generally cast as either a cowboy or an army officer.

John Wayne (centre) with Dan Rowan and Dick Martin, creators of Rowan and Martin's Laugh-In.

He was usually a goodie chasing the baddies.

Throughout the 1940s and '50s Wayne made such great films as *Flying Tigers, Tall In The Saddle, Fort Apache, Sands Of Iwo Jima* and *Rio Grande.*

One of the most sought-after names in Hollywood, his successes continued into the 1960s with such classics as *The Alamo* (which he also directed), *El Dorado, The Green Berets* and *The Longest Day.*

Despite his great talent, Wayne was only twice nominated for the best actor Oscar — for his portrayal of Sgt. John Stryker in *Sands Of Iwo Jima* in 1949 and for his portrayal of the tough Marshall Rooster Cogburn in *True Grit* in 1969. It was for the latter role that Wayne eventually won his one and only Oscar.

Wayne became one of Hollywood's wealthiest actors and invested money in agriculture amongst other things. He overcame lung cancer in 1964 but Hollywood's most popular cowboy died at Los Angeles on 11 June 1979 at the age of 72. His last film was *The Shootist* three years earlier.

The films of John Wayne in the 1960s:

North Of Alaska	(1960)
The Alamo	(1960)
The Commancheros	(1961)
The Man Who Shot Liberty Valance	(1962)
Hataral!	(1962)
The Longest Day	(1962)
How The West Was Won	(1962)
Donovan's Reef	(1963)
McLintock	(1963)
Circus World (The Magnificent Showman)	1964
The Greatest Story Ever Told	(1965)
In Harm's Way	(1965)
The Sons Of Katie Elder	(1965)
Cast A Giant Shadow	(1966)
The War Wagon	(1967)
El Dorado	(1967)
The Hellfighters	(1968)
The Green Berets	(1968)
True Grit	(1968)
The Undefeated	(1968)

WHICKER, Alan

ALAN Whicker is one of the best known and wealthiest television personalities. He is also one of the most travelled as his popular programmes have taken him to all corners of the globe.

Born in Cairo in 1925 he was a war correspondent, foreign correspondent, novelist, writer and broadcaster before embarking on a television career in 1957 as one of the *Tonight* team. He was one of the reporters on the first *Telstar* two-way transatlantic transmission.

His popular series, *Whicker's World,* first appeared in 1959 and ran until 1960. It was then replaced with *Whicker Down Under.* Other series like *Whicker On Top Of The World!, Whicker In Sweden, Whicker Down Mexico Way* and so on followed and kept him busy during the 1960s. *Whicker's World* returned for three seasons in 1965 but in 1968 he left the BBC, having become the biggest private individual shareholder of the new Yorkshire Television company and he took his talent to the new company where he featured in more than 80 documentaries, starting with *Whicker's New World.*

He returned to the BBC in 1982 when he fronted *Whicker's World — The First Million Miles.*

A millionaire, he lives a lifestyle to suit on the beautiful island of Jersey.

WHO, The

DESPITE never having a British number one, The Who have been one of the biggest rock bands since their formation in the early 1960s.

They started life as The Detours and then The High Numbers before changing to The Who in 1964. The following year they had their first big hit *I Can't Explain* and follow-up hits like *My Generation, Substitute* and *I'm A Boy* have all become classics of the rock era. *My Generation* was regarded as the rock anthem by the anti-establishment youngsters in the 1960s.

The group's line-up remained unaltered throughout their long career and consisted of Pete Townshend on lead guitar, John Entwistle on bass, Keith Moon (now deceased) on drums, and lead singer Roger Daltrey. Each was an outstanding

The Who (from left) Pete Townshend, Roger Daltrey and John Entwhistle, with Keith Moon on drums.

individual talent, but together they formed one of the great bands of the last 25 years.

The Who were typical of the 'Mods' of the 1960s and did a lot to popularize the mod-style type of dress. They were also responsible for composing the classic rock opera *Tommy* which was a 1960s musical masterpiece. They followed that with *Quadrophenia* in the seventies.

Sadly, many will remember The Who for the wrong reasons. Admittedly they went over the top at times and of course the media picked up on such stories as hotels being wrecked, their equipment-smashing routine on stage, and so on. But ignore those stories and you were left with a tremendously talented and popular band.

Top Ten hits of The Who in the 1960s:

Year	Record	Pos
1965	I Can't Explain	8
1965	Anyway Anyhow Anywhere	10
1965	My Generation	2
1966	Substitute	5
1966	I'm A Boy	2
1966	Happy Jack	3
1967	Pictures Of Lily	4
1967	I Can See For Miles	10
1969	Pinball Wizard	9

WILSON, Sir Harold

IF Acker Bilk was famous for his waistcoat, bowler hat and clarinet in the 1960s, then Harold Wilson was just as identifiable by his *Gannex* raincoat and pipe.

Born in Huddersfield, he spent all his political career serving northern constituents, first at Ormskirk and then Huyton, not a million miles from the famous jam butty mines of Ken Dodd.

Wilson was educated at Oxford and entered Parliament in 1945 as MP for Ormskirk. He was appointed President of the Board of Trade in 1947, becoming the youngest Cabinet Minister (31) since Pitt. He resigned in 1951 at the time of Bevanism and re-entered the Commons in 1955 as MP for Huyton. He succeeded Gaistkell as Party leader in 1963 and led Labour to victory in the 1964 General Election. Despite a majority of only four he held on and his

Government was re-elected 18 months later with a considerably larger majority of 97.

Harold remained in power until losing at the 1970 General Election, but returned as Premier in 1974 before eventually retiring in 1976 when he was made a Knight of the Garter.

Constantly at Wilson's side during his time at Downing Street (and both before and after) was his devoted wife Mary. He also received the support of his political secretary Marcia Williams, whom Wilson controversially created Lady Falkender upon his retirement.

WOODSTOCK

THE WOODSTOCK festival took place on 16, 17 and 18 August 1969 on a 600-acre dairy farm near the town of Woodstock, New York State. The festival was scheduled for 72 hours and torrential rainstorms did not dampen the enthusiasm of the estimated 450,000 youngsters who came to listen to rock and blues music, drink beer, smoke pot, and make love (not war). Despite being cut to 'just' 60 hours it was the biggest single youth happening of the 1960s.

The festival saw some of the top artistes of the day give outstanding performances. Among the well-known singers and groups who played at the festival were: Arlo Guthrie, Joan Baez, Crosby, Stills, Nash and Young, Santana, Jefferson Airplane, The Who, Creedance Clearwater Revival, Blood Sweat and Tears, Sly and the Family Stone, Jimi Hendrix and many more.

The song *Woodstock* was a number one for Matthews Southern Comfort in 1970. It was written by Joni Mitchell, who did not appear at the festival. She wrote the song based on reports of the event that she read.

WORLD CUP 1966

THE finest hour in English soccer history came at Wembley Stadium on 31 July 1966 when England, led by Bobby Moore, beat West Germany in a thrilling game to lift the Jules Rimet Trophy, better known as the World Cup.

As the host nation, England was exempt from qualifying for the competition and opened their campaign at Wembley where they played out a goalless draw with Uruguay. Goals from Bobby Charlton and Roger Hunt set up a 2-0 win over Mexico in the next match and they made sure of winning the group when they beat France 2-0.

Argentina were England's opponents in the quarter-final and it was a fierce battle with the South Americans showing their usual display of physical play which resulted in their skipper, Antonio Rattin, receiving his marching orders. Not that he marched too quickly. He disagreed with referee Kreitlein's decision and decided to stay on the pitch for eight minutes before FIFA officials finally persuaded him to leave.

The semi-final saw Bobby Charlton score two goals against Portugal, one an absolute gem from outside the penalty area. England hung on to win 2-1 and were in their first ever World Cup Final.

West Germany, skippered by Uwe Seeler, and containing such talented youngsters as Franz Beckenbauer and Helmut Haller, were the opposition in what turned out to be a thrilling and tense match.

Obviously, most of Wembley's 96,000 fans were willing on the England XI, but their hopes received a set-back in the 13th minute when full-back Ray Wilson failed to connect properly with a header. The ball fell straight to the feet of Haller who made no mistake. But it was not long before England were level. Bobby Moore took a quick free-kick. He found his West Ham teammate Geoff Hurst, who headed past the motionless German defence.

With West Germany tiring and England's hearts raised by their own fans, Martin Peters, another West Ham star, made it 2-1 in the 78th minute and an England victory looked assured. With the game going into injury time, the Germans won a free-kick. The ball came off the defensive wall and arrived at the feet of Weber, who stabbed the ball over the line.

The England players could only drop their heads. The fans were in disbelief. Suddenly the celebrating stopped as despair set in and everybody had to endure another 30 minutes play.

After ten minutes there came one of the most controversial incidents in World Cup history. Alan Ball pulled the ball back to Geoff Hurst. His fierce shot hit the underside of the bar and bounced back into play. Referee Dienst consulted his Russian linesman, Bakhramov, and they ruled the ball had crossed the line. The West Germans protested but it did no good. England led 3-2.

Geoff Hurst sealed the victory with a final goal in the dying seconds to complete his hat-trick — the first ever in a World Cup Final.

Moments later the England team collapsed on to the Wembley turf, some crying, some just numbed. England were the World Champions as Bobby Moore led Alf Ramsey's gallant men up Wembley's famous 39 steps to collect the most cherished prize in football.

The 1966 World Cup certainly belonged to England, but let's not forget the little North Koreans who came as complete underdogs but left as heroes and great favourites of the British fans.

Not only did they oust Italy from the tournament but they also reached the quarter-finals where, after 24 minutes, they led Portugal 3-0 before the 'Black Pearl', Eusebio, single-handedly destroyed them with four goals.

WORLD CUP 1966 ~ RESULTS
Group 1

England 0	Uruguay 0
France 1	Mexico 1
Uruguay 2	France 1
England 2	Mexico 0
Uruguay 0	Mexico 0
England 2	France 0

	P	W	D	L	F	A	Pts
England	3	2	1	0	4	0	5
Uruguay	3	1	2	0	2	1	4
Mexico	3	0	2	1	1	3	2
France	3	0	1	2	2	5	1

Group 2

West Germany 5	Switzerland 0
Argentina 2	Spain 1
Spain 2	Switzerland 1
Argentina 0	West Germany 0
Argentina 2	Switzerland 0
West Germany 2	Spain 1

Geoff Hurst completes his historic hat-trick for England in the 1966 World Cup Final.

	P	W	D	L	F	A	Pts
W Germany	3	2	1	0	7	1	5
Argentina	3	2	1	0	4	1	5
Spain	3	1	0	2	4	5	2
Switzerland	3	0	0	3	1	9	0

Group 3

Brazil 2	Bulgaria 0
Portugal 3	Hungary 1
Hungary 3	Brazil 1
Portugal 3	Bulgaria 0
Portugal 3	Brazil 1
Hungary 3	Bulgaria 1

	P	W	D	L	F	A	Pts
Portugal	3	3	0	0	9	2	6
Hungary	3	2	0	1	7	5	4
Brazil	3	1	0	2	4	6	2
Bulgaria	3	0	0	3	1	8	0

Group 4

USSR 3	North Korea 0
Italy 2	Chile 0
Chile 1	North Korea 1
USSR 1	Italy 0
North Korea 1	Italy 0
USSR 2	Chile 1

	P	W	D	L	F	A	Pts
USSR	3	3	0	0	6	1	6
North Korea	3	1	1	1	2	4	3
Italy	3	1	0	2	2	2	2
Chile	3	0	1	2	2	5	1

Quarter-finals

England 1	Argentina 0
West Germany 4	Uruguay 0
Portugal 5	North Korea 3
USSR 2	Hungary 1

Semi-finals

England 2	Portugal 1
West Germany 2	USSR 1

Third place play-off

Portugal 2	USSR 1

Bobby Moore kisses the World Cup after England's famous victory.

Final

England 4   **West Germany 2**

Hurst 3, Peters   *Haller, Weber*

England: Banks; Cohen, Wilson, Stiles, J.Charlton, Moore, Ball, Hurst, Hunt, R.Charlton, Peters.

West Germany: Tilkowski; Hottges, Schnellinger, Beckenbauer, Schulz, Weber, Held, Haller, Seeler, Overath, Emmerich.

Attendance: 96,924

Referee: Gottfried Dienst (Switzerland)

Receipts £204,805 (world record for any football match at the time).

WYNGARDE, Peter

PETER Wyngarde, alias Jason King, was one of the heart-throbs of the late-1960s in the days of the flared trousers.

Born in Marseilles, France, he started his working life in advertising before going into showbusiness and working with the Bristol Old Vic. He made his New York stage debut in 1960 and appeared in such movies as *The Innocents, Siege Of Sidney Street* and *Flash Gordon.* But it was as secret agent Jason King that he made his name.

King first appeared in the popular series *Department S* which was about an unusual police department which was a branch of Interpol. King was called in to solve a variety of mysteries ranging from blackmail to espionage and murder. He was constantly surrounded by a bevvy of beautiful girls. The series ran from March 1969 to March 1970 and Wyngarde appeared as King in the spin-off series, *Jason King* but it was not a patch on *Department S.*

After his jaunt into the world of television, Wyngarde returned to the theatre.

YOUNG, Jimmy, OBE

ONE of the great radio personalities of the last 30 years, Jimmy Young, better known simply as 'JY', was a Radio Luxembourg disc jockey, then one of the original Radio One DJs, before transferring to Radio Two in 1973. Since then he has become the housewives' favourite, as well as developing into one of the most knowledgeable interviewers and broadcasters on the station.

Born in Cinderford, Gloucestershire, in 1924, Young was a proficient musician as a youngster and performed as a singer/bandleader in the West End in the early-1950s. As a singer he had seven Top Twenty hits in the 1950s, including two chart toppers: *Unchained Melody* and *The Man From Laramie.* A re-recording of *Unchained Melody* was released in 1964 and spent another three weeks in the charts, but only reached number 43.

His first radio broadcast was for the Light Programme in 1949 and his first programme as a DJ was *Flat Spin* in 1953. In 1955 he stood in as the presenter of *Housewives' Choice* for two weeks, and it was after that stint that he was offered a job at Radio Luxembourg.

Having interviewed leading political figures and members of the Royal Family, for which he earned a great deal of respect, Young was given his own television series, *The Jimmy Young Television Programme,* which

Two characters from Z Cars: Inspector Barlow (right) and Sergeant Blackett, who took over from Sergeant Twentyman as desk sergeant.

confirmed further his skill and experience as an interviewer.

Young is well remembered for his great inter-show banter with Terry Wogan on Radio Two, and also for his catchphrases like: "Orf we jolly well go" and "BFN" (Bye for now). He was awarded the OBE in 1979.

Z CARS

THIS popular series was set in the fictional Liverpool district of Newtown, but most of the filming was in the Kirkby district of the city. It ran for more than 650 episodes and was first seen in 1960. It spawned such actors as Frank Windsor, Stratford Johns, Jeremy Kemp, Brian Blessed, James Ellis, Colin Welland and many more, who went on to find fame in other programmes.

Z Cars was centred around the workings of the Newtown police station and in the Panda cars, Z-Victor

1 and Z-Victor 2, which patrolled the streets of the town. The desk Sergeant was Sergeant Twentyman, played by the likeable Leonard Williams and he was well known for his saying:"Get it down in the book lad!"

> The theme tune was entitled Johnny Todd *and was played by the Johnny Keating Orchestra. It reached number eight in the charts in 1962 and was also adopted by Everton FC as their theme song.*

Other dominant figures were Detective Inspector Barlow (Stratford Johns) and his aid John Watt (Frank Windsor). Stratford Johns took his character into two spin-off series, *Softly, Softly* and *Barlow At Large.*

Z Cars had a great influence on subsequent television police series and testament to its popularity lay in the fact that it lasted for 18 years.